Metacinema

Metacinema

*The Form and Content of Filmic
Reference and Reflexivity*

Edited by

David LaRocca

OXFORD
UNIVERSITY PRESS

Oxford University Press is a department of the University of Oxford. It furthers
the University's objective of excellence in research, scholarship, and education
by publishing worldwide. Oxford is a registered trade mark of Oxford University
Press in the UK and certain other countries.

Published in the United States of America by Oxford University Press
198 Madison Avenue, New York, NY 10016, United States of America.

Library of Congress Control Number: 2021935072
ISBN 978–0–19–009535–2 (pbk.)
ISBN 978–0–19–009534–5 (hbk.)

DOI: 10.1093/oso/9780190095345.001.0001

1 3 5 7 9 8 6 4 2

Paperback printed by Marquis, Canada
Hardback printed by Bridgeport National Bindery, Inc., United States of America

Contents

Foreword

The Cinematic Question—"What Do You Want from Me?"

Anything filmed—fictional narratives, documentaries, experimental films, animated films—and offered for viewing is inherently reflexive. That is, it embodies a concept of itself and assumes there is some point in displaying the film to viewers, some end to be achieved. One dimension of that reflexivity is an identification with genre categorization; first of all, with one of these broad types and then within each, with an established genre like romantic comedy, melodrama, western, political critique, anime. Often this is straightforward. The film can be said to "take itself to be" an action-adventure film, a musical, a slapstick comedy, and its point in being displayed is to amuse, please, entertain, and thereby to be consumed for a price. And there can certainly be more ambitious agendas. These typological and genre identities (which, as Stanley Cavell pointed out, exist mostly to be redefined each time, for the boundaries to be reset) also signal an audience, suggest assumptions that ought to direct attentiveness; that is, suggest a modality of attentiveness or the reflective self-understanding inherent in a kind of viewing. "Embodied" and "inherent" and the like suggest difficult philosophical questions about just how a reflective form can be at work in such an aesthetic object even if not prominent and not attended to in the experience as such.

But one way it can be at work is for the issue itself to be attended to within the world of the work, and sometimes in the world depicted in the work, either as a general issue, or, in the most complex cases, in an internal interrogation of its own particular cinematic form. The film itself can be said to be metacinematic and attention can be directed to elements of cinematic form or to the pragmatic dimensions of display and presentation, whether as a so-called art film or a commercial vehicle. The most familiar examples are films about filmmaking, either explicitly, like François Truffaut's *Day for Night* (1973) or Federico Fellini's *8½* (1963), or more indirectly and in a way as much about Hollywood as about film, as in Nicholas Ray's *In a Lonely Place* (1950), Vincente Minnelli's *The Bad and the Beautiful* (1952), Robert Altman's *The Player* (1992), or David Lynch's *Mulholland Drive* (2001). Both Michael Powell's *Peeping Tom* (1962) and Alfred Hitchcock's *Psycho* (1960) thematize the psychological meaning and attraction of observing while being unobserved (a key element in all film: the film world is present to us; we are never present to or in the film world). My candidate for the most complicated and thoughtful reflection on cinematic form in general and its own psychological stake in cinema is Hitchcock's *Rear Window* (1954), which culminates in a character, Thorwald (Raymond Burr) exiting the representation of the "watched world" (the window-framed scenes as watched from the opposite apartment building), entering the viewer's world, and asking Jeff (James Stewart), "the viewer," plaintively, as an avatar of Hitchcock himself: "What do you want from me?"

The same sort of double viewing is possible in documentaries. I mean attending to the object of the documentary, while also noting that the documentary is questioning either the documentary form itself (e.g., its possibility, the possibility of nonfiction) or the point of its own recording and display. Perhaps the finest and most subtle example is Joshua Oppenheimer's *The Act of Killing* (2012, the subject of an essay in the following), where the murderous death squad members' own self-display in the film is folded into an interrogation of the ethical tone of the documentary itself, its display and relation to the beholder. Godfrey Reggio's *Koyaanisqatsi* (1982) embodies this double viewing in a different way, given that our attention is constantly drawn to the aesthetic form of the documentary itself, as well as the question of whether it is a documentary. Errol Morris's films are also so made as to raise the question, often left unresolved, about the point of the documentary and "what we want" by watching it. Since Ari Folman's *Waltz with Bashir* (2008, also the subject of an essay in this book) combines both the documentary form of autobiography with animation, that form itself, animation, is immediately thematized as an issue, its appropriateness and point.

Experimental films, like the works of Louis Buñuel, Stan Brakhage, Kenneth Anger, Bruce Conner, or Martin Arnold, are unavoidably metacinematic. The very concept of experimental, which signals an attempt to make something that will not fit standard typological or genre classifications, or any classifications, signals a metacinematic interest by requiring the viewer, in effect, to find the object's distinctive, even unique, cinematic form and wonder about the point of the object being made and displayed.

A general question is raised by all such metacinematic attempts. What is distinctive, especially distinctively valuable, about such cinematic self-explorations, as opposed most obviously to a standard, discursive philosophic-aesthetic inquiry into the same issues? Answering that question would require we first identify the nature of the aesthetic form of cinematic self-consciousness, in itself quite a complicated issue, but whatever answer we suggest, we will have to preserve that element of interpretive free-play, breadth of possible meaning, and affective involvement opened up in an aesthetic experience. Its own thematization of itself, as itself aesthetic, could thus be ironic, deliberately misleading, could capture the point of view of a character or an ideology. That is, we need to respect the fact that such a form is not just a shorthand expression of propositional claims. At the minimum, whatever cinematic attention is directed at the object's own form, it remains cinematic attention, not an invitation or spur to independent philosophical reflection, and as such it requires the same sort of polysemous interpretive work and affective involvement as any aesthetic form, as is all so ably demonstrated in this collection.

Robert B. Pippin

Contributors

J. M. Bernstein is University Distinguished Professor of Philosophy at the New School for Social Research. His writings include *The Fate of Art: Aesthetic Alienation from Kant to Derrida and Adorno* (1992); *Recovering Ethical Life: Jürgen Habermas and the Future of Critical Theory* (1995); *Adorno: Disenchantment and Ethics* (2002); and *Against Voluptuous Bodies: Late Modernism and the Meaning of Painting* (2006). His most recent book is *Torture and Dignity: An Essay on Moral Injury* (2015). He is working on a manuscript with the tentative title *Of Ecocide, Sustainability, and Human Rights: Ethical Life in the Anthropocene*.

Timothy Corrigan is Professor Emeritus of Cinema and Media Studies and English at the University of Pennsylvania. Books include *New German Film: The Displaced Image*; *The Films of Werner Herzog: Between Mirage and History*; *Writing about Film*; *A Cinema without Walls*; *Film and Literature*; *The Film Experience* (coauthored with Patricia White); *Critical Visions: Readings in Classic and Contemporary Film Theory* (coauthored with Patricia White and Meta Mazaj); *American Cinema of the 2000s*; *Essays on the Essay Film* (coauthored with Nora Alter); and *The Essay Film: From Montaigne, after Marker*, winner of the 2012 Katherine Singer Kovács Award for the outstanding book in film and media studies. He has published essays in *Film Quarterly*, *Discourse*, and *Cinema Journal*, among other collections. In 2014 he was awarded the Society for Cinema and Media Studies Award for Outstanding Pedagogical Achievement and the Ira H. Abrams Memorial Award for Distinguished Teaching at the University of Pennsylvania.

Laura T. Di Summa is Assistant Professor of Philosophy at William Paterson University. She earned a PhD in philosophy from CUNY, The Graduate Center, under the supervision of Noël Carroll. Her book publications include *The Palgrave Handbook for the Philosophy of Film and Motion Pictures* (Palgrave Macmillan), coedited with Noël Carroll and Shawn Loht, and she is currently working on a volume entitled *A Philosophy of Fashion through Film: On the Body, Style, and Identity* (Bloomsbury).

Shoshana Felman is Robert Woodruff Distinguished Professor of Comparative Literature and French at Emory University, Thomas E. Donnelley Professor Emerita of French and Comparative Literature at Yale University, and a member of the American Academy of Arts and Sciences. Among her works: *The Claims of Literature: A Shoshana Felman Reader* (2007); *The Juridical Unconscious: Trials and Traumas in the Twentieth Century* (2002); *The Scandal of the Speaking Body: Don Juan with J. L. Austin, or Seduction in Two Languages* (2003); *Writing and Madness: Literature/Philosophy/Psychoanalysis* (2003); *Testimony: Crises of Witnessing in Literature Psychoanalysis and History* (1992, coauthored with Dori Laub, MD); *Jacques Lacan and the Adventure of Insight: Psychoanalysis in Contemporary Culture* (1987); *Literature and Psychoanalysis: The Question of Reading—Otherwise* (1982, editor); *La "Folie" dans l'oeuvre romanesque de Stendhal* (1971); *Barbara*

Johnson: A Life with Mary Shelley (2014); *La Folie et la chose littéraire* (1978; to be reissued, in 2021, with two new prefaces, by the College International de Philosophie, Paris, France).

Ohad Landesman is Lecturer in Film Studies at the Steve Tisch School of Film and Television at Tel Aviv University. He holds a PhD from the Department of Cinema Studies at New York University, where his dissertation focused on aesthetic implications of digital developments in contemporary documentary cinema. His recent publications appeared in several anthologies on documentary culture, and in peer-reviewed journals such as *Visual Anthropology Review, Studies in Documentary Film, Projections: The Journal for Movies and Mind*, and *Animation: An Interdisciplinary Journal*. He is currently working on a monograph about travelogues in Israel, and is coediting the anthology *Truth or Dare: Selected Essays on Documentary Cinema*, forthcoming from Am-Oved Publishing House.

Joshua Landy is Andrew B. Hammond Professor of French and Professor of Comparative Literature at Stanford University, where he co-directs the Initiative in Philosophy and Literature and cohosts the NPR show *Philosophy Talk*. His books include *Philosophy as Fiction: Self, Deception, and Knowledge in Proust* (Oxford, 2004), *How to Do Things with Fictions* (Oxford, 2012), and (as coeditor) *The Re-Enchantment of the World: Secular Magic in a Rational Age* (Stanford, 2009).

David LaRocca is the author, editor, or coeditor of a dozen books. He edited *The Thought of Stanley Cavell and Cinema*; *Movies with Stanley Cavell in Mind*; *The Philosophy of Documentary Film*; *The Philosophy of War Films*; and *The Philosophy of Charlie Kaufman*. He has contributed book chapters and articles on the films of Werner Herzog, Terrence Malick, Michael Mann, Sofia Coppola, Casey Affleck, Kelly Reichardt, Errol Morris, Rithy Panh, Martin Arnold, Christopher Nolan, Lars von Trier, Olivier Assayas, Douglas Sirk, Spike Lee, Joel and Ethan Coen, David Cronenberg, Steven Spielberg, Robert Zemeckis, Tim Burton, and Charlie Kaufman. His articles have appeared in *Afterimage, Conversations, Epoché, Estetica, Liminalities, Post Script, Transactions, Film and Philosophy, The Senses and Society, Midwest Quarterly, Cinema: The Journal of Philosophy and the Moving Image, Journalism, Media and Cultural Studies, Journal of Aesthetic Education*, and *Journal of Aesthetics and Art Criticism*. As a documentary filmmaker, he produced and edited six features in the Intellectual Portrait Series, directed *Brunello Cucinelli: A New Philosophy of Clothes*, and co-directed *New York Photographer: Jill Freedman in the City*. He studied in the Department of Rhetoric at Berkeley, was Harvard's Sinclair Kennedy Traveling Fellow in the United Kingdom and participated in a National Endowment for the Humanities Institute, a workshop with Abbas Kiarostami, Werner Herzog's Rogue Film School, and the School of Criticism and Theory at Cornell. He has taught philosophy and cinema and held visiting research or teaching positions at Binghamton, Cornell, Cortland, Harvard, Ithaca College, the School of Visual Arts, and Vanderbilt.

Eleni Palis is Assistant Professor of English and Cinema Studies at the University of Tennessee. Her work focuses on the intersections between classical and post-classical American cinema as well as race and gender in contemporary American cinema, adaptation, genre, and videographic criticism. Her work has appeared in *Screen, The Journal of Cinema and Media Studies* (*Cinema Journal*), *[in]Transition: Journal of Videographic Film and Moving Image Studies*, and *Oxford Bibliographies Online*.

Robert B. Pippin is Evelyn Stefansson Nef Distinguished Service Professor at the University of Chicago. He is the author of several books on modern German philosophy; a book on philosophy and literature, *Henry James and Modern Moral Life*; a book on modernist art, *After the Beautiful*; and five books on film and philosophy. He is a past winner of the Mellon Distinguished Achievement Award in the Humanities and a Guggenheim Fellowship, is a fellow of the American Academy of Arts and Sciences and of the American Philosophical Society, and is a member of the German National Academy of Sciences, Leopoldina. His latest books are *Filmed Thought: Cinema as Reflective Form*, published by the University of Chicago Press, and *Douglas Sirk: Filmmaker and Philosopher*, published by Bloomsbury.

Paul Schofield is Assistant Professor of Philosophy at Bates College in Lewiston, Maine. He earned his PhD in philosophy at Harvard University, specializing in ethics, political philosophy, and action theory. Since then, he has developed a professional interest in film. He has published on Powell and Pressburger's *The Red Shoes* in the journal *Film-Philosophy*, on Elaine May's *A New Leaf* in *Movies with Stanley Cavell in Mind*, and he regularly teaches a course called Film as Philosophy. He has also written extensively about what a person owes to themselves; his book *Duty to Self: Moral, Political, and Legal Self-Relation* is published with Oxford University Press.

Yotam Shibolet is a doctoral candidate and teacher in the Department of Media at Utrecht University. He is a *cum laude* graduate of Utrecht University's Media, Art and Performance Research program and of the Marc Rich Honors program in the Humanities and Arts at Tel-Aviv University. His interdisciplinary research on "embodied narrativity" spans media phenomenology, the 4E approach to cognition, narrative theory, and the study of interactive new media and somatic practices. He aims to analyze how the perception of movement and embodied interaction give rise to the experience and interpretation of stories. Shibolet has a background in filmmaking and remains fascinated with the ways by which the experience of cinematic imagery constitutes an active process of making meaning.

Garrett Stewart is James O. Freedman Professor of Letters at the University of Iowa, and member of the American Academy of Arts and Sciences since 2010. He has published four cinema books with the University of Chicago Press. *Between Film and Screen: Modernism's Photo Synthesis* (1999) was followed by *Framed Time: Toward a Postfilmic Cinema* (2007) and *Closed Circuits: Screening Narrative Surveillance* (2015). He has rounded out this analytic trajectory from the celluloid era through digital recording to CCTV and CGI thematics with the appearance in 2020 of *Cinemachines: An Essay on Media and Method*, whose final paired chapters on visual special effects (VFX) are extended here with more recent Hollywood evidence in reviewing the long tradition of metacinematic reflexivity on the narrative screen.

Thomas E. Wartenberg is Professor of Philosophy Emeritus at Mount Holyoke College. His main areas of focus are aesthetics, the philosophy of film, and philosophy for children. Among his publications are *Thinking on Screen: Film as Philosophy*; *Big Ideas for Little Kids: Teaching Philosophy through Children's Literature*; *A Sneetch Is a Sneetch and Other Philosophical Discoveries: Finding Wisdom in Children's Literature*; *Existentialism: A Beginner's Guide*; and *Mel Bochner: Illustrating Philosophy*. He has published numerous papers on the philosophy of film, including "Dramatizing Philosophy" and " 'Not Time's Fool': Marriage as an Ethical Relationship in Michael Haneke's *Amour*." His philosophy for children website, teachingchildrenphilosophy.org, was awarded the 2011 APA/PDC Prize for Excellence and Innovations in Philosophy Programs. He received the 2013 Merritt Prize for his contributions to the philosophy of education. He served as President of Philosophy Learning and Teaching Organization (PLATO) from 2016 to 2018 and is Film Editor for *Philosophy Now*. He recently created a website for teaching philosophy through works of art: *Philosophy @ The Virtual Art Museum*.

Daniel Yacavone is Senior Lecturer (Associate Professor) at the University of Edinburgh, where he has been the Director of the Film Studies Program within the School of Literatures, Languages and Cultures. Currently a Fellow-in-Residence at the Netherlands Institute for Advanced Study in the Humanities and Social Sciences (NIAS), in Autumn 2021, he will be Senior Research Fellow at the Cinepoetics Center for Advanced Film Studies at the Free University Berlin. He is the author of *Film Worlds: A Philosophical Aesthetics of Cinema* (Columbia University Press, 2015) and is currently writing a book on the cognitive, affective, and inter- and transmedial dimensions of reflexive cinema for Oxford University Press.

Introduction

An Invitation to the Varieties and Virtues of "Meta-ness" in the Art and Culture of Film

David LaRocca

> The highest minds of the world have never ceased to explore the double meaning, or, shall I say, the quadruple, or the centuple, or much more manifold meaning, of every sensuous fact: . . . the masters of sculpture, picture, and poetry.
>
> **—Ralph Waldo Emerson**

> A representation that alienates is one which allows us to recognize its subject, but at the same time makes it seem unfamiliar.
>
> **—Bertolt Brecht**

A prefix inherited from Greek antiquity, *meta*, has in the last couple of generations gained traction as an independent word, one that denotes—in popular and critical discourses—those instances when a work of art makes an internal reference or invokes an external referent, both of which have the power to highlight the work's status as art.[1] The oddness of agency here—that art somehow can "make" or "invoke"—provides a first clue to the special sense of this unprepossessing preposition. A modest prefix, then, has come not only substantively but also inventively to augment the creation of art and our critical conversation about it. Given the expansive scope of the term's use, our gathered labors in what follows in this book are aimed at clarifying and developing the radiating significance of meta for the study of motion pictures and their sonic correlates—how images and sounds relate to the form and content of film itself. Despite the widespread invocation of meta as a concept—or perhaps because of it, and especially with respect to cinema—it remains relatively undertheorized; and as sometimes happens, excellent existing theorizing

David LaRocca, *Introduction* In: *Metacinema*. Edited by: David LaRocca, Oxford University Press. © Oxford University Press 2021. DOI: 10.1093/oso/9780190095345.003.0001 remains presumed, hidden, neglected, or unknown. Compensations and recalibrations are in order. And since there is such an abundance of meta material to address beyond scholarship, and because the name has become a go-to cultural shorthand, a double invitation abides: to take stock of the diversity of content and to take care with the multiplicity of senses at work in varied contexts. Indeed, while meta has gone mega, metacinema has for the most part been incorporated (fully digested even) to such an extent that its deployment appears uncontroversial and its meaning assumed to be apparent. Not so fast. In our efforts here, we aim to make compensations and contributions that provide a foundation for the everyday and professional use of meta in the context of cinema studies and film philosophy and more generally in our engagement with a range of media across the arts. From the celluloid origins of motion pictures to the latest developments in digital representation, we wish to articulate how these independent phenomena—*meta* and *cinema*—have distinct as well as overlapping and mutually reinforcing identities.

The contemporary recovery of "meta" (as a prefix), and subsequent use as an adjective, adverb, and noun (and in these modes achieving status as a stand-alone term of art), can be traced to several sources, but perhaps most conspicuously for film scholars to landmark writing by Gérard Genette and Christian Metz, critics who employed "meta" terminology often borrowed from linguistics and literary theory, and repurposed it for discussing and understanding cinema.[2] To be sure, William H. Gass—who coined the term "metafiction"—is an essential part of what Werner Wolf retrospectively deemed a broad-based "metareferential turn" in the creation of art and media—from fiction to literary criticism to cinema and more.[3] Mikhail Bakhtin remains a fecund reference for our enduring interrogation of heteroglossia, dialogism, and the chronotype—in short, how text relates to context, how storyworlds connect to reality, and so on.[4] Erich Auerbach's legendary conceptualization of mimesis is pertinent, yet even more than its familiar sense of imitation, the particular charge of the meta is interactivity: what has traveled under the name self-reflexivity (one type) and intertextuality (another type).[5] Writers of and on the theater, perhaps most essentially Bertolt Brecht, also bear cardinal importance, since his reflections highlight the theatrical nature of performance—namely, its artifice; accordingly, making or breaking the spell of fiction becomes an intriguing potential of acting, including when acting winds up on celluloid or is digitally captured.

By now, the memefication of meta has allowed it to go rogue, so one can feel confident about using the word correctly even as one may be hard-pressed to define its meaning in specifics.[6] Thus, in keeping with William Safire's observation about the "separatist rebellion of the prefixes," we find "meta-" transitioned into wide circulation as an independent adjective ("The play is so meta"), adverb ("Contemporary audiences have been trained to think meta"), or noun ("The stratified narrative proved to be a lively example of meta"), and especially in relation to our interpretation of cultural objects, such as films.[7] Once the prefix is pointed out, though, a dozen or more examples of its varied application can be identified—and across time, disparate disciplines, and categories of inquiry (metascience, metahistory, metaphilosophy, metacognition, metatheater, metamusic, metajournalism, metamaterial, metatext, metalepsis, and perhaps most commonly, metaphor, and even, as feels inevitable, metametaphorism).[8] Metalepsis is "maddeningly but accurately, a metonymy of a metonymy," as Harold Bloom glossed it in a famous metaformulation.[9] As with metaphor (which encodes a sense of transit, transfer, or "carrying across"), when "meta" is prefixed to a word, it regularly denotes a change of position or condition (metamorphosis, metabolism, metagenesis); an orientation after, behind, or beyond (metaphase, metacarpus, metadata); or an indication of something conceptual, of a higher or second-order nature (metalanguage,[10] metafiction, metamodernism,[11] metapsychology, metagnosis,[12] métamatics/metamachines/metamechanics,[13] metaethics, metamathematics, meta-analysis, metatheory, and the website Metacritic, which functions as an aggregator of criticism/assessment achieved by a data metasearch, that is, a metacrawl).[14]

When we turn to instances of creative production, such as the art of movies, "meta" typically denotes work that either refers to genre conventions or to itself—though sometimes, in fact many times, to both. In these ways, the meta trades on the potencies of citation and allusion (a gesture that looks outward from the text at hand to some other source or frame of reference), or folds back upon itself (making its very existence an issue). There is telescoping in both cases: to distant reference points, in the first scenario; to internal ones in the second. Imitation, impersonation, parody, satire, etc., often lead to doubling, repetition, or sequential replication; to transgeneric and transmedial crossings, while the structure of *mise en abîme*, for instance, encourages modes variously of recursion and regression "placed in abyss." Consequently, cinema that is meta appears especially effective at parodying or satirizing at the level of both form and content—imitating styles, iterating traits that bring attention at once to the means of fabulation as well as to storytelling trends (aspects already well known and widely used in metafiction). As a broad methodology, or even within a single work of art, the meta provides a compacted, layered space for semiological investigations—indeed, often distractingly so, since we can be deluged with features (such as film stock, lighting, shooting style, graphics, the presence of stars, the cadence of dialogue, ambient sound, musical motifs, etc.) that send our minds in many directions, seemingly at once. The technological and artistic attributes of film (as a medium) and film (as an art) are wonderfully, if aggressively, suited to such dimensionalities.

To wit, our focus in the ten entirely new chapters collected here (all invited and written expressly for this occasion), joined by a crucial set of four now-essential touchstones, is works of art that may be grouped under the category—and notion—of metacinema. What "metacinema" means as a category and a notion, how it is used, where it is invoked, and why it might be advantageous to carefully theorize the concept for cinema, media studies, and related meta studies, constitutes our primary task. Given the prevalence and prominence of meta, our efforts should be a worthy, engaging, and (as befits the structure of the meta) an inexhaustible errand. As we have benefited from our ongoing examination of the influence of other culturally resonant prefixes—auto-, extra-, inter-, multi-, retro-, self-, trans-, and the like (whether long-ago "pre-fixed," still attached, or, as with meta, newly liberated to independent existence), similar illuminations should attend our explorations here of the "meta-ness" that pervades the objects and methodologies—namely, films and audiovisual modes—that draw and hold our attention.

Consulting the *Oxford English Dictionary*, we learn that in ancient Greece, *meta* (μετα) meant "after" as in a temporal or conceptual order: "Aristotle wrote the *Physics*, and then later, the *Metaphysics*."[15] Metaphysics, in this case, is "after" physics sequentially but perhaps not conceptually. Verily, despite its position "after physics," Aristotle deemed metaphysics "first philosophy." The *OED* includes an illuminating gloss on what has happened since that distant usage, namely, that metaphysics has been "misapprehended as meaning the science of that which transcends the physical." No such connotation was meant to be suggested by the prefix "meta." Still, the misapprehension has only gained momentum in modernity, since such an allusion "has been followed in the practice of pre-fixing 'meta' to the name of a science to a designation of a higher science (actual or hypothetical) of the same nature but dealing with ulterior and more fundamental problems." For instance, in his *English Traits*, Ralph Waldo Emerson wrote: "It seems an affair of the race or meta-chemistry"—namely, as the *OED* phrases it, "the chemistry of the supersensible."[16] Thus, the meaning of "meta" as "after" has shifted over time to mean "higher." Looking to the most widespread use of the prefix in contemporary parlance, that is in postmodernity, we see how it has *also* come to mean self-aware or self-referential, since both of these descriptions require a mental move understood as a view from a separate, perhaps elevated, position. Baruch Spinoza's perception of things *sub species aeternitatis* may be a first glimpse of the dawning of our present-day notion of meta, for when we look at phenomena "from the standpoint of eternity," we are, no doubt, on higher ground—or perhaps none at all.

Describing something as "meta" has become a default, highly economical and thus convenient linguistic shorthand for locating the characteristics of a work of art, and in turn, assessing its value and virtues; indeed, as a meme it has become a conspicuous tick of interpretation, both casual and professional. Since authors in mainstream periodicals continually invoke meta as an accepted stand-alone concept, they must assume it is intelligible to their readership. Yet how did this reliable usage and prevailing assumption develop, take hold, and to what end? Richard Dyer psychologizes astutely: "Intellectuals tend to be drawn to the meta-discursive in art; since what they do is a meta-activity, they take special comfort from other things that are meta, like self-reflexive art."[17] The book in hand may be one more submission of evidence for Dyer's cogent observation about intellectual obsessions.

Yet are we not *also* hearing the ascription "meta" more and more because art has, in fact, *become* more meta? What are people talking about in the first place? And why do more and more circumstances seem to offer, or demand, an appeal to the meta? This quality of "meta-ness," as critics at the *New York Times* put it, addresses the feeling that many cultural and art objects—and perhaps *especially* films—can be understood and enjoyed in part, or in whole, by their connection to other things, say other films, or, indeed with a special reference to themselves.[18] The work of art we experience, on this account of the meta, either depends upon some previous work of art—and thereby implicitly or explicitly stands in a citational relationship to that earlier work—or undermines some of the cardinal traits that make art absorbing (and for many people, entertaining). On the latter point, the (potentially) entrancing qualities of a work of art are replaced with alienating effects, thus exchanging the pleasures of immersion with an awareness of artifice (perhaps, as we will see, offering a different sort of pleasure). In short, when something is meta, when it is imbued with "meta-ness" or has "gone meta," we are no longer (solely) engaged with the work of art that stands before us—including its characters, its storyworlds, and so on—as something to "enter," "get carried away by," and remain within, but instead are called upon to think about and remember the various references the work makes to realms beyond it, or to its very status as a work of art (e.g., its stars, its participation in a genre, etc.). Instead of encountering a stand-alone work of art, meta-art opens up a museum; rather than reading a novel, metafiction insists on a library; quite apart from watching a single film, an audience for metacinema is directed to consider the full expanse of cinematic history. Thus, and all at once, the meta work of art cleaves: it abides as an object to be studied *and also* introduces us to new, manifold points of reference—within the work, yes, and often well beyond it. The metawork endures on at least a double register, and often insists on many more levels.

Once readers engage the terms of art and salient film examples in play in this collection, it will be readily apparent just how widespread meta-ness—and metacinema, in particular—has become. Indeed, as cultural production speeds up—with stand-alone feature films giving away to abundant series, serials, episodic works, and franchises—metatraits proliferate. And once one is tipped off what to look for when studying "movies about movies,"[19] or "films within films,"[20] a consumer of art may soon be inundated and feel overwhelmed by the sheer quantity of metatexts and metareferences.[21] We are often asked to address our attention to more than one thing at once—as if to simultaneously focus on what is screened in the present *and* on what that content calls to mind from the past; thus, somehow to achieve full presence with a single work (be attentive to it), while also allowing for one's absence from it by way of distraction by many other works (private reflection on that contingent collection that lives precariously in one's personal, mental experience). The pleasures of remembering and making connections from retrieved memories, linking present to past, tying the here to the elsewhere, however, is periodically offset by frustrating lacunae and misrememberings revealing themselves along the way. To aid some recovery from such a vertiginous predicament, this book has been created by metacinematicians laboring to offer terminological clarity and close readings of representative works of meta-art. In its capacity as a guide for the interested (and perhaps also justifiably perplexed), the collection of dispatches may also function as something of an announcement or "call to theorize" among those who care to think about such things. In this way, the volume participates in an emergent subfield—and perhaps more than one: metastudies, generally, and metacinema, specifically. (Once such endeavors find a grounding, a further series of related domains present themselves for our consideration: metatheater, meta-performance art, metatelevision,[22] meta-video games, meta-social media, and so on through the ranks of cultural and technological production.)

As part of the present terminological and disciplinary investigation, then, let us ask ourselves how we have come to use the word "meta" and its filmic compound "metacinema." Does it denote a technique of filmmaking or a genre—or something of both? The question reminds us that we are, undoubtedly, seeking criteria for discussing metacinema. As we cast about, looking intently at discrete moments of the meta in a film, or assessing entire films or collections of films, we may borrow from Stanley Cavell's sentiment that there is "nothing one is tempted to call *the* features of a genre which all its members have in common."[23] Since there is no de facto definition on hand, or as suggested earlier, perhaps many competing and overlapping ones persist, we seem in need of a clinic on usage and its variants: "Nothing would count as a feature until an act of criticism defines it as such."[24] If metacinema is a case of knowing it when one sees it, what, in fact are *some* of the qualities or cases that call for its conceptual invocation? Such a question points up the way that the present volume is *reflecting* on the topic of metacinema while also, concomitantly, trying to *invent a critical conversation* about it. Akin to the re-building of the ship of Theseus, this project can quite fittingly be thought of as a meta enterprise: an expression of metatheory and metaphilosophy—how we go about doing theory and (film) philosophy while aboard—since it is an inquiry into existing methods and terms that nevertheless are deployed to define a still evolving and for that reason inchoate field of inquiry.[25]

That said, the principal hermeneutic of this series of meta studies involves close attention to a more generally available approach to cinema, what Cavell called "reading"[26] films—a trope admitting yet another terminological import from longstanding habits of relating to the literary arts. Moreover, that reading is undertaken with another Cavellian claim and motif in mind—namely, that "film exists in a state of philosophy: it is inherently self-reflexive."[27] The implication of inherency is startling, in part, because it would follow that all cinema is metacinema; such a global statement may be a compelling curiosity of the medium, but it also risks being an unhelpful bit of hyperbole (especially for skeptics and novitiates). Moreover, the claim doesn't necessarily aid an urgent interest in the mode in which (specifically) metacinematic traits are emphasized and made prominent (above and beyond the standing condition of medium-specific self-reflexiveness).

We critics must contend, therefore, with alternations between thoughts on the ontology of film as such (the medium in which movies arrive and persist, now expanded, of course, to acknowledge digital) and the encounters we have with specific films (including what Cavell named the "inflectionality" of the camera—"what it is responding to inside or outside of itself").[28] Dana Polan has shrewdly framed a similar double inventory that guides our work here: "On the one hand, . . . cinema exists to transcend itself in the articulation of theoretical questions," and on the other hand, there remains an interest in "individual films in all their aesthetic specificity."[29] Cavell, as if in reply to these two aspects, said that his "guiding assumption is that everything we know of [*mise en abîme*, in this case] must be derived from its function in particular films."[30] This tandem methodology, as applied in our collection, makes both aspects better: theory is clarified and amplified by attention to concrete examples, while particularly vexing filmic instances stand in need of theory. Film theory, then, is rightly beholden to filmic expressions. To that end, while each chapter calls the method and meaning of theory into question, as befits a metaphilosophical enterprise, the authors do so in the company of particular, discrete works of film art. Consequently, as a way of finding her bearings with respect to a range of metaphilosophical expressions (in art and in the criticism of art), a reader of this volume will find regular recourse to the "reading" of specific films, or as necessary, film genres (understood as groups or cycles of individual films with shared and overlapping "static and dynamic"[31] characteristics).

From Arnheim, Bazin, Cavell, Corrigan, Deleuze, and Elsaesser to Felman and onward to Landy, Metz, Mulhall, Mulvey, Peretz, Pippin, Rothman, Silverman, Sinnerbrink, Stewart, and Wartenberg, among many others, we have been told that film is an inherently philosophical medium. In point of fact, film's very ontology suggests that "film was as if made for philosophy" (and, admitting the achronology, vice versa).[32] Yet if we are by now convinced that film is a philosophical *medium*, perhaps—given the great breadth of its expressive exemplifications—we remain in need of a term that will help us understand when film is used philosophically or announces its philosophicality, that is, when we seem to have an encounter with what may be called the philosophical mode or register of films and filmmaking. It is to these latter terms, their definitions, explications, and illustrations that we are reliably devoted in this book. Put tersely, while film can be said to "do" philosophy and encode, embody, depict, or otherwise express various philosophical themes and problems, we are embarked on a project aimed at articulating the special category of metacinema: that is, as the book's subtitle announces, when film *form* or film *content* calls itself into question—a philosophical move if ever there was one. A governing interest in what follows, indeed, an implied investigative goal, then, is to become more aware of the way we speak of a kind of art that makes *awareness* (either internally, i.e., reflexively; or externally, i.e., referentially) a hallmark of its attributes.

It is precisely in the uncanny parallel with our own (human) self-consciousness that we find a peculiar correlate in the movies. The resemblance would seem to suggest, in short, that films think, or better that they entreat us to think about them or with them—instead of, as fiction is often wont to do, get lost in them (hoping for distraction, submitting to immersion). Timothy Corrigan has described the phenomenon "when films interrogate films" as "refractive cinema."[33] Implied in Corrigan's formulation is an overture to the viewer to join the interrogation (otherwise thought of as the work of the film's cast and crew). It is thus a measure of the metacinematic when one notices that one is *thinking* about what one is watching instead of, say, being caught up in it, carried along by it. To be stopped, thrown back upon the work of art, to realize that it is, indubitably, a work of art that one faces (and not, say, a world to enter and remain in) is to experience an encounter with the metacinematic. Joshua Landy, like Corrigan, also a contributing voice in this conversation, describes the phenomenon as "mental calisthenics." Whether this effect is received as a welcome labor or a tiresome chore will sift audiences; the metacinematician, of course, already manifests a claim for the conceptual intrigue of such consequences. Yet, the invitation to (improved?) cognitive—and metacognitive—acuity presents something of a conceptual, and in time, hermeneutic surplus to the act of mere absorption. Working out the meanings of metafilms can be a rewarding workout.

When watching any film, but especially movies that make an effort to announce their createdness, we may be positioned, as Cavell commended in *The World Viewed*, to "discov[er] how to acknowledge a fundamental fact of film's photographic basis: that objects participate in the photographic presence of themselves; they participate in the re-creation of themselves on film; they are essential in the making of their appearances. Objects projected on a screen are inherently reflexive, they occur as self-referential, reflecting upon their physical origins. Their presence refers to their absence, their location in another place."[34] First, note Cavell's serial adducement and clustering of core terms: self-referential/reflexive/reflecting. Moreover, if the mental life of humans is *also* "inherently reflexive" (or in the more colloquial expression for thought, "reflective"), then cinema—and especially metacinema—makes a match. It turns out that films "think" in ways that resemble human cognition. Just as a mind can become aware of its thoughts, so a film can express awareness of its sounds and images. Metacognition and metacinema are kindred phenomena.

Such a resemblance is not without points worthy of worry. Just as being (too) self-conscious may be an impairment to better living, we may wonder if the metacinematic mode leads to better—or worse!—movies (and for that matter better or worse film criticism). As the child plays immersively, absorbed in durational expanses of time (in Henri Bergson's sense of *durée*), the creative artist finds an "optimal experience" through what Mihaly Csikszentmihalyi calls "flow," or the gifted musician or athlete enters and remains "in the zone," so the "naive" filmgoer (simply) enjoys the dreamlike, even womblike, qualities of the movie theater—as a sound chamber in surrounding darkness, offering a frame of light, bracketing the offscreen world, focusing on an object beyond or outside one's own mind, and so on. Here cinema, in its everydayness, presents an opportunity for an escape from narcissism, a certain momentary lostness from the life one left at the theater door. But what of a cinema that pushes its audience to keep close track of the screen *and* the life beyond the screen, the "inside" of film and one's own inner life—the lived reality of ethical significance and conflict, of epistemic crisis, of ontological seriousness? This is movie watching with the lights on. Such doubleness (or layeredness, what Christian Metz styles "imbrication, braiding, or entanglement")[35] lies at the core of metacinema: to experience the work of art and see how it pushes back upon itself, indeed, upon the audience, and thus to a world of art and lived reality beyond the theater, at the very surface of the screen—where worlds make contact. Cavell wrote compellingly that "we come to think of our viewing as gazing inward. A good film or text will try to make us self-conscious, or to re-create self-consciousness."[36] And assuredly, as Stephen Mulhall has noted, Cavell's own writing provides a model for "prose that is continuously responsive" to "multiple, complex, and idiosyncratic conditions," of which an engagement with film—along with the task of using language to account for film—must be counted.[37] In addition to agitating self-consciousness, metacinematic works *also* invite us to gaze outward: to see the work of art as art, perhaps to recover some of the playfulness and invention suggested in Fluxus artist Robert Filliou's circular and thus reflexive remark that "art is what makes life more interesting than art." (The traditions of Dada, surrealism, and other modernist conceptions of the work of art intimately neighbor many incarnations of the meta, including metamodernism.) In *The Treachery of Images* (1929), in his painting of a pipe, René Magritte would seem to have given us a bona fide emblem of meta-art in modernity by declaring on the surface of the very same work: *Ceci n'est pas une pipe.*

Metacinema presents an alternate reality in order to give us back to our own reality anew, differently; it serves as a perpetual reminder that we must process what befalls us, transform it—think and then rethink it—and then return again to extra-filmic experience with its conditions remade. Having trouble writing a story? How about a story of a writer trying to write? Struggling to make a film? Consider making a film about the struggle to make a film. (Film directing, acting, and screenwriting are vocations prominently featured in metacinematic films.) And whatever else unsettles us—love, work, friendship, children, health, and so on—can be folded into the meditation and mediation as well. So it can *also* be the case that Cavell's "unembarrassed propensity for continuous self-reference" in his own writing exemplifies these trying, often troubling conditions: namely, that we as viewers are called to respond to metacinema in ways that would seem to require a persistent metacritical dimensionality for our thinking—that consciousness too remains aware of its createdness.[38]

Quite consequentially, metacinematic works challenge us to consider the merit of self-consciousness as such—both as an attribute of human cognition and with respect to its purpose in, or as, a work of art. After hundreds, even thousands, of years, some may feel (depending on the tradition and frames of reference) that the discourse about "the self" has become antiquated, moribund, counterproductive, and wrongheaded. As a species, we may be finally moving away from the metaphysical question "What is a self?" to the after-the-fact anthropological inquiry: "When was the self?" Metacinema, however, seems to be one spot in which we are forced to remain in contention with our sense of the positive, productive significance of the viewing, hearing, and experiencing subject—for example, having a point of view (even as a *camera* is said to have one), being attuned to what is presented/re-presented, cultivating an aware of our awareness, and so on. At the same time, the fact that the conversation about the meaning of meta preserves and deploys "self"-centric phrases when adducing qualities in a work of art (instead of a person)—e.g., self-consciousness, self-awareness, self-reflexiveness, etc.— intimates potentially problematic (and archaic) anthropomorphisms; with a touch of irony firmly in place, should this attribution—or potentially un-verified translation—be something we become (more) aware of, and beyond that, seek to resist or change?—For a start, "self-reflexive" may be redundant, since "reflexive" encodes a circular logic of relation. Many audiences intuitively account for this feature, since metacinematic films, perhaps more than films aiming to seduce us into immersive storyworlds (realms admittedly in which one may *want* to lose or forget one's self, or diminish one's chattering inner narration), create a continual frisson between the viewer and viewed, hearer and heard, thought and thought about thought. In these fractious moments, the relationship between medium, representation, and audience will suggest that in the company of certain films, as "we come to think of our viewing as gazing inward," we are also looking outward, that is, into the "self-consciousness" of the film. No wonder time spent with metacinematic works so often feels like being in the company of another mind.

As found in the chapters collected here, the metacinematic mode is one that involves a certain set of thematics (e.g., doubleness and multiplication— "the quadruple, or the centuple";[39] repetition and recursion; nesting, levels, layers; the constructedness of art; genre conventions; a contest between al-ienation and immersion) in conjunction with technical/technological parameters and potentialities (e.g., medium type, combinations and inter-activity of media, aspects of display). To sort out and sort through these cat-egories and conditions, among other factors, we have the fortune of making ourselves familiar with the capable and compelling labors of our gathered critics. As noted, ten essays appear in print here for the first time; to these are added selections and updated versions of earlier, now indispensable work by Robert B. Pippin, Timothy Corrigan, Joshua Landy, and Shoshana Felman. Bringing these fourteen contributions together, a new chorus on metacinema coalesces.

Part I aims to provide conceptual and theoretical reorientation to metacinema—not just bringing us up to speed on how cinema as such is metacinematic, but also, more especially how the sometimes inconspicuous or subsumed traits of self-conscious cinema can be amplified by the manipulation of reference and reflexivity. To consider an inimitable instance of such aggressive experimentation, we begin with Robert B. Pippin's recent, if already, canonical chapter from *Filmed Thought: Cinema as Reflective Form*, "Cinematic Self-Consciousness in Hitchcock's *Rear Window*." The interaction between the referential and the reflexive in *Rear Window* (1954) is not only satisfying as entertainment, but also as an education in cinema itself, and Pippin duly appoints (and anoints) it one of our touchstones for thinking about reflectiveness-as-thought and filmic reflexiveness.

Pippin's observations on the observational unsettle our relationship to undisputed masterworks of the medium: why doesn't Jeff use film to take photographs of the alarming things he sees, or thinks he sees, through his telephoto lens?—that is, apart from a flowerbed! Pippin reminds us of prototypes such as Buster Keaton's *Sherlock, Jr.* (1924), with its understated allusions to the era of silent film as well as to the finer points of theatrical dramaturgy and production design, thereby sending us on our way to the further consideration of Hitchcock's oeuvre, including *Vertigo* (1958) and *North by Northwest* (1959). Pippin's close reading of *Rear Window* as an exemplary icon of mid-twentieth century metacinematic moviemaking, sets up the cascade of pieces to follow. For instance, Timothy Corrigan reclaims insights from André Bazin about how the "refractive environment" we have inherited includes both cinema and literature—and in increasingly interdependent and generative ways. Here metacinema and metafiction collide. Thus we find Corrigan placing Bazin at the center of a (prophetic) discussion of Charlie Kaufman's *Adaptation.* (2002, dir. Spike Jonze) and Lars von Trier's *The Five Obstructions* (2003). Titular notions such as adaptation and obstruction become master terms for our contemporary understanding of metacinema, including its evolving definitions and uses.

Like Pippin, Garrett Stewart turns, or returns, our attention to an indelible, iconic film text—*Citizen Kane* (1941, dir. Orson Welles)—to both illuminate the film's potent metacinematic traits and to enrich our capacity to understand them. Beginning with an onslaught of pseudo-newsreels in the service of backstory on Charles Foster Kane, Welles is a filmmaker amplifying film's expositional power in the service of a soaring portrait and searing critique of the melodrama of American capitalism. As he does a generation later in *F for Fake* (1973), Welles's hall of mirrors beckons our assessment of actor, star, and character; and of diegesis and extradiegesis. Consider how *Citizen Kane*'s film within a film innovates with a veritable film *before* a film, a prologue repeated many times since to amplify by means of so-called documentary footage the reality credentials of all that follows it (ersatz home movies are a go-to norm). As with later experiments, such as *Adam's Rib* (1949, dir. George Cukor), in which a home movie intervenes early on to allow us and the characters a moment of self-critique and group analysis, so too in *Citizen Kane*, as Stewart notes, we find "the frame of reflex reference through which we see not just the eponymous American tycoon but, at our own spectatorial off-angle, the exposed celebrity fetish of a mass attention that the imaged fictional Kane shares, for instance, with movie stars (like Welles) in their larger-than-life aura, optic duplication, and limitless visual distribution."[40] Welles, in short, provides a lesson on how "medial *technique* directs each episode of narrative *text* toward its reflex *context*." Hence film style offers a first encounter, while its achieved referent pushes outward to actor, audience, history, and the famous film known as *Citizen Kane*.

The categories and concepts at work in the opening trinity of chapters—by Pippin, Corrigan, and Stewart—are given taxonomical order and elegant exegetical definition in Daniel Yacavone's handy, highly nuanced contribution to the subfield of metastudies. At a pivotal moment in the volume, in his careful organization and assessment of theoretical approaches to the varied terms and rarefied distinctions scholars have employed when discussing meta works, Yacavone's abcdiary not only refines how we can speak of reflexive works but, as should be expected, also transforms how we may experience them. As part of a larger project to come, Yacavone here generously shares a first look at a refreshed typology for understanding works of art that make reference to themselves and the world beyond themselves.

Eleni Palis closes out this opening salvo of conceptual and theoretical reorientations to metacinema by steps—first by taking up Martin Scorsese's *Hugo* (2011) as that film draws us back to cine-origins and the preternaturally inventive George Méliès. Uncustomary in the context of Scorsese's usual fare of (and flair for) criminal life, but completely in keeping with his archivism and cinephilia, *Hugo* is a movie about moviemaking that, like *Holy Motors* (addressed in chapter 8), aims to think through the contemporary life of films in company with both the first stirrings of the medium and the latest cutting-edge technologies: here computer-generated imagery is put into service for exhibiting the marvels of the photochemical experiments of the French fin de siècle cinematic innovator. In the company of film critic-cum-director Alexandre Astruc, Palis incites our thinking about the *caméra-stylo*, and thus about authorship (especially of films) and therefore about the director as auteur, as "signatory" of/on the work of art. With *Hugo*—a mash-up of Méliès and Scorsese—we are positioned to think anew about inscription in its variable senses (a theme that will recur in chapter 14 on the films of Martin Arnold).

Unmistakably, the very notion that metacinematic works compel us to reflect on their creation—their authorship—is central to their vitality, a vexing aliveness. Where we had been happily ensconced, distracted, and immersed in a work of art, we are suddenly jolted to think about who made the film, how it was made, who the actors are, and how the finished film relates to the culture that created it and the history that contains it. *Hugo*, as one instance of this phenomenon, is a multiauthor film that achieves this consciousness in us by presenting a "videographic" style—one that is defined by reference to and thus reliance upon prior works of film. This informative category—the videographic—will radiate throughout the remainder of the volume as it is revealed in serial instances of implementation and reconceptualization. Similar to the making of metacinematic works and the subsequent study of them, there is much that remains in flux, part of an ongoing project of hermeneutic discovery and theoretical invention.

Part II follows the analytic approach modeled in Part I, namely, of sustained, perspicacious analysis of specific films (and their distinctive qualities and characteristics) in the service of identifying perhaps more general traits as well as strategies for theorizing kindred works of metacinematic art. Joshua Landy begins the new series, whose portions together create a scene of continental exploration: with Landy in Italy studying Federico Fellini's *8½* (1963), Laura T. Di Summa hiking with Olivier Assayas beneath the *Clouds of Sils Maria* (2014), and Ohad Landesman tracking Leo Carax—or more conspicuously, Denis Lavant (in a performance of fervent energies and fractal results)—through the streets, cemeteries, and sewers of Paris in *Holy Motors* (2012). This sequence of selected films and these astute readings prove revealing insofar as we are made to contend with the nature of actor, character, star; director, auteur, membership in a creative guild; figure/figuration, performer/performance; and related attributes of the humans who represent reality and fiction on screen.

In *8½*, Marcello Mastroianni plays a film director, Guido Anselmi, who not only spends his diegetic time negotiating his relationship to being a film director, but—under *Fellini's* direction—these doubled presences press the viewer into a multivalent consideration of memories, dreams (daydreams? nightmares?), and one's own sense of being, acting, playing, and even establishing the texture of inner/outer reality itself. Landy takes up the *mise en abîme* as an occasion to consider the service such art provides for what he calls "mental calisthenics," drawing in part from empirical psychology. Film, in short, gets us thinking, but metacinematic film—and the metafictions that animate it—keeps us agitated to ask further questions, reminding us of the "double consciousness" that is required of us in such encounters, such thinking; awareness is partnered with a perception of awareness. Moreover, in assessing types and kinds of reflexivity, we are positioned to consider the differences between "challenging and facile" exemplifications. Some works of metacinema prompt reflection more than others, and thereby reward our enduring, endlessly renewed contemplation. For Landy, *8½* is one of the metaworks that is worth our time.

The fraught fiction/nonfiction divide that stirs much metacinema is in bold evidence as Laura T. Di Summa considers how another refractive environment propels our group investigation. In *Clouds of Sils Maria*, an iconic French actress, Maria Enders (played by iconic French actress, Juliet Binoche) is served by Valentine (former American ingénue, Kristen Stewart), and studied by Jo-Ann Ellis (yet another former American ingénue, Chloë Grace Moretz). In this arrangement, the familiar doubleness and refractiveness of character/star is collapsed by meta motifs in the story and by means of meta casting; two identities—one diegetic, one nondiegetic—overlap and intermix. In these pairings and parallels, repetitions and reconceptions, not only are we summoned to remember La Binoche as ingénue (famed early on, from Jean-Luc Godard's *Je vou salue, Marie* [*Hail Mary*, 1985] and Krzysztof Kieślowski's *Trois couleurs: Bleu* [*Three Colors: Blue*, 1993]), but also the serial archetypes of the theatrical backstage or offstage, for example, when this actress/ingénue, character/star dynamic has played out on screen—from *All About Eve* (1950, dir. Joseph L. Mankiewicz) to *All About My Mother* (2000, dir. Pedro Almodóvar) and the obsessive repetition of *A Star Is Born* (1937, 1954, 1975, and 2018) and before all of them, *What Price Hollywood?* (1932, dir. George Cukor). Assayas's own earlier work, *Irma Vep* (1996), provides yet another set of conspicuously relevant refractive references that inform *Clouds of Sils Maria*—commentary on the history of French cinema (from silent film to Truffaut's *Day for Night*); closely-held convictions—for good and for ill—about Hollywood movies; the unity and doubleness of the actor/celebrity; the nature of making a remake, an adaptation, or an iteration—and perhaps most pointedly, becomes a resource for tracking Assayas's long-standing fascination with "cinema about your navel."

If Landy has made a case for the continuity of metafiction and metacinema and Di Summa has us renew our appreciation for the influence of film (and theatre) history on the creation of new works of film art, Ohad Landesman's study pushes us to dwell on film's medium specificity—especially as we continue to negotiate the transition to digital capture, distribution, and projection. As Amy Villarejo has said, "Cinema is about everything and always about itself."[41] Landy, Di Summa, and Landesman have given us reason to see why this condition is at once a cause for frenzy and a standing solicitation to explore cinema's capacity for conceptual and artistic generativity. To exemplify the matter, in *Holy Motors*, and within a few minutes of each other, we encounter "short excerpts from Étienne-Jules Marey's late nineteenth-century chrono-photographic experiments" and then another human figure who, in the present age, "shows how postproduction capacities of digital manipulation can nonetheless retain photographic indexicality and remain entirely dependent on old-fashioned physical performance." Though we may feel very far from the origins of cinema, Landesman's metameditation highlights the unities and affiliations that shrink the temporal and conceptual distance. Film is film whenever film is.

Part III finds a trinity of metacinematic works that aver representations of human bodies in some form of pain, turmoil, contestation, or trial. If film's character as a (mere?) projection of light makes it seem insubstantial, ephemeral, truly a product of the "dream factory" it is said to emerge from, what do we make of substantive encounters with self-inflicted harm, sadistic torture, or industrial-scale mass genocide? Moral, political, and personal aspects of metacinema are therefore duly pronounced in J. M. Bernstein's Trump-era rereading of David Fincher's *Fight Club* (1999), the scene of which becomes laden with the potentialities inherent to art's creation and meaning (as well as to the portentous threat of moral deterioration, political destruction, and physical annihilation that attends such creation). In short, with first initials reversed, Donald Trump is our Tyler Durden; to unpack and explain this canny if troubling equivalency, Bernstein draws pointedly from Plato, Freud, Adorno, and the critical literature on the film (including its indebtedness to the eponymous Chuck Palahniuk novel). Since the chapter was composed before Trump's defeat, Bernstein added a coda in the wake of the first successful breaching of the U.S. Capitol in the nation's history, on January 6, 2021, in which a new "alt-right fight club" fulfilled the "pattern of charismatic bonding becoming political fascism becoming political violence." Though the Trump presidency may be over, the Trump era—or some variant of it—may not.

In his daring return to Michael Haneke's *Funny Games* (1997 and 2007), Paul Schofield productively applies and develops the moral philosophy of

Richard Moran. The ethical strain of Schofield's research intersects with the study of rhetorical affect found in Christopher Carter's "reflexive materialism," for instance, the way films can formally build in critique—or beckon consciousness—of their morally weighty content.[42] A master of meta, Haneke adds yet another twist: the remake. Thus, before we even get to explore "multiple Brechtian moments" in *Funny Games*, we are struck by the duplication and replication of Haneke's work—that the film is not one but two; made, then remade. And by the same filmmaker. Structurally, these two works stand in communication with one another, but, of course, thematically, the diegesis reveals a deep interest in what lies at the limit of the screen: the audience, the viewer "safe" in her seat. The film is alive to our presence. Thus, to (material) duplication is added (thematic) duplicity, where the perpetrators' efforts to hurt the characters "in" the film are coupled with the attempt to make viewers contend with their status outside the frame—innocent and yet somehow also implicated. For his part, Schofield aims to extend Moran's argument for the role of imagination in our encounters with art, concluding that *Funny Games* "isn't simply an exercise in moralistic finger-wagging, but an invitation to reflect on the way narrative films prompt us to 'try on' points of view, and on how we in the audience become," in turn, "morally complicit." Indeed, we viewers are told by the characters that they are doing what they are doing *for us*—for our entertainment. Perhaps they also do it for our edification? Thus, pain is inflicted—and protracted—in the film by exploiting and exploding genre conventions and by teasing audience taste by testing it.

Concluding Part III with a lifetime's worth of reflection on human suffering and trauma, Shoshana Felman's essential remarks on Claude Lanzmann's *Shoah* (1985) feel as pertinent as ever, especially as we continue to struggle to make sense of the nature of "the event," witnessing, accounting for trauma, documenting loss, and undertaking related measures of compensation for the gravest aspects of history: human fallibility, failures of empathy, and the burden of mourning. With *Shoah* in mind, Felman draws the act of film spectatorship into communion with very notion of witnessing history (e.g., watching the firsthand, "eyewitness" testimonies of Holocaust survivors; listening to a multiplicity of languages that must be translated—and yet acknowledging whose languages, or experiences, may or must remain "untranslatable"). Felman asks: "What does it mean to be a witness to the process of the film?" The survivors are witnesses, but so also seem the filmmaker and the audience. Like so much metacinema, Lanzmann's landmark film achieves a "double task"—of breaking silences and also of complicating the audible discourses around them. As Lanzmann says, he doesn't regard *Shoah* as a "historical film" so much as an "incarnation" or "resurrection." Hence, "The whole process of the film is a philosophical one." Such a filmmaker, it is clear, like others attuned to the riches and resources of film, is aware of the medium—its complicity and complications—even as it is used to make art and testimony.

In all three cases—*Fight Club*, *Funny Games*, and *Shoah*—the very nature of filming and watching is under critical consideration: What does it mean to be an audience? How does viewing involve complicity? Can one testify to what one has seen (e.g., as a vital historical proxy from the profilmic "time of the event" or merely when casually catching a Sunday matinee)? As we cultivate replies to these questions, we may appreciate how Felman's work provides a hinge between Bernstein's and Schofield's chapters and those three to come in Part IV, that is, where performance ("acting"), re-enactment, "playing oneself," direct witnessing, testimony, and more are brought into conversation with animation, the manipulation of found footage, the intimacy of fiction and nonfiction, and the troubled status of the documentary index. For instance, thinking of genocide, what would constitute proof of it—encountering visible evidence, sharing witness accounts, having perpetrators dramatically re-enact their deeds (trading memories of real horrors for a playful retelling)? Such questions, which were enriched by the investigations of Part III, propel us forcefully into the metacinematic creations under analysis in the final segment of the volume.

Part IV continues and concludes our multivalent investigation by pushing beyond the iconic, canonical, mainstream films of Part I; the celebrated "foreign films" and "indie darlings" of Part II; and the audience-oriented provocations of Part III, to further modes and genres, namely, documentary, animation, experimental, and avant-garde cinemas. Thomas E. Wartenberg, who has become an instructive interpreter of Joshua Oppenheimer's *The Act of Killing* (2012)[43]—a film that was executive-produced by both Werner Herzog and Errol Morris—returns here to refine the metacinematic attributes and achievements of this disquieting masterwork. Striking among the topics and techniques addressed is the way Oppenheimer hands over the tools of expression to the subjects of his film, namely, inviting the perpetrators of genocide to "act out" their relationship to the real-world, violent events they were complicit in. Instead of the documentary "study"—whether as interview, as ethnographic report, as cinema-vérité, as observational, as "direct"—here we have an experimental *method*: documentary as the site of fantasy and true confession, of propaganda and its reckoning.

Likewise, Yotam Shibolet takes us to the location of another atrocity—the Sabra and Shatila massacre in Lebanon, 1982. Yet when addressing this historical moment, the director of *Waltz with Bashir* (2008), Ari Folman, doesn't hand over the camera so much as displace it altogether: we are in the realm of animation. Fantasies and confessions, nightmares and hallucinations, memories and traumas, are rehearsed here as well, but to different effect—especially at the end of *Waltz with Bashir*, when the viewer experiences what might be deemed "the return of the index." Animation gives way to video footage and where we had spent eighty-odd minutes accustomed to the dance of colorful, mostly two-dimensional shapes, the screams find their bodies and the blood is suddenly far from cartoonish. An animated take on the documentary becomes a documentary of animation's powers and its (apparent) competition/complementarity with photographic representation.

Finally, in the concluding chapter of the book, I add one more category for the reader's consideration, namely, avant-garde filmmaking in the instance of Martin Arnold's *Alone. Life Wastes Andy Hardy* (1998) and its parent project, *The Cineseizure*. If Oppenheimer has us considering the nature of agency, narration, and genre, and Folman conjures a new mode for "documentary" filmmaking about history, Arnold forces a deep dive into the varied significations of manipulated audiovisual media. In his accomplished, hip-hop remixes of found footage from Hollywood's golden age, we appear to be given new, unintended meanings. But are these latent or imposed? X-rays of the psychoanalytic content of until now hidden desires, or epiphenoma of metaformal experimentation? The stakes of such metacinematic questions are urgent in their own right: what inheres and what is added? Intention and reception become uncannily intermingled, perhaps to the point of an indistinguishable union. And if the implications of such an inquiry have been duly fraught since Arnold's *Cineseizure*, the pronounced arrival of CGI, AR/MR/VR, NFTs, deepfakes, and GANs promises to send metacinematic panic into an entirely novel stratosphere.[44]

To our great fortune, the discerning, generous critics gathered on this occasion provide a remarkable set of indispensable interventions into the landscape of metacinema, from the early innovations of George Méliès through standard-bearers by Orson Welles and Alfred Hitchcock to the latest manifestations in this illustrious sequence. Moreover, these labors not only illuminate the forms and functions of specific films, but also yield language we can use to speak of other existing works of metacinema—and those to come. We are given the terms and conditions to negotiate individual and collective encounters with the reflexive and referential art of film, and in effect, invited to roam beyond cinema—to meta media and modes that can be drawn into this conversation or benefit from its findings.

While the use of meta as a stand-alone word is a fairly recent development—invoking at once a contemporary feeling of postmodern self-awareness, acts of capacious textual referencing, and atemporal hyper-connection—the origins of the meta impulse are ancient, antediluvian; they have been, there-fore, only magnified, enriched, and made more culturally apparent by the modern technology of cinema and its media heirs. That is to say, humans have been seeing their reflections in the surface of water and struck—troubled—by the existential implications ever since becoming human (and likely well be-fore). If there is trouble, however, there is also comfort: we should be sensible to nostalgia as a guiding force in the motivation to create and consume art. Admittedly, the disquiet and the reassurance may travel together—as when a remake, prequel, adaptation, spinoff, sequel, series, or even a brief instance of media sampling at once fractures our sense of relation to the film *and also* rewards us for loyalty to the history of intellectual property and the industrial products that package it. Film has, from the start, provided humans with the impression of traveling temporally and spatially; of encountering revenants, proxies, and doppelgängers; of indulging in the pleasures and terrors of vi-carious experience; and of exercising empathy, or failing to. The varied and inventive deployment of cinema for these several purposes—as it were in re-sponse to primordial psychological needs and desires—has made the inter-face between audience and sonic spectacle the signature of the medium. Not surprisingly, then, there is seemingly a brand of metacinema for everyone—high, low, kitsch, camp, avant-garde, well-trodden, globally distributed, or privately presented. In all cases, something in the work makes us feel a certain way and, in turn, invites us to think about our reaction.

In these ways, "reflection" has always been a punning problem for homo sa-piens, an admission of how consciousness (or self-consciousness) introduces us to ourselves as beings *and* as the type of being who has an awareness of that being. Fathoming how self-awareness is the kind of "thing" it is is precisely what we have come to call "thought" (or a "self" having a thought). We see a *reflection* and then *we* reflect. We face—and are faced with—an indication of our existence, and so thinking itself finds a new dimension. Cinema—as the art of reflection and, indeed, the reflexive—created a material basis for the on-going artistic and philosophical exploration of these indelible facts.

If the instinct that renders self-awareness and self-reference is primeval, cinema remains a novel art—one that is transformed continually by evolving technologies and the uses we put them to. "Seeing ourselves"—giving rise to narcissistic and nostalgic tendencies—remains persistent, pervasive, and thus undeniably vital. Yet could it be that after more than a century of hyper-obsessive exploration of cinematic possibilities of or for the meta, there is a sense that our fascination with the *mise en abîme* has been exhausted? Has this self-eating become self-defeating? Are we left with what Werner Herzog calls "inadequate imagery"?[45] More than celebrating the double, the proxy, the nested, hasn't the art *itself* become repetitive—drawing us full circle to the origins of cinema in magic and thus gimmick? Our initial and considered replies to such questions may lead us to the observation that the meta has become, at last, banal, moribund, decadent, culminating in a culture of hand-me-downs, recycled properties, and ceaseless surrogates, substitutions, and synecdoches—a perhaps fitting outcome of postmodernism and its apparent capacity to pulverize foundations, forms, and formulations until there remains only impotent debris (and a lot of conceptual confusion to boot).

Seeking a counter-response to the chagrin that might be felt under these conditions, however, we can point out that repetition, recycling, and recirculation are crucial elements of the art at hand and only activate further the cognitive and emotional potency of the meta move; that is, while meta-ness may at times present itself like an outmoded parlor trick (and thus seem easily dismissible), it is in fact an ontological attribute of cinema as such (therefore undeniable and interminable) and an essential aspect of what would give credence to its artistic achievement. For these reasons, the meta is necessarily, that is, structurally, a self-feeding mechanism, and it is also a means of production. Such functioning can take the shape of the auto-cannibalizing ouroboros, or it can manifest as a perpetual motion machine, endlessly regenerating. To be sure, these allegories—like the metacinematic works that bear them out—may not always sustain our fascination, or earn our praise, though they are situated to sustain themselves.

The capaciousness of the meta can be intimidating: once one catches sight of the provocations it affords, it demands, one can feel overwhelmed. But then the comprehensiveness—as pictured and parodied, for example, in *Synecdoche, New York* (2008, dir. Charlie Kaufman)—is a reminder to us that *anything* can become a subject for our considered interest. Some understand reflexivity in art, or in philosophy, as an urge, or perhaps better a willingness, to "study the differences," as Ludwig Wittgenstein counseled, or to discover the extraordinary in the ordinary, as Henry David Thoreau prescribed. As part of this Socratic tradition, Cavell proposed "[that] philosophy is at all times answerable to itself, that if there is any place at which the human spirit allows itself to be under its own question, it is in philosophy," and—imperative for our thinking about cinema, this sentence and its sentiment end this way— "that anything, indeed, that allows that question to happen *is* philosophy."[46] Consequently, we cannot help but recognize the pronounced *philosophical* credentials of metacinematic works: if cinema is an art that is naturally, as we have said ontologically, reflexive and referential, then metacinema adds a new degree of intensity to the cinematic status quo. Hence the generativity, hence the fatigue. Since metacinema is cinema that exists perpetually "under its own question"—insistently foregrounding its status *as* art and as art that contains or refers *to* art—we are continually invited to consider its reflexiveness as we reflect on it and on ourselves. In a word, metacinema exemplifies a tendency of art, for art, to take itself seriously and by extension to remind us of the seriousness—the consequentiality—of our own lives. (Not to be missed, of course, is the attendant risk of self-importance, and its common associations with narcissism, undue self-regard, and pretentiousness. Yet even that seemingly unfavorable suite of afflictions can be profitably reflected upon.)

If the expanding abundance of the meta in our lives is proving exhausting, it may also be an indication of it exhaustiveness. Compiling some of the conspicuous qualities of the meta, we quickly recognize the spirit of its expansion: namely, how it is acquisitive, consuming, drawing all and everything into its vortices. Text, history, myth, memory: anything and all can be aggregated and integrated.

> [The movie] studio lot was one in the form of a dream dump. A Sargasso of the imagination! And the dump grew continually, for there wasn't a dream afloat somewhere which wouldn't sooner or later turn up on it, having first been made photographic by plaster, canvas, lath and paint. Many boats sink and never reach the Sargasso, but no dream ever entirely disappears. Somewhere it troubles some unfortunate person and some day, when that person has been sufficiently troubled, it will be reproduced on the lot.[47]

Drawn from a moment of Nathanael West's brazen, often caustic Hollywood novel, *The Day of the Locust*, we are reminded that no matter how much we are "troubled," anything photographed, filmed, performed, or engendered by digital means may become a future subject for our obsessions—cinematic, cultural, psychological, philosophical. We are ever navigating and negotiating the sea and seaweed (*sargassum*) of the situation. West's book courts our deliberation on this long-lasting fact about fiction and, of course, about the movies; cinema is always alive to our remembering, recovering, and repurposing. Robert Stam's image of the "Hollywood *combinatoire*" comes boldly to mind.[48] Metacinema—whether from a mainstream studio, an independent collective, or homespun from iPhones—is a fundamentally reproductive mode of art: seemingly all of its offerings are quotations and in turn subject to further quotation. Derivation and appropriation are now established, respected methodologies for transfiguring or otherwise repurposing prior works into new works. In contest with aspirations to originality, citationality has become the predominant posture with respect to existing material culture. Cinema has not escaped this fate; instead its practitioners—mobilizing

latent attributes of the medium—have made such an acquisitive and derivative orientation a primary feature of its aesthetic, thereby aiming to perpetually intensify the allure (and necessary membership) of each subsequent film,
series, or episode.

Since metacinema seems to be everywhere—from the movie house to
home theater, from blockbuster feature to social media clip, from experimental short to documentary film, from commercial advertisement to mixed
reality—it is our question to ask and answer how metacinema matters to us
in our time and the time to come (for instance, how will post- or perma-
pandemic art interact with pre-pandemic meta practices? Will new work
be regressive in the wake of trauma or innovative in the space of shattered
norms?). Admittedly, the volume presumes an audience—readers (and
cineastes) already savvy enough to notice why metacinema is a worthy topic.
Yet even with an arsenal of experiences to draw from, it may be difficult to find
one's orientation to such bounty. How, for example, is addressing the fourth
wall different from "breaking" it? Are "movies about movies"[49] always (and
necessarily) metacinematic, or can they take moviemaking as a topic without
admitting much, if any, reflexiveness? Can a film that feels very far from the
studio soundstage or backlot nevertheless be dynamically self-referential?
These types of questions—and dozens more permutations thereof—are given
careful vetting in the chapters that follow, with each contributor isolating an
aspect of metacinematic art and then doing the hard work of offering a series
of potent, tractable replies.

Nathanael West's sense of the human—artistic—impulse to collect dreams,
to be "troubled" by images, to "reproduce" as a response to both the hoarding
and the anxiety—is part of a long tradition of meta-expression in literature,
reaching back to Apuleius's *Metamorphoses* and Lucian's *Philosophies for
Sale* and onward to Miguel de Cervantes, Lawrence Sterne, Thomas Carlyle,
Herman Melville, and Luigi Pirandello, with numerous innovations in contemporary metafiction and autofiction (among them, Vladimir Nabokov's
Pale Fire, Saul Bellow's *Herzog*, Philip Roth's "Philip Roth" novels, and itemized
dispatches from Karl Ove Knausgaard[50]); percolating up in philosophy from
Plato to Friedrich Nietzsche and in the exhilarating use of pseudonymous
authorship by Søren Kierkegaard; and in contemporary screenwriting, functioning perhaps most notably in the work of Charlie Kaufman (master of *mise
en abîme*) and Quentin Tarantino (maven of metareference).[51] Directors—
from George Méliès to Werner Herzog—continuously test what Cavell (in
response to Erwin Panovsky) called the "aesthetic possibilities of the medium."[52] With Méliès we are reminded of cinema's origins in proximity to
magic—that it *remains* magic for us is likely not news. With Herzog (and his

inheritors, such as Joshua Oppenheimer) we are repeatedly buffeted against the charged border of fiction and nonfiction, forced to contend with where the "real" (and "true") and the "fabricated" mix, mingle, reverse positions, and otherwise upset any settled notion of representation. The rise of deepfakes, issuings from generative adversarial networks, and the radical provocations of non-fungible tokens are present-day harbingers for a media—and meaning— landscape that is already presenting increasingly elaborate challenges to inherited, perhaps obsolete categories. If metacinema has been a reliable fix- ture of image-making since its nineteenth-century origins, perhaps we can draw from its tuitions as we front twenty-first century conditions.

As we have benefited from ever-emerging installments devoted to well- worn but not worn-out questions—found in films by Chantal Akerman, Agnès Varda, Abbas Kiarostami, and Hong Sang-soo, and more recently in ventures such as Olivier Assayas's *Non-Fiction* (2018), Quentin Tarantino's *Once Upon a Time . . . in Hollywood* (2019) and its metaliterary companion, a novelization of the same name (2021), Hirokazu Kore-eda's *The Truth* (2020), Werner Herzog's *Family Romance, LLC* (2020), and David Fincher's *Mank* (2020)—the meta abides. That said, even a high-profile film critic such as Manohla Dargis confesses to her readers parenthetically, as if sharing a transgressive bit of commiseration out of earshot: "(Filmmakers love making movies about movies more than many of us like watching them.)"[53] Essayist Phillip Lopate noted, in a similar vein, that "academic film critics . . . overrate cinematic self-reflexivity."[54] How would we know? Perhaps by observing, in the spirit of Sianne Ngai's inquiries, how metacinema—as a permanent and prominent feature of cinema and among the most definitive aesthetic cate- gories of postmodernity—may present itself as a gimmick yielding momen- tary pleasures and insights ("entertainment"), yet also enriching, sustaining ones.[55] The intrinsic meta-ness of cinematic form united with compulsive interests in re-circulating and repeating existing content (as if renewing the lease on Genette, Propp, and Todorov's structuralist approaches to narrative mores and archetypes), would counter most critiques that metacinema must, at last, admit of decay or triviality, or both. Rather than a durable, but now de- funct fashion, metacinema seems to be a permanent part—and potentiality— of movies, whatever their provenance in time and space.

One of the surprises of this collection, we hope, is that reading about these metacinematic works—with their elaborate traits and entrancing techniques— in the company of such versatile, informed, and nimble critics, readers will feel rewarded for their fascination with the medium and its capacity to take an interest in itself. No doubt, readers will be newly equipped to face a present and future demanding the astute interpretation of such works, known and yet to be created. Given the longevity of the metacinematic instinct, we can recognize at once the talent needed to create such films about films and also the appetite among audiences to experience and understand them—but have we been provided sufficient and intelligent companionship in sorting and sifting the virtues and varieties of such works and their effects on our lives? Though theorizing metacinema admits general attributes and telltale characteristics, we likely have to decide, perhaps on a case-by-case basis, which films of this sensibility are worthy of study, admiration, even love. One after another, the contributors here assess the accomplishments and, in turn, recommend the compensations for studying these exemplary instances. If it is true, on occasion, that some metacinematic works are closer to fodder or stunt than superlative art, cinephiles should wish to find ways to articulate the differences. And while making such distinctions, as we do in what follows, we can be grateful for anything—any work of art, any film, however seemingly facile or slight—that provokes and sustains serious philosophical reflection. Guided and challenged by film's capacity for reference and reflexivity, we may come to regard metacinema as a genre, a mode, and an elemental attribute of the medium that prompts us perpetually to an awareness of what we experience.

Notes

1. Ralph Waldo Emerson, "The Poet," in *The Complete Works of Ralph Waldo Emerson*, Concord Edition (Boston: Houghton, Mifflin, 1903–4), 3:4; Bertolt Brecht, *Brecht on Theatre: The Development of an Aesthetic*, ed. and trans. John Willett (New York: Hill and Wang, 1957), 192.
2. See, e.g., Gérard Genette, *Métalepse: De la figure à la fiction* (Paris: Seuil, 2004) and *Palimpsests: Literature in the Second Degree*, trans. Channa Newman and Claude Doubinsky (Lincoln: University of Nebraska Press, 1997); and Christian Metz, *Impersonal Enunciation, or the Place of Film*, trans. Cormac Deane (New York: Columbia University Press, 2016).
3. William H. Gass, *Fiction and the Figures of Life* (New York: Alfred A. Knopf, 1970), 24–25; Werner Wolf, ed., *The Metareferential Turn in Contemporary Arts and Media: Forms, Functions, Attempts at Explanation* (Amsterdam: Rodopi, 2011) and earlier, *Metareference across Media: Theory and Case Studies* (Amsterdam: Rodopi, 2009). See also R. M. Berry, "Metafiction," in *The Routledge Companion to Experimental Literature*, ed. Joe Bray, Alison Gibbons, and Brian McHale (New York: Routledge, 2012), ch. 10, 128–40.
4. See Mikhail Bakhtin, *The Dialogic Imagination: Four Essays*, ed. Michael Holquist, trans. Caryl Emerson and Michael Holquist (Austin: University of Texas Press, 1983; originally published, 1975).
5. See Erich Auerbach, *Mimesis: The Representation of Reality in Western Literature* (1946), trans. Willard R. Trask (Princeton: Princeton University Press, 2003) and also *Time, History, and Literature*, ed. James I. Porter, trans. Jane O. Newman (Princeton: Princeton University Press, 2014).

6. See, e.g., the "Meme" entry in *Keywords in Remix Studies*, ed. Eduardo Navas, Owen Gallagher, and xtine burrough (New York: Routledge, 2018), 202–16.

7. William Safire, "On Language: What's the Meta?," *New York Times Magazine*, December 25, 2005, Sec. 6, 30. See also Noam Cohen, "Meta-Musings," *New Republic*, September 5, 1988, 17–19.

8. Nathaniel Hawthorne used the term "metascience" in "The Birth-mark" (1843). See Hayden White's *Metahistory* (1973). Metamusic includes not just highbrow, high-modernist work by Arnold Schoenberg and John Cage, but also contemporary instances, such as Father John Misty's inserted chorus of (mocking) laughter on "Bored in the USA" (2014) and his thirteen-minute meta-reflection "Leaving LA" (2017). For "metametaphorism," see Ian Bogost, *Alien Phenomenology, or, What It's Like to Be a Thing* (Minneapolis: University of Minnesota Press, 2012), 80, 82.

9. Harold Bloom, *A Map of Misreading* (Oxford: Oxford University Press, 1975), 102.

10. See Louis Hjelmslev, *Prolegomena to a Theory of Language*, trans. Francis J. Whitfield (Madison: University of Wisconsin Press, 1961).

11. See *Metamodernism: Historicity, Affect, and Depth after Postmodernism*, ed. Robin van den Akker, Alison Gibbons, and Timotheus Vermeulen (New York: Rowman & Littlefield, 2017).

12. See Danielle Spencer, *Metagnosis: Revelatory Narratives of Health and Identity* (New York: Oxford University Press, 2020).

13. Jean Tinguely (1935–91) designed machines that could make art. This extension of a Dadaist tradition offered as a satire of automation can be traced to present-day works by the consortium Obvious, which designed a generative adversarial network (GAN) that, in turn, created *Edmond de Belamy* (2018, 70 cm × 70 cm), a GAN portrait painting that sold at Christie's for $432,500. Here Tinguely's métamatics meets *acheiropoieta*—works of art "made without hands."

14. Definitions are drawn from a series of entries available in the *Oxford English Dictionary*, *American Heritage College Dictionary*, and the online dictionary aggregator—what we can call a metadictionary—dictionary.com.

15. *Oxford English Dictionary*, 1971. Not to be confused with the Pali word *mettā* (from the Sanskrit *maitrī*), commonly translated as loving-kindness, benevolence, amity, or good-will. See Peter Harvey, *An Introduction to Buddhism: Teachings, History and Practices* (Cambridge: Cambridge University Press, 2012), 278–79.

16. Ralph Waldo Emerson, *English Traits* (1856), in *Complete Works*, 5:238. See also my *Emerson's English Traits and the Natural History of Metaphor* (New York: Bloomsbury, 2013), 118; and Emerson, *The Journals and Miscellaneous Notebooks of Ralph Waldo Emerson*, ed. Ralph H. Orth and Alfred R. Ferguson (Cambridge: Belknap Press of Harvard University Press, 1977), vol. 8 (1852–55), 246.

17. Richard Dyer, *The Culture of Queers* (New York: Routledge, 2002), 201.

18. Wesley Morris and A. O. Scott, "The 10 Best Actors of the Year," *New York Times*, December 9, 2019.

19. Christopher Ames, *Movies about the Movies: Hollywood Reflected* (Lexington: University Press of Kentucky, 1997).

20. Metz, *Impersonal Enunciation*, esp. Part II, ch. 8.

21. See Patricia Pisters, *The Matrix of Visual Culture: Working with Deleuze in Film Theory* (Stanford: Stanford University Press, 2003); see esp. ch. 1, "The Universe as Metacinema,"

14–44; see again Wolf, *Metareference across Media* and *The Metareferential Turn*; Décio Torres Cruz, *Postmodern Metanarratives: "Blade Runner" and Literature in the Age of Image* (New York: Palgrave Macmillan, 2014); Eyal Peretz, *The Off-Screen: An Investigation of the Cinematic Frame* (Stanford: Stanford University Press, 2017). See also Timothy Corrigan, "Adaptations, Refractions, and Obstructions: The Prophecies of André Bazin," *Falso Movimento* 1, no. 1 (Fall 2014); and Joshua Landy, "Mental Calisthenics and Self-Reflexive Fiction," in *The Oxford Handbook of Cognitive Approaches to Literature*, ed. Lisa Zunshine (New York: Oxford University Press, 2015), 559–80. For Corrigan and Landy, see in this volume respectively, chapters 2 and 6.

22. Some prominent examples of metatelevision include *The Muppet Show*, *It's Garry Shandling's Show*, *Curb Your Enthusiasm* (see esp., "Seinfeld," s7:e10), *The Office*, *30 Rock*, *Community*, *BoJack Horseman*, *Fleabag*, *Russian Doll*, and *WandaVision*. The meta-ness of television is explored in, among other places, Jen Chaney, "When Did TV Get So Meta?," *Vulture*, February 10, 2017, and Scott R. Olson, "Meta-television: Popular Postmodernism," *Critical Studies in Mass Communication* 4, no. 3 (1987): 284–300.

23. Stanley Cavell, *Pursuits of Happiness: The Hollywood Comedy of Remarriage* (Cambridge, MA: Harvard University Press, 1981), 28.

24. Cavell, *Pursuits of Happiness*, 28.

25. Daniel Yacavone, *Film Worlds: A Philosophical Aesthetics of Cinema* (New York: Columbia University Press, 2015), xiv.

26. Cavell, *Pursuits of Happiness*, 2, 202–5; and Stanley Cavell, *Cities of Words: Pedagogical Letters on a Register of the Moral Life* (Cambridge, MA: Harvard University, 2004), 116, 272.

27. Cavell, *Pursuits of Happiness*, 13. See also 14, 14 n. 1.

28. Cavell, *Pursuits of Happiness*, 203.

29. Dana Polan, "Afterword," in Metz, *Impersonal Enunciation*, 181.

30. Cavell, *Pursuits of Happiness*, 206.

31. Thomas Schatz, *Hollywood: Critical Concepts in Media and Culture* (New York: Routledge, 2004), 1st ed., 691.

32. Stanley Cavell, *Contesting Tears: The Hollywood Melodrama of the Unknown Woman* (Cambridge, MA: Harvard University Press, 1996), epigraph and xii. See also "Reflections on a Life of Philosophy: Interview with Stanley Cavell," *Harvard Journal of Philosophy* 7 (1999): 25. For further exploration of the notion, see *The Thought of Stanley Cavell and Cinema: Turning Anew to the Ontology of Film a Half-Century after "The World Viewed,"* ed. David LaRocca (New York: Bloomsbury, 2020). See also Catherine Wheatley, *Stanley Cavell and Film: Scepticism and Self-Reliance at the Cinema* (New York: Bloomsbury, 2019) and Robert B. Pippin, *Filmed Thought: Cinema as Reflective* (Chicago: University of Chicago Press, 2019).

33. Timothy Corrigan, *The Essay Film: From Montaigne, after Marker* (New York: Oxford University Press, 2011), 181–204.

34. Stanley Cavell, *The World Viewed: Reflections on the Ontology of Film*, Enlarged Edition (Cambridge, MA: Harvard University Press, 1979), xvi.

35. Metz, *Impersonal Enunciation*, 76.

36. Cavell, *Cities of Words*, 325.

37. Stephen Mulhall, "Introduction," in *The Cavell Reader*, ed. Stephen Mulhall (Oxford: Blackwell, 1996), 1.

38. For more on Cavell and cinematic self-reference, see Wheatley, *Stanley Cavell and Film*, 89–90.

39. Emerson, "The Poet," in *Complete Works*, 3:4.

40. See also my "On the Aesthetics of Amateur Filmmaking in Narrative Cinema: Negotiating Home Movies after *Adam's Rib*," in *The Thought of Stanley Cavell and Cinema*, 245–90.

41. Amy Villarejo, *Film Studies: The Basics*, Second Edition (New York: Routledge, 2013), 11.

42. See Christopher Carter, *Metafilm: Materialist Rhetoric and Reflexive Cinema* (Columbus: The Ohio State University Press, 2018).

43. See, e.g., Wartenberg's "Providing Evidence for a Philosophical Claim: *The Act of Killing* and the Banality of Evil," *NECSUS: European Journal of Media Studies* (2017) and "Contemporary Philosophical Filmmaking," in *The Palgrave Handbook of the Philosophy of Film and Motion Pictures*, ed. Noël Carroll, Laura T. Di Summa, and Shawn Loht (New York: Palgrave Macmillan, 2019).

44. CGI (computer-generated imagery), AR/MR/VR (augmented reality/mixed reality/virtual reality), NFTs (non-fungible tokens), and GANs (generative adversarial networks). And with GANs, the age of *acheiropoieta* is upon us—art "made without hands."

45. See *Werner Herzog: A Guide for the Perplexed; Conversations with Paul Cronin* (New York: Faber & Faber, 2014), 81–3. See also my *Emerson's English Traits and the Natural History of Metaphor*, 209–10.

46. Stanley Cavell, "An Interview with Stanley Cavell," by James Conant, *The Senses of Stanley Cavell* (Lewisburg: Bucknell University Press, 1989), 59.

47. Nathanael West, *The Day of the Locust* (New York: Library of America, 1997), 326.

48. Robert Stam, *Reflexivity in Film and Literature: From Don Quixote to Jean-Luc Godard* (New York: Columbia University Press, 1992), 26.

49. See again Ames, *Movies about the Movies*.

50. See my "Autophilosophy," in *Inheriting Stanley Cavell: Memories, Dreams, Reflections*, ed. David LaRocca (New York: Bloomsbury, 2020), 275–320.

51. See, e.g., *The Philosophy of Charlie Kaufman*, ed. David LaRocca (Lexington: University Press of Kentucky, 2011; updated with a new preface, 2019); *Quentin Tarantino's "Inglourious Basterds": A Manipulation of Metacinema*, ed. Robert von Dassanowsky (New York: Continuum, 2012); *Quentin Tarantino's "Django Unchained": The Continuation of Metacinema*, ed. Oliver C. Speck (New York: Bloomsbury, 2014); Eyal Peretz, "What Is a Cinema of Jewish Vengeance?," in *The Off-Screen: An Investigation of the Cinematic Frame* (Stanford: Stanford University Press, 2017), ch. 4; and David Roche, *Quentin Tarantino: Poetics and Politics of Cinematic Metafiction* (Jackson: University of Mississippi Press, 2018).

52. Cavell, *The World Viewed*, 31.

53. Manohla Dargis, "Being Catherine Deneuve," *New York Times*, July 2, 2020.

54. Phillip Lopate, "In Search of the Centaur: The Essay-Film," in *Beyond Document: Essays on Nonfiction Film*, ed. Charles Warren (Middletown, CT: Wesleyan University Press, 1996), 260.

55. See Sianne Ngai, *Theory of the Gimmick: Aesthetic Judgment and Capitalist Form* (Cambridge, MA: Harvard University Press, 2020) and her earlier *Our Aesthetic Categories: Zany, Cute, Interesting* (Cambridge, MA: Harvard University Press, 2015).

PART I
CONCEPTUAL AND THEORETICAL
REORIENTATION TO METACINEMA

1

Cinematic Self-Consciousness in Hitchcock's *Rear Window*

Robert B. Pippin

> Tell me everything you saw and what you think it means.
> —**Lisa Freemont**, *Rear Window*

Spectatorship: Lived and Cinematic

Filmed fictional narratives seem to most viewers to create some minimal transparency illusion, the illusion that the viewer is somehow magically present at various events, that she is an unobserved observer in the scenes.[1] But of course we also know that this cannot be literally true. We are not *in* the action, cannot be affected by what happens, cannot intervene. We occupy far too many points of view, including those of several characters, that no one present could. We are in some sense aware that what we are seeing is being narrated, has been photographed and is being told to us in a visual way, and when this feature is unavoidably obvious, as when we are whisked back in time, or transported suddenly in one cut to another country, or are flying through the air, we easily accept a widespread convention. That is, we have learned to ignore for the most part that someone is purposefully showing us what we are seeing, has decided what we will not see, that the events are not simply magically present in front of us. But some directors do not want us to ignore this feature. They are able also to draw our attention to the director's narrational control, and so to the presence of the camera, not just to what the camera is photographing. When we do notice, the visible narrational element is what gives the film its reflective form. Such a narrative form cannot but suggest a purposiveness, its point, and so manifests that the aesthetic object bears a conception of itself, a source of unity and ultimately interpretive meaning. It seems odd to say that filmed fictional narratives are in this sense

Robert B. Pippin, *Cinematic Self-Consciousness in Hitchcock's* Rear Window In: *Metacinema*. Edited by: David LaRocca, Oxford University Press. © Oxford University Press 2021. DOI: 10.1093/oso/9780190095345.003.0002

"self-conscious," embody an awareness of themselves, but this is just an ellip-
tical way of saying that the director is self-conscious of the point of the determinate narrative form.[2] That point may simply be "to create funny situations"
or "to scare the audience in a way they will enjoy," but it can clearly be more
aesthetically ambitious; for example, to help us understand something better.
This all corresponds to our own implicit awareness in experiencing an aesthetic object that that is what we are doing. "Implicitly aware" also requires a
lot of philosophical unpacking, but there is a natural sense of something like
such potential attentiveness becoming explicit when we find ourselves asking
why we are first shown a character by a camera seeming to swoop in through
a window (*Psycho*) or why there are so many close-ups of backs and backs of
heads in the Dardenne brothers' films. But such aesthetic attending already
embodies a norm. It can be done well, or it can be done lazily, sloppily, indif-
ferently, in a biased way, or self-righteously. That issue will ultimately be the
topic of the following.

There is no clearer example of this set of issues than Alfred Hitchcock's
1954 film, *Rear Window*, and this has occasioned a good deal of discussion
about the purpose of Hitchcock's triply thematizing all at once (1) the voyeurism in the plot, (2) the striking similarity between the main character's
immobile position watching the "framed" dramas he sees in the windows of
the apartments opposite his and the viewer's position in cinema, unquestion-
ably the most commented-on feature of the film,[3] and (3) Hitchcock's calling
attention to his control of what we see and when and how we see it, his insistent breaks from what is established as the main point of view established,
Jeff's.[4] Further, when, in the last twenty minutes of the film, Jeff, the photographer, begins intervening and "directing" the actions that occur (Jeff, afraid
a suspected murderer is pulling out, finally sends him a note and then calls
him and sends his friends on a mission), we have a final allegorical connection made, (4) between Jeff's (the photographer's) position and Hitchcock's.
(This is a photographer, though, who, looking for evidence of a murder, takes
no pictures; never loads his camera although he is always looking through it.
We shall have to return to that.) This last allegorical connection also reminds
us that it was Jeff's vivid narration, with its intensity, passion, and unwavering
conviction, to Stella, his nurse, and Lisa, his girlfriend, and his friend, the detective Tom Doyle, that initially brought into being the possibility of murder,
creating an event out of several disconnected nighttime events. He created, out
of what he saw, what it meant. Put another way, he edited together the various
scenes he saw to make his own imagined film narrative, a murder thriller. He
put together, in a kind of coherent sequence, a tense marital situation, angry
arguments, long-distance phone calls, three nighttime trips by the neighbor,

Thorwald (Raymond Burr), with his metal sample case, and no sign the next day of the wife. (This is all he has at first, but he thinks it enough.) Then he saw a large box, tied with thick ropes and carted away, saw some knives, and a saw a dog digging in the dirt and then being killed, Thorwald washing down the walls of his bathroom, and finally his wife's jewelry still at home.[5] His deep investment in what he wants to be true is also signaled by the strange fact that Jeff is, from the very earliest stages, absolutely and passionately certain that a murder has been committed and immediately, dogmatically rejects any alternate explanation. When he is informed that he had been asleep when a crucial event occurred that disconfirms his entire theory—Thorwald had been seen by the superintendent leaving with his wife the next morning[6]—he is unfazed. This persists even after he hears more disconfirming information from the detective-friend. (Mrs. Thorwald was seen being escorted to the train that morning; seen picking up the trunk, which turned out just to contain her clothes. All of this emphasizes, to the point of obsession, Jeff's investment in the narrative he has constructed.) When it is explained to him that when one observes people unaware they are being observed, not presenting themselves to others as they want to be seen, one does not at all necessarily see some truth about them—they could be presenting themselves to themselves in a way that is just as theatrical and a kind of self-pretense—he is indifferent to such cautions as well.[7]

This manner of Jeff's constructing the suspicion is obviously also linked to what we do when we try to understand what is happening in a film. We are guided by the director and the editor, but we have to do some work, remembering past scenes, deciding which should be remembered, interpreting how one past scene might or might not bear on a recent one, anticipating possibilities. Usually this is no problem in commercial films because we are given very clear visual "advice" about how to do this. Even more to the eventual point here, it is also often what we do when we try to understand someone or some event in ordinary life. If we need to work at the understanding, if something does not make initial sense to us, one of the main ways we go about that work is to create this sort of narrational sense. We try to put what a character said or did into some sort of coherent pattern of remarks or actions in the past, requiring us to decide which might be relevant or not, bring to bear what we have heard other people say about the person, what we know about remarks and deeds we might not have experienced, all in the hope that all of this might reveal what was intended and so what the words or the action meant. This is usually much more revealing than isolating the words or deed in that moment and trying to "plumb the depths" by some deeper insight into their inner life, as if in search of some isolated truth-maker, the fact of the matter. But there are ways of doing this sort of "editing" that are better or worse, and even though Jeff turns out to be right in this case, his way of going about this is quite problematic, and that fact touches on both ethical and aesthetic issues. This is because, inevitably, as noted, we are also often invested in some way in the clarification, and that investment can be self-interested, self-deceived, biased, subject to wishful thinking, and so forth. One of the ways this can become impossible for us to avoid acknowledging is when our views intersect in some way with the lives of others and they respond, intervene in some way to challenge us. And, of course, one of the ways this can be *avoided* is by preventing such challenges, keeping our distance, staying inside our dollhouses or cages, psychological as well as spatial.

The Hitchcockian cinematic self-consciousness that we are interested in happens at the very beginning of the film and is dramatically signaled. Jeff, a photographer immobilized by a broken leg, is asleep (we soon learn) in the early morning heat. He is alone. But the bamboo blinds in his modest apartment rise like theater curtains on the courtyard scene and apartment windows visible from his "rear window," as the credits roll. Staged drama, which the curtain and the open windows suggest, effaces even more any indication of a narrator.[8] The fourth wall has simply disappeared and we take ourselves to be simply watching what the characters do and say.[9] Hitchcock seems to be introducing this "theater convention" into a movie in order subtly to contrast this transparency illusion we indulge more easily in theater with the contrasting but often unnoticed control of narration by a director.[10] (There is another indirect allusion to the theatrical experience. In a departure from Hitchcock's brilliant use of music in his other films, there is no nondiegetic music in the film.)[11] I think Hitchcock is alluding to this difference again when he makes his cameo appearance. He is in the apartment of the composer and appears to be repairing or setting his clock. In the theater, the author "winds everything up" and it plays out without intervention. But a movie director can control the pace and timing of everything we see, intervening frequently, has control of "the clock" throughout. As if to emphasize his control even more, he turns directly in our direction, something I believe he does in only one other cameo, in *Marnie*. Moreover, it is almost as if we are to believe he is giving instructions to the composer about what is the theme music of the film, the piece he is composing that we hear throughout and that eventually is finished as—what else?—"Lisa.")[12] Here, the blinds rising makes no diegetic sense; there is no one who could have raised them (except the director). Then the camera emphasizes its presence and control even more by taking the viewer on a little tour of the outside scene, all until we finally settle on a perspiring James Stewart, L. B. Jeffries, asleep in his wheelchair. (If we are to come later to have some doubts about the propriety of Jeff's voyeurism, we by and large do not at first notice our own compromised position, that our first look at Jeff is rather invasive, a man in a most vulnerable state, unable to look back, to project himself as he wants; asleep.[13] The film is "rounded by a sleep" again at the end, when Jeff is asleep once more, even more immobilized and unable to assert or project himself, and Lisa is awake, now even more able to manipulate her own appearance.[14] (This is the beginning of what Lisa will call "rear window ethics," and, as is emphasized here, it will have something to do with the ethical dimensions implicit in cinema itself.) As if all that weren't emphasis enough, the camera shows us, calling attention to what will be important later in the plot and to the cinematic theme, Jeff's broken 8×10 view camera (no doubt a souvenir of his injury, caused when he stood in the middle of an automobile racetrack to snap the photo we are also shown) and, mysteriously, a framed negative of a woman's face, the positive magazine image of which we are also shown on the cover of a stack of the magazines in which it appeared. (Every positive image starts as a negative, and for some reason never explained Jeff keeps the negative framed and displayed. Is he able to connect the negative with the positive sides of human existence, or is he stuck in "negative viewing," especially, as we shall see, a negative view of marriage, of domestic life, perhaps of women?)[15]

And what we are shown involves the narration of a triple plot, a feature that always raises the issue of the meaning of the interrelation of the three. There is first the minimal plot, Jeff's growing obsession with voyeurism. He is recovering, immobilized by a broken leg, and he spends his days and many of his nights looking out his window and into the apartments of his neighbors. (There is a heatwave and everyone has windows open and blinds up.) He follows the little dramas of people he gives names to: Miss Lonelyhearts, apparently a spinster looking forlornly for love; Miss Torso, an acrobatic dancer usually in various stages of undress, and apparently naively (but not credibly) uninterested in who sees her twirling, stretching, or wiggling her backside as she bends over; a childless couple who dote on their dog; a family with children (normal and apparently happy; they do not catch Jeff's attention and we see very little of them); a newlywed couple; a middle-aged woman who lives alone and sculpts; a composer who also lives alone. Aside from a neighbor who Jeff comes to suspect has murdered his wife, Jeff, his girlfriend, Lisa, and his nurse, Stella, pay most initial attention to the sad plight of the older, unmarried woman, watching her pantomime having a dinner guest, struggling with and rejecting a young, aggressive would-be lover, and contemplating suicide. They are all clearly embarrassed by what they see, but they do not turn away and they watch eagerly. In the second plot, they watch a couple across the way, the wife, an invalid, and her caregiver, her husband, a costume jewelry salesman who seems the object of much criticism by the wife and apparently with good reason. Our early suspicion is that he is having an affair. (There are phone conversations that she overhears and becomes enraged at.) Jeff will come to suspect that the man, played by Raymond Burr, finally murdered, cut into pieces, and disposed of his wife, and that becomes the central plot. Almost as important as the murder plot is the third, what appears to be a long-standing resistance by Jeff to marriage to Lisa, played by Grace Kelly. Kelly, obviously in the running as the most glamorous and beautiful movie star in the history of cinema, and always gorgeously dressed in couture in the film, is nevertheless unable to get Jeff over his deep resistance to marriage. She even seems unable to arouse much sexual desire in the cold fish. He is visibly much more aroused "spectatorially," at a scopophilic distance, by Miss Torso than he ever is by Lisa, no matter her explicit request for a bed for the night, no matter her negligée.[16] Lisa wants Jeff to quit traveling the world photographing disasters and settle down in New York, where he can become a fashion and portrait photographer. He refuses and also refuses to allow her to travel with him, which she claims she is willing to do. Their relationship appears headed for a breakup.

What appears to connect all three plots is the issue of domestic married life, and especially Jeff's view of its horrors. Eventually what connects the narratives to the allegorical dimensions of film watching and filmmaking will be the problem of spectatorship in human relations, how things look, like romance, gender relations, and marriage, from the "outside," not the "inside." When Stella, the nurse played by Thelma Ritter as the voice of common sense, says at the beginning that "we've become a nation of peeping Toms," she cannot mean that we literally spend so much time spying on our neighbors through their windows. We have, though, become a notion of moviegoers, and beginning at around the time of the film, 1954, in a way suggested by the tiny, framed windows, television watchers. I don't think this just means to suggest that filmed drama and comedy interest us because we like to be voyeurs, unobserved observers, but that we watch these screens *like peeping Toms*. That is *the uninvolved spectatorial way* we watch them, as if what we see asks nothing of us, is simply there "for us"; and therein lie both the aesthetic and ethical issues that will be discussed in the next section. Moreover, in a way that will link up to the spectatorship theme, the whole broader issues of gender politics, male power, and the limited options for women's resistance are all emphasized quite explicitly at the beginning and throughout the film. In a conversation with his editor, who has forgotten when Jeff gets his cast off, Jeff asks the editor how he ever got to be a big editor with such a small memory, and the editor responds, "Thrift, industry, and hard work, . . . and catching the publisher with his secretary." (This occurs as a helicopter hovers over two women who are sunbathing on a roof, and as Jeff watches the scantily clad dancer practicing her routines in front of the window.) Jeff is asked why he doesn't marry, and Jeff paints a picture of boredom, routine, and a "nagging wife." In fact, what little we see of the suspect's, Thorwald's, domestic life seems to reflect Jeff's view of the typical entanglements of marriage. From his point of view, we see a man prepare a meal for his wife, carry it to her, and kiss her lovingly, only to see her contemptuously toss aside, with some remark, the flower with which he decorated her tray. He makes a phone call and is then berated by the wife he must attend to constantly. (Tellingly, Jeff is just as unappreciative and ungrateful for the elaborate meal Lisa has arranged for him from "21" as Thorwald's wife is for hers. Jeff is as much an ungrateful nag as any wife we see in the film.) There is thus ample justification for Fawell's characterization: "*Rear Window* represents an unambiguous, sometimes even vicious broadside on the male psyche and male sexual insecurity."[17] (This is all clearly contrasted ironically with the fact that the cleverest, wittiest, and bravest character in the film is Lisa. She also has the most reliable moral compass.)

It is also possible that his initial passionate investment in the murder suspicion has something to do with a projected fantasy of liberation from what Jeff thinks marriage is, what he imagines he might be tempted to do if married to a "nagging wife." The fantasy even has two sides, and the less obvious is more complex. That is, aside from seeing in Thorwald's marriage his possible fate being tied to a wife and yearning to be free, he sees someone immobilized, like him, being served a meal by a loved one, like him, and he sees her reject it unfeelingly; again, like him. He is drawn to attend to a scene of what he likely feels is his own ingratitude and insensitivity in the "21" dinner scene just noted and in his general whiny attitude about Lisa. And more generally, as has been often noted, seeing things so much from Jeff's point of view lets us feel his own anxieties about involvement with women. Virtually every small drama he attends to reflects this concern about marriage and domesticity, as well as a mostly unacknowledged anxiety that, in its absence, one suffers a soul-crushing loneliness. His perception already embodies what it means to him; it is intensely *projective* in a way reminiscent of Proust's observations in *À la Recherche*. The distinction embodied in Lisa's remark quoted earlier, "Tell me everything you saw and what you think it means," is a distinction or separation of moments undermined by what we learn about Jeff in the film. "What it means" to Jeff *is* what he sees. It is also a convenient diversion from Lisa's persistent questions about their future.[18] Given the anecdote about the publisher and what Jeff thinks he

sees around him, it would appear that Jeff much prefers his current position, at least as a mode of life: merely watching, external, photographing
surfaces, spectacles, only to move on to another visual excitement. But to
return to my epigraph, in our case as viewers, this is all just what we see, or
what we think we see. We don't know enough to have much investment, yet,
in what we see, so for us, what it all means is another question. And nothing
in Hitchcock goes unqualified. Jeff's self-involved, projective voyeurism is
also what draws him, probably for the first time, into the lives of the others,
diverts him for a while from the spectacle and danger he prefers and forces
him to simply look at the human condition in middle-class urban New York.
As noted, he at first sees, in effect, only himself in various possible domestic
situations, but that will change dramatically.

Finally, the fact that Hitchcock parallels our initial look at the Thorwalds
at dinner with Jeff's dinner with Lisa has a number of psychological
dimensions. The invalid parallel with Jeff is a figure of his own anxiety about
being "femininized" by domesticity (one of the things he oddly complains
about to the editor is the whir of electric appliances on returning home to a
married life every day), and that is no doubt a reflection of his anxiety about
his own masculinity, in Freudian terms his fear of his own desire for such
feminization, which, finally, seems connected with his own need to demonstrate his masculinity by wild and reckless bravery, another exaggerated sign
that he fears not being as masculine as he should be, and so needs constantly
to prove it.

"What it means" for us has something to do with the context of Hitchcock's
work, and what we have been discussing thus far is not an isolated theme in
Hitchcock. In what are often regarded as his three greatest films, *Rear Window*
(1954), *Vertigo* (1958), and *North by Northwest* (1959), the central character is
a man north of forty (Stewart was forty-six and fifty in the first two; Grant was
fifty-five), unmarried (a bachelor in the first two; many times divorced in the
third), no doubt anxious about entering middle age and the future of his romantic life, and each of the three is quite skeptical of and so deeply resistant to
marriage. They are all attracted to and attractive to beautiful, younger, blond
women, but despite happy-enough endings in *Rear Window* and *North by
Northwest*, there is little hope that a stable marriage with any of these men
will result. *Vertigo*'s ending is of course unqualifiedly tragic.[19] And in each,
some features of moviemaking and even what we might call the ontological
presuppositions of cinematic experience and their relation to ordinary life
are present in some way, again suggesting some link between the romantic
theme and the cinematic one. In *Rear Window*, it is the "externality" of the
viewer's (or most viewers' assumed) position and the manipulative power

of the director. In *Vertigo* it is the fantasy creation of a fictional character, largely by means of "external" aids, clothes, make up, gait, style. Both Elster and Scottie play the figurative role of director and character-creator. And in *North by Northwest*, the emphasis is on acting and pretense, Roger Thornhill pretending to be a nonexistent character, Kaplan, because some rather incompetent spies believe the fictional character is real and is the advertising executive Cary Grant, advertising itself being some sort of figure for the creation of cinematic illusion.[20]

Rear Window Ethics

We've become a race of peeping Toms. What people ought to do is get outside their own house and look in for a change.
                                    —**Stella,** *Rear Window*

The ethical question Lisa raises when she says, "I'm not much on rear window ethics" appears to be the straightforward and obvious one that Jeff had just mentioned: is it right, "ethical," to spy on people just because one can ("even if one proves that someone did not commit a murder"). But the film is raising a deeper and more complicated ethical question, and it is already suggested by Stella's remark just noted, that one needs to go outside and look in, not just stay inside and look out. Dramatically the issue is introduced subtly, in the famous scene when Grace Kelly first appears in the film. Jeff awakens to see her luminous, gorgeous face, as if conjured up in his dream state (a movie star from the "dream factory," but also a faint suggestion of her fantasy status, perhaps her merely fantasy status, for Jeff), and he asks what appears to be a humorous, ironic question after some romantic banter and a slow-motion kiss (actually a so-called step-print technique was used): "Who are you?" Lisa answers by turning on, one by one, the lights in the room, as if in answer, "illuminating" who she is, and saying, "Lisa. Carol. Freemont" until she stands, posed to-be-looked-at, fashion model that she is, in a lovely thousand-dollar gown. And that *is* the answer, for Jeff, at this point anyway. She is a model, a to-be-looked-at woman. He does not, in other words, immediately or in most of the film, acknowledge in any serious way her view of him, allow himself, in any serious sense, to be seen by her, imagine him from her point of view, see himself from the outside, as in Stella's recommendation. And she is not just a model for him, but a mere type, a Park Avenue, rich, spoiled girl, he says. That deeper ethical question concerns the appropriateness of this sort of spectatorial relation to others in general, not just in spying situations, not necessarily reifying or objectifying. It is more a matter of blindness and resistance, and it is a blindness toward others that cripples Jeff's own self-knowledge (it insulates him from others' view of him, a much more valuable potential source of self-knowledge than introspection), leaves him a bit smug and already tending toward that "old, bitter" unmarried man his editor warned him against. Of course to a large degree (at this point) Lisa has accepted that role and function, as have the dancer and Miss Lonelyhearts. But she is already chafing under Jeff's thoughtless presuppositions about her and what she can and cannot do. She'll show him soon how wrong he is.

And all this too is all connected to the cinematic allegory, with Jeff's position as viewer of those several mini-films he sees across the courtyard, as that aesthetic theme becomes entwined with this issue of spectatorship. That doubling is not just meant as a remark on the rather banal explanation of what attracts us to cinema, the possibility of seeing while unseen. And this is not, at least not wholly, a cautionary critique of what cinema can do or what a mistake it would be to ignore the limits of cinema.[21] It is rather, I want to suggest, a critique of a common and not at all necessary or unavoidable form of *cinematic viewership*, of the *way* Hitchcock clearly thinks that people watch movies, especially his movies, what they expect from them, and most importantly what they imagine (overwhelmingly what they do not imagine) that an intelligent film expects *from them*. In this respect a question is being raised that is larger than one specific to cinema and includes all the arts, and embodies a relation to the viewer that also bears on interpersonal relations. But it will take a closer look at some elements in the film before that claim can be defended. We will need to prepare for what I want to suggest is the most important "ethical" question in the film, the one asked by Thorwald when he first enters Jeff's apartment, "What do you want from me?"

This stage of the film is marked by a break in the enthusiasm and excitement that Jeff, Lisa, and Stella have felt in figuring out how Thorwald murdered and disposed of his wife. The detective, Doyle, a smug, indifferent presence throughout the film who cannot hide his weary contempt for these amateurs, informs them that the mysterious trunk was retrieved by Mrs. Thorwald after all. She is very much alive. Jeff and Lisa are severely disappointed. The murder possibility had obviously drawn them together, given them a bond, in a way that the next scene in the Miss Lonelyhearts drama does not. In their dejection, they watch her bring home a man she has picked up. She lowers her Venetian blinds, but before she can close them he assaults her and she has to fight him off. They watch, do not look away, do not even look alarmed or surprised, but they are clearly embarrassed, and even ashamed of themselves. (Later, Jeff and Stella see her prepare to attempt what they think is suicide and they are ready, finally, to intervene in Miss Lonelyhearts' life, but by then the plot developments—the police arriving in Thorwald's apartment—distract them. She might have died if it had not been for a mere accident. She hears what appears to be the finished tune the composer had been working on, and that music seems to turn her from suicide.)[22] Lisa is also appropriately embarrassed that they are sad that a woman is *not* dead. They are, she claims, a couple of "ghouls." They had spent so much of their time together looking out the window, and Jeff had spent so much time avoiding Lisa's serious attention to their future, that this is their first serious engagement face to face, and about a weighty topic. They have begun to deal with each other, rather than co-viewing these little films. So a phase of the film does seem over. They finally confront the fact that the expectation of privacy is a human entitlement, and we sense some closure as, after this conversation, Lisa ceremonially closes all three blinds, announces that "the show is over," and prepares for the "preview of coming attractions," her negligée. (She still uses the language of spectatorial cinema to describe their relationship.) Jeff even resolves, starting tomorrow, to take seriously the imperative "Love thy neighbor." But then a neighbor screams.

The third-floor couple with the little dog has discovered him dead, and Miss Lonelyhearts announces that he has been killed, his neck had been broken. It will turn out that Thorwald had buried part of his wife (probably her head) in the garden, and the dog had gotten too curious, was sniffing and digging in the wrong spot. The wife in the couple then makes a speech decrying the lack of humanity in the apartment complex, their indifference to each other, the fact that they are not at all neighbors, they do not watch out for each other, care at all for each other. Hitchcock clearly stages this as a voice from an older generation, decrying (rightly we are given to believe) what has happened to more recent urban culture: that the younger generation has become alienated from each other, even indifferent to each other. The couple sleep outside on the fire escape during the heat, figuring that they are the only tenants not so isolated, always inside what Narmore calls their "doll's houses,"[23] and what Chabrol called "a kind of human rabbit hutch, a variety of cages in which humans live in close proximity to one another but in isolation nevertheless."[24] The speech is obviously a reflection on Jeff's isolated, spectatorial position as well, although he is being drawn out of this isolation by the murder; eventually, literally *tossed* out of his window. However, what connects all this with the cinema theme emerges when the dog's owner, in her justifiable rant about her so-called neighbors, asks an extremely odd question: "Did you kill him because he liked you, just because he liked you?"

This is an extraordinary suggestion about a killing motive. One can (I suppose) imagine killing a pesky dog who is destroying one's garden, or yapping all day, or biting one's children, or even a dog so friendly that he bothers one constantly and so forth, but none of that is relevant here. Who would kill a dog "just because" the dog was affectionate? It suggests immediately by contrast a great resistance to being loved.[25] That of course brings Jeff and his resistance to Lisa to mind. That, in turn, raises again his spectatorial position, looking out but "letting no one in," enjoying his godlike perch above it all, just as he had enjoyed the kind of action photography that made up his professional life. And all of that, in turn, returns us not only to Jeff's position as a figure for cinema viewing, but to the question of *how* he watches. I noted previously that, at the interpersonal level, our interpretive attempt to understand each other, involving as it often does an attempt at some narrational sense requiring our own editorial skill, can be done well, or poorly, lazily, or simply stupidly, informed by insufficient experience, little sense of how it might be done. And we can find all sorts of ways of preventing any external interference with the narrational pattern we have established in the little dramas we have narrated for ourselves. In this case, we have seen Jeff's overinvestment in the very idea of "Thorwald murdering his nagging ball and chain" (we can imagine him saying it if he were ever honest with himself), as well as his overinvestment in the sense he thinks he has made of the isolated dramas in each of the apartments he has selected for attention. It turns out that he will be wrong about Miss Torso. She was not playing the field, but was no doubt dealing with professional contacts ("juggling wolves," as Lisa puts it sympathetically) while awaiting a boyfriend's return from the army, a short, nerdy-looking man whom Jeff would never have anticipated in his clichéd attitude toward her.[26] He cannot come up with any view of the composer, invokes a romance magazine stereotype for Miss Lonelyhearts, and clearly (and it turns out wrongly) thinks of Thorwald as simply a sociopathic killer. The fact that he was "right" about the murder is no result of any interpretive finesse. He has *the plot* right, just as many viewers of Hitchcock watch and follow the plot successfully, and take great pleasure in the technical brilliance of the editing, pacing, intersecting threads and so forth. But they see nothing else, or they casually adopt some cliché about Hitchcock as their interpretive result, the meaning of the narrative: he is a perverse voyeur, a sadist, a cold, manipulative technician, a champion of the male gaze, a Catholic director convinced of universal and profound sinfulness, a cynic, or even the much more accurate cliché, but still a cliché, that he is a "humanist" at heart, and so forth. Many of his films, but especially *Rear Window* and *Vertigo* (above all *Vertigo*), seem to me great protests against this. The final turn of this screw occurs when the windows, the screens, of both apartments, Jeff's and Thorwald's, are breached.

Involvement: Lived and Cinematic

After the dog's death, Jeff and Lisa notice that the only light that did not come on was Thorwald's, as if, they think, he already knew what happened and who did it. As they try to figure out why he would kill the dog, Jeff remembers that he had taken several slides of the courtyard in the weeks of his confinement. As he unpacks the slides, he mutters, "I hope I didn't take *all* leg art." This is a reference to a shot we had just seen a few minutes before of Miss Torso's apartment. All the viewer can see are her two legs exercising. So we know Jeff had been taking photographs, and that he has an overdeveloped interest in Miss Torso's body (not, apparently, in her), but we don't know why he took no photos recently with his huge telephoto lens: none of any of the potentially incriminating scenes he has seen, and none just now of Thorwald washing down his bathroom walls or, soon, packing to leave, his wife's jewelry and so forth. (He surely must have high-speed film and knows how to take photos in low light.) It is as if he wants to keep his involvement *purely* observational, as if even the imprint on his film is too much of an intrusion from the outside. At any rate, it is an odd omission by a professional photographer, especially since we now learn that he *has* bothered to take photos even *of the garden* and the row of flowers that were the cause of the little dog's death. The two yellow zinnias in the flower bed are shorter, and "Since when do flowers grow shorter in two weeks?" This realization and the sudden sight of Thorwald packing begin the first intervention in the outside world.

Jeff writes a note. Hitchcock shifts to an overhead shot and dramatically zooms in as Jeff writes, "What have you done with her?" and puts the note in an envelope with Thorwald's name on it. There could be a score of explanations for why the zinnias are shorter, aside from Thorwald having dug up what he had buried there (which no one has seen him do), but this "discovery" and the dog's death and now the sight of Thorwald packing up have moved Jeff to this staged intervention. The first stage is this note, still a pretty non-involved in-volvement, although it is Lisa, clearly enjoying the role, as she had called it, of the private eye's "girl Friday," who must deliver the note and is almost caught. When she returns, Jeff obviously looks at her with new respect and desire. (All of his is going on while Miss Lonelyhearts—noticed by Stella—is preparing for her suicide.)

Then another stage of involvement, a bit closer. They need Thorwald out of the apartment so Stella and Lisa can dig up the flower bed unseen; Jeff, to get Thorwald out, calls Thorwald on the phone, pretends to be a blackmailer, and arranges to meet him. Still no risk to Jeff, as he notices when he stumbles on the word "we" and admits the women are taking all the chances. Meanwhile Miss Lonelyhearts' suicide preparations go on apace, unnoticed by our thrilled amateur detectives. The phone call works, Thorwald leaves, and the coast is clear.[27]

The final act begins. Jeff keeps watch as they dig. They find nothing, but Lisa, in an extraordinarily risky and brave move, climbs up and into Thorwald's second-story flat, and, given all the associations built up, it is just as if she is leaving one world, the world of the audience, and literally entering the fictional world of the "Thorwald movie," as dramatic a moment as any that has occurred so far. I don't know of any way to prove the point, but given the detective theme and this moment, Lisa's climbing into the Thorwald world must be a reference to Buster Keaton's great 1924 film, *Sherlock, Jr.*, where essentially the same conflation of worlds occurs and a character climbs into a movie screen. In this case, we keep our attention divided between the dangerous "merged" world Lisa has created and Jeff, the viewer, helpless, reacting like a terrified movie audience, squirming, grimacing, no longer just a distant spectator, but unable to help, still in the audience world, connected to his beloved, now in mortal danger.

The involvement/non-involvement dynamic reaches a crisis level when Thorwald discovers Lisa in the apartment and begins to struggle with her. She calls out to Jeff, but, in an astonishing last sign of Jeff's immobility, distance, reticence, and all that entails, even though for all they know she could be being murdered, neither he nor Stella calls out *to Thorvald*! They don't yell at him to leave her alone, that they see him, that they have called the police. (Perhaps Jeff is still in full "cinematic mode," assuming that doing so would make as little difference as the person who yells out, "Don't open that door!" at a horror film. Perhaps he is simply afraid of giving away his position.) The police do arrive, and Lisa indicates to Jeff that she has found and managed to keep Mrs. Thorwald's wedding ring, but in signaling him, she also alerts Thorwald to Jeff's observing presence, and the most tense part of the film begins. That other "outside" world invades Jeff's. The phone rings. It is obviously Thorwald but he says nothing, is clearly only checking that he has the right apartment, and we soon hear Thorwald's slow, heavy, and for Jeff and for us, terrifyingly ever closer footsteps climbing the stairs to Jeff's apartment, and he enters. Lisa has penetrated that outside cinematic world, and now, in a stunning move, the counterpart involvement occurs, as if a character steps out of the screen and into the viewer's world. (We are shown that Jeff, with his heavy full leg cast, can't get out of his chair to lock his door; he is defenseless against this intrusion.)

"What do you want from me?" Thorvald asks, and then, "Your friend, the girl, she could have turned me in. Why didn't she? What is it you want? A lot of money? I don't have any money. Say something! Say something! Tell me what you want. Can you get me that ring back?" Jeff tells him the police have it by now, and Thorwald advances at Jeff. As many commentators have pointed out, Raymond Burr's pained, suffering, and pathetic tone instantly humanizes what Jeff and we had considered a stereotypical monster-murderer; the voice virtually creates another character, the real Thorwald, not the character in Jeff's film, albeit still a murderer. Then in a cinematic staging of astonishing brilliance, Hitchcock enacts visually the culmination of the themes of cinematic viewing and the lived-out dimensions of the spectatorship/involvement relation in a single scene.

Jeff's protective strategy is to use what would normally be his "illuminating" flashbulbs to *blind* Thorwald momentarily, to keep him from seeing where to advance. This of course figures Jeff's general resistance to "being seen," to anyone "looking in," to allowing even Lisa to see him honestly; all this, even though he is of course also trying to save his life. But for this to work, he *must also "blind" himself*, shield his eyes from the flash so he can see how to work the next flash efficiently. The extraordinary, even somewhat childish image of Jeff with his hands over his eyes, flashing his blinding bulbs in blinded self-protection, makes a complex point in a densely compressed way, all in a single image: that his "peeping Tom," external, spectatorial relation to the world has resulted in his own infirmity, a kind of willed self-blindness to others but especially to himself.[28]

And this bears directly on the cinematic theme. It is as if "the Thorwald film" has come alive, invaded a world Jeff had thought of as ontologically separate, sealed off, and has challenged the way he has watched his "films." "What do you want from me?" is a question I think of as one Hitchcock poses to his audience, and it implies another: what do you think I, my films, want *from you*? "To assault you"—to toss you out of your insulated, sealed-off world, to involve you—might be a general answer, but more specifically, here and throughout the film, he appears to be signaling a demand for a kind of cinematic involvement, an interpretive one.[29] Throughout, we have seen all sorts of cinematic signs of the limitations and distortions in Jeff's mode of viewing, that it is self-involved, anxious, negative, but mostly everywhere based on an assumption of a strict, walled-off separation between the world of the viewer and the movie world, an inside-Jeff world and an outside-to-be-viewed world.

We saw aspects of that assumption in his relation to his work and to Lisa and certainly to any romantic entanglement. But the assumption has also been revealed to be a distortion of virtually every scene he watches, and in the terms we introduced to at the beginning, this is a result of the simplicity and laziness of his mode of narration, how he attends to what he sees. He can be said to have an impoverished notion of cinematic form, like a reader who reads "only for plot." Hitchcock was always so careful in his films to include visual details that repay multiple viewings[30] that he is clearly demanding something from his audiences, a mode of attending he must feel (on the evidence of *Rear Window*) that he is not getting, that the formal devices alone, all of which quickly become Hitchcock stereotypes, do not for most viewers (at least until the French discovered him) inspire any depth of interpretive involvement, raise any question about the point of the stories he tells. The cinematic object is just treated as there to be viewed, an occasion for the viewer's experience, of significance only for that.[31] And of course, if we start off assuming that that is what commercial films are exclusively for, objects made for consuming subjects, designed to cause experiences that will entertain in various ways, will cause who cares what sort of experiences so long as they encourage consumption, then, given that Hitchcock was certainly deeply interested in the financial success of his films, and so actively encouraged audiences to think of his films as mere scary entertainment, it might appear that the assumption is justified. But this film itself suggests otherwise; it highlights an implicit demand on the part of Hitchcock's films to be "let in" to the viewer's world, so that "what we see" and "what it means" can be worked at beyond working at how the plot events fit together, and beyond the self-involved meanings the events seen had for Jeff and audiences like him. And just as in *Vertigo*, where Hitchcock links the creation of fantasy characters by Elster and Scottie with the creation of fantasies by the Hollywood "dream factory" in order to show the limitations and dangers of such an attitude to others as well as to cinema, the dynamic of spectatorship and involvement plays out at both levels, cinematic and social, in the film's conclusion.

At the film's conclusion we are shown that the temperature is twenty degrees lower now, perhaps a sign that there will be a less feverishly projective attitude by Jeff toward others as well as to what he sees across the way in the new seven-week period he will be laid up with his second broken leg, suffered when Thorvald pushes him out the window. Or at least that this would be possible. The composer's song has been finished, and we are reminded that for some artists, the only consideration is the one he expresses: "I hope it's gonna be a hit." That is *not* "what it means" to Miss Lonelyhearts, as she tells him, "I can't tell you what this music has meant to me." (The contrast drawn between commercial success and another kind of success continues to be made.) Thorwald's apartment is being repainted. The older couple has a new dog. Miss Torso's boyfriend, Stanley, comes home and, after a long time away from his gorgeous girlfriend, is only interested in what she has in her refrigerator. In line with that little Jeff-like joke, the very last dialogue we hear is from the newlyweds, whose initial romantic flame had been shown to cool to a boring, routine duty, at least for the husband. The wife says, "If you had told me you had lost your job, we would have never gotten married." Much of the Jeff world of boring domesticity and futility seems still available if the mode of attending remains the same. And then we are shown there is little hope of anything really different. Again, as at the beginning, we see Jeff asleep, this time smiling, but now with two broken legs, even more immobile, emphasizing his continued position as mere non-involved spectator. As we hear the composer's recording ironically intone its last phrase, "Lisa," we see her in jeans, pretending to be reading a book called *Beyond the High Himalayas*, as if ready to travel the world with Jeff. But when she notices Jeff is asleep, she pulls out a *Harper's Bazaar* and smiles. Nothing has changed much, except for the viewers who notice that Hitchcock wants to show us that nothing has changed, that it should have, that that lack of change misses a potential both for the couple and for Hitchcock's audience—except for those who see a different way to connect what they see and what it means.[32]

Notes

1. An earlier version of this chapter appeared in my *Filmed Thought: Cinema as Reflective Form* (Chicago: University of Chicago Press, 2019), 23–48.

2. I don't mean that the director necessarily has a determinate "message" or "theme" explicitly in mind, and always constructs everything to making such a point, or that the film must have such a message. (Louis B. Mayer was right: if you want a message, call Western Union.) The "sense" embodied in the narrative, and so the form's determinacy, can be intuitively at work; e.g., simply in seeing that such and such a narrational move would "make sense" in the context of the overall film or that it wouldn't; that such and such an action on the part of a character should be experienced as troubling; that a kind of self-blindness should be portrayed as destructive, not merely naive, and so forth. The idea that a work must be formally self-conscious about itself, bear a conception of itself, is worth a separate study in itself. For more on the issue, see my *After the Beautiful: Hegel and the Philosophy of Pictorial Modernism* (Chicago: University of Chicago Press, 2013).

3. This has been suggested by several commentators. See especially Jean Douchet, "Hitch et son public," *Cahiers du Cinéma* 19–20, no. 113 (1960–61): 7–15; John Fawell, *"Rear Window": The Well-Made Film* (Carbondale: Southern Illinois University Press, 2001), chs. 8 and 9; John Belton, "The Space of *Rear Window*," in *Hitchcock's Rereleased Films*,

ed. W. Raubicheck and W. Strebnick (Detroit: Wayne State University Press, 1991); Robert Stam and Roberta Pearson, "Hitchcock's *Rear Window*: Reflexivity and the Critique of Voyeurism," in *A Hitchcock Reader*, ed. M. Deutelbaum and L. Poague (Ames: Iowa State University Press, 1986).

4. For the most part, such a cinematic narrator is, in George Wilson's phrase, "minimal," effaced; certainly not usually present in the film, as if a character. And nothing about the biographical details of the actual makers of the film are needed to infer the intentions of the narrator. The intentions are what can be seen in the film. See *Seeing Fictions in Films: The Epistemology of Movies* (Oxford: Oxford University Press, 2011), 129.

5. This all of course mirrors what we see and largely what we also do when watching a film; we are always implicitly asking what it means that one sequence follows another, and we form our hypotheses the same way as Jeff, usually with more tentativeness. The film itself is, as usual with Hitchcock, quite cinematic in this sense; 35 percent of it is without dialogue, as noted by S. Scharff, *The Art of Looking in Hitchcock's "Rear Window"* (New York: Limelight Editions, 1997), 2, 179. It is often as if we were watching silent films, and one long scene is even a pantomime. See James Narmore, *Acting in the Cinema* (Berkeley: University of California Press, 1988), 241. Scharff's book has a useful shot-by-shot summary of the film's 796 shots, and is a valuable resource for its subject: Hitchcock's "symmetries and subsymmetries, contrapuntal arrangements, trigger releases, slow disclosures, familiar images and those ominous transitions by way of fades; each scene is woven out from these elements, and their presence is detectable in different combinations—they are the poetics of his cinema" (180).

6. This must have been his confederate/lover, and it takes Lisa, not the detective and not Jeff, to surmise that the woman could have been anyone. (Mrs. Thorwald is an invalid and rarely seen.) The confederate likely got into the building when both Jeff and the super were sleeping.

7. This is my suggestion about why one should be cautious. All Doyle says is, "That's a secret, private world you're looking into out there. People do a lot of things in private they couldn't possibly explain in public."

8. See again Wilson on this point in *Seeing Fictions in Films*, and my discussion in a review article of Wilson's book, "*Le Grand Imagier* of George Wilson," *European Journal of Philosophy*, 21, no. 2 (June 2013), 334–41.

9. The scenes are also separated in the film by a black screen, not dissolves, again suggesting the separation of acts in a theater, with the curtains closing.

10. There is an illuminating discussion by Belton in "The Space of *Rear Window*" of the way Hitchcock makes use of the techniques of both "showing" (as in theater) and "narrating" or "telling" (as in the novel), or mimetic versus diegetic narration, and especially how he mixes the two in his use of the spatial arrangement of the outside apartments and in the inside world of Jeff's. See also Éric Rohmer and Claude Chabrol, *Hitchcock: The First Forty-Four Films*, trans. S. Hochman (New York: Unger, 1992), where they call the film "a reflexive, critical work in the Kantian sense," and state that the "theory of spectacle" implied in the work requires a "theory of space" that implies a "moral idea" that "derives from it" (124). (Their sense of the "moral idea" at work is "Christian dogma" [126]. See their all-too-pat summary of their whole approach to Hitchcock [128]. That can be contrasted with the approach taken here.)

11. There is, though, plenty of music coming from the apartments, and it has several functions at various points in the plot. See Fawell, *Rear Window*, 120–22.

12. Lisa suggests that it is their song, and she is right: he is having a lot of trouble "completing" it. (She says of the music that it's "as if it's written expressly for us." It was.)

13. This is certainly not the only time Hitchcock reminds the viewer that he or she may be complicit with the actions of a character the viewer may also be tempted to judge morally. The most humorous treatment of the theme is our invitation to laugh at Joe and Herb in *Shadow of a Doubt* for their fascination with gruesome murder plots; this in a film that we have paid to see about a serial killer.

14. The 360-degree pan is repeated as well.

15. For an especially good treatment of Jeff's obsession with "the negative" see George Toles's fine piece, "*Rear Window* as Critical Allegory," in *A House Made of Light: Essays on the Art of Film* (Detroit: Wayne State University Press, 2001), especially this remark:

> No space for reflection is created in which the mesmerizing labor of the negative reveals its potential for infecting the knowledge and claims of social justice or truthseeking that are its putative higher ends. In other words, Jefferies's (or anyone's) capacity to envision the ideal, to act credibly in the name of a truth better than the radically imperfect "givens" of the present[,] can be subtly deformed by a consistent reliance on a terminology obsessed with negation and hidden tyranny. (169)

> The photography issue appears to have something to do with the argument between Jeff and Lisa about the future. Jeff wants to photograph spectacles, events that require no deep interrogation of or involvement by the photographer. She wants him to become a fashion and portrait photographer, a job where, presumably, much more psychological investment in understanding the subject is required. That that dialectic between mere spectatorship and involvement will be crucial in the film is an early indication of Jeff's skepticism that there is much more to know in any such depths than "the negative," and it is not worth the bother. On the other hand, the fashion photograph is an indication that he *can* do and has done what Lisa is asking.

16. When she is in his lap and they are kissing at the 45:27 mark in the film, things do seem to be getting romantic, but she actually has to plead with him to pay attention to her, has to say that she wants all of his attention, and when he says, smiling, that he has a problem, which seems to be a reference to an erection, everything changes when he explains his problem: "Why would a man leave his apartment . . . etc." Lisa is crestfallen.

17. Fawell, *Rear Window*, 6.

18. Douchet, "Hitch et son Public," 8.

19. There are a number of deliberate echoes of *Rear Window* in *Vertigo*, starting with the fact that the same actor plays the marriage-resistant male. Both men begin the film injured and immobile to some degree (by a back "corset" and a leg cast), both voice satisfaction with their bachelor life, and Hitchcock even echoes in the opening of *Vertigo* at the end of *Rear Window*: the aloof bachelor played by Stewart dangling from a ledge. See my *The Philosophical Hitchcock: "Vertigo" and the Anxieties of Unknowingness* (Chicago: University of Chicago Press, 2017) on Scottie's resistance.

20. The "reluctant, skeptical male" and the modern marriage theme is certainly not limited to these three films. There is the wife's poignant speech about her marriage in *Shadow of a Doubt* (1943) ("You sort of forget you're you" in a marriage); Cary Grant's suspicions and

skepticism about Ingrid Bergman's character in *Notorious*, and, in a class completely by it-self, the strange brutality of the marriage in *Marnie* (1964).

21. It is true, as Toles notes, that the cinema is limited to what can be made visible, but what is made visible can also "show us" what might be invisible, although that requires work on our part. This is the issue of cinematic irony. See my "Cinematic Irony: The Strange Case of Nicholas Ray's *Johnny Guitar*," in *nonsite* 13 (September 2014), and "Love and Class in Douglas Sirk's *All That Heaven Allows*," *Critical Inquiry* 45, no. 4 (2019): 935–66.

22. This is in keeping with Hitchcock's own obvious enormous faith in music, I suppose one would have to call it, in both its powerful role in narrative and its closeness to what he strove for, "pure cinema," visual images packed with content, with as little dialogue as possible.

23. Narmore, *Acting in the Cinema*, 374.

24. Claude Chabrol, "Serious Things," in *Cahiers du Cinéma: The 1950s, New Realism, Hollywood, New Wave*, ed. J. Hiller (Cambridge, MA: Harvard University Press, 1985), 139. The sculptress also sits outside and even speaks to Thorwald, but only to criticize him for the way he is gardening. We also see her sleeping with a newspaper over her face. At the end of the film, she is asleep again.

25. This of course brings the project of Stanley Cavell to mind, especially "The Avoidance of Love: A Reading of *King Lear*," in *Must We Mean What We Say: A Book of Essays* (Cambridge: Cambridge University Press, 1976), 267–356 and his treatment throughout his work of the problem of skepticism as a form of resistance. But this passage from *The World Viewed: Reflections on the Ontology of Film* (Cambridge, MA: Harvard University Press, 1979) seems written with *Rear Window* in mind: "Our condition has become one in which our natural mode of perception is to view, feeling unseen. We do not so much look at the world as look *out at* it, from behind the self" (102).

26. No doubt this is Hitchcock's comment on the viewer's expectations too.

27. Thorwald puts on a ridiculous white hat as he leaves that immediately makes him look far less threatening, much more ordinary, than in Jeff's obvious fantasy. This prepares us for the pathos created when he appears soon in Jeff's apartment.

28. Toles, in "*Rear Window* as Critical Allegory," has argued that this image of self-protective blinding is meant to suggest "the drastic limits of the camera's power to image truth" (179). I have been suggesting throughout that the limit at stake for Hitchcock arises from modes of attending more than the limits of cinema, but the two positions are not incompatible.

29. Is it a coincidence that he chose for the actor who plays Thorwald an overweight Raymond Burr, or that Burr, thirty-seven at the time, was made up to seem older, perhaps about Hitchcock's age at the time, fifty-five?

30. For some evidence, see D. A. Miller, *Hidden Hitchcock* (Chicago: University of Chicago Press, 2016), especially his chapter on *Strangers on a Train* ("Hidden Pictures"), and my account of the difference multiple viewings of *Vertigo* makes in *The Philosophical Hitchcock*.

31. This touches on a very complicated problematic prominent in reflection on modern art from the time of Diderot until the advent of minimalism, postmodernism, the rejection of all appeal to authorial intention, and beyond. It is the problematic that Michael Fried has called "theatricality," and it touches on all sorts of ethical and political issues as well as aesthetic ones. For an account of how, see my "Authenticity in Painting: Remarks on Michael Fried's Art History," *Critical Inquiry* 31, no. 3 (2005), 575–98, and ch. 3 in *After the Beautiful*.

32. Robin Wood argues that overall the film is "therapeutic" for both Jeff and for the viewer, but it is hard to see how, since in his concluding paragraph Wood emphasizes quite rightly the deliberate, almost mocking superficiality of the "loose ends tied up" summaries of the various plots, that the "semi-live puppets enclosed in little boxes" are still subject to the "frustrations and desperations" that "can drive them to murder and suicide" and that "we are left with the feeling that the sweetness-and-light merely covers up that chaos world that underlies the superficial order." See his chapter on *Rear Window* in *Hitchcock's Films Revisited* (New York: Columbia University Press, 1989), 107.

2

Adaptations, Refractions, and Obstructions

The Prophecies of André Bazin

Timothy Corrigan

This essay is a rather odd look at a particular shape of adaptation today as what I'll call a "refractive environment," a look that may seem slightly less peculiar if we keep in mind that I'm poaching my fundamental terms and ideas and what they suggest from essays by André Bazin. Alongside my abiding respect for traditional pathways into adaptation studies, my direction here has little to do with cinematic adaptation in most of the usual senses. Instead I want to follow Bazin's terms as dynamic metaphors for some ways of thinking about adaptation studies today and, as a somewhat more provocative move, of raising some questions about the advancement of adaptation studies into today's environment as an evolutionary shift that might be best served by looking backward. Here is where I locate the intersection of adaptation and metacinema.[1]

Here is where the 2002 film *Adaptation.* becomes a clever allegory for metacinematic adaptation studies and a reminder that there's no escaping our cultural environment and that even we textual scholars are capable of surviving. If this Spike Jonze/Charlie Kaufman film identifies the danger of adaptation as a psychological and textual narcissism blocked and obstructed by its commitment to singularity, the film follows that danger along a Darwinian path that moves from a romantic and solipsistic individualism to its commercial transformation, from passionless fidelity to passionate infidelity. The twins Charlie and Donald Kaufman become both an aesthetic and a biological image of adaptation, two figures whose struggle to define and differentiate themselves madly expands and redirects a tortured character study into a mystery about drugs and death, an action film with car crashes and man-eating alligators, and ultimately about the triumph of life as the triumph of commerce and industry. While infidelity permeates the plot involving Susan Orlean and her orchid thief lover, in the end fidelity is ultimately reconstituted in the film as a personal and textual commitment to faithful change, personal

Timothy Corrigan, *Adaptations, Refractions, and Obstructions* In: *Metacinema*. Edited by: David LaRocca, Oxford University Press. © Oxford University Press 2021. DOI: 10.1093/oso/9780190095345.003.0003 passion, and environmental transformation. If Donald's lesson is that "change is not a choice," it is a learned lesson through which his paralytic insistence on authorial expression and textual integrity gives way to the demands of a social and industrial environment as the always-evolving prism of both. The horror of mere duplication embodied in twins becomes the triumph of continual environmental adaptation where to survive is to follow your passions about "what you love" and, as Donald's puts it, "not what loves you." As the strangely hilarious climax of the film suggests, you can adapt to the world or be eaten by an alligator.

Trends since 2000: The Environment of Multiplication

For me three recent trends stand out in adaptation practices of the last two decades. First, the proliferation of the adaptation of classical texts from Shakespeare to Austen and beyond has increased to a noticeable degree across different venues and different cultures. Second, blockbuster adaptations, most notably of the *Harry Potter* and *The Lord of the Rings* series, have figured as the most economically and commercially reliable force in the industry today, generating sequel after sequel, as serial duplications that advance canonized literary texts through a seemingly inexhaustible series of reincarnations. Third and most distinctive, graphic novels, comic books, and video games have now become primary and popular sources for films and repositories themselves for adaptations that respond to the unique representational overlap between source and adaptation as they recycle both visual images and graphic mise en scènes.

Related to this last trend have been the social and industrial changes of the last twenty years that in turn have often impacted and provided the environment for these textual directions. Here I'm referring to the multiplication and proliferation of technologies and contexts, across computer games through internet sites, through which adaptations now circulate as part of a so-called convergence culture, a cultural environment that has inflected, if not defined, how films and other media are now received as a series of "remediations," "transmutations," and "intertextualities" that transpose and translate texts as replications, interactive exchanges, and more importantly as "adaptations" in the broadest and most resonant sense.

This particularly contemporary movement toward proliferation and replication has, I'd argue, been part of the adaptation evolution at least since Bazin's work in the 1950s. Since the 1940s, in fact, modern narrative cinema has provided numerous examples of where the activity and thematic of adaptation have been about remediation as survival. Witnessed in Laurence Olivier's movement between the stage and the cinematic scene at the celebrated transitional moment in *Henry V* (1944), later in Godard's crashing of cultures and texts in *Contempt* (1961), and more recently in R. W. Fassbinder's 1980 epilogue in his *Berlin Alexanderplatz* (1980) that transforms the Doblin novel into a personal psychic landscape, in each adaptations have aggressively reshaped, distorted, condensed, extended, and repositioned literary texts as a self-conscious testings of the material and social limits of those texts and, concomitantly, of the films themselves. For me, these three films act as exempla, calling (exaggerated) attention to a definitive, if less obtrusive, evolution in modern adaptation and its theories: as the redistribution of texts through different technologies, as a recognition that betrayal may be as cinematically productive as fidelity, and as the dissipation of authorial expressivity within the social and material fabric of reception. For me, each of these films anticipates the charged state of adaptation today in which adaptation for both filmmakers and critics is ultimately about multiplication, not as repetition or duplication but as a productive refraction that is ultimately an act of criticism, an act of criticism in which critics of adaptation have an obvious and important role to play.

A contemporary environment of redundancy and duplication can thus not only be seen as subverting the traditional status of adaptation as a singular dialogue between two primary texts but also, more importantly I think, be seen as bringing into high relief adaptation as an act of critical intervention in their historical and cultural environment. Rather than some sort of crisis, this state of adaptation might be seen as a salutary call to re-examine questions of value through the lens of adaptation, to ask in new ways what matters in this cultural field of multiplying adaptation. And why. This becomes no longer a theoretical question about source texts or transtextual movements in adaptation. It becomes a question of how adaptation practices, texts, and studies answer or provoke new and old questions about the material world in which we live. It is a question of how the adaptations that today suffuse a cultural environment and of how the adaptation studies that identify them can and should assume the stance of critical interventionist within that environment. Let's recall that famous scene in *Clueless* where that surfer of postmodern images, Cher, correctly counters an academic debate about Shakespeare's *Hamlet* by assuring her graduate student opponent that while the rival may think she knows her *Hamlet*, Cher knows her Mel Gibson.

Adaptation studies are more important than ever and are more difficult and challenging than ever in our contemporary environment for the very same reason: adaptation has more shapes, wider boundaries, and much vaguer definitions than ever before and, in this environment, has become pervasively about reflecting meaning and values in a far larger sense perhaps than ever before.

Backward Evolution: Bazin, Refractive Cinema, and Aesthetic Biology

It's in this contemporary context that I wish to draw on what I tongue in cheek refer to as Bazin's prophetic observations and specifically his notion that adaptation is a "refractive" activity that redirects, multiplies, and disperses different texts and perspectives. Writing in the 1950s, Bazin introduces this notion of refraction as a model for a kind of adaptation when he describes Robert Bresson's adaptation of *Diary of a Country Priest* (1951) as a "dialectic between cinema and literature" that includes "all that the novel has to offer plus . . . its refraction into the cinema." He insists that there "is no question here of translation. Still less is it a question of free inspiration with the intention of building a duplicate. It is a question of building a secondary work with the novel as foundation. . . . It is a new aesthetic creation, the novel so to speak multiplied by the cinema." Adaptation requires, Bazin says in another essay, "a scientific knowledge" associated with the "field of optics" in which the complexity of an adaptation can be seen as compensation "for the distortions, the aberrations, the diffractions" of the lens. With Resnais's brilliant 1948 *Van Gogh* as a primary example, adaptation as refraction becomes, in short, a symbiotic multiplication of forms, putting into play a productive interaction of different kinds of what Bazin calls aesthetic biologies. This last phrase obliquely suggests the physical and material terms of adaptation and the evolutionary pressure that dogs it. More importantly, Bazin's sense of adaptation as refraction anticipates, I believe, a contemporary climate in which hierarchies and precedents lose their privileges as texts as they create a prismatic environment of intersections, overlappings, and misdirections. As Bazin notes in another essay, adaptations "do not derive from the cinema as an art form but as a sociological and industrial fact."[2]

The environmental nature of this refractive climate is spelled out more boldly by Bazin in his essay on adaptation as digest. The majority of adaptations, he says, "are condensed versions, summaries, film 'digests,' " and adaptations as refraction then become not so much about "the actual condensing or simplification of works" as about "the way they are consumed," the ease of "physical access" creating "an atmospheric culture."[3] Bazin's example of this atmospheric culture and the evolving proliferation of cultural texts and practices within it is radio, whose environment of consumption is a dim foreshadowing of our contemporary technological environment, notably lacking the interactivity of the internet and other delivery systems today. The emphasis on the consumption of a film adaptation within this environment is, however, most critical here, as it relocates the expressive singularity that has always underpinned traditional adaptation in the material environment of its reception. Well before it became both obvious and fashionable, this environment brought seriously into question the traditional cornerstones of adaptation: "The ferocious defense of literary works," Bazin argues,

> is to a certain extent, aesthetically justified; but we must also be aware that it rests on a rather recent, individualistic conception of the "author" and of the "work," a conception that was far from being ethically rigorous in the seventeenth century and that started to become legally defined only at the end of the eighteenth. . . . [We observe] the birth of the new aesthetic Middle Ages, whose reign is to be found in the accession of the masses to power (or at least their participation in it) and in the emergence of an artistic form to complement that accession: the cinema. . . . All things considered, it is possible to imagine that we are moving toward a reign of adaptation in which the notion of the unity of the work of art, if not the notion of the author himself, will be destroyed.

Sounding a bit like Walter Benjamin here, he argues: "The aesthetic energy is all there, but it is distributed—or, perhaps better, dissipated—differently according to the demands of the camera lens"—or, I would add, the many other cultural and material lenses through which adaptations now pass.[4]

In extending and re-adapting Bazin's term "refractive" and emphasizing a practice of deflection or dispersal, I am differentiating these films from the common characterization of films as (self-) "reflexive" or "reflective" cinema, according to which works typically turn back on themselves or a literary precedent to comment on their own making. "Refractive" suggests a kind of "unmaking" or disturbance of an equilibrium of the work of art or the film.[5] Like the beam of light sent through a refractive cube, refractive cinema breaks up and disperses the art or object it engages, splinters or deflects it in ways that leave the original work scattered and redirected through a world outside. This refractive cube of social, media, and material challenges provide, I believe, the productive obstructions of contemporary adaptation.

Bazin's remarks ask us not to think only about the aesthetics of adaptation— the genius behind it, artistic strategies, or its emotional and imaginative communications—but instead to emphasize *value* as a fundamental part of adaptation studies. He suggests that adaptation is an additive process, and refractive cinema makes adaptation an exponentially additive process that demands, especially in today's climate, the additions of critical value.[6] As in the films of Olivier, Godard, and Fassbinder, refractive adaptations in our prismatic environment tend, in a variety of ways, to draw attention to where the material and social environment act as productive *obstructions*, a term I'm using in a large sense. Obstructions here test the limits of different kinds of textualities and the strategies for understanding of them—from the technological to the political and aesthetic to the historical subject formations, textual, social, and material obstructions clarify that what counts and what doesn't is a crucial mission for how criticism reacts to and adapts those practices. In one sense, we textual scholars need today to sometimes be sociologists and scientists, discovering the flashpoints and crashpoints that adaptations reveal in the world. To adapt Bazin's wonderful analogy for the adaptation of theater on film: without a central historical and critical chandelier today, we'd do well to move through media culture with historical and cultural flashlights that choose to illuminate our evolutionary future through a past where adaptation studies had little direction and fewer models. What matters then and now is why adaptation studies are important in a fundamental and broad sense.

Surviving Obstructions

In her *Theory of Adaptation*, Linda Hutcheon has sharply updated Bazin within what she calls a "continuum model" that "positions adaptations specifically as (re-) interpretations and (re-) creations." At the opposite end of this continuum from fidelity, adaptation now appears as various forms of "expansion." At this expanding site on her continuum a film like *Play It Again Sam* (1972, dir. Woody Allen) that "offers an overt and critical commentary on another prior film (in this case, *Casablanca* [1942]) finds a place here," but so do, Hutcheon continues, "academic criticism and reviews of a work."[7] This far end is where the contemporary culture of adaptation seems to be settling, I believe, and I'd extend Hutcheon's suggestions even further to include the continual flow of adaptive commentaries and recreations as DVD supplements and other reinventions and interventions as one or more texts, palimpsests, or social commentaries—including the work we do as critical scholars adapting texts and films to the world and journals we live in. Meanwhile this refractive consciousness and movement find its way into the practice of specific films, not just recognizable adaptations but even less literary films, as what I will call a refractive cinema in an effort to distinguish it from the usual characterization of certain self-conscious films as reflexive cinema. Sometimes these films do not look or act like adaptations in a conventional sense, yet this is, in large part, because they work to dramatize the fault lines of adaptation less as a textual practice than as a social practice, opening itself up to the obstructions of a material world and its multilayered cultures. Adaptations are about surviving the technological, social, political, and economic obstructions, and one of the key opportunities in adaptations studies today, I'd argue, is about identifying what the encounter with those obstructions tells us our environment and world.

My model for this project might be Lars von Trier's *The Five Obstructions* (2003), a film about a refractive dialogue between von Trier and film-maker Jørgen Leth. A tongue-in-cheek inversion of cinéma-vérité, the film describes an encounter in which von Trier proposes that Leth adapt his avant-garde classic *The Perfect Human*—a 1967 film that features the minimalist movements and abstracted living patterns of a "perfect human" and perfect text—adapting it to five precisely defined requirements or "obstructions." Von Trier quite literally "tests" Leth's abilities by asking him to remake his original film according to specific experiential conditions proposed by von Trier as five "obstructions": (1) in Cuba with no take longer than twelve frames, (2) in "the most miserable place in the world," for Leth the red-light district of Bombay, (3) as either a return to Bombay to remake his failed first effort or a film without rules, (4) as an animated film, and (5) as a text composed by von Trier and read by Leth.

The film interrogates Leth's and by implication the film's representational system to adequately adapt to a world beyond its prescribed borders. Manufactured appropriately by a Dogme 95 director with a flair for announcing theoretical rules, each of the obstructions or systemic rules or "laws" tests and exposes, "goads" and "examines" Leth's aesthetic. Von Trier, for instance, rejects the second film for not following his instructions when it shows a crowd of Indian onlookers, and then insists Leth remake it with "complete freedom" by returning to Bombay. Leth, however, wants and needs those rules, and the film becomes punctuated by the director wandering, confused, or dumbfounded, caught in his own long takes. With each failure, von Trier demands that Lethe needs to make a film that "leaves a mark on you."

As a series of adaptations that follow a refractive trail of obstructions, the film becomes at once a game and a trial: a game in which film, especially the "perfect film," will inevitably lose to its adaptive world and not survive. If von Trier's project is to adapt "a little gem that we're now going to ruin," that "plan is to proceed from the perfect to the human." In this series of adaptations there can be no textual success since the human always exceeds the aesthetic.

As one commentator put it, *The Five Obstructions* is "a hall of mirrors, shot through with ambiguities" that aims "to open the cinema to the outside, to the flesh-and-blood richness of human life," and so becomes a "work of thinking as problematizing."[8] Or in von Trier's words, the film seeks "to see without looking, to defocus!"[9] I suppose what I'm suggesting here is to think of adaptation studies as a critically defocused activity.

A critical refrain in both the original film and von Trier's game of adaptation is "I experienced something today that I hope I understand in a few days," and the relentless urging of that understanding to think through the aesthetics of adaptation and the experience of adaptation is all that remains when one is forced to see oneself finally as Leth does as an "abject" human being, constantly "obstructed" and excluded from some essential truth, where the essence of knowledge may be only, as the film's conclusion indicates, "how the perfect human falls." If the commentator of Leth's original perfect human concludes wondering, "What is the perfect human thinking?" and von Trier's film opens with the query "What was I thinking?" the unspoken question that lingers at the end of von Trier's film and points for me toward adaptation studies today might be "How now do we rethink the imperfect artist through the resistant medium that is our world?"

Conclusion

Although we are still some decades away, Bazin provides us with this proleptic suggestion, slyly sneaking in a futuristic reference to the film *Adaptation*: the "critic of the year 2050," he says, "would find not a novel out of which a play and a film had been 'made,' but rather a single work reflected through three art forms, an artistic pyramid with three sides, all equal in the eyes of the critic. The 'work' would then be an ideal point at the top of this figure, which is itself an ideal construct. The chronological precedence of one part over another would not be an aesthetic criterion any more than the chronological precedence of one twin over the other is a genealogical one."[10] That three-sided pyramid has expanded appreciably in the fifty years since Bazin imagined the next fifty years of our future; and now, with still forty years to go, it may be better conceived as a many-sided prismatic cube through which films and other texts adapt and refract continuously. What we look at and the paths of adaptation we critically engage are now more varied and less predictable. We need to explore the cube, as it tells us about the environment in which we live and the best ways to adapt to it. We need to encourage the refractive spread of adaptation studies where evolutionary progress can also be a return to positions that we may have archived too quickly—from Vachel Lindsay and Béla Balázs to Bazin and Bellour and well beyond. For one way to see and value adaptations is as part of a project of survival in which we need to find what historically matters, not just textually but as the intellectual and social material of our lived experience. Remember Donald's words: that it's "what you love, not what loves you" that counts; remember, as von Trier suggests, seek out adaptations whose obstructions "leave a mark on you" as a mark on our culture. That may be, I think, the best way for all of us to avoid that alligator.

Notes

1. For an anticipation of this metacinematic foundation in Kaufman's films, see David LaRocca's "Inclusive Unscientific Postscript: Late Remarks on Kierkegaard and Kaufman," in *The Philosophy of Charlie Kaufman*, ed. David LaRocca (Lexington: University of Kentucky Press, 2011), 269–94.
2. André Bazin, *What Is Cinema?*, trans. Hugh Gray, vol. 1 (Berkeley: University of California Press, 1967), 143, 42, 69, 142, 69.
3. André Bazin, "Adaptation, or the Cinemas Digest," in *Film and Literature*, 2nd ed., ed. Timothy Corrigan (New York: Routledge, 2012), 57–58.
4. Bazin, "Adaptation," 60–62.
5. Bazin, *What Is Cinema?*, 68.
6. Bazin, *What Is Cinema?*, 70, 75.
7. Linda Hutcheon, *A Theory of Adaptation* (New York: Routledge, 2006), 172, 171.
8. Hector Rodriguez, "Constraint, Cruelty, and Conversation," in *Dekalog 01: On the Five Obstructions*, ed. Mette Hjort (London: Wallflower Press, 2008), 53, 40, 55.
9. Hjort, *Dekalog 01*, xvii.
10. Bazin, "Adaptation," 62.

3

A Metacinematic Spectrum

Technique through Text to Context

Garrett Stewart

Mirror Mirror Mirror . . . It is surely among the handful of most famous shots in American film history. Charles Foster Kane (in the person of Orson Welles—or vice versa, in the mirror of screen impersonation), deserted by his wife and destroying her bedroom in a blind fury, then trudges robotically past the byzantine arched moldings of a vast hall of mirrors in his mansion as the camera tracks his rightward dead march.[1] But wait—back that up, not in reverse action but in the retracing of its flamboyant optic recess in those Xanadu mirrors. Rather than lumbering numbly past the camera in a steady rightward motion, Kane immediately disappears frame left behind a pillar, the camera holding in place until his mirror image emerges from that stone occlusion into the dropback of its optic recess. It is only then that his *actual* body (though it's one ontological notch harder, now, to think of it that way) follows behind, and up on, the reflected double into a nearer close-up on his stricken person as sole (but already compromised) anchor of this infinite regress. The camera's clean-edged rectangular bordering—stabilized, after its initial lateral glide, only at this turning point in the record of external motion—is thus passively asserted against (though in figurative association with) the inset Moorish framing of the *other* reflective surfaces receding inside its own light-sensitive mechanical rectangle.

This gripping ocular parable of subtracted spatial presence—and its renewal as embodied image—has turned the abyssal hall of mirrors not just into a generalized figure for cinema as an apparatus of secondary imaging but into a metanarrative mirror of the film's abiding irony as fictional biopic. There are indeed more parallels, narrative rather than optic, than those confined to these imprisoning parallel mirrors. For the film's antihero Kane—seldom more than a mere image, even to himself—has earlier been mirrored in dancing celebration (phantom-like, as mobile vanishing point) in the reflective window glass of his newspaper office between the flanking heads of his two chief minions in debate over his motives and methods. Moreover, this redoubling (even while

Garrett Stewart, *A Metacinematic Spectrum* In: *Metacinema*. Edited by: David LaRocca, Oxford University Press. © Oxford University Press 2021. DOI: 10.1093/oso/9780190095345.003.0004 thinning) of image is a motif of derivative rectangular depiction that has been with the film from the beginning of its real plot. It is sprung from the jump-cut launch of the narrative's epistemological quest by our drastically sudden side view of the screen on which the working draft of Kane's documentary obit (for "News on the March") is blaringly projected in the production screening room—in all its superficial thinness, material and journalistic. And beyond a first sense of the iconic mogul in repeated ironic reduction to a skin-deep optic mirage, this film-before-the-film is one to which all subsequent montage answers as *meta*cinema—in deep-focus tropes *about* its own contrastive powers of penetration.

So it is that this canted angle on the newsreel screen delimits, by synecdoche, the whole outward field of the movie's beveled narrative mirroring. This is the frame of reflex reference through which we see not just the eponymous American tycoon but, at our own spectatorial off-angle, the exposed celebrity fetish of a mass attention that the imaged fictional Kane shares, for instance, with movie stars (like Welles) in their larger-than-life aura, optic duplication, and limitless visual distribution. In all these camera-angle trick reframings (in reverse order across *Kane*'s plot: mirror, window, screen)—and to anticipate the template proposed and developed in this chapter—medial *technique* directs each episode of narrative *text* toward its reflex *context* not just as machinated specular object but as stargazing American mythography in visual realization.

In the tilt of story toward the inferences of its mass mediation, technological on one side, ideological on the other, the real issue begins. When mapped from fiction onto supposed biographical forensics in the documentary picture show within *Citizen Kane*, what can such a mere set of edited pictures really show? And show forth about their own process in doing so? How, within the larger frame of *Kane*'s narrative fiction, do we understand emblematically the actual trajectory of optical replication, including the place of both reflective glass and earlier sideways screen within the broader pattern of iconic newspaper shots and election posters? The vectors of irony are quite pointedly ours to track: from inaugural inset screen *acutely* viewed—debunking the metaphoric windowed vista on history it might be thought to simulate—through the enforced reminder of superimposed reflection rather than transparency in that triangulated office shot midway through the plot. From there, with that optical pivot point of public man versus mere image, visual narrative drives on down, right before the end, to the nadir of Kane's splintered authenticity in that climactic shot of his mansion's mirror setting—and figural setup. Dead-ending there is not just the stark replication of a factitious public profile in multiple delivery. Although the mirror recession is angled just barely to miss the cinematographer's exposed position in our imaginary place, what we see "captured" nonetheless—at a calculated angle of viewer implicature—is the raw fascination of our own spectatorship at risk of being thrown back in our face: in reflective recognition. For what we're teased with by the chance of seeing it in the just-deflected angle of incidence—in that later hall of mirrors that *is* Xanadu—is not our image, of course, but nonetheless, in near-miss, a glancing reminder of any naive hope we may have harbored about even this surrounding narrative film, let alone the skin-deep "News on the March," working to single out the "real Kane" from his mass-media image.

Terminology is of no decisive help in all this—except when placed under investigation in its own right. Metacinema? Even for starters, the tired quip takes us nowhere: I never met a cinema I didn't like. For one thing, its categorical ambiguity gets immediately in the way: cinema as place versus visual event, movie palace versus motion picture, screen site versus screened sights. Though preventing the jejune wordplay, *metafilmic* will no longer do, either, in marking certain moments of self-reflexivity in motion pictures, since the pictures move via pixels now rather than filmic frames, algorithmic code rather than celluloid. More flamboyantly all the time, movies are postfilmic. Even in the consideration of mainstream cinema, then, a sense of the *meta* needs to be more specific (medium-specific) about material causes as well as narrative gestures or their extratextual reverberations. Any one "film" (as such projections are still atavistically called), or say each movie, is of course unique—even as it may choose to avow, or generalize about, its own status as image system, narrative format, or cultural artifact.

Adducing just those three aspects in adjacency and overlap—image flow, storyline, sociopolitical or commercial context—this chapter focuses on how cinematic motion, with its machine-gunning of images, pictures its dramatic narrative show only by a typical elision of exactly the separate frames that nonetheless sometimes show through. It is in this sense that the anomalous manifestations—these apparitions of the apparatus—seem to have exceeded what they narratively constitute: to have become *meta*. But even then the unique nodes—rather than just modes—of such acknowledgment or generalization are too various to categorize, and sometimes too intertwined to isolate. Increasingly in Hollywood blockbuster cinema, for instance, the palpable force of "production values" tends to collapse a narrative's admitted status as socially embedded commercial product into its material generation as digital composite. And quite apart from brandished CGI (computer-generated images) when their manifest financial outlay, in its full extravagance, is implicitly taken up in the layout of screen action, cinema has often tipped its technical hand in more traditional ways as well. Familiar forms of dissolve, match cut, slow motion, rear projection, what have you, are to be numbered, especially when exaggerated, among the most pointed local triggers of cinema's reflexive recognitions in the movies-about-movies vein—when that category is understood more broadly than just to include backlot narrative storylines. And to speak of such a tipped hand is, of course, to imply the kind of narrative reflex that, in the momentary override (or revealed underwriting) of plot, gestures back to the structuring technical image even while beyond it to supplemental cinematic inferences for the sociopolitical setting—or reception—of the story thus visualized.

A question is thus left open. What "about" the movies—in such metacinematic recognition—is being noted or negotiated? About which conditions of their existence as motion pictures do the techniques of visual generation, the arcs of plot, or some third term of socioeconomic context tend to deliver a reflexive inference? Or ask again what, in the first of the threefold distinctions floated earlier, a given film can (to repeat the triad) work to manifest about "its own status as image system, narrative format, or cultural artifact"? Put otherwise—though still with an emphasis on that orienting division of labor—to what possibilities does a given screen effect, text, or cultural (as well as corporate) product tend to revert, turn back upon in reflex? The issue can't be determined in advance, but the embedded structural mirror is likely to be angled in one of those three suggested directions: toward pronounced visuals, narrative pressures, or industrial dissemination without a monetized social arena. Optical process, story, manufacture and distribution: these, then, anchor the artifact in its theatrical display. Materiality, narrative depiction, exhibitionary circuit: such a cross section can, of course, be variously sliced and tested. Traversing the image system, the storyline generated by it, and its public interface, one may therefore cut the distinctions, if seldom cleanly, this way: screen *effect* as technique, narrative *text* as audiovisually articulated storyline, circulation *context* as social space of reception, even as that third public dimension may open out by allusion to the broader surround of its own spectatorial moment in relation to mass culture or political climate at large.

In my four books on narrative cinema in particular, rather than on the broader aesthetics of time-based imagery, few episodes of concentrated discussion have ever been more than a page or two away from some measure of metacinematic uptake or speculation of this sort: regarding first, in *Between Film and Screen*, the mechanical evolution of celluloid film from its chemical basis in photography, as evinced by the recursive returns of that still medium within the screen image; next, in *Framed Time*, concerning the transformation of screen practice in a postfilmic cinema's new orientation, among other cognitive adjustments, both in frame shifts and in narrative topics, toward the much-debated "time-image" in the work of Gilles Deleuze; then, in *Closed Circuits*, focusing on the relation of fictional visualization to surveillance—frame to frame-up, montage to espionage, passive spectatorship to bodies spied/eyed-upon inside the narrative world—including all the inset secondary screens (increasingly the banks of remote digital monitors) arrayed to thematize just this correlation; and then, in *Cinemachines*, involving an explicitly methodological reassessment, under the name "apparatus reading," of the approach I had come to call "narratography."[2] In this mode of applied narratology, the apparatus itself becomes legible in tracking the microplots articulated by disclosed gestures of cinematographic device—what Stanley Cavell calls "assertions in technique"[3]—and not least in their reflexive connection to the wider parameters of screen imaging. After that book's renewed emphasis on the machinations of the celluloid, then digital, apparatus in sustaining and inflecting the cinematic mirage, the present effort is to widen further the purview in categorizing the basic threefold range of metacinematic features that this shifting image system tends to foreground.

Metamedial: A Sliding Scale

Again the partitioned but interpenetrating template in this spectrum analysis: technique; its textual manifestation at the narrative level; then its contextual reverberation in industrial production or programmed reception (contemporaneous allusions included, where text finds its dominant terms of interpretation). Traditional narrative cinema can be understood as *medial* in all three dimensions—and directions: whether pointed inward to the technology of its material support, forward along the narrative arc of its storytelling conveyance (genre included), or outward to mediating context (industrial distribution, on the one hand, or political topicality, on the other). Increasingly, as noted, this third register may also appear to be pointing back again—inward—at the same time, via the manufactured audiovisual composite, to scrutinized material conditions: as when a movie is found adverting to—and advertising—its own implicit CGI budget in relation to a broader spectrum of computer technology in social deployment. (Much more subsequently.)

So it is worth stressing, up front, not just the slippage from technique to text to context, but the comparable drift, exerting a reverse pressure upon narrative textuality, when some tacit contextual surround is understood first of all via technical reflex: edging the inference of the narrative toward a zone of auto-imaging that connects in that way with the round and *about* of metacinema as structuring given. So what sort of thing does narrative have to project, if not explicitly to say, about the medium by which it is manifested, either technically or industrially? Once plastic and electric in the era of celluloid mechanics, since then electronic and pixel-driven—and often showcased as such in either phase—this technical aspect of the motion picture medium has perhaps never been more baldly asserted than in recent franchise cinema. Canonical formalism speaks of "baring the device," exposing the works of a given work. That sense of device isn't limited to technique. All three dimensions of response proposed here have their way of devising their own bearings in response, orienting us as we go. In the exponential computerization of the Hollywood action picture, certainly, an overt subterfuge of CGI in the deployment of VFX (visual special effects) can be readily exposed, then reincorporated, by some denaturalized twist of narrative sequence that may also incorporate a knowing sidelong nod at genre slotting or cultural intertext. All may reflect back on cinematic operations in a formative if not formalist manner.

Even if one were to force the proposed dovetailed triad involved in metacinematic registration (technical\textual/contextual) into the more familiar formalist dichotomy of form versus content, style versus substance, all subtlety of gradation would not be lost. When movies are found reflecting on either their manufacture as image system or their manifold narrative complex, the either/or doesn't stay put. In undoing this dichotomy, for instance, there is always the "content of the form"—where densities of style spill over to narrative increments in their own right; or, in turn, the form of the content—where broader structuring functions of genre and social coding come into play. So we're back with the triadic schema after all: call it, under a specifying adjustment, technique\text/intertext, with that third term locating the very process of contextual inference—and with the narrative reflexes of the textual system pointing either out toward it or back upon the material and montage *techne* of plot's own composition. And while we're at it, in this consideration of a formative versus a formalist logic, note how one may rethink another structuralist touchstone in cinema studies that folds any bared device back into narrative as an adjunct of operational process. In David Bordwell's influential definition of screen *narration*, as opposed to the extractable narratives it transmits, "Narration is the process whereby the film's *syuzhet* and style [sequential structure plus technique] interact in the process of cueing and channeling the spectator's construction of the *fabula* [the fable, the story]."[4] Under the adjusted lens of the threefold refraction I'm proposing, style can momentarily divert structure away from its ongoing story function and back to the reflexive exhibition of screen narration's own technical provisions. So, too, may story at any moment reveal, by metanarrative aside, its shaping conditions in certain contextual rather than technical "cues" that also operate in "channeling" further inferences—cinematic and social alike—beyond the formatting of plot.

Subtlety of gradation, then, even though not intrinsically forgone in taking on board the binaries of formalist analysis, remains a matter of overlap rather than delimitation, where one level of self-reflection transgresses upon and energizes another. The metacinematic leverage entailed may well give new purchase on theme or its cultural memes. That leverage, that "moment" in its sense from physics, is precisely the reflex exertion at stake in metacinematic detection. But "precisely" is too easy there—except on a case-by-case basis. How does one really think the "meta" in self-reflexivity? The dictionary might seem at first too democratic on this score to be definitive, but in fact its spread of derivation helps subdivide a whole range of effects. It can, though, certainly appear rather amorphous at the first scanning of options. *Meta*: "a prefix appearing in loanwords from Greek, with the meanings 'after,' 'along with,' 'beyond,' 'among,' 'behind.'" When translated to the field (or plane) of the screen's material origins and effects, that array of prepositions samples the various pre-positioning (or premising) aspects of the cinematic condition (however defined) in regard to the multifaceted screen object. This is the "meta" in its full shifting spread of manifestation. *After* but *along with*: the so-called internal supplement, where some cinematic self-acknowledgment completes the narrative picture. *Beyond, among, behind*: exceeding while underlying and interleaved, involving a certain broad sense of underlay or support (electronic substrate, generic format, financial backing, cultural moment, etc.) made immanent on screen.

Recall here the rhetorical device of metalepsis—as when authors suddenly appear as speaking characters in their own stories, intervening to interrogate another or to redirect the action. First cause is thereby manifest in a secondary effect, at the narrative rather than stylistic level, in any such mode of author interpolation—or in its more common kindred effects on screen. Famously in film, or infamously, a character's breaching the "fourth wall" by apostrophizing the audience is one way to expose the public-address system of cinema at large—as a set of directed narrative messages, couched ordinarily in dramatic enunciations, and rendered commercially available in the transmit of projection. But there are, of course, other disclosures of cause in effect, technical rather than overtly rhetorical, that pivot cinema back on itself in reflexive twists within the narrative flux—other, many, innumerable, and not easy to categorize. But the effort alone can clarifying.

So far, this chapter has been organized to correlate related terminological distinctions across several sliding triadic scales, all of them parallel to each other in their linkages. With each triad separately, the adjacency—or tangency—of emphasis locates a latent transposition from one zone of notice to another: call it an internal "othering" of cognitive strata. Such an othering of effect from within its own manifestation is what may well give rise to a sense of these metacinematic nodes as allegorical: not just figuring some cinematic given but emblematizing it in the form of a circumscribed minor parable. The dictionary's received wisdom once more: "*allēgoria*, from *allos* 'other' + -*agoria* 'speaking.'" And since, etymologically again, the "behind," "beneath," and "after" of the *meta*, as well as the "among" and "between," are all versions of the other within—operating as flashpoints of resident alienation on the dematerialized underside of unfolding process—it is clear why metacinema often comes across as a mode of auto-allegory.

The variable bandwidths of registration distinguishing the technique\text/context nexus are not hierarchical or even topological; they are logical, categorical, and thus permeable—open across each other's delineations (not borders) to a perception analogical or metaphoric. One may best think of the recurrent schemata here in terms of Venn diagrams. Such is the unique interpretive value of the metacinematic when conceived according to this overlapping triadic model, where the turns of its reflexes may coincide with—or incur—each other at certain points of perceptual friction. Accordingly, when the reflexive axis of a given dimension of response reverts, for instance, from the immediacy of generated image or event—optical technique or narrative text—to its abstracted parameters as such, its "turn" may also at the same time be outward to context (to commercial, social, or political conditions as well as to genre norms) along a linked scale of calibration and implication. Linked—and interpenetrating. It is in this sense that one stratum of apprehension "tropes" the other in the etymological sense, *diverts* into it, or, by another etymological route of figurative understanding, is *carried over, trans-ferred* (*meta-ferein*) to it. An obtruded technical gesture often, that is, becomes not just a nudge to plot, or a roughening of its route, but a metaphor for some organizing dynamic or building theme in the storyline. At the same time, a narrative paradox may trope some political contradiction in the contextual (become intertextual) field. Such, then, are the metatropes at play across continuous dimensions of response, trans-ferried from one field of recognition to another in an auto-allegorical circuit of inference. Think (by seeing) *Kane* again. As far as the eye can see via incremental distortion, there are still far fewer visible mirror duplicates of Kane on screen than are required in near-duplicate photograms, or photo cells, on the strip (technique) to track these few seconds of irony (text) in their epitomizing of a narrative motif—self as image—whose capitalist valence (context) is the very world of media circulation in which Kane and Welles together participate.

Testing: 1941, 1979, 2019

To clarify further, in its metamedial scope, the scalar triad technique\text/ context in screen narration—or, if preferred, to certify an alternative formulation as substrate\structure\intertext—let me briefly subdivide such terrain in examples from three motion pictures approximately four decades apart across the technological eras of celluloid, video, and CGI. These initial exhibits are, to say the least, technically invested screen narratives—ranging from the prewar *Citizen Kane* again (1941, dir. Orson Welles) through the topical Vietnam epic *Apocalypse Now* (1979, dir. Francis Ford Coppola) to the postfilmic dystopian spectacle of *Blade Runner 2049* (2018, dir. Denis Villeneuve). The substrate in each case, the materiality of audiovisual record, sets off a kind of figurative chain reaction in their variable cinematic allegories.

In *Kane*, we can back up now to the beginning rather than the end of the "News on the March" film, the latter marked with that diminishing side-angled screen view just as the projector was gratingly turned off. In contrast, the first moving footage of the newspaper magnate is introduced to viewers (to us and to those, within the plot, privy to this rough cut of the documentary metafilm made just after his death) only once a dossier of headline photographs and a childhood daguerreotype have been filed past, along with the loot of his wealth, in a series of rapid cross-fades and wipes that figure—in a deliberately clichéd rhetoric of transience—the blatant ephemera of his fortune. The photojournalist ironies of these two montage sequences are, in their tumult, also mixed with quick cuts between static images of his discrepant aggregations. All told, three distinct techniques of cinematographic punctuation, serial and fixative, operate in a correlated intersection of media metaphors. All is *image*, display, including the simulated paparazzi shots of the title figure under the contradictory voice-over "aloof, seldom visited, never photographed," its shaky footage filmed through the forbidding X of protective wire fencing. Internally reframed in this way, (1) the figurative reflexivities of technique are then immediately equivocated by the metatext of filmic access to the private confines of wealth and power. This happens when the flat grainy images of invaded privacy are put in contrast with the deep-focus treatment of the "News on the March" production team in the screening room, to which we cut abruptly across that satiric view of the documentary's skin-deep scrim. At an emerging metanarrative level, then, with the reflexive ironies of technique behind it, this is where (2) the first-draft storyline of the film-within-the-film is postmortemized along with its human subject, the commercial journalistic purpose being to deepen its narrative charge—and by this motive precipitating the five-part frame structure of separate investigative interviews that organize the rest of the main narrative, with no return to any screen-within-the-screen. The resulting puzzle-piece ensemble of subsidiary points of view (3) tropes in turn, and not just through the intertext of William Randolph Hearst's similar career, the broader social context of fame and overexposure in pursuit of the American dream, where the superficial trappings of public figures yield themselves up, metafilmically or otherwise, to no stable explanatory gaze.

After Kane, Kurtz, where (quite apart from the fact that Welles wished to play both Kurtz and his double Marlow in a film version of Conrad's *Heart of Darkness*) we can trace out a metamedial domino effect that ends up manifested in Coppola's version of the same classic novel. Crucially, an early reflexive flashpoint in *Apocalypse Now* is ignited from a clutch of mere images divorced from recorded voice. Even before this, however, in the technical salience of the opening scene, (1) an unorthodox blitz of figurative jump cuts submits Captain Willard (the new Marlow) to the fracturing of his screen image after he bloodies himself in smashing its (and his) mirror equivalent in a Saigon hotel room. From there we move to an equally thematized technology in that crucial—because technologically primal—dichotomy of image and sound, where Willard, recruited for a new murderous assignment, is made privy to separate visual and audial information regarding a proudly uniformed Colonel Kurtz. On the one hand, he is offered dossier photographs (actually 8 × 10 publicity shots of Marlon Brando's previous roles as disturbed or brutal military officers); on the other, he is unnerved by reel-to-reel tape (spinning in close-up) of the colonel's intercepted mad ravings (this, historically backdated, before mainstream digital recording in Hollywood production, and thus invoking the spools of film that will finally fuse voice with image in the plot's climactic phase). These definitive medial ingredients in picture and speech, divided against themselves, thus pass from technical conditions to the guiding terms of (2) the ensuing narrative text, where it is only with the vanishing point of closure in sight hours later, after the ongoing fissure between Willard's sometimes violent expedients on screen and his own intermittent voice-over in the reading of Kurtz's dossier, that convergence will have been achieved. Only when plot's trajectory has brought Willard into Kurtz's compound—and quite literally face to face with the soliloquies of his rogue derangement, through sutured chiaroscuro close-ups and their bifurcating shadows—will the divided audio/visual matrix of that launching scene have been dialectically resolved. And only then will both dialogue and voiceover have been suspended together in the intercut execution montage to follow. All of this, of course, in its Vietnam update of the imperial violence in the African colonial setting of Joseph Conrad's source novel, operates as revisionary narrative text within (3) its contemporary context of genocidal conflict and the ravages of American power. Moreover, this outward turn is punctuated reflexively by a pointed intertextual trope. This is a famous fleeting moment of documentary metalepsis (rather than, as in *Kane*, affording an entire framing motive). Whether we tag it as contextual or intertextual, the moment transpires when Coppola himself, cast as a video documentarian, appears on a beachhead instructing his own cast not to look at the camera, but just to look like they're fighting. As a dramaturgic more than a technical turn—a metamedial irony cinematographic, yes, but only because on camera as such, as a second-order filming—the effect lodges within the plot a metamedial reminder of the Vietnam mayhem and its video spectacle as the "first TV war."

After Kane and Kurtz, K, the replicant hero of the *Blade Runner* sequel. He negotiates a world of futurist audiovisual technology well beyond the screen-encased pleasures of the cinematic, whether filmic or digital, being solaced in his humanoid emptiness only by a hologram housewife more penetrable than desire necessitates. His fleshly satisfaction remains balked at the level of the audience's own before her sheer (both senses) scintillating image. (1) The uneven shimmer and variable transparency of Joi's digital manifestation in the inhabited space of the film's 3D world, whether she is beamed from a "home entertainment" projector or later streamed remotely, comments via contemporary media options on the post-millennial telos of optical technology as well as AI. Her speaking image, her hologram, serving K his dinner, represents the phonorobotic kitchen helper as erotic surrogate. At the same time, the riveting metamedial (or auto-allegorical) specter of her CGI hovering and break-up up is a reflex that, we may say, *tropes over* into (2) the vexed cyborg narrative of K's existential crisis, the hero clutching at the possibility of his lone humanity among a cadre of replicants—with Joi only a more pointed reminder that you can't tell by looking (on screen or off) what someone really is, or even whether, in an anthropocentric sense, they really are. This is a sustained dramatic irony centered, in terms of classic narrative epistemology, on tactical flashbacks to a human past that are discursively real for us (as a staple of narrative anachrony) whether they are the hero's own or an implanted memory. At the metatextual level, this technique of flashback montage works to expose the inevitably constructed storyline that makes up any supposed autonomous lifeline in retrospect. But the narrative reflex is sociocultural as well as biographical and existential. This is to say that the plot-bound ruse of false memory as visual illusion in the text is at the same time (3) rendered further metaphoric—in contextual extrapolation to the exponential electronic infrastructure of our own social systems—for the proverbial crisis of authenticity in a wired culture of rampant simulacra, prosthetic virtualities, and vicarious affordances. To say nothing of VR's reflex action in regard to the Hollywood audience's ongoing inculcation into the ruses of postfilmic screen imaging—in ways that come to a dead end in our final exhibit, to follow.

In summarizing the sliding scale of these three differently "medial" examples so far, before looking more closely at the latest extravagance of metamedial CGI, we may say that (1) the manifestation or emblem of the material medium—at whatever stage in its evolution from photography through celluloid projection, then on past videotape to digital and laser streaming, and by however dramatic an eruption of technique—may at the same time become (2) a metaphoric reflex within the encompassing textual structure of the narrative medium as plot format. And it is there that (3) an extra contextual torque may further evoke a specific cultural intertext or zone of association (the opacity of fame, the artifices of staging in photojournalism, the corruptions of power, financial or military, the fragility and lurking misnomer of electronic "presence") in the media surround of a given historical moment—as typically exaggerated in the sci-fi genre by its futurist projections—projections often in the double reflexive sense: optical and historical.

In the variant configurations of such a threefold breakdown as applied so far, the stratum of marked technique, in its disclosed medial substrate, is exactly the focus of my methodological argument for "apparatus reading"—as distinct from the kind of psychoanalytic apparatus theory, and its ideological critique, that once put a film like Hitchcock's *Vertigo* through its paces as a parable of the phallic gaze. Looking back briefly to that classic text, I would instead call out a central moment that—in yielding almost inevitably to apparatus reading—is readily extrapolated to a metacinematic crux as well, the visuals of its plot twist triggering a forceful, almost flagrant, reflexive signal. Apparatus theory to one side, there is no question that Hitchcock's narrative allegorizes the way in which the seductions of a plot artifice (the husband's contrived narrative of the Carlotta haunting) can induce investments in a character (the hero's fixation on Madeleine) that exceed the reality principle—and that may further produce a desire to make another female body over into the image of the idealized mystery woman. Spurred by the faked conspiratorial backstory, the film's unfolding plot proceeds by tacitly reflecting on its own erotic fetishism in fueling our fascination with the blonde *femme mortale*—and precisely in metafilmic connection with Hollywood standards of coiffed and costumed glamor (including the insider Hollywood intertext about remolding Kim Novak herself from shopgirl to star). Yet the storyline as text repeatedly ties these narrative-cum-industrial inferences back to cinematographic ironies, pins plot to image, in aspects at least as technological as psychological.

One turning-point example. At the crisis of identification between the hero's libido on life support and the supposedly self-slain object of his desire, when his surrealist nightmare retraces Madeleine's fall from the mission bell tower onto the tiled roof below, the oneiric image recalls the several previous process shots (or rear projections), with their undisguised artificial backdrops, that have rendered equivocal—and figurative—the nature of the hero's own erotic "projections." Now, as his own imagined body is about to splatter against the tiles, his slamming awake is figured by a sudden switching off of the rear projection behind his artificial dream avatar (a kind of emblematic cardboard cutout). In the medial irony induced there, we revert in a single split second from narrative dreamscape at the textual level to the technical *abyme* of the production site, where cinematic "special effects" are exposed at the machinated basis of the so-called dream machine. Again the triadic spectrum becomes a vicious circle—as is the case even more unabashedly in my coming example from the far more "sophisticated" (and, in narrative context, infinitely less subtle) trick effects of Marvel Universe CGI.

Paratext as Metatext

Few films are more famous for their main title sequence than is *Vertigo* for the spiraling vortices of Saul Bass's animated graphics, the film's one-word title emerging from a giant eye, as does "Directed by Alfred Hitchcock" at the end of the dizzying (vertiginous) sequence—the Master of Suspense *directing* the gaze from within as usual. In this way a film about disabling voyeurism opens, in its extranarrative paratext, with the look of looking per se. Such a common interface between cinematic technique and main narrative text, brokered by the technical inflections of copyright and credit sequences, has, long since *Vertigo*, entered a new millennial phase. Now this technical and thematic bridgework has been edged back into tampered with corporate logos as well, a tendency begun with the apocalyptic darkening and warping of the Warner Brothers studio image in digital distortion for 1999's *The Matrix* (dir. Lana and Lilly Wachowski).

In *Vertigo*, for all the credit sequence's front-loaded optical disorientation, the Para/mountain remains intact, even as overlain by the VistaVision logo. In the latest iteration of this branding icon as punning "mount," however, abstract geometric stars sweep into view from the sky behind its gleaming peak, orbiting as a kind of halo in this upgraded industrial imprimatur. Such was the case, for instance, in the first four films in the *Transformer* series, with only tantalizing hints of alien cyber noise on the soundtrack accompanying the whizzing astral shapes. But by 2017, for *Transformers: The Last Knight*, with its chivalric throwback twist, the same cookie-cutter star-shaped forms now hydroplane toward the mountain on a reflective body of water extending out toward the theater audience before creating the logo's star-power aureole. Then suddenly, from the distant zone of these astral graphics, a barrage of meteor-like forms rocket toward us from behind the mountain—easily mistaken for asteroid visitations or, of course, attacking extraterrestrial weaponry. But they are actually catapulted balls of fire vaulting not just the mountain but straight into a flashback on a medieval battlefield—as millennial prequel to the alien invasion master plot. Primitive aerial weaponry undergoes digital manifestation (of course) in order to snap us out of our high-tech expectations—only momentarily (of course)—and then only at the plot level, doing nothing (of course) to impugn the credibility, just obtrude the ingenuity, of those impinging CGI fireballs. Again, imploding the threefold nexus of the metamedial spectrum, collapsing its sliding scale into a self-confirming circuit, in this case (and others like it) a *text*, as if jumping its own narrative gun, has broken through—by foregrounded *technique*—into the framing corporate *context* itself as an extra advert for (and to) its own high-tech finesse.[5]

Looking back for a moment to the latest *Blade Runner*—and returning there all the way to its opening credits as well, we note how, more histrionically than ever, they manipulate the production company logos that flash past—Warner Brothers, Alcon, Sony, and Columbia. Each seems to be invaded in anticipation by the diegesis—this through a digital glitching easily read as leaked in advance from the instabilities of a high-tech dystopia in the plot to come, with its repeated evocation of optic data fields and their fragile electronic manifestation. Here, as the industrial advertising logos seem themselves to advertise, is a plot so intense that it can't be contained, its metatechnical blowback already felt on merely routine corporate approach. This familiar trope of a narrativized paratext, so to say, together with its thematized technique— foregrounding the electronic apparatus at its inaugural apparition—is in danger lately of becoming a distribution cliché: in our terms, the studio imprimatur already imprinted with the technical traces of a text still in promotional abeyance.

Yet such slick involutions of corporate "investment" in the narrative's own technological intensity find understandably little place, up front, in the latest overblown and metamedial VFX spectacle. It would be too much, too soon, by way of CGI chicanery. As it unfolds, the film in question marks a quantum leap in thematized technique even beyond Villeneuve's *Blade Runner 2049*, risking as such a kind of dead end for this mode of showcased computer graphics—even if not, of course, for the Marvel franchise already proleptically rebooted by the film's final credits with an in-built teaser. I refer to *Spider-Man: Far from Home* (2019, dir. Jon Watts), which settles in its precredit logo for the cycle's routine kinetic montage of graphic frames from the comic series, digitally shuffled but bearing no electronic wear and tear. Never in the familiar studio-branding of this franchise, however, has this quarantine of pulp source from CGI plot been more apt, even tactical. We'll soon see why. The only logo irony this film can sensibly permit itself seems based on Steven Spielberg's famous match fade, in *Raiders of the Lost Ark* (1981), between the Para/mountain, still untampered with as in Hitchcock, and its imposing diegetic double in the exotic precincts of the launching scene. In *Spider-Man*, we fade even more quickly from the Columbia torchbearer to a briefly glimpsed outsize statue of the Virgin Mary, driven rapidly past, at the site of Mexican devastation after a recent and mysterious weather disaster. Any erosion of the female Columbia icon by digital noise, for instance, would have compromised too soon another kind of optical faith—with which the film narrative is multiply caught up through its timely story of a manufactured global menace facilitated by electronic data subterfuge.

Reflecting the escalating CGI aesthetic of the Hollywood action film over the last two decades, here is a movie that comes down to the wire of this present media-reflexive commentary almost by being cornered on the ropes of its own technical expertise, slapped all but silly in the ricochet of the special-effects ironies it unleashes. And it can best be comprehended in this framework under one final rephrasing of the sliding scale of such reflexive functioning—with technique\text/context translated on the spot to apparatus\plot/production, each of these zones of response being shot through—as a further zone of contextual reverb—with intertextual links to the epidemic of mass manipulation in contemporary politics. This outer range of contextual reference is secured only once a midpoint reveal has reset our terms of engagement with the film: namely, that in regard to (1) the VFX bravura on display so far, we've been watching the medium's digital apparatus generate, as in the normal operation of VFX, a cataclysmic series of trick effects to materialize (2) narrative threats that are in fact, diegetically, just that: deceptive effects, tricks—or, in other words, (3) explicitly projected illusions of Hollywood-style industrial technique, as well funded but unreal as the self-styled superhero who vanquishes (vanishes) them. The overriding trick of the plot, then, can only be to banish the risk of tech disaffection by a metaphorics of damage control within a familiar genre pattern of unrest and restoration.

Optical Allusion: Causes and F/X

One rule of action genres—western, detective, and sci-fi especially—is that they melodramatize broader cultural anxieties before laying them to artificial rest through some variety of heroic intervention or sacrifice. Franchises, a kind of subgenre all their own, work somewhat differently. In this they resemble serial TV. With the "tag scenes" familiar from the final credit rosters of the Marvel series, these loose ends—despite intermittent narrative plateaus of resolution in a single film plot—keep refueling the cycle from within its own peripheral flexibility. It is all the more likely, then, that broader cultural parameters of intended audience response—rebooted with each new wrinkle of geopolitical anxiety—will coincide with narrative and technological reflexivity in a franchise devoted almost exclusively to digital "marvels" at the cutting edge of technological empowerment—or its revenge upon us.

Certainly this is the case with this latest *Spider-Man*, including its trumpeted critique of Trump-era demagoguery linked directly to global technological deception (think Russian hacking) in a plot of nefarious VFX technique. The distinction this chapter began with, between cinema as mediatized spectacle (once filmic, now digital) and cinema as designated site of exhibition, has perhaps never been more reductively addressed than in this film's plot about Hollywood-style illusionism in its strategically remote deployment. Plot, did I say? Intertwined with a thin rom-com about a high school trip through European tourist sites—attended, among the usual typecast suspects, by our secret spiderboy, a sidekick or two, and a would-be girlfriend—is the frail narrative thread of the story's thriller premise. According to which: a maestro of technological illusions generates and projects the CGI mirage of monstrous urban catastrophes (Venice, Prague, London) that only he can fend off, becoming in the process a global hero. The unleashed Spider-Man, with all his teen powers on offer, is recruited to the villain's assistance before the former, our true hero, discovers the ruse. Reduced to the simplest logic of genre showdown, and to near pun on the prosthetic efficacy of the eponymous hero (his *web*-spinning miracles)—as well as backed in turn by much repeatedly loaded dialogue to this end—the auto-allegory of *trucage* (what Christian Metz saw as the "special effect" that is cinema all told)[6] is impossible to miss. The panic fostered by high-tech "propaganda" (in this case the illusory images of elemental forces out to destroy the world as we know it)—a paranoia to which a self-styled fascistic superman and avenging scourge is the fake antidote—can in the long run be bested rather than abetted, in its campaign of big-budget illusory disinformation, only by the spidery net of our *web*master hero.

Anything we might call the apparatus disclosures of the metacinematic spectrum in all this are so surfeited and manic, almost comic, in their Hollywood overtones that one feels compelled to work backward from (3) the production end of the sliding scale we've been contemplating toward (2) the plot-transacted structural sense of its own (1) generative electronics. Though deliberately avoiding any logo contamination by a glitched d/effect—precisely the pixel break-up that will be climactically incarnated in the plot—this latest *Spider-Man* enterprise wallows in an almost uncontainable level of digital reflexivity. Computerized technique has swallowed all action. This is just where the overarching paranoia plot must kick in, displaced from its own comic-book source, so that now the updated glancing barbs at fearmongering and fake news never let up for long. When the wunderkind Spider-Man—fostering in his own right a false cover story to keep one of his heroic interventions under wraps so as to protect his empowering anonymity—suggests that people should always believe what they see on the news, the audience's mild sniggering is merely de rigueur. In the age of "post-truth," the plot's whole premise, including a villain pretending to hail from a supposed parallel universe within a wide array of "multidimensional worlds," feels pitched at the idea of Trump-era alternate realties—and not just when this fake superman is anointed as patron saint of terrestrial *border defense* in coming to society's collective rescue. Duping the news outlets with his announced arrival from another version of Earth, where Elementals have slain the populace, the con artist Mysterio is the embodiment of group-think mystification. And what he promises, one simulated alien invasion after another, is only a protective ballistic scrim, exposed eventually as a mere CGI interface, between the spectacle of encroaching horrors and its riveted but vulnerable public audience.

With climate change unsaid but inescapably pressing in the allegory, the worldwide elemental disasters—explicitly subdivided as those of air (emissions), earth (quakes), water (floods), and fire (exponential heat)—all "have a face" in Mysterio's artificial mobilization of their threats. All are incarnate as oversized demons. But here, as so often, is where sci-fi dystopias can get caught up in inverted transpositions of the anxieties they are manifestly extrapolating from. Paranoia is a double-edged sword. The enormity of Mysterio's trumped-up threat is rendered with an enormous and vaguely humanoid form, that is, not because rampant cataclysmic forces are the embodiment of human-induced meteorological disaster, but rather because in this case (phew!) they are all fake: staged flashpoints in a climate of fear itself, stoked with advanced electronic enhancements by the wannabe Avenger. In a no doubt accidental facet—and fallout—of a typically lightweight political parable, climate deniers may thus take some cold comfort even from within the denigration of their parodied hero. "I control the truth," boasts Mysterio (aka Beck, who thinks he has the world at his beck and call). "It's easy to fool people when they're already kidding themselves." Finally overmastered by the "web"-adept Spider-Man once the latter wins back his billion-dollar experimental upgrade of Google Glass, it is up to Mysterio to repeat one more time, with his dying words, his earlier confidence in mass gullibility. "People need to believe," says this vicious genius of a computer-boosted confidence game, and "nowadays they'll believe anything."

Especially their own eyes. What tucks all this limply scripted topicality back into the coils of cinematic self-reference in the cognitive force field of the postfilmic screen apparatus is that Mysterio is, in fact, a maestro of what one of the teen heroes calls, in knowing industry lingo, "illusion tech." So designated is the whole panoply of marauding demons and heroic resistance that gets staged—make that virtually screened—before gullible mass crowds in Mysterio's digital enactment of his own image as savior. He accomplishes this sci-fi feat by manipulating, from a remote electronic hub, a collaboration of weaponized drones (military-industrial anxiety du jour) and gargantuan laser holograms. These we see him testing out under laboratory conditions in the CGI rendering room—and then implementing in real-world capitals by the remote voice-activation of such Hollywood argot as "cue the lightning."

Beyond narcissistic megalomania, his particular vendetta stems from a festering resentment against his ousting by onetime boss Iron Man. This detail marks the film's most obvious strategic dodge, at the plot level, in avoiding what would have been too explicit a corporate reflex if drawn from the villain's actual backstory in the Marvel comic source. In his original paper incarnation, Mysterio's perverse illusionist credentials are more, so to say, medium-specific in their visual deceits than the film would be likely to withstand without toppling into satire or black comedy. In the original serial pages, Mysterio is an unlikely double-threat as maverick agent: having lost his Hollywood jobs as at once a top FX engineer and a valued stunt man (combining Christian Metz's separate categories of visual and invisible tricks: the fantastic illusions you do see, and the substitutions you don't). In that original commix premise, Beck's deceptive tech becomes the incarnate revenge of the system against its own benign commercial spectacles, turning them to a new kind of conviction and notoriety as global terrors. But the movie doesn't offer up such Hollywood employment practices to be sacrificed on the altar of plot, just its hallowed VFX technology to be implicitly borrowed from—and, of course, signally misused. In his filmed version as antihero, Mysterio's CGI stunts, both physical and pyrotechnical, are nonetheless studio signatures: feats of motion capture, green screen, CGI infill, and the rest. Incautiously enough, in this version of the Marvel Universe, everything keeps reverting to a reflex of its own electronic marvelous. So it is that form and content implode upon each other, with any clean delineations in the matter of social or political critique being the first victims of this collapse.

Even the immediate narrative backstory (rather than comic-book genealogy) of the franchise confirms such metacinematics—and does so explicitly at the border between technological and corporate contrivance, CGI and the casting department. Explicitly rehearsed, early in this *Spider-Man* plot, is its position in the wake of *The Avengers: Infinity Wars* (2017), where superpower heroes suffer pixelated decimation along with half of the human race. These dissipating ash-gray digital variants of a dust-to-dust paradigm in mortal disintegration remind us, of course, that the splintered, then obliterated, heroes have in fact been constituted, in their flashiest exploits, by CGI simulation to begin with. Five years later in narrative time, though only one year in the fast turnaround of the lucrative franchise, we learn of a remission in this galactic "Blip." The chronological mismatch is itself, one suspects, part of the metanarrative inference. The fact that many other victims of the Blip have been restored (after this half-decade hiatus) to their former stations, their bodies unaged, and thus lagging behind their cohorts, is a kind of industry in-joke. It doesn't take much to see this as a reflection of such franchise filmmaking at large, which can only keep rebooting itself (the James Bond cycle being quintessential and exemplary) if it replaces plot agents every few years with younger actors in comparable roles.

But it isn't just the age of the narrative agents, but that of the intended audience, that is figured in this film as well. What turns out to be the ultimate threat to Mysterio's computerized disinformation campaign is part of the closely calibrated Hollywood metatext, around which the last phase of the plot revolves. Two friends of Spider-Man have come to learn, along with him, that the humungous Elemental predators are just digital simulations beamed by a "very advanced projector," some high-powered portable gadget (streamlined progeny of the lumbering apparatus of IMAX 3D). What it can generate are looming hallucinations that are finally discerned, under climactic duress, as "coming apart" by explicit pixel break-up—and thus confirming, for all to see, their basis in mere optical trickery. That, plus more. For these three teen agents of potential debunking—in a kind of tacit generational parable— serve to concentrate the audience demographic whose aggressive doubts (as opposed to merely suspended disbelief) would demolish the whole Marvel Universe, let alone the thrills, however deceptive, of this one plot. If these kids don't fall for the spectacle, who will? They are in this regard, aptly enough, the intended victims of Mysterio's final lethal retaliation: the renegade target audience as target. Again, in the variable interchange of this chapter's three-fold template, the corporate logic, even as it enfolds (3) the political intertext of fake territorial invasions and their self-appointed superman of nativist resistance, circles back via (1) the CGI screen's own technical apparatus when "read"—that is, when figured or troped in the plot, or say allegorized—as (2) a narrative reflex, at the textual level, of aggressive computer manipulation (not just on Facebook or in the voting booth, but as the very *specter* of mass paranoia).[7] At the plot level, of course, redemption is pure Hollywood celebration in the formulaic happy ending—yet, in this extreme case, won from within the surprise vilification of its own industrial selling point in compelling special effects.

In my earliest writing on cinema, I had occasion more than once, in identifying the reflexive escalation of visual technology in the sci-fi genre, to observe that "movies about the future tend to be about the future of movies." If one were tempted to update this for the transition from the hologram in 1956's *Forbidden Planet* to Mysterio's digital demons, in positing that "VFX cinema is about the future of illusions," the question would remain, in the face of the present dead end, what future? In the normal run of CGI spectacle, we in the audience, like a credulous public at large, will believe anything too, as long as it's expensively enough generated on screen—and not least, in the closed circuit of the fan appreciation sublimated here, when it parades itself as such. In the digital poetics of the Marvel franchise in general, cinema loses nothing in brand loyalty by adverting to the artifice of its own signature effects. But the risk exposed by an unavoidable "apparatus reading" of the pixel substrate in this hypertrophic case has been, if almost too obvious to mention, all the more serious for that. Where can sci-fi screen invention possibly go from here—in bringing VFX along in motivated genre tow—when plot has become all apparatus?

What persuasions remain once the tail has wagged the dog in this blatant way—or the metatale been so egregiously flagged: exposing the frayed heels of narrative originality dogged by exclusively industrial resources in "illusion tech"? What story is left to tell, what narrative challenges left to face, but those of industrial production and its self-congratulatory sleights of hand? That's one question such an exacerbated case of pop metacinema can't avoid being met with. But to rescue the structural from the judgmental, clear the mind's eye of *Spider-Man* by thinking back to Coppola, or to *Kane*: to the genuine force of their optical flashpoints both of cinematography and of near-miss viewer address by the camera. And here's the main point to stress. Just as there was, is, no way to specify in advance what exactly about literary fiction the classic metafiction is about—or what in respect to narrative form the self-referential narrative, even at its postmodern cynosure, tends to put under tacit study—so too, in movies before or since, with any hermeneutic attention to the localized "reflex action" of incorporated stylistic response. The node of cued intake—as self-conscious uptake—reflects back on itself in ways not just ad hoc but already incorporated by form. Yet not disappeared into it. Such moments are the uniquely legible way film has of "picturing back" to us the paths of meaning unique to its own medium.

Notes

1. "Quoted" here in its full "textual" complexity: *Citizen Kane* (1941, dir. Orson Welles), 01:51:04–24.
2. Stewart, *Between Film and Screen: Modernism's Photo Synthesis*; *Framed Time: Toward a Postfilmic Cinema*; *Closed Circuits: Screening Narrative Surveillance*; and *Cinemachines: An Essay on Media and Method* (Chicago: University of Chicago Press, 1999, 2007, 2015, 2020), with a subsequent turn to motion picturing as a gallery aesthetic in *Cinesthesia: Museum Cinema and the Curated Screen* (Montreal: caboose, 2020). Regarding the media-focused method of *Cinemachines*—with its stress on the techno-historical factors of the apparatus in the "reading" of its technique as text—I'm not advertising that study (any more than the previous commentaries of mine that led to and fed into it) as a necessary preliminary reading on the shift from celluloid to postfilmic cinema reviewed in summation here; I'm merely borrowing the gist of its fuller account to license a discussion propelled in this case by a more recent instance of medial disclosure turning up in the digital machinations of the Marvel franchise.
3. Stanley Cavell, "Assertions in Technique," ch. 18 of *The World Viewed*: Enlarged Edition (Cambridge, MA: Harvard University Press, 1979), 133–45.
4. David Bordwell, *Narration in the Fiction Film* (Madison: University of Wisconsin Press, 1985), 53.
5. These metabrandings—these above-and-beyonds of the logo—are variants of the small-scale corporate allegories detected by J. D. Connor in *The Studios after the Studios: Neoclassical Hollywood (1970-2010)* (Stanford, CA: Stanford University Press, 2015) and closely related to the exploration of studio (rather than *authorial*) intentionality in Jerome Christensen, *America's Corporate Art: The Studio Authorship of Hollywood Motion Pictures* (Stanford, CA: Stanford University Press, 2011).
6. Christian Metz, "*Trucage* and the Film," trans. Françoise Meltzer, *Critical Inquiry* 3, no. 4 (Summer 1977): 657–75, his work revisited and marginally revised in my *Cinemachines*.
7. In exploring such meta-for(ens)ic "beyonds" of the image system, one notes as well that the teen conviction dramatized in default in this Marvel installment would extend to a courted willingness to "play along" in the franchise's interactive gamer tie-ins. It is in that context— along that corporate spectrum from computerized screen action to digital interactivity— that the desire to inhabit the virtual, versus the will to expose it, is the organizing tension of Spielberg's *Ready Player One* (2018).

4

Recursive Reflections

Types, Modes, and Forms of Cinematic Reflexivity

Daniel Yacavone

> Reflection on reflexiveness, like the topic itself, can be a labyrinthian experience for both writer and reader.
>
> **—Don Fredericksen**

There is considerable consensus concerning cinematic reflexivity in broad terms. Few, if any, critics and theorists are likely to dispute that *Man with a Movie Camera*, *Breathless*, and *Mulholland Drive* are highly reflexive films; that the film within the film and breaking the proverbial "fourth wall" are conventional reflexive devices; and that there are substantial differences, whether of *nature* or *degree*, between reflexive and non-reflexive films, styles, and their experiences. Beyond such general characterizations, however, one finds a marked diversity of views on the detailed workings of reflexivity as a form of signification, communication, and artistic expression. These include its specific effects on viewers; its historical and stylistic evolution; its relation to cinematic realism and illusionism; and the political and social critical dimensions of reflexivity.

Over a number of decades film theorists have addressed these and related issues through the creation of more or less detailed typologies of reflexivity rooted in various, often implicit, ideas and assumptions concerning it. As one would expect, together with reflecting shifting movements in the tectonics of film and media theory, these schemes have mirrored changes in reflexive practice in cinema and allied forms of moving-image representation. Recognizing, like David Bordwell, that "in any discussion of reflexivity as a theoretical concept, a great many distinctions have to be made," literary and media theorists, narratologists, and semioticians have also provided typologies of reflexivity,

Daniel Yacavone, *Recursive Reflections* In: *Metacinema*. Edited by: David LaRocca, Oxford University Press. © Oxford University Press 2021. DOI: 10.1093/oso/9780190095345.003.0005 self-reference, and "metareference" in works and media.[1] Some of these explicitly encompass cinema, and others are applicable to it.

This chapter offers a critical overview of certain of these classifications of types of cinematic reflexivity, under the headings of which fall a number of reflexive devices. As is typical of all classificatory enterprises, what these frameworks leave out is in some cases as instructive as what they include; and the points where they overlap are as illuminating as where they diverge. Divided here, for the purpose of analysis, into three general categories—focused on reflexivity's referential content, communicative structures and functions, and intended effects on viewers—together these typologies highlight recurring tendencies in its theorization, including certain lacunae with respect to some of reflexivity's underanalyzed features and effects.

In the interest of beginning to fill in a few of these theoretical gaps, and as one step toward a more comprehensive account of cinematic reflexiveness, I will also sketch the outlines of a new, transmedial typology.[2] This is centered on reflexive "forms," as distinct from specific devices and general modes. So as to not put the conceptual cart before the horse, however, it is best to begin with some general definitions and distinctions concerning reflexivity and related processes. It is only once we have a clear handle on what cinematic reflexivity actually is, and what connects it with, and differentiates it from, other features of films, that we may begin to better understand its diverse manifestations.

Reflexivity and Self-Reflexivity

Amid what Robert Stam aptly calls the "swirling galaxy of satellite terms pointing to specific dimensions of reflexivity," some writers have sought to distinguish it from overlapping concepts and practices.[3] These include *metafiction*, *metacinema*, *metalepsis*, *self-consciousness*, *mise en abîme*, and *allusion/intertextuality*. More basic still, the terms *self-reflexivity* and *reflexivity* are most often used interchangeably. Nevertheless, one may, like Jean-Marc Limoges, attempt to separate them. For Limoges, *self-reflexivity* entails a film specifically foregrounding its own artifactual nature and technological and significatory "apparatus." Whereas *reflexivity* is any reference on the part of a film to "the medium" in general.[4] The suggested distinction immediately runs into conceptual difficulties, however. "Reflexivity" (sans prefix) still involves a film drawing attention to *itself as a film*, even if implicitly. Since any film, as a specific instance of cinema in general, stands in close metonymic relation to it; and thus, a fortiori, to any medium properties, aspects of filmmaking and viewing, screen history and culture, and other generic features of cinema a given film references. Moreover, the only vehicle at a film's disposal for evoking these in the minds of viewers is its concrete audiovisual presentation, aspects of which it foregrounds for this purpose. In this sense the reflexive "signified" always contains the "signifier." Or, as Christian Metz puts it, while extranarrative, cinematic reflexivity is always "textually enclosed" within the work.[5]

Entailing all of the circularity, recursiveness, and double articulation frequently associated with reflexivity in other artistic and non-artistic contexts, such combined *reference to cinema through self-reference* and *self-reference through reference to cinema* on a film's part is perhaps as suitable a general definition of all cinematic reflexivity as is possible.[6] And, strictly speaking, it renders the term "self-reflexivity" redundant. Certainly, in practice there is considerable co-presence and fluidity between a film drawing special attention to features of itself, and to cinema more generally, at times through the same image, sequence, and device. For these reasons, I shall maintain the tacit convention and conceive of these as poles of the same basic phenomenon (reflexivity) rather than insisting upon what would amount to a rather artificial categorical distinction between them. Nonetheless, in the analysis of the specific emphasis and primary function of reflexivity in individual cases the reflexive/self-reflexive division is a useful one. It is also a clear example of categorizing cinematic reflexiveness on the basis of its *referential content*, an approach to which we will shortly return. Thankfully, differences among reflexivity in general and often related features of films are somewhat more straightforward. Although here, again, one finds a number of contrasting concepts and definitions.

Metafiction and Metacinema

Some literary texts address their own fictional status. Frequently termed *metafiction*, as, most basically, "fiction about fiction," this is widely considered to be a defining feature of "postmodern" literature.[7] Exemplified by Nabokov's *Pale Fire*, Calvino's *If on a Winter's Night a Traveler*, and John Barthes's *Lost in the Funhouse*, among other novels and stories, metafiction, Patricia Waugh maintains, is a sustained exploration of the "relationship between the world *of* the fiction and the world *outside* of the fiction," which necessitates a higher-order level of discourse within works on the model of metalanguage, as language used to speak about language.[8]

Numerous films foreground aspects of their own narration and fiction, and fictionality and storytelling, more generally. This sometimes extends to generic, stylistic, and technological factors germane to constructing and experiencing film and television narratives and storyworlds, as seen in the metafictional play of Crichton's *Westworld* (1973) and Nolan and Joy's large-budget television remake of it (2016–). In both cases, the conspicuously high-tech narrative world-making taking place *within* the fictions—providing certain characters in the eponymous fantasy theme-park with a genre cinema-like, yet three-dimensionally immersive and interactive experience—closely parallels the high-tech (for the respective times) narrative world-making of their productions.[9] While here and elsewhere cinematic metafiction has a clear reflexive aspect, not all, or even most, reflexivity in films is metafictional. Some works foreground medial, formal, stylistic, or contextual features that do not turn on fictional reference making and storytelling.[10] Clearly, it is on these other aspects of film-making/viewing that reflexivity in *nonfiction* cinema, both documentary and experimental, is focused. Thus, metafictional reference, where present, is best thought of as a particular sort of cinematic reflexivity, broadly construed.

While some writers employ the term *metacinema* as shorthand for cinematic metafiction, other "meta-" descriptions of films with different, if sometimes related, meanings have been put forward.[11] These include Marc Cerisuello's understanding of a "metafilm" as one that "deals *explicitly* with cinema through representing those responsible for production" (my italics). And Metz's diametrically contrasting employment of "metafilmic" to refer instead to a film's *implicit* evocation of cinema, for example through visual *mise en abîme* figurations (as will be discussed shortly).[12]

Metalepsis

Citing Marx Brothers comedies, Allen's *The Purple Rose of Cairo*, and Altman's *The Player*, among other films, the widely influential French narratologist and literary theorist Gérard Genette (2014) extends his concept of narrative *metalepsis* to cinema.[13] Subsequently modified in various ways by other writers, in Genette's original formulation metalepsis is a "paradoxical . . . transgression between the world of the telling and the world of the told"[14] resulting from "any intrusion by the extradiegetic narrator or narratee into the diegetic universe (or by diegetic characters into a metadiegetic universe, etc.), or the inverse."[15] As John Pier, Marie Laure Ryan, and Werner Wolf, among others, point out, metalepsis is a highly transmedial narrative device. It is found in some plays, films, television shows, graphic novels and comics, and video and computer games. Like metafiction, metalepsis is particularly prevalent in postmodern fiction and drama. However, as modern and modernist novels and plays like Sterne's *Tristram Shandy* (adapted, with cinematic equivalents for its metaleptic conceits, in Winterbottom's *Tristram Shandy: A Cock and Bull Story*), Gide's *The Counterfeiters*, and Pirandello's *Six Characters in Search of an Author* demonstrate, it is by no means confined to it.

Metalepsis is undoubtedly a useful concept in theorizing the reflexive structure and content of films where there is such direct and specifically "paradoxical" movement between ontological and narrative levels, on the part of a narrator, characters, or the narration itself.[16] Extended (as in Genette's analysis) to certain occasions of actors stepping out of their roles and real people appearing as themselves in films, metalepsis is still too restrictive a concept and occurs relatively too infrequently in film practice to be the basis for a general theory or classification of cinematic reflexivity. Which, as already mentioned, also takes many other and quite different forms.

Self-Consciousness

Since the mid-nineteenth century, it has been common to regard some artworks as figuratively evidencing *self-consciousness*, or *self-awareness*, analogous to the reflexive capacities of human thought and consciousness; a relation between art and mind influentially elaborated by Hegel and Friedrich Schiller. In film theory and criticism, however, and with an analogue in literary studies, self-consciousness has another, more precise sense. Here it refers to styles and techniques that draw particular attention to themselves. Thus, one finds frequent descriptions of Max Ophüls's and Stanley Kubrick's self-conscious camera movements, the self-conscious, tableau-like compositions of Peter Greenaway's and Wes Anderson's films, and so on. Film theorists have associated such formal and stylistic self-consciousness, which varies widely in degree, intent, and effects, with cinematic modernism (versus classicism), formalism (versus realism), and contemporary, "post-classical" Hollywood cinema in contrast to the so-called invisible style of classical Hollywood productions.

Some scholars, including Stam, deem such self-consciousness to be a general type of reflexivity. If so, it represents a low grade, or what Metz calls "weak," reflexiveness. Consider the relevant differences between the equally unconventional and attention-drawing, long-take traveling shots that open Welles's *Touch of Evil* and the aforementioned *The Player*. In keeping with

Stam's notion of reflexiveness as a matter of degree, and of films' variable "coefficient of reflexivity," the latter is considerably more reflexive, quantitatively and qualitatively (i.e., experientially), than the former. Since *The Player*'s traveling shot also depicts a film studio, occurs in a film explicitly about filmmaking, and includes characters discussing the length and intricacy of *Touch of Evil*'s opening shot.

When self-conscious presentation is pervasive throughout a film, it may translate into what Bill Nichols identifies as "stylistic reflexivity" as a category in its own right. Disrupting "received conventions" through "gaps, reversals, and unexpected turns that draw attention to the work of style as such," it is contrasted with the less emphasized operation of style typical of more illusionistic, plot and story-centered, cinema.[17] Nevertheless, in their basic forms, the primary difference between reflexiveness and stylistic/narrative self-consciousness is that the latter, as pertaining to the *way in which* a film presents what it does and tells a story, is contentless, in this sense. Whereas, in broadly semiotic and cognitive terms, reflexivity *is* (self-)referential content, in the form of a symbol of the film, or a part of it, as a film.[18]

Mise en Abîme

The French term *mise en abîme*, "put into [the] abyss," traditionally denotes (a) images embedded within the same or similar images, as in some heraldic emblems; or (b) stories within stories. In cinema, by extension, it pertains visually to images, screens, and frames contained within the film's image and frame, and the screen on which it is viewed; or narratively, to nested sequences and stories and attendant narrative framing devices. Films such as Weine's *The Cabinet of Dr. Caligari*, Has's *The Saragossa Manuscript*, Buñuel's *The Discrete Charm of the Bourgeoisie*, and Tarantino's *Pulp Fiction* indicate the wide range of innovative ways in which filmmakers have employed the latter.

Whether or not all visual *mise en abîme* structures in films—such as the multiple mirror-reflected images within images of central characters in Welles's *Citizen Kane* and *The Lady from Shanghai*—are reflexive, or if this meaning depends on the narrative and thematic context in which they occur, hinges on how cinematic *mise en abîme* and reflexivity are more specifically theorized. Beyond a mere duplication and mirroring of elements, some writers, like Stam, build a strong microcosmic aspect into the very definition of *mise en abîme* ("by which a passage, a section, or sequence *plays out in miniature the processes of the text as a whole*" [my italics]). This entails that at a minimum such features always amount to self-reference on the part of the films that contain them, regardless of whether and how they are further foregrounded.[19] If, however, one places emphasis on the spatial-temporal and narrative situation of the *mise en abîme* compositions in the two Welles films, for instance, and their range of possible (non-reflexive) diegetic and thematic meanings—and works with the general definition of cinematic reflexivity I have suggested—in these and other cases it represents another relatively weak form of it.[20] Something closer to what Metz analyzes as "metacinematographic enunciation." Wherein an element of a film's mise en scène "merely" duplicates certain perceptual characteristics of the cinematic image (e.g., its rectilinear framing; the rectangularity of the screen on which it is viewed), amounting to a "semi-involuntary witnessing of the cinematic mechanism."[21] Most of the images of the doorway of the Edwards's homestead in Ford's *The Searchers*, framing the view outside it, are examples of what Metz seems to have in mind. This stands in contrast to what he terms "metafilmic" *mise en abîme* structures, including some "secondary screen" configurations.[22] Such structures generate much stronger, if still figurative, reflexive associations with cinema, and with the film as a whole, not only through their visual form, but through aspects of their represented content, *and* the narrative and thematic context in which they appear. The final appearance of the doorway, and the image-within-the-image it frames in silhouette, in the last shot of *The Searchers* –before the door ceremoniously closes in the film's equivalent of a final curtain – clearly belongs to this latter category.

In actual critical practice, historical, stylistic, and interpretative context often has the last word, if there is one, on the matter in more borderline, or open, cases (a point that Francois Jost stresses repeatedly).[23] Nonetheless, while too large a topic to be adequately addressed here, and while *all* reflexivity (as referential) involves a contextual interpretation of what appears on screen and on the soundtrack, such ambiguity—if seldom outright indeterminacy—also indicates a need to try to distinguish in principle features and devices in films that, to borrow an Aristotelian distinction, are *intrinsically* reflexive and those that are *instrumentally*, that is, contingently and contextually, reflexive.[24]

Allusion/Intertextuality

Whether characterized as quotation, *allusion*, or, bracketing issues of authorial intention, *intertextuality*, a film's reference to another film (such as, *Touch of Evil* in *The Player*), is ipso facto reflexive on the general definition

I have offered. This may or may not be the case concerning a film's reference of works in other media and art forms, or representation of those media/forms more generally. The test here, again, is whether such cross-modal reference and representation on the part of a film involves significant self- and cinema-related meaning, even if implicit, and the spectator's corresponding awareness of it. Bearing this in mind, Stam is right to maintain that together with drawing attention to their "production," "authorship," "reception," and "textual procedures," reflexive films often foreground their "intertextual influences."[25] This may center on adaptation, as he points out with reference to Godard's *Contempt*, in relation to its film-within-the-film's adaptation of Homer's *Odyssey*, and Reisz's *The French Lieutenant's Woman*, scripted by Harold Pinter, in which Fowles's eponymous novel is presented as a film in the process of being made.[26] Also at work in these films, and highly significant both theoretically and historically, are what may be termed *intermedial* and *trans-art* reflexivity. These reflexive forms, to which I will return, operate through the cinematic representation of other art forms and media as vehicles for reflection on cinema from at least one ontological remove.

Proceeding from these basic definitions and distinctions to more detailed classifications of cinematic reflexivity, these may be divided into three main areas of focus: the representational and referential *content* of reflexive features; their effects on viewers, or *reception*, in this sense; and the *communicative structures and functions* of reflexivity, understood in terms borrowed from linguistic semantics and pragmatics. Just as these working, higher-order categories unavoidably overlap, so to do the specific typologies I have placed under these headings. This is not surprising, given that past theorists have tended to repeatedly classify, and reclassify, many of the same reflexive phenomena, including in some of the same films, often making relatively minor but nonetheless significant conceptual and descriptive modifications.

Reflexivity as Reference

Since reflexivity is, among other things, a referential process, it seems natural to analyze its cinematic occurrences according to that to which they refer. In other words, to the semantic content of reflexive features of films, to the extent that it may be generalized. To this end, Don Fredericksen appropriates a distinction originally proposed by Gilbert Cohen-Séat, later taken up by Metz, between the "filmic" and the "cinematic." Some films refer to "cinematic facts" that, strictly speaking, are outside of their own "signifying discourses."[27]

Such reference may pertain to filmmaking and film projection (or playback) technology; the people involved in the work's creation (a common focus of the Hollywood-film-about-Hollywood genre); the rituals and context of film viewing; narrative and genre conventions; historical and cultural factors of context and reception (e.g., the phenomenon of film stardom); and the logistics and economics of production. This last category calls to mind Gilles Deleuze's provocative, if clearly reductive, notion that at base all cinematic reflexivity concerns the time and the money required to make a film and their special, often conflictual, equivalence in this context.[28]

Alternatively, a film's reflexivity may be centered on "filmic facts" pertaining to its status as a perceptual and "signifying object."[29] Writing in 1979, Fredericksen observes that it is this latter category of reflexivity that is of most interest to film theorists who, drawing on structuralism, poststructuralism, and semiotics, are "concerned primarily with constructing the codes and systems that explain how and why messages and texts are meaningful."[30] This is certainly true of the narration-focused, textual "enunciation" paradigm under which reflexivity has long been subsumed in French film theory. From a contemporary vantage point, however, the pendulum has swung some way in the opposite "cinematic" direction. Film scholars are increasingly attuned to films' engagement with extra-work (i.e., real world) cultural, historical, and technological realities of production and reception—including those sometimes lumped together under the heading of "industrial reflexivity"—in a postmodern, and what is now referred to as a "post-cinema," moving-image environment.[31] Aside from evolutions internal to academic film and media studies, part of the reason for this is a general shift in reflexive film practices over the past forty years, as conjoined with wider stylistic and technological developments. As Thomas Elsaesser, Steven Shaviro, and others observe, this includes a movement away from a self-regarding, form- and medium-oriented reflexivity characteristic of the global cinematic modernism of the 1950s and 1960s "New Waves," and toward a more outward-looking engagement with film cultural and contextual dynamics. The latter has sometimes taken the form of a substantial critical exploration of these realities. Far more commonly, however, in mainstream narrative cinema and television, they are acknowledged through mere duplication, pastiche, homage, playing with genre conventions, and copious intertextuality.

Such broad generalizations aside, as is clear from Fredericksen's examples of both categories of reflexivity, the history of cinema is too long and varied with respect to reflexive content to be divided in binary fashion chronologically, stylistically, or on any other basis. Moreover, highly reflexive films from all periods often combine visual and/or aural reference to the "filmic" and the "cinematic," sometimes in a single shot or sequence. Furthermore, and as is crucial to remember in these contexts, while watching films viewers are sometimes well aware of what falls under both of these headings in the *absence of any reflexive signaling of them* on the part of films.

Bordwell also provides a reference-based typology of reflexivity, albeit of a metatheoretical kind. It forms part of his polemical critique of "implicit" and "symptomatic" interpretations of films, centered on "symbolic" and "repressed" meanings seen to reflect various social and cultural processes, and the workings of the unconscious, respectively.[32] On Bordwell's view such readings frequently lack empirical falsifiability and a self-critical dimension, and often neglect close historically-informed, analysis of film form and style. They are supported and sanctioned, however, by various constructed "semantic fields" of meaning, that is, interpretative paradigms, which film criticism and academic film studies have institutionally accepted as valid. Reflexivity, which licenses "the critic to link virtually any object on-screen—windows, curtains, light bulbs—to some aspect of cinema," is singled out by Bordwell as the "most powerful semantic field shared by all schools of criticism," including psychoanalytic, semiotic, feminist, Marxist, and auteurist approaches.[33]

In this context, Bordwell identifies seven "attributes of cinema" that critics and theorists routinely appeal to in diagnosing reflexivity. Partly overlapping with Fredericksen's designations, these are the film industry, film technology, film history, the "role of the filmmaker," the film "screening situation," the spectator, and "doctrines or theories concerning cinema."[34] His examples of such interpretations, drawn from writings stretching back to the 1920s, confirms the prominent role of reflexivity in film theory and criticism from its early stages. While other film theoretical approaches have since superseded those Bordwell targets, scholars and critics continue to regard films as foregrounding these same attributes, in part to buttress their favored conceptual frameworks. They frequently point to the metaphorical representation of cameras, projectors, and screens; films' references, sometimes disguised, to the lives and works of their makers as a key to unlocking their deeper meanings; and to their purported meta-level address of cinematic history and filmmaking technology. Exemplifying the latter, Amy Taubin and Zara Dinnen separately read the plot of Fincher's *Zodiac* (2007), involving characters' decoding cryptic bits of information contained in the eponymous serial killer's cyphers, as a "coded" commentary on its and other films' then innovative use of digital image manipulation (i.e., also through coded bits).[35] With reference to the last of Bordwell's categories—films' suggested evocations of *theories of* cinema—despite his skepticism concerning overarching reflexive interpretations of films, he elsewhere appeals to the now canonical reading of Hitchcock's *Rear Window* as an allegory of cine-matic spectatorship in using the film to illustrate (rather persuasively) his own constructivist account of cinematic narration.[36]

Setting its metatheoretical agenda aside, Bordwell's classification, like Fredericksen's, helpfully indicates the very wide—and, by virtue of cinema's ceaseless evolution, continually expanding—range of aspects of cinema that films, and those who think and write about them, may engage with as the "target domains" of reflexive reference, to borrow the terminology of meta-phor theory. Even if, as some of his choice examples of far-fetched interpret-ations demonstrate, these sometimes say more about the interpreter and his or her theoretical-critical biases than about the work in question. However, like all other exclusively referential classifications of the signified content of reflexivity separated from its visual and auditory form (i.e., the "signifier"), and diverse intentions and functions, this typology is fundamentally partial.

Reflexivity as Reception

Traditionally, discussion of reflexivity in cinema has been preoccupied with its effects on viewers' attitudes and beliefs, for convenience sake here termed *reception*. Bound up with notions of illusionism, medium awareness, and films calling attention to their artifactual status, this concern is one of the persistent legacies of the ideology-centered perspectives of French apparatus theory, "*Screen* theory," and related writings, which have been collectively la-beled "post-structural film theory."[37] In these contexts, emphasis is placed on reflexivity's role in fostering a more critical attitude toward narrative cinema, especially on the classical Hollywood model and what Noël Burch calls its "Institutional Mode of Representation."[38] This prioritizes the viewer's percep-tual and psychological immersion in a film both as a simulacrum of ordinary spatial-temporal experience and as an autonomous storyworld. In breaking this illusion—variously referred to as "diegetic" (Burch; Metz), "aesthetic" (Limoges; Wolf), and "projective" (Richard Allen)—of an unmediated, al-ternative reality, some films' reflexive forms and devices draw contrastive at-tention to its audiovisual manufacture.[39] While simultaneously laying bare their own counter-operations in what may be perceived as a more honest way, the most radical "political modernist" films, to borrow D. N. Rodowick's phrase, also deconstruct the problematic (e.g., Western, late capitalist, im-perialist) cultural-ideological attitudes seen to underpin the representations of characters and situations in most popular cinema. These attitudes, on this view, are reflected not only in the representational and narrative content of many Hollywood and Hollywood-style films, but in their realist-illusionist style. A style that is the moving-image descendent of Western perspectival painting and nineteenth-century realist literature and drama, with its *effet de réel* (reality effect), in Roland Barthes's famous phrase.[40]

While agreeing on these perhaps intuitively plausible and yet, in their details and suggested implications for film theory and practice, contentious, premises, certain writers have sought to further delineate this use of reflexivity in contrast with others. Nichols forwards a primary distinction between "formal" and "political" reflexivity, applicable to narrative, documentary, and experimental cinema.[41] Citing the precedent of Peter Wollen's and Dana Polan's arguments, he understands this division in two ways.[42] The first is the difference Polan emphasizes between political reflexivity and that motivated by "purely formal" concerns, including the playful self-referentiality of some classic Warner Brothers cartoons (in Polan's example). The second, following Wollen, is a way of thinking about two different sorts of political reflexivity and their respective "materialisms."[43] One, more formal in orientation, centered on the "materiality of the cinematic signifier," is embodied in the pan-European avant-garde cinema of the 1920s. The other, a "second avant-garde" exemplified by the "Brechtian cinema" of the 1960s and 1970s, is concerned with "the materiality of social practices including that of viewing and of the cinematic apparatus."[44]

Like Wollen, Nichols sees the spirit of the first avant-garde, which attempts in a romantic, "visionary" fashion to alter the world through creating new ways of perceiving it, as continuing in the works of experimental filmmakers such as Stan Brakhage.[45] This dovetails with Noël Carroll's description of the "apperceptive reflexivity" of Brakhage's works, Snow's *Wavelength*, Frampton's (*nostalgia*), and other form- and medium-centered experimental films.[46] In what amounts to another functional, *reception-focused* theorization, Carroll emphasizes how these works' foregrounding of perceptual processes involved in film viewing opens a privileged window for viewers onto perception, and perception-derived knowledge more generally.

As acknowledged in such distinctions and categories, just as reflexivity per se is compatible with some forms of realism, as well as escapist entertainment—as its long, varied history in the popular comedy and musical genres attests—its intended effects are by no means confined to explicitly or implicitly political ones. Stam places particular emphasis on these facts, and they are reflected, if in a very general way, in his division of all "reflexive art" into three broad, sometimes overlapping, modes: "didactic," "aggressive," and "ludic."[47] Corresponding to the aforementioned conceptions of modern political reflexivity, the *didactic* is here understood in the terms of Brechtian "materialist fiction." Exemplified, for Stam, by *Tout va bien*, one of Godard's most overtly Brechtian works, in cinema it involves "exposing" the technological and cultural apparatus of film viewing: an idea that was elevated to the point of "fetishization" in 1970s film theory, as Metz retrospectively observes.[48] An equally transmedial category, *aggressive* reflexivity, is characterized by an attempt to shock viewers into critical awareness through "modernist dehumanization," among other means, as in a number of Buñuel's films (*L'Age d'Or*; *The Exterminating Angel*).[49] As something of a catch-all category for any reflexivity that is not primarily political or satirical, and thus in need of finer parsing, what Stam terms *ludic* reflexivity is characterized by aesthetic and conceptual playfulness. Familiar across narrative film styles, modes, and periods, for example silent film comedy, as well as television, it takes both popular and more intellectually challenging forms.

Nichols astutely observes that the *same* reflexive tropes and devices—such as the actor's/character's address of the spectator, the visible presence of the (or *a*) film crew and camera, and certain voyeuristic situations mirroring the conditions of filmmaking and viewing—may be part of either political or nonpolitical (e.g., formal) reflexivity.[50] And this is equally true of Stam's suggested modes. In metatheoretical terms, this underscores that no matter how closely wedded, indeed inseparable, they may be within films and their experiences, in theory it is necessary to logically differentiate reflexive *devices*, *modes* (including those defined by their purported effects), and what I will go on to describe as reflexive *forms*, together with classifications operating on these three distinct levels.

Likewise approaching the subject from a transmedial perspective, media theorist Werner Wolf provides what is likely the most comprehensive account of reflexivity operating in numerous media, including cinema and television. He does so, however, under the more specific term and concept of "metareference," as the process underlying the seemingly ever-increasing "metaization" of all media. Metareference is distinguished from (1) basic "self-reference," whereby a work draws attention to its formal features, such as through repetition and contrast of elements; and (2) basic "semantic" (content-based) "self-reflection," for example, when characters or narrators in a novel or film refer to other characters. Metareference, in contrast, is semantic self-reflection with an additional "metadimension."[51] This enables a work to foreground its medium and its "fictionality" (where present), "from a higher level of reflection . . . that exists or is implied to exist in the work."[52] As well as transmedial, Wolf's metareference is yet another functional, reception-based category. Since the suggested evidence of its presence is the generation of substantial "medium awareness" on the reader's or viewer's part. In fact, Wolf identifies no less than twenty (!) distinct aims and effects of metareference and the resulting awareness in works. All applicable to cinema, these include undermining aesthetic illusion; a work's attempting to assert the truth and "authenticity" of its representations; providing perceptual and cognitive amusement; gratifying the audience's intellect as being capable of grasping the reference in question; inculcating a more sophisticated awareness and appreciation of media; serving the social function of creating "experts," and generating "a particular in-group pleasure" as a result; and attuning audiences to the ways in which we live in an increasingly media-constructed reality.[53] As this partial list indicates, a merit of Wolf's highly detailed scheme is its acknowledgment of at least some of reflexivity's emotional and affective qualities.

In sum, many of these and other reception-centered categories are applicable to both fiction and nonfiction cinema. They thereby remind us of the pan-cinematic nature of a number of reflexive modes and techniques. And also of currents of influence and imitation in this respect across narrative, documentary, and experimental film practice. Finally, this spectator-based approach to the topic highlights an array of ideas and attitudes that reflexive features may prompt in audiences, as desired by filmmakers for a similarly wide range of reasons. Wolf's broader classification aside, however, it is of most use in better understanding films that are clearly intent on communicating relatively specific messages. Typical of politically motivated and, as Stam's term implies, "didactic" reflexivity, this diverges from more subtle, semantically ambiguous, or polysemic manifestations of reflexivity, including as part of a film's aesthetic explorations and expression. This said, in rightly recognizing the manifest diversity of the formal, stylistic, and tonal means of critical-political reflexivity specifically, some of these classifications also wisely caution against any overly monolithic conception of it in cinema and beyond.

Of course, like all reception theories, those mentioned here are confined to broad intuitions and hypotheses concerning spectators' psychological responses to reflexiveness in films. Given the perpetually evolving habits, knowledge, and expectations of cinema audiences—along with familiar problems concerning generic appeals to "*the* audience," and both the "average" and "ideal" viewer, including in the absence of empirical research – such approaches are open to considerable challenge on methodological and conceptual grounds.

Reflexivity as Communication

Discussions of reflexivity's intended effects on spectators emphasize that, like other forms of cinematic meaning, it is, at base, a communication—albeit of a very particular kind—from the work and its makers to audiences. Semiotic theory, as the analysis of (the structures of) communication through material signs, together with allied linguistic, narratological, and rhetorical concepts and categories, is thus prima facie well suited to provide means of classifying reflexive constructions.

Metz, in his last major work, critically (re)appropriates Émile Benveniste's and others' aforementioned concept of "enunciation," as the act of "utterance" by an "enunciator" for an "addressee." Enunciation is understood as a relation of subjectivities marked by shifting *deictic* (context-dependent) personal pronoun positions; for example, in Francesco Casetti's cinematic model, "I" (the filmmaker), "you" (the spectator), and "he/she" (characters).[54] In light of Bordwell's, Edward Brannigan's, and other theorists' objections to applications of traditional enunciative frameworks to cinematic narration (criticisms that Metz largely endorses), Metz argues that cinema instead involves acts of "*impersonal* enunciation" on the part of the filmic "text" itself. Embedded in the work during its creation, and reflecting back upon it, the acts in question are foregrounded as such. Avoiding appeals to implied narrators and other such projections of subjectivity onto films (the pronoun-based and anthropomorphic, or "humanoid enunciation," approach to cinema Metz rejects), this self-referential address is a one-way stream of communication from film work to spectator. Encompassing, although not limited to, reflexivity, as traditionally understood, it operates either through a film's fictional storyworld or outside of it (i.e., nondiegetically), but always by way of conventional, historically evolved semiotic devices. These include voice-over narration, intertitles, direct address, and several varieties of the film-within-the-film, the use of which Metz traces from early cinema to the time of his writing in the early 1990s.[55]

Predating Metz's account, in theorizing cinematic reflexivity Don Fredericksen draws on Roman Jakobson's synthesis of C. S. Peirce's and Ferdinand de Saussure's foundational *semiotics* and language-based *semiology*, respectively. Unlike Saussure, who famously brackets the actual speech act and its pragmatic contexts, instead focusing on the historically unchanging, "synchronic" structures of language (*langue* rather than *parole*)—but in common with Peirce—Jakobson was concerned with its concrete uses. Fredericksen transposes Jakobson's posited six basic functions of language to suggested functions of reflexivity. Although both Bordwell and Stam cite the resulting, and still highly relevant, "six-fold categorization of reflexive modes" in cinema (Table 1) for its fundamental approach to the subject, it has not received the attention it deserves.[56]

To briefly summarize each of the modes in question, in "emotive" speech acts, emphasis is on the expressed state of the speaker, that is, his or her feeling or attitude. Fredericksen takes this to correspond to the "attitude" of a film, as reflecting that of the filmmaker, and expressed through its "tone."[57] Following Elsaesser's characterizations of the "indirect" reflexivity of a good deal of post–New Wave art cinema, he regards the tone in question as reflexive if it is ironic, understood as creating a perceived distance between the filmmaker, or narrator, and what appears on screen.[58] As is also discussed by Nichols, in relation to documentary cinema, such self-referential irony implicitly raises "the question of the author's own attitudinal relation to his or her subject matter."[59] Taking many different, more or less reflexive forms, this expressed authorial distance has increased markedly since Fredericksen's writing. It is now widely regarded as a characteristic trait of postmodern cinema, with its tendency to place story and narration in figurative quotation marks.

Jakobson's "conative" function of language is the opposite of the emotive in that it is the listener who is the object of the message, as in a command or a question requiring response. Fredericksen identifies this function with a character's/actor's address of the camera and with voice-over narration. In both instances, the cinematic fiction is bypassed in favor of a more direct

Table 1 Fredericksen's Six Reflexive Modes (from Jakobson's Semantic Functions of Language)

Linguistic function	Emphasis of the speech act	Reflexive cinema equivalent
Emotive	Expressed attitude of speaker	Irony
Conative	The addressee	Direct address and voice-over
Referential/Denotative	Empirical and practical context	Foregrounded ontology of medium and/or fiction
Phatic	Speaker/addressee social relation	Attention on the film/viewer relationship
Metalingual	Linguistic codes	Reference to cinematic signs/codes
Poetic	Expressive form/materiality of language	Foregrounded formal/material features (spatial, temporal, rhythmic, graphic, auditory)

communication between film and audience. He links Jakobson's third category, the ubiquitous "referential" (or "denotative") function of language—e.g., to convey factual information about the world—with a film's drawing attention to the ontology of the cinematic image and of fictional characters and events. In other words, this is a film's probing of "existence relations" between cinematic representation and fiction, on the one hand, and extra-work reality and standards of truth – as correspondence with this reality – on the other hand.[60] In common with a good deal of modern film theory, this reflexive mode is concerned with the "psychological and ideological" ramifications of these relations. For Fredericksen it is frequently overtly political and often involves films' use of Brechtian-style alienation (*Verfremdungseffekt*) devices.[61]

The social relationship between speaker and hearer, and the channel of communication itself, is the object of Jakobson's "phatic" function (similar to the conative one, yet less direct). Fredericksen associates it with various ways that films acknowledge the audience as engaged in an active relationship with them and with cinema more generally. This includes characters watching films (within the film) and other represented situations that circularly mirror the activity of the viewer. Here we may add that some films foreground their dynamic relationship with spectators in a highly confrontational way: less a figurative conversation than an all-out assault on the audience's senses and beliefs. Such is the case in Michael Haneke's *Funny Games*, both the original German-language film and Haneke's own Hollywood remake, whose aggressive reflexivity is centered on its depiction of graphic, senseless violence as a means of exploring the fraught ethics of film spectatorship. Under the phatic heading, Fredericksen also aptly singles out a film's invitation or demand, as it were, for more active viewer participation than is otherwise common, thereby placing the viewer in the position of a virtual co-creator.[62] This strategy has a special relevance for what has been more recently analyzed as the contemporary (i.e., post-1990) "puzzle" and "mind game" film.[63] The reflexivity quotient of the cognitively challenging narratives of Nolan's *Memento* and *The Prestige*, Carruth's *Primer*, Villeneuve's *Arrival*, and other works that have been placed in these categories may be usefully understood in such participatory and ludic terms.

Like other semioticians and linguists, Jakobson identifies a specific "metalingual function" whereby a statement reflexively refers both to itself and to the codes of language it instantiates. In common with Metz, Barthes, and other theorists, Fredericksen sees a cinematic equivalent in reflexive films that foreground their semiotic structures of signs and codes or, contrastively, those of conventional illusionist cinema. Unlike the ontological nature of the "referential" reflexivity mentioned previously, this mode, which notably overlaps with others, is cast as largely *epistemological*, concerned with knowledge and meaning relations. Given metalanguage's demonstrated subversive capacities, such reflexivity is also frequently critical-political. It may involve the previously noted audiovisual deconstruction of the connotative codes of classical Hollywood cinema, which (on this view) not only shape the viewer's understanding of what is represented on screen but the realities to which they refer.[64]

Widely credited as a highly original and influential contribution to semiotic and semantic theory, Jakobson's last posited function—the "poetic"—applies to the specifically *aesthetic* use of language or other system of communication. Here the signifier does not disappear in the signifying process, as a transparent pointer to the signified, but draws attention its own expressive perceptual form and "materiality," thereby deliberately rendering the signifying relation opaque.[65] Owing to its aesthetic emphasis and its stress on language's concrete materiality (e.g., read and spoken rhythms), in many respects this is the most directly applicable of Jakobson's categories to cinema. Fredericksen allies it with a film's drawing particular attention to the "material" aspects of the medium. These include spatial, temporal, rhythmic, and graphic features, and, more literally, the celluloid film strip.[66] To his examples of avant-garde films of the 1920s and parts of canonical New Wave works (*Persona*; *Breathless*) we may add the mature films of Ozu, which in this way famously diverge from the conventions of classical Hollywood-style cinema and the institutional mode of representation (IMR);[67] together with formally experimental twenty-first-century narrative films, such as Lynch's *Inland Empire*, Glazer's *Under the Skin*, and Wheatley's *A Field in England* (to cite a few English-language cinema examples). Fredericksen associates such formal-poetic reflexivity with what the Russian Formalist critics and Bordwell, applying their concepts to cinema, describe as defamiliarization (*ostranenie*). In the sense of a work's use of unconventional forms and techniques that disrupt habitual patterns of perception and provoke heightened awareness of the conventions violated, as well as of the ordinary realties artistically transformed.

Reflecting upon this schema as a whole, Fredericksen justly maintains that it is a mistake to confine reflexivity and "metacinema" to the "meta-discursive functions" alone.[68] In other words, to the *phatic, referential*, and *metalingual*, as the focus of most semiotic, structuralist, and post-structuralist accounts, in contrast to the *poetic, conative* and *emotive* ones. Clearly, all six posited modes of cinematic communication and expression may be the significant object/vehicle of reflexivity.

Along with this and other insights, Fredericksen's classification also use-fully identifies a specifically "rhetorical" category of reflexivity—comprising the *conative* and *phatic*—alongside tonal, formal, ontological, and semiotic types.[69] As my supplementary examples in the foregoing indicate, all are very much present in contemporary fiction (and nonfiction) cinema. Where they also appear in the complex, overlapping combinations that Fredericksen acknowledges. Some, such as ontological reflexivity, have gained added im-petus and a new significance amid the sea change from celluloid to digital film-making and viewing—including specific technologies like CGI, HD formats, and contemporary 3D—and filmmaker's, as well as theorist's, explorations of constitutive properties of both of these moving-image media and their expe-rience. In this vein, Laura Mulvey analyzes the deliberately anachronistic use of celluloid rear-projection techniques in some contemporary films. These foreground conventional relations among cinematographic representation, stylistic realism, and three-dimensional reality in the current digital era.[70]

A chief merit of Fredericksen's account is its showing that the "reflexive film can address itself to all constitutive parts of the 'film event.'"[71] Like other semio-linguistic approaches to cinema, more generally, however, *his classifi-cation* does not, and cannot, address numerous perceptual, expressive, and affective aspects of the "film event." As many writers over the past decades have pointed out from their respective cognitivist, phenomenological, and Deleuzian perspectives (among others), linguistic semiology does not map directly onto the cinematic form, which in the first instance *shows* rather than *says*, with the crucial and much-discussed differences this entails (this being, ultimately, the crux of the debate concerning the applicability of enunciation theories to cinematic narration). Thus, his classification gains its value (as Metz, for instance, admits) only at the price of considerable omissions and a high degree of abstraction from any film's presentation and experience.

Although Fredericksen's identification of an emotive mode of reflexiveness is salutary given theorists' underemphasis of its multiple feeling dimensions (beyond humor and amusement), he unduly restricts it to tone and irony. In both mainstream and art cinema, however, reflexive forms and devices some-times generate, or are entangled with, a wide range of spectator emotions. Closer to tone, but not identical with it, reflexivity may be a major contributor to non-object-specific constellations of feeling, or "affect," as Shaviro suggests with respect to some twenty-first century "post-cinema" works. But it may also create feeling specifically toward, and about, the represented worlds of films. As Torben Grodal has argued with an emphasis on interlinked pro-cesses of cognition and emotion, V. F. Perkins has shown in relation to film style and fictional worldhood, and some empirical research also supports, some reflexive forms and devices may result in greater emotional "intimacy" with a film's characters and drama, and a consequent psychic immersion in its diegetic reality.[72] This stands in sharp contrast with the proverbial critical distance and forced imaginative and emotional removal from the fictional storyworld with which reflexivity and medium awareness are often simplistically associated.[73] Although an accurate extrapolation of Jakobson's definition of the emotive mode of language as pertaining to the feelings of the *speaker*, hence figuratively the filmmaker, rather than the *listener*—on this model, the spectator—the restrictiveness of this function in the context of cinematic reflexivity is indicative of a larger methodological issue.

Cherry-picking only those aspects of films that somehow match up with Jakobson's general semantic categories, this scheme is also straitjacketed by them. His careful qualifications aside, any attempt such as that of Fredericksen to fit all cinematic reflexivity into the prefabricated mold of a theory of largely practical communication in another medium, especially discursive language, seems bound to entail considerable conceptual tensions. Not least as a result of the numerous points at which cinema and language, artistic and non-artistic representation, and reflexive and non-reflexive communication sharply diverge. For these reasons, although along with Metz's typology of enunciative devices, Fredericksen's remains the most detailed and systematic classification of cinematic reflexivity yet offered, it presents an at once admirably broad (in strictly communicative, if not experiential, terms) and problematically narrow picture of the phenomenon in toto.

Reflexive Forms: A New Typology

A differently oriented understanding of cinematic reflexivity involves positing recurrent types, which, although they frequently feature in the analysis of individual films, are not identified explicitly in any of the classificatory schemes that have been surveyed here. As we have seen, theorists have largely written about reflexivity as if there were nothing in between, so to speak, conventional reflexive *devices*, on the one hand, and highly general functional *modes*, on the other. A familiar and oft-remarked example may suffice to show the plausibility and usefulness of a mid-level classification that is neither inappropriately abstract nor limited to work- or creator-specific forms and meanings.

One widely suggested function of the multilayered reflexivity of Antonioni's *Blow-Up* is to probe and problematize the nature of perception as affording access to objective truth and reality. As in Fredericksen's referential and semiotic-epistemic reflexive modes, this questioning notably extends to the perception of art, cinema, and the film itself. Building upon elements present in Julio Cortázar's eponymous short story upon which the film is loosely based, Antonioni and his collaborators employ a number of conventional reflexive devices to achieve this aim. These include physical objects within the mise en scène figuratively signifying cinema and its technological apparatus; numerous images-within-the-image and frames-within-the-frame; and highly self-conscious staging, camera movement, and editing. The last of these culminates in the iconic final sequence, in which, harkening back to the trick effects of Georges Méliès, Thomas, the photographer protagonist, disappears from a field of grass (i.e., the 'visual field') via a slow dissolve and is replaced by the film's end title—a dramatic instance of extradiegetic enunciation as theorized by Metz.

Additionally, however, *Blow-Up* features a markedly *reflexive use* of (a) space, location, and ambiance, for example, the photographer's studio and darkroom with connotations of film studio, editing suite, and viewing space; the London park and adjacent tennis courts, as circumscribed spaces of voyeurism and performance, including in front of Thomas's camera; (b) other art forms and media (still photography; abstract painting) explicitly and implicitly contrasted with the photographic and cinematographic image; and (c) various mystery and suspense film conventions, which recall the mystery-based reflexivity of Feuillade's *A Tragic Error* (1912) and Marston and Thanhouser's *The Evidence of the Film* (1913), made some fifty years earlier, as much as they anticipate that of Coppola's *The Conversation* (1974) and De Palma's *Blow Out* (1981).[74] As in Antonioni's *L'Avventura* and *The Passenger*, *Blow-Up* self-consciously subverts familiar elements of these genres to consistently undermine viewer expectations. The film also includes (d) a surrogate directorial figure (Thomas) involved in proto-cinematic creation and a filmmaking-like manipulation of sequential images; and who, like other characters in the film, shares certain known interests and traits with Antonioni; and (e) various acts of self-aware performance and role-play on the part of the protagonists and other characters, including the student mime troop, reflecting and refracting cinematic performance.

Beyond their specific operations in *Blow-Up*, these aspects correspond to certain reflexive formations that are familiar across a broad range of films. Based on their characteristics, and with reference to the above, they may be correspondingly termed

(a) Environmental
(b) "Trans-art" and intermedial
(c) Generic

(d) Creator centered
(e) Performance based

Each of these forms, which are also notably transmedial, have, in turn, a number of distinct, classifiable subtypes.[75] *Creator-centered* reflexivity, for instance, ranges from directors' major roles and cameo appearances in their own films and others to their acting as voice-over or on-screen narrators; from actors playing filmmakers (or characters metaphorically representing them) to the most reflexive pole of films' use of "free indirect" narration;[76] among other forms of reference to the lives, personas, and works of creators and collaborators.

Reflexive "formations" or simply "forms" are here understood as complex configurations of elements—representational, formal, thematic—rather than structures lacking content. They are more akin to literary *tropes*, as found in numerous guises across a number of works, genres, and styles, than to *modes*. As means and manifestations of reflexive meaning in films, these forms are likewise distinct from specific reflexive *devices*, including those through which these forms work and which the latter may modify.

The first point to notice is that different devices may be part of the same reflexive forms in their instantiations in specific films. Second, with reference back to the typologies we have surveyed and their principal focuses, and as the terms "form" and "formation" are also intended to suggest, the species-level types proposed differ from reflexive modes defined primarily in terms of their intended *functions*, as in Stam's and Fredericksen's reception- and communication-centered classifications. Thus, in different films a given form may be utilized to different purposes: formal or political, intended to foreground ontological or ethical realities, generate humor or irony, comment upon conventional cinematic practices, and so on—with different resultant effects. Last, while some of the forms that I wish to draw attention to specify the representational and referential content of reflexive features, they also implicate themes, structures, styles, and inter- and transmedial aspects of works.

Typically, these forms are integrated with conventional reflexive devices and with the other reflexive, or sometimes reflexive, features discussed earlier (such as allusion and self-conscious presentation), to form complex referential wholes. A few relevant examples illustrate these sorts of relations.

The familiar film-within-the-film figuration is instantiated in all of the forms identified. With respect to *intermedial* and *trans-art* reflexivity, it often takes the alternative guise of a television broadcast or internet stream within the film (*The Truman Show*; *Demonlover*); the play within the film (*Opening Night*; *Marat/Sade*); the novel or screenplay within the film (*Providence*;

Adaptation.), and so on.[77] In *creator-centered* reflexivity, the film within the film telescopes connections between it, the work containing it, and the filmmaker's (or maker's) life and/or other works. Thus in Fellini's fictionalized cinematic autobiography *Intervista* (1987), framed as a documentary being made on the director, one of the multiple (fictional) films shown in the process of being made at Rome's Cinecittà studios is a magical realist account of the young Fellini's first experiences of the film industry; while the projection of sequences of his *La Dolce Vita* (1960) on a makeshift screen in Anita Ekberg's villa brings "the maestro's" earlier and later style and career into the same experiential field for both the audience and *Intervista*'s motley crew of fictional and real-life personages watching it.

In reflexivity's *performance-based* manifestations, the film within the film draws special attention to diegetic and nondiegetic roles, casting, and performances. In Tarantino's *Once Upon a Time . . . in Hollywood* and its partial inspiration, Rush's *The Stunt Man*, the witnessed making of a Hollywood television series and a film, respectively, affords the opportunity to explore the curious relationship between actors and their stand-ins and stunt-doubles, within the narratives and in production practice. In *Intervista*, the primary narrative focus of *La Dolce Vita*'s above-mentioned screening is its stars, Ekberg and Marcello Mastroianni (here playing versions of themselves) nostalgically watching their younger selves. As also pertains to other reflexive devices, along with whatever ideas and feelings a film within the film structure *per se* may generate, its meaning and experience in given works are shaped by the higher-order forms of reflexivity enumerated, which (shades of Plato's forms and their copies) films partake in concretely actualizing.

As *Intervista* and *Once Upon a Time ... in Hollywood* also demonstrate, the forms of reflexivity that I have specified, and likely others, are frequently combined in films and even in individual sequences. And their conjunctions create conceptually and experientially powerful reflexive dynamics. The epiphanic conclusion of Scorsese's *Raging Bull* is a clear instance of overlapping, or in contemporary parlance, networked, *creator-centered, performance-based*, and *allusive/intertextual* reflexivity, as perceptually conveyed through a secondary screen device, also with echoes of a film within the film.

Near the end of his method-acting tour de force performance as Jake La Motta, Robert De Niro sits in front of a mirror in which the former boxer is rehearsing a set piece for his one-man nightclub act prior to going on stage. To his own reflection, captured in a medium-close shot, La Motta / De Niro enacts former boxer Terry's (Marlon Brando's) half of the back-seat conversation with his brother Charlie in Kazin's *On the Waterfront*, one of the most celebrated sequences, and method-inspired performances, in American cinema. De Niro here plays both La Motta *and* La Motta playing Brando/ Terry. Through association, the pair of physically and emotionally wounded former boxer characters (La Motta and Terry), the real Jake La Motta, whose story *Raging Bull* tells, and the two screen acting greats (De Niro and Brando) are brought together in a fivefold configuration of intertextual and performance-based reflexivity. This not only occurrs in the same extended sequence-shot and diegetic situation, but the same embedded image and "screen," that is, the dressing room mirror, framing De Niro's / La Motta's face and voice. Into this bravura, audiovisual *mise en abîme* construction, the thematic implications of which are far too numerous to be detailed here, comes Scorsese, credited as the club's stagehand. Glimpsed in the mirror and calling to mind his haunting appearance with De Niro's Travis Bickle in *Taxi Driver*, he gives La Motta a five-minute warning that the show is about to start, just as the film, and its portrayal of La Motta, is about to end: with a dramatic fade to black, a titled quotation from the Gospel of John, and a dedication to Scorsese's film teacher. In an instance of creator-centered reflexivity, the auteur, as an "intercessor" (in Deleuze's term) within his own cinematic world, metaphorically announces the conclusion to his film and, thereby, further underscores its intensely personal nature, as manifestly informed by Scorsese's customary themes, professed religious beliefs, film school experience, and so on.

On the whole a far more reflexive film than *Raging Bull*, in *Intervista* ("an almost unequaled source for enunciative moves and reflexive fireworks"), the amount of reflexive forms and subforms, and their combinational complexity, was exceptional, if not wholly unprecedented, in narrative cinema.[78] Today, however, such a dense, global, and often deliberately bewildering abundance of reflexive forms, modes, and devices throughout films, both comic and dramatic, is increasingly common. Indeed, together with emphasis on the affective valences of reflexivity, this is one of the defining features of the transgeneric cinematic phenomena I have elsewhere labeled twenty-first-century "hyper-reflexivity."[79]

The forms of reflexiveness I have mentioned work through formal, representational, medial, narrative, and performative features and capacities of cinema. While not inherently reflexive, all of these aspects of films have a powerful, latent potential in this direction that some works actualize. Although more specific in their empirical reference than the theoretical postulation of general reflexive modes, again like literary tropes these forms resist the degree of systematization and inventory to which more concrete, self-contained, and conventionalized reflexive devices are amenable. Nonetheless, there is much more to be said about them in theoretical terms and as exemplified in particular films and bodies of work. Moreover, mapping the mutable dynamics between such forms and reflexive functions, devices, and objects of reference, including those recognized in existing classifications, may significantly aid in the analysis and interpretation of reflexive films. Finally, as appearing in works in other art forms and media, these types provide clear focal points for comparing reflexiveness in cinema with that found in novels, plays, paintings, comic books, new media productions, and so on. In affording common variables by which to gauge differences, they may thereby reveal possible cinema- and moving-image-specific reflexive properties and effects.

In sum, despite its greater utility in these respects, for the reasons indicated this classification, which requires further elaboration, neither can nor should replace any of the typologies I have here briefly appraised. Rather, it is offered as one more systematic viewpoint from which the conspicuously multifaceted, and—in the face of perpetual stylistic and technological change in screen art and media—remarkably persistent phenomenon of cinematic reflexivity may be framed and contemplated.

Notes

1. David Bordwell, *Making Meaning: Inference and Rhetoric in the Interpretation of Cinema* (Cambridge, MA: Harvard University Press, 1989), 11.
2. This chapter is part of a larger project devoted to rethinking the theory and practice of cinematic reflexivity as the subject of a forthcoming monograph.
3. Robert Stam, *Reflexivity in Film and Literature: From Don Quixote to Jean-Luc Godard* (New York: Columbia University Press, 1992), xiv.
4. Jean-Marc Limoges, "The Gradable Effects of Self-Reflexivity on Aesthetic Illusion in Cinema," in *Metareference across Media*, ed. Werner Wolf (Amsterdam: Rodopi, 2009), 392.
5. Christian Metz, *Impersonal Enunciation, or The Place of Film* (New York: Columbia University Press, 2015), 19.
6. See also Daniel Yacavone, "The Cognitive and Affective Dimensions of Cinematic Reflexivity," in *La furia umana* (multilingual quarterly of the theory and history of cinema), forthcoming 2021.
7. Brian McHale, *Postmodernist Fiction* (London: Methuen, 1987), 27.
8. Patricia Waugh, *Metafiction: The Theory and Practice of Self-Conscious Fiction* (New York: Routledge, 1984), 3.
9. Long before the sophisticated CGI effects that the *Westworld* limited television series showcases, Crichton's film holds the distinction of being the first feature film to contain entirely computer-generated images.
10. Based on these and similar considerations, some literary theorists also suggest a distinction between metafiction and "self-reflexive," or "self-conscious," fiction, which Stam extends to cinema. See Stam, *Reflexivity*, 73–74, 127–31.

11. Fernando Canet, e.g., suggests that reflexivity is a defining feature of "metacinema," as the larger category. Canet, "Metacinema as Cinematic Practice: A Proposal for Classification," *L'Atalante*, July–December 2014, 24.

12. Cerisuello quoted in David Roche, *Quentin Tarantino: Poetics and Politics of Cinematic Metafiction* (Jackson: University of Mississippi Press, 2018), 8; Metz, *Impersonal Enunciation*, 55.

13. Gérard Genette, *Métalepse: De la figure à la fiction* (Paris: Seuil, 2014).

14. John Pier, "Metalepsis," in *The Living Handbook of Narratology* (Hamburg: Hamburg University Press, 2011), http://wikis.sub.uni-hamburg.de/lhn/index.php/Metalepsis, no pagination.

15. Gérard Genette, *Narrative Discourse: An Essay in Method*, trans. Jane E. Lewin (Ithaca, NY: Cornell University Press), 234–35, quoted in Pier, "Metalepsis."

16. See, for instance, Jeff Thoss, *When Storyworlds Collide: Metalepsis in Popular Fiction, Film, and Comics* (Leiden: Brill-Rodopi, 2015) and Dominic Lash, *The Cinema of Disorientation* (Edinburgh: Edinburgh University Press, 2020).

17. Bill Nichols, *Representing Reality* (Bloomington: Indiana University Press, 1991), 70. Accordingly, for Bordwell, a high degree of self-consciousness is a defining feature of what he posits as "art cinema" narration, in contradistinction with "classical [i.e. Hollywood-style] narration". See *Narration in the Fiction Film* (Madison: University of Wisconsin Press, 1985), 209–13.

18. On this basis Metz distinguishes reflexivity from a film's narrative or stylistic "commentary." See *Impersonal Enunciation*, 133–34.

19. Stam, *Reflexivity*, xiv. On these points, see Werner Wolf, "Metareference across Media: The Concept, Its Transmedial Potentials and Problems, Main Forms and Functions," in Wolf, *Metareference across Media*, 60.

20. This is not to suggest that a given aspect of a film cannot have both significant reflexive and non-reflexive meaning. But to the main point here concerning *mise en abîme*, Wolf helpfully points out that "it would be difficult to argue that *all* instances of this device are at the same time *metareferential*, that *all* reflections of (a part of) a work or performance [in a work] are also reflections on its mediality, structure and so forth" (my emphasis). Wolf, *Metareference across Media*, 60.

21. Metz, *Impersonal Enunciation*, 55.

22. Metz, *Impersonal Enunciation*, 55.

23. In Francois Jost, "The Authorized Narrative," in *The Film Spectator: From Sign to Mind*, ed. Warren Buckland (Amsterdam: Amsterdam University Press, 1995).

24. This is in addition to recognizing that reflexive features may be more or less significant with respect to a film's experience, intentions, and interpretation, as a whole.

25. Robert Stam, *Film Theory: An Introduction* (Oxford: Blackwell, 2000), 150; Stam, *Reflexivity*, xxi.

26. Stam, *Film Theory*, 27–32.

27. Don Fredericksen, "Modes of Reflexive Film," *Quarterly Review of Film Studies* 4, no. 3 (1979): 306.

28. Gilles Deleuze, *Cinema 2: The Time Image*, trans. Hugh Tomlinson and Robert Galeta (Minneapolis: University of Minnesota Press, 1989), 77–78.

29. Fredericksen, "Modes of Reflexive Film," 307. Partially inverting Fredericksen's dichotomy, for Canet "cinematic reflexivity" is centered on the "creative process itself," and "filmic reflexivity" on film history and intertextuality ("Metacinema as Cinematic Practice," 18).

30. Fredericksen, "Modes of Reflexive Film," 307.
31. See Steven Shaviro, *Post-cinematic Affect* (New York: Zero Books, 2010).
32. Bordwell, *Making Meaning*, 8–10, 250–55.
33. Bordwell, *Making Meaning*, 252, 110–11.
34. Bordwell, *Making Meaning*, 113. Categorizing objects of reflexive reference according to Étienne Souriau's posited seven levels of "filmic reality"—of which the "diegetic" and the "profilmic" are the most cited—results in a classification similar to Bordwell's.
35. See Amy Taubin, "Nerds on a Wire," *Sight and Sound* 17, no. 5 (May 2007): 24–26; Zara Dinnen, *The Digital Banal: New Media and American Literature and Culture* (New York: Columbia University Press), 2018. Taubin thus places *Zodiac* in a category of "films that contain metaphors for their own making" (24).
36. See Bordwell, *Narration in the Fiction Film*, 40–47.
37. Warren Buckland, *The Cognitive Semiotics of Film* (Cambridge: Cambridge University Press, 2009).
38. For an early account of IMR, see Noël Burch, *To the Distant Observer: Form and Meaning in Japanese Cinema* (Berkeley: University of California Press, 1979).
39. See Richard Allen, *Projecting Illusion: Film Spectatorship and the Impression of Reality* (Cambridge: Cambridge University Press, 1995). From a perspective sympathetic to its wider interests and goals, D. N. Rodowick and Jacques Rancière, together with Metz, have analyzed various tensions and contradictions concerning the suggested role of reflexivity in the film theory discourse in question on its own ideological terms, whereas Carl Plantinga (among others) has challenged it from a cognitivist perspective. See, e.g., Rodowick, *The Crisis of Political Modernism* (Berkeley: University of California Press, 1995); Rancière, *The Emancipated Spectator*, trans. Gregory Elliott (New York: Verso, 2011); and Plantinga, *Screen Stories: Emotion and the Ethics of Engagement* (New York: Oxford University Press, 2018). On the numerous problems entailed in theorizing medium awareness, and pronounced psychological immersion in cinematic fiction, in strictly binary, oppositional terms, see Yacavone "The Cogntive and Affective."
40. See, e.g., Stephen Heath, "Narrative Space," *Screen* 17, no. 3 (1976): 68–112.
41. Nichols, *Representing Reality*, 64.
42. See Peter Wollen, "The Two Avant-Gardes," *Studio International* 190, no. 978 (November–December 1975): 171–75; and Dana Polan, "Brecht and the Politics of Self-Reflexive Cinema," *Jump Cut* 17 (April 1978): 28–32.
43. Nichols, *Representing Reality*, 64.
44. Nichols, *Representing Reality*, 64.
45. Nichols, *Representing Reality*, 64.
46. Noël Carroll, *Interpreting the Moving Image* (Cambridge: Cambridge University Press, 1998), 306.
47. Stam, *Reflexivity*, xii, 9.
48. Metz, *Impersonal Enunciation*, 55.
49. Stam, *Reflexivity*, xi, 7.
50. Nichols, *Representing Reality*, 69.
51. Wolf, "Metareference across Media," 30.
52. Wolf, "Metareference across Media," 30.
53. Wolf, "Metareference across Media," 66–68.

54. Metz, *Impersonal Enunciation*, 1–24; and Francesco Casetti "Face to Face" in *The Film Spectator: From Sign to Mind*, ed. Warren Buckland (Amsterdam: Amsterdam University Press, 1995), 118–40.

55. See Metz, *Impersonal*; and Daniel Yacavone, "The Expressive Sign: Cinesemiotics, Enunciation and Screen Art," in *The Anthem Handbook of Screen Theory*, ed. Hunter Vaughn and Tom Conley (London: Anthem Press, 2018), 245–62.

56. Fredericksen, "Modes of Reflexive Film," 305; Bordwell, *Making Meaning*, 111 n. 29.

57. Fredericksen, "Modes of Reflexive Film," 308.

58. Fredericksen, "Modes of Reflexive Film," 308.

59. Nichols, *Representing Reality*, 73.

60. Fredericksen, "Modes of Reflexive Film," 309–10.

61. Fredericksen, "Modes of Reflexive Film," 309–10.

62. Fredericksen, "Modes of Reflexive Film," 313.

63. See, e.g., *Puzzle Films: Complex Storytelling in Contemporary Cinema*, ed. Warren Buckland (Oxford: Blackwell, 2008); and Miklós Kiss and Steven Willemsen, *Impossible Puzzle Films: A Cognitive Approach to Contemporary Complex Cinema* (Edinburgh: Edinburgh University Press, 2017).

64. Fredericksen, "Modes of Reflexive Film," 307.

65. Fredericksen, "Modes of Reflexive Film," 316.

66. Fredericksen, "Modes of Reflexive Film," 316.

67. See Burch, *To the Distant Observer*; and Bordwell, *Narration*, 285–89.

68. Fredericksen, "Modes of Reflexive Film," 305.

69. Fredericksen, "Modes of Reflexive Film," 305.

70. Laura Mulvey, "Rear Projection and the Paradoxes of Hollywood Realism," in *Theorizing World Cinema*, ed. Lucia Nagib, Chris Perriam, and Rajinder Dudrah (London: IB Tauris, 2012), 207–20.

71. "Modes of Reflexive Film," 306.

72. V. F. Perkins, "Where Is the World? The Horizon of Events in Motion Pictures," in *Style and Meaning: Studies in the Detailed Analysis of Film*, ed. John Gibbs and Douglas Pye (Manchester: Manchester University Press, 2005), 36–38, 40 n. 6. See Plantinga, *Screen Stories*; Torben Grodal, *Moving Pictures: A New Theory of Film Genres, Feelings, and Cognition* (New York: Oxford University Press, 1999). Within a cognitive psychological framework there has been some relevant empirical study of the effects on viewers of reflexive devices, such as breaking the fourth wall's impact on narrative absorption and spectator emotion. See Daniela M. Schlütz, Daniel Possler, and Lucas Golombek, "'Is He Talking to Me?' How Breaking the Fourth Wall Influences Enjoyment," *Projections* 14, no. 12 (2020), 1–25.

73. For further analysis of emotion generating and amplifying reflexivity in films, including a number of examples, see Yacavone, "Cognitive and Affective Dimensions."

74. My thanks to Livio Belloï for bringing these early films' similarities to *Blow-Up* to my attention through his presentation at the reflexivity and metafiction conference hosted by Université Blaise Pascal / Université Clermont-Ferrand, in Auvergne, France, November 14, 2019.

75. Elsewhere I discuss a number of distinct types of *creator-centered* and *trans-art/intermedial* reflexivity at work in von Trier and Leth's *The Five Obstructions* and Clouzot's *The Mystery of Picasso*. See Yacavone, "Doubled Visions: Reflexivity, Intermediality, and Co-creation

in *The Mystery of Picasso* and *The Five Obstructions*," *New Review of Film and Television Studies* 18, no. 4 (2020): 452–79.

76. See, e.g., Pier Paolo Pasolini, "The 'Cinema of Poetry,'" in *Heretical Empiricism*, ed. Louise K. Barnett, trans. Ben Lawton and Louise K. Barnett (Bloomington: Indiana University Press, 1988), 167–78; and John Orr, *Contemporary Cinema* (Edinburgh: Edinburgh University Press, 1998).

77. See also Metz, *Impersonal Enunciation*, 85.

78. Metz, *Impersonal Enunciation*, 82.

79. Yacavone, "Cognitive and Affective Dimensions."

5

Méliès, Astruc, and Scorsese

Authorship, Historiography, and Videographic Styles

Eleni Palis

When the title character in *Hugo* (2011, dir. Martin Scorsese) repairs his mysterious, inherited automaton, the machine springs to life with a pen at the ready. Extreme close-ups catalog moving cogs and gears before resting expectantly on the poised pen. Reaction shots of Hugo (Asa Butterfield) and Isabelle (Chloë Grace Moretz) provide an emotional barometer for the scene, prompting us to mirror their excitement when the automaton moves and then crestfallen confusion when the machine sputters and stops. Both on-screen characters and audience expect written prose because, in flashback, Hugo's father introduced the automaton saying, "This one can write." The automaton disappoints these authorial expectations when it falters after only a few, seemingly random marks on the page. When the automaton magically moves again, Hugo exclaims with relief, "It's not writing, it's drawing!" Yet this is not entirely true. The automaton draws and signs the synecdoche for Georges Méliès's *A Trip to the Moon* (1902): the man in the moon with a spaceship piercing one eye. In recognition, Hugo exclaims, "It's the movie my father saw!"—citing an inherited cultural memory, though neither Hugo nor Isabelle can identify the source text or filmmaker through image alone. Fortunately for them, the automaton *both* writes and draws. After a brief pause, the poised pen clicks back into motion and writes with a flourish: "Georges Méliès."

The central conflict here, inspiring hope, disappointment, and relief, rests on the technological capability for simultaneous word and image, or rather authorial signature and image. Narratively, the signature is the crucial clue, revealing the disgruntled toyshop owner, Isabelle's Papa Georges, as silent cinema auteur Georges Méliès (Ben Kingsley). Metacinematically, however, this moment hyper-literally approximates the cinematic apparatus in general and auteur theory rhetoric in particular. With varying rigor, popular and scholarly auteurist discourse often cite the "signature" as the auteur's metaphorical mark. John T. Caldwell summarizes this trope, remarking, "Authorship assumes that artist works are signed (explicitly, implicitly, or

Eleni Palis, *Méliès, Astruc, and Scorsese* In: *Metacinema*. Edited by: David LaRocca, Oxford University Press. © Oxford University Press 2021. DOI: 10.1093/oso/9780190095345.003.0006 figuratively).”[1] Here, Hugo and Isabelle take authorial identification via signature literally. French film theorist Alexandre Astruc is often credited with the idea of filmmaker as signatory, wielding the camera as a pen. Astruc’s “The Birth of a New Avant-Garde: *La Caméra-Stylo*,” an early work in the French auteur theory canon, proclaims that “[the cinema] is gradually becoming a language . . . a form in which and by which an artist can express his thoughts, however abstract they may be, or translate his obsessions exactly as he does in the contemporary essay or novel. That is why I would like to call this new age of cinema the age of *the caméra-stylo* (camera-pen).”[2] Astruc continues, demanding literal rather than metaphoric interpretation; he is not comparing the camera to a pen, but rather, “Direction is no longer a means of illustrating or presenting a scene, but a true act of writing. . . . The filmmaker/author writes with his camera as a writer writes with his pen.”[3] In the scene described earlier, the automaton *literally writes* with his pen to reveal both the film image *and* its filmmaker/author. The pen performatively stands in for Méliès’s camera, mechanically reproducing the image and marking its author as signatory. Hugo at once metacinematically demonstrates Astruc’s *caméra-stylo*, staunchly upholds Astruc’s gender pronouns (and emphasizes male lineage far more than its literary source text), and, most troublingly, uses its metacinematic *caméra-stylo* to present myopic and exclusionary historiography.

Hugo’s plot unfolds along a “paper trail” of books, writing, drawings, and quotations, a journey through personal and official archives. Jennifer Clement and Christian B. Long diagnose “*Hugo*’s bibliophilia” evinced by the books, scholarship, and written words cluttering screen and narrative space.[4] More to my point, a search for authorial identity propels *Hugo*’s bibliophilic preoccupations. Scorsese’s narrative returns obsessively to authorial identity and ownership. Hugo is a young orphan living clandestinely in Gare Montparnasse in 1931, who supports himself by stealing from train station vendors. In his spare time, he secrets mechanical parts from the train station toyshop to repair the mysterious automaton. Hugo’s deceased father (Jude Law) “adopted” the automaton after finding it abandoned in a museum. When Hugo finally repairs the automaton, its combination of word and image reveals Isabelle’s godfather, “Papa Georges,” as silent cinema auteur Georges Méliès. With the help of friendly film historian and author René Tabard (Michael Stuhlbarg), the Film Academy recovers many Méliès films and restores Méliès to his rightful film-historical glory. The film ends with the gala celebrating Méliès restored auteur status.

The automaton, producing words and images, provides one metacinematic representation of the digital *caméra-stylo*. Scorsese transposes Astruc’s *caméra-stylo* into the twenty-first century, demonstrating digital cinema’s capacity for writing *on film about film* through what I call "film quotations," or fragments of past film reappropriated and recontextualized into subsequent films. Film quotation as a label deliberately invokes the rich interdisciplinary discourse mapping literary strategies onto film—from auteur theory and Astruc, to film semiotics, to adaptation theory, and beyond. Catherine Russell's etymological definition of "archiveology" invokes similar linguistic metaphors, saying that archiveology "when applied to film practice, . . . refers to the use of the image archive as a language."[5] *Hugo*'s metacinematic *caméra-stylo* writes with Méliès's image archive, especially the man-in-the-moon synecdoche, and other early cinema fragments.[6] Scorsese's metacinematic film quotations constitute what Russell calls "critical cinephilia," when filmmakers creatively use "archival material to produce knowledge about how history has been represented."[7] *Hugo*'s deserves interrogation for the way Scorsese "writes" with his metacinematic, "critically cinephilic" *caméra-stylo*. His use of "archival material to produce knowledge" is neither politically neutral nor historiographically objective.

    Hugo marks a departure from Scorsese's other metacinematic "essayistic" works. Timothy Corrigan theorizes the "essayistic" as "a kind of encounter between the self and the public domain . . . [that] acts out a performative presentation of self as a kind of self-negation in which narrative or experimental structures are subsumed within the process of thinking through a public experience."[8] Corrigan highlights the personal, the in-progress, the self-conscious performance of authorial subjectivity acting through essayistic work. Drew Morton delineates between the subjective essayistic mode and "videographic" style. Videographic works, which re-edit footage from preexisting films, often adding either on-screen text or explanatory voice-over, to reinterpret, reframe, or reconsider the moving images under consideration. Discussing the evolving labels for digital videographic work (sometimes called video essays, audiovisual essays, and now often videographic criticism), Morton explains that he "[does] not view [his] expository videographic efforts (supported by research and vigorously structured) as being particularly subjective."[9] Morton then turns to "Scorsese's essayistic moments," when characters offer self-conscious, subjective commentary on on-screen action.[10] For me, *Hugo* as a metacinematic treatise writes videographically rather than essayistically. Like Morton's videographic work, Scorsese's *caméra-stylo* is expository, "supported by research and vigorously structured," and wields enunciative authority.

    Positioning videographic criticism as a digital manifestation of Astruc's *caméra-stylo* situates *Hugo* within a larger conversation about new technologies and film studies. Christian Keathley connects Astruc and videographic criticism in "*La Caméra-Stylo*: Notes on Video Criticism and Cinephilia," published the same year that *Hugo* hit theaters. Therein, Keathley argues that "due to developments in digital technology, film scholars also find themselves in a position to respond to Astruc's call—using new technologies to invent new audio-visual critical forms."[11] These critical forms now populate digital, scholarly forums, like the peer-reviewed *[in]Transition: Journal of Videographic Film and Moving Image Studies*. In *[in]Transition*'s inaugural issue, Laura Mulvey transposed her written analysis of *Gentlemen Prefer Blondes* (1953, dir. Howard Hawks) from her book *Death 24× a Second: Stillness and the Moving Image* into videographic criticism—demonstrating the productive overlap and shared aims across textual and videographic film-scholarly "writing." Central to both Mulvey's book and videographic work is the concept of "delay." Mulvey argues that delaying the film image is "the essential process behind textual analysis."[12] The analytical opportunity in "delaying the image, extracting it from its narrative surroundings, also allows it to return to its context and to contribute something extra and unexpected, a deferred meaning."[13] *Hugo* "delays" a single, central image—the man in the moon with the rocket in his eye—subjecting it to repeated scrutiny as central clue, as artistic signature, as synecdoche of *A Trip to the Moon*.[14]

Reading *Hugo*'s auteurist enunciation expands existing scholarship on Scorsese's authorial signature. As Sandra Annett summarizes, "The media has tended to position [*Hugo*] through auteurist discourses, working with or against Scorsese's signature style."[15] Guerric DeBona fits this model, arguing that "Scorsese has left his indelible imprint in *Hugo*."[16] Attention to Scorsese's signature ultimately obscures *Hugo*'s considerable metacinematic writing, which demonstrates the *caméra-stylo*'s historiographic capabilities. Victoria Duckett comes closest when she hesitantly remarks, "*Hugo* is largely a story about how we need to find and make sense of drawings and other visual records. It is also . . . perhaps about the re-writing of film history."[17] I argue that *Hugo*'s metacinematic writing is *precisely* about rewriting film history. As Janet Staiger argues, "filmmakers are involved in canon formation. Those films chosen to be reworked, alluded to, satirized"—here I add, quoted— "become privileged points of reference, pulled out from the rest of cinema's predecessors. As ideal fathers, these select films are given homage or rebelled against."[18] Staiger's paternal invocation precisely fits the characterizations of patriarchal authority in both classical auteur criticism and Scorsese's characterization of Méliès in *Hugo*. *Hugo* participates in canon formation through metacinematic, quotational *caméra-stylo* "writing" that wields totalizing, videographic confidence, presenting film historical "facts" that argue for both Méliès's *and* Scorsese's status as auteurs. Or, said another way, Scorsese evinces no "awareness of the politics of the chosen criteria" or of "a politics of eliminating power of some groups over others, of centering at the expense of marginalizing classes, genders, sexual orientations, or cultures."[19] Such "awareness" or "politics" would demand authorial self-consciousness, an authorial subjectivity and awareness more aligned with the essayistic, rather than videographic, mode. This chapter expands studies of Scorsese's auteurism, analyzing *Hugo*'s metacinematic demonstration of Astruc's *caméra-stylo* and the canon-formation politics videographically expressed.

Following the man-in-the-moon image across *Hugo* reveals a pedagogy crafted through repetition. Scorsese's metacinematic writing affirms Astruc's claim that film is "a means of writing just as flexible and subtle as written language."[20] The man in the moon's progressive reveal—from description to drawn sketch to still image to moving image—primes Scorsese's audience to experience a rush of familiarity when *A Trip to the Moon* is finally projected as a motion picture.[21] Thus, Scorsese *constructs* his filmic readers, preparing spectators with planted visual "memories" that fabricate collective expectations that pay-off when the spaceship finally collides with the moon. Or, in Patricia White's terms, Scorsese crafts an experience of "retrospectatorship," a "film reception which is transformed by unconscious and conscious past viewing experience."[22] In a totalizing way, Scorsese supplies "past viewing experience" via descriptions, sketches, and stills that prefigure and precede moving-image quotations from *A Trip to the Moon*, simulating re-viewing and rediscovery for Scorsese's young audience, even if most had no previous experience of Méliès. More nefariously, the pleasurable familiarity of "retrospectatorial" recognition confers cultural capital and canonical status upon Méliès by fabricating collective cultural memory around him.

The first mention of *A Trip to the Moon* invokes masculine genealogy and inherited spectatorial memory. Strolling through Paris with Isabelle, Hugo explains, "My father took me to the movies all the time. He told me about the first one he ever saw. He went into a dark room, and on a white screen he saw a rocket fly into the eye of the man in the moon. . . . The movies were our special place. . . . Where we didn't miss my mum so much." This introduction to the man-in-the-moon synecdoche fits larger film critical/theoretical assumptions in which, as Duckett argues, the "moon-face has largely come to represent the magic and illusion of film. [Tom] Gunning's article "The Cinema of Attractions: Early Film, Its Spectator and the Avant-Garde" is largely responsible for this."[23] The correlation between film scholarship and narrative feature film quotation (here as description rather than appropriated footage) emphasizes the *caméra-stylo*'s capabilities for critical, theoretical enunciation. As Hugo speaks these lines, he and Isabelle cross a bridge over the Seine, visually evoking how the movies bridge the chasm between past and present, life and death, father and son. Hugo inherits cultural memory, remembering through his father's eyes, and thereby genders the movie theater as a "special place" for father and son. This gendering extends to all film institutional spaces in *Hugo*. As a respite from "miss[ing] mum," *Hugo*'s cinema is a boys' club of escapism and masculine camaraderie—almost predicated on mother's absence. In contrast, Brian Selznick's novel keeps Hugo's cinematic memories quiet. Selznick's Hugo silently thinks "about the times he had gone to the movies with Father."[24] Later, talking with Isabelle "made Hugo remember something Father had once told him, about going to the movies when he was just a boy, when the movies were new."[25] No mention of "special" male bonding or maternal absence. Scorsese's emphasis on masculinity and paternity fits with the tone of Astruc's polemic, as encapsulated in the statement: "The filmmaker/author writes with his camera as a writer writes with his pen."[26] The traditional Romantic filmmaker/author wields masculine pronouns.

Scorsese emphasizes masculine gendered art/artistry by literally and metaphorically giving Hugo the keys—or rather, the power to break in—to the movie theater. In the novel, Isabelle beckons, "Follow me," deftly picks the lock, and "then [holds] the door open for Hugo."[27] In contrast, Scorsese's Hugo picks the lock and shrugs off Isabelle's trepidation ("We could get into trouble!"). Allowing Hugo to "break in" casts the cinema as a male dominated space and metacinematically reflects Scorsese's movie brat past "breaking into" post-classical Hollywood. The theater's controlling masculinity manifests again in the angry theater manager, who discovers and expels Hugo and Isabelle. Masculine oversight echoes across the film's institutional spaces: the station inspector (Sasha Baron Cohen) patrols the train station; Monsieur Labisse (Christopher Lee) imperiously surveils the bookstore in aggrandizing low angle; Rene Tabard controls access to the archive.

The synecdochic man-in-the-moon image next appears in the automaton's pen-and-ink drawing, described at the outset, and continues metacinematic contemplation of the cinematic apparatus while upholding its consistent masculine gendering. The *caméra-stylo*, represented as a pen drawing the cinematic image, also reflects Méliès's own auteurist pronouncements. To publicize the gala in his honor, Méliès published a theory of film authorship in 1929, almost twenty years before the *Cahiers du cinema* writers' *politique des auteurs*, saying,

> The author must know how to work out everything by himself on paper, and consequently he must be the author [scriptwriter], director, designer, and often an actor if he wants to obtain a unified whole. The person who devises the scene ought to

direct, for it is absolutely impossible to make it succeed if ten different people get involved.[28]

Conceptualizing the film author as director, scriptwriter, designer, and actor, Méliès anticipates Astruc's claim that "the scriptwriter directs his own scripts; or rather, that the scriptwriter ceases to exist, for in this kind of film-making the distinction between author and director loses all meaning.... The filmmaker/author writes with his camera as a writer writes with his pen."[29] For Méliès and Astruc, the auteur's totalizing control blurs conventionally distinct production roles. Méliès' emphatic individualism, "work[ing] out everything by himself on paper," and the textual language of paper and pen invoke the classical, Romantic author that Astruc's *caméra-stylo* uses nineteen years later. The automaton scene's pacing also signifies metacinematically. When the automaton initially grinds to life, making indecipherable markings on the page, Hugo sinks into despair. Just when Hugo loses hope, the automaton unexpectedly continues to draw, contextualizing the previously illegible markings. This two-step process creates dramatic tension and, more importantly, reflects the temporality and construction of cinematic writing; like these pen-and-ink markings, ideas written on film rely on assemblage, on the joining of disparate images to create cumulative meaning.

Echoing the rhetorically masculine author in Astruc's and Méliès's writing, the automaton wields a "paternally infused" pen.[30] The automaton sutures paternal lineage across an odd interplay of abandonment and adoption: like a metaphoric mechanical son, Méliès creates and then abandons the automaton, and then Hugo's father adopts it. Hugo's father introduces the automaton, saying, "I found him abandoned in the attic at the museum," immediately gendering the inanimate object.[31] Later, when Hugo expects the automaton to transmit a message from his father, Isabelle receives a paternal message too. In strange kinship, Isabelle stares at the automaton's writing/drawing and wonders, "Why would your father's machine write Papa Georges's name?" The unaccountable association of paternal signifiers, the moon image, and the signature creates something like shared paternity between Isabelle and Hugo. This foreshadows their official kinship by film's end, when Méliès adopts Hugo, making Isabelle and Hugo adoptive siblings. Oddly, Hugo's happy-ending adoption achieves sole male parentage. After the station inspector apprehends Hugo and the automaton (despite Hugo's offensive, ableist appeal to the inspector), Méliès appears just in time, bellowing, "Monsieur! This child belongs to me!" This speech act constitutes Méliès's unilateral decision to adopt Hugo, without any input from or consideration of Méliès's wife, "Mama Jeanne" (Helen McCrory).[32] Thus, Méliès achieves asexual, solely male reproduction. Méliès embraces his progeny, cradling the automaton in one hand and Hugo in the other. Méliès's own goddaughter and ward, Isabelle, stands awkwardly behind, the embodiment of an afterthought.

Following the man-in-the-moon's progressive reveal, from spoken description to sketch (and eventually to stills, moving image, and then 3D rendering), crafts *Hugo*'s deliberate pedagogy. With lesson-plan orchestration, Scorsese shepherds his audience to increasing familiarity, approximating a student's re-viewing study tactic. Metacinematically, moving from spoken word to sketch to still to moving image reflects the progressive techno-historical capabilities for quoting film on film in general, and across Scorsese's oeuvre in partic-ular. Scorsese integrates film quotation into almost all his films. His direc-torial debut, *Who's That Knocking at My Door* (1967) begins this career-long preoccupation and anticipates *Hugo*'s quotational aesthetics. Produced be-fore Scorsese had industry contacts, lawyers, and budgetary capability to li-cense film quotations, *Who's That Knocking* resorts to describing *The Searchers* (1956, dir. John Ford).[33] Protagonist J. R. (Harvey Keitel, in his first film role) chats up a girl (Zina Bethune, named only "Girl") holding a "French movie magazine," invoking but not naming *Cahiers du cinema*, the publication that popularized auteur theory.[34]

Scorsese continues his metacinematic film pedagogy with a glimpse inside an unofficial, early film archive. Isabelle and Hugo take the automaton's signed sketch to the Méliès household, seeking the auteur behind the signature, and while hiding in a bedroom, they discover an armoire's secret compartment. When Isabelle topples from a chair, the compartment bursts open and a swarm of paper erupts. The explosion both showcases digital 3D capabilities, as papers fly toward the viewer (no such explosion appears in the Selznick text), and models proto-cinematic, paper-and-ink toys: the flipbook and the thaumatrope. These optical games, popular in the decades before cinema, combine drawn images and paper in motion to create the illusion of move-ment. The thaumatrope combines images drawn on the front and back of a card by alternating rapidly between the two sides (often by twirling a string). One of Méliès's fluttering pages somersaults, end over end, and at first, like the thaumatrope, each flip of the page makes the drawn image move. But enhanced by 3D, the winged girl on the first side magically becomes a but-terfly and takes flight. Integrating digital and proto-cinematic technologies positions 3D within a longer history of technological and aesthetic innova-tion.[35] Metacinematically, Scorsese models proto-cinematic toys to a young audience of digital natives.

Yet Scorsese's most pronounced change in adapting this scene from novel to film concerns gender. In the novel, "Within moments [of the paper explosion] the bedroom door flew open. 'Isabelle!' yelled her godmother as she ran to the girl."[36] This scene centers female interaction, expressing the action between "god*mother*," and "girl." In the film, however, this scene hinges on "father-son" betrayal. After Méliès's angry outburst (the same in the novel), ripping and crumpling the strewn sketches, he points and speaks directly to Hugo in low, wounded tones, saying, "I trusted you. This is how you thank me?" From a medium shot of Méliès, the reverse shot frames Hugo in close-up. What began as an interaction among four people shrinks to one-on-one confrontation. The focus on Hugo is surprising. Shouldn't Méliès's greater trust, and thus greater betrayal, rest with Isabelle? Instead, Mama Jeanne and Isabelle fade, visually and metaphorically, into the background. A subsequent long shot positions Hugo and Méliès closest to one another, while Isabelle stands behind Hugo and Mama Jeanne sits timidly behind Méliès. Physically and metaphorically, Scorsese sidelines the women, foregrounding conflict in masculine lineage and archive.

After this altercation, Hugo collides with Monsieur Labisse, the bookseller, who leads Hugo to an "official" archival space: the Film Academy Library. Here, *Hugo*'s metacinematic engagement with Astruc's *caméra-stylo* and "filmic writing" comes to greatest fruition. Paired with an extreme long establishing shot, Labisse's imperious drawl introduces the space, "The Film Academy Library," conveying gravitas, solemnity, "authority," and masculinity, repeating and emphasizing each word. Whereas in the novel, Labisse simply suggests, "You might have more luck [finding books on early cinema] at the Film Academy library," in Scorsese's adaptation, Labisse provides a voice-of-God sound-bridge: "You'll find all you need to know about movies there."[37] The inflated, totalizing claim of completeness is striking, even for an auteur as self-aggrandizing as Scorsese. As Janet Staiger argues, "Claims for universality are disguises for achieving uniformity, for suppressing through the power of canonic discourse optional value systems. . . . It is a politics of power."[38] The Film Library sequence demonstrates Scorsese's auteurist politics of power, written with a metacinematic *caméra-stylo*.

Scorsese's library conveys a frustratingly misleading "illusion of consensus."[39] Labisse's voice-over guides Hugo and Isabelle through the library, intoning, as if from memory, "second level, fourth row, section three, and, yes, top shelf." Unlike the novel's parallel scene, in which a friend "helped Hugo navigate the card catalogue so he could find the book he needed," resources in Scorsese's library seem accessible only through inherited or oddly word-of-mouth information, rather than any organizational system.[40] Labisse's voice-over continues, intoning book title, author, and subtitle: "*The Invention of Dreams* by Rene Tabard, *The Story of the First Movies*." Authorship is central: inserted between title and subtitle. This single volume, offering "the story of the first movies," fulfills Labisse's problematic claim to contain "all you need to know" and fulfills Astruc's aspirational *caméra-stylo* with hyperliteral accuracy—this paper book integrates film quotation within its pages, demanding to be read as historiographic film *writing*.

Scorsese's metacinematic book of *filmic writing on film* springs from a real-life childhood film book. In "Introduction to Modern Library: The Movies," Scorsese explains, "When as a small boy I first fell in love with the movies, I discovered a book by Deems Taylor entitled *A Pictorial History of the Movies* at our local branch of the New York Public Library. It was the only film book that I knew about, and I borrowed it time and time again. . . . It was the first course in my film education."[41] While a "first course" of film study suggests that this book was only Scorsese's starting point, *Hugo* performs Scorsese's boyhood mistake by positioning this single volume as "the only film book" Hugo/*Hugo* knows. Even Deems Taylor acknowledges his limitations, introducing the book with "no pretense of being a critical survey, nor is it, except in the most summary sense, a history of the movies . . . the series is inevitably incomplete and far from detailed."[42] However, its cinematic corollary, *The Invention of Dreams*, makes no such disclosure, and conversely, claims to contain "all you need to know about the movies."

Scorsese's real-life *Pictorial History* also sutures film writing and authorial signature. Scorsese explains that *Pictorial History* spent years out of print, and he eventually found a copy previously owned by child actor Roddy McDowall, who

> would take it on the set and get the cast and crew to sign the stills of the movies on which they had worked. The *How Green Was My Valley* page, for instance, was eventually signed by John Ford, Maureen O'Hara, and Walter Pidgeon. This treasure book awoke in me the desire to collect as many film books as possible. There are one thousand or so books in my library, covering the past one hundred years of movie history, which I use constantly for information and inspiration.[43]

Scorsese describes in prose what Hugo's automaton draws on paper, a decade before *Hugo* was made. The Taylor volume becomes a "treasure book" by combining film image and signature. The signature's auratic power mimics the largely bygone autograph book collections of celebrity signatures (replaced by the "selfie" visual record of self and celebrity). For Scorsese, the autograph-film-book awakens a voracious "desire to collect as many film books as possible," a personal archive of stills and signatures, words and images—or, iterations of the automaton's prototype: visual sign and authorial inscription. For Scorsese, then, the greatest inspiration springs from the imbrication of film text and authorial trace.

As Hugo flips through the *Invention of Dreams*, film stills like those in *A Pictorial History* spring to life as full-screen film quotations, performing a deceptively inaccurate pedagogical historiography. The sequence begins with *The Arrival of a Train at La Ciotat Station* (1895, dir. Auguste and Louis Lumière). In a smoothly edited sequence, the paper-and-ink still becomes a quotation, and the camera pulls back to reveal the diegetic, 1895-audience's apocryphal "group flinch" as the train approaches the camera; as Duckett remarks, Scorsese "enact[s] a film historical myth."[44] Méliès's reminiscing flashback later dramatizes this cinema legend a second time, providing another pedagogy of repetition, teaching one of the most well-worn cinema legends. Next we see several film quotations, including W. K. L. Dickson's early sound test, a boxing match, *The May-Irwin Kiss* (1896, Edison, dir. William Heise), and the final, jarring head-on shot from *The Great Train Robbery* (1903, dir. Edwin S. Porter)—the latter two also appear in the first pages of *A Pictorial History*.[45] While these quotations appear and disappear quickly, pacing deliberately slows on a tinted extreme long shot from D. W. Griffith's $2 million *Intolerance* (1916) set. Scorsese further underscores the Griffith quotation by immediately inserting a reverse shot of the book's "spectators" Hugo and Isabelle who, delighted and engrossed, marvel "Wow!" in unison.

Griffith's privileged place in montage reflects similar adulation in Scorsese's written prose—and many other canon-forming critics. Writing in 2015, Scorsese credits Griffith and *Intolerance* with "cross-cut[s] through time, something that had never been done before. [Griffith] tied together images not for narrative purposes but to illustrate a thesis."[46] Scorsese's language echoes Astruc's, attributing literary (specifically, "thesis"-driven) enunciation into Griffith's filmmaking. Scorsese rehearses what Janet Staiger calls canonical "sloppy thinking," in which "Griffith's feature films and contemporary publicity (for which he was in part responsible) led some writers to the conclusion that he was first to achieve a number of technical innovations and, following that, that he was the only one and thus influenced the rest of the industry."[47] While Staiger roundly refutes such claims, Scorsese's "sloppy thinking," perpetuated more than twenty-six years after Staiger's writing, upholds an exclusionary, inaccurate, prejudicial canon. Falsely positioning Griffith as a father of "thesis"-driven filmic writing fits Scorsese's myopic obsession with white masculine authorship. Alice Guy-Blaché's magical gags, Lois Weber's splitscreen cinematography, achieving simultaneity across disparate locations in *Suspense* (1913, three years before *Intolerance*), or Oscar Micheaux's racially revisionist cross-cutting in *Within Our Gates* (1920) has no place in Scorsese's historiography. I risk belaboring this point because *Hugo* continues to be used *as a pedagogical tool*, co-opting/amplifying Scorsese's metacinematic pedagogy for students in high school and college film studies classrooms. Only by interrogating the *caméra-stylo*'s uses, and the prejudices perpetuated therein, can *Hugo* render truly thoughtful students of film history and the film canons being upheld.

Hugo and Isabelle continue "reading" the quotation-filled, metacinematic text, and the sequence accelerates into a montage of flipping pages and dizzying silent cinema survey quotations. A page turn prompts a full-screen film quotation of *The General* (1926, dir. Buster Keaton). Another page turn, and Louise Brooks springs to life. Intercut with quotation and book pages, Hugo's upturned, awed face appears, illuminated in flickering projector light (Isabelle temporarily forgotten). Montage integrates the reading and viewing experience into a hybrid reader-spectator for the metacinematic film. The montage crescendos to its culmination, the printed film-still of the "man in the moon." Emphasized with jarring stillness, Méliès's still is the pinnacle among preceding legends, conferring unequivocal auteurist pedigree. Crucially, Selznick's novel does not integrate film quotation into book format. The many stills from Méliès and others appear on discrete, full pages, held apart from the novel's drawn diegesis. Scorsese's adaptive addition demonstrates the *caméra-stylo*'s capacity to meld literary form and film quotation into metacinematic historiography.

Accepting *The Invention of Dreams* as "all you need to know about the movies" teaches a deceptively limited film history. As Isabelle reads aloud, "The filmmaker Georges Méliès was one of the first to realize that films had the power to capture dreams." However, "If the film became the main manipulator of the American dream," Ralph Ellison writes, "for Negroes that dream contained a strong dose of such stuff as nightmares are made of."[48] Ellison reminds us that Scorsese's (and Méliès's) dream of film history depends profoundly upon the dreamer's identity and unconscious. The metacinematic book's claims totalizing completeness (containing "all you need to know") and access (the author appears after this montage, welcoming Hugo and Isabelle to his Méliès archive) and imagines a history that forgets the problems of historiography, archive, and inclusion to which Ellison alludes. Scorsese conveniently flips past the decades of exclusion, excision, and caricature perpetuated against the raced, gendered, classed, and abled Other, of silent cinema's frequent forays into blackface, minstrelsy, and whitewashing, and of the film medium's technological prejudices—especially white-balancing for Caucasian skin tones. As Richard Dyer notes, "All technologies are at once technical in the most limited sense (to do with their material properties and functioning) and also always social (economic, cultural, ideological)," and photographic media were "developed with white people in mind and habitual use and instruction continue in the same vein, so much so that photographing non-white people is typically construed as a problem."[49] Scorsese avoids this "problem" by including only white actors and quoting only white, male filmmakers. Scorsese's metacinematic, videographic claims clash with recent works like the Women Film Pioneers Project, a collaborative digital archive that "features silent-era producers, directors, co-directors, scenario writers, scenario editors, camera operators, title writers, editors, costume designers, exhibitors, and more to make the point that they [women film pioneers] were not just actresses."[50] This evolving, multiauthored work emphasizes female film pioneers' multiplicity and multifaceted work and proves, for me, that the most accurate volume of film-quotational writing is that which dramatizes the impossibility of compiling "all you need to know about movies" in any single volume—or film.

Scorsese's metacinematic book provides intellectual, visual, and physical access to the film archive. As if summoned by the visual "reading" experience, the author appears. Fittingly, Tabard is revealed as the author by the inside-back-cover author photograph. As a white man, he looks the part. When Hugo and Isabelle insist that Mélies is alive and well, contrary to the book's claims, Tabard invites them to his private archive. The archive doors open as if by magic, creaking but untouched. Tabard's archive, which has no corollary scene in the novel, models Scorsese's own archival interests, and Tabard ventriloquizes Scorsese's pedagogical tone throughout, showcasing Mélies's cameras, handbills, and photographs. At one point, Tabard exclaims, "This is one of his *actual* cameras!" Scorsese's videographic explication of Mélies and his works showcases Mélies's *caméra-stylo* implements. Further, Tabard as film scholar emphasizes *Hugo*'s videographic investment in research, pedagogy, and enunciative authority.[51]

Finally, *A Trip to the Moon* appears in moving image quotations during an at-home screening, bookended between two flashback sequences—first through Tabard's memory and then through Mélies's—providing pedagogical contextualization and production history for the *A Trip to the Moon* quotation. Tabard's reminiscence introduces Mélies's glass studio, elaborate set-work, and layered frames, which explicate and enrich the *A Trip to the Moon* quotations about to unfold. Mélies's flashback details his "substitution trick" strategies, his background in magic, and his development of mechanical and cinematographic special effects. As Kyle Meikle points out, the substitution trick, followed by Mélies cutting and splicing frames around the trick, is "redundant—Mélies' trick is complete when he asks the actors to step out of the frame and then resumes filming—but it is intentionally redundant. Scorsese seeks to show us how film, in its earliest incarnations (and for much of the twentieth century) was film, was material, was tactile."[52] This intentional redundancy fits Scorsese's pedagogical aims throughout, as these flashbacks function like metacinematic, instructional "lessons." Then the videographic, pedagogical tone gives way to an oddly gendered screening space. Tabard convincing Mama Jeanne to screen A Trip to the Moon diverges markedly from the novel. In the source text, curiosity prompts Mama Jeanne to permit the screening, as "her eyes shimmered momentarily with curiosity. At least that's what Hugo thought he saw . . . then she shook her head and said, 'Be quick with it.' "[53] In Scorsese's version, Tabard makes two significant gendered appeals. The first, as in the novel, articulates Hugo's auteurist reverence, as Tabard acknowledges "the profound debt of gratitude I owe your husband . . . your husband is a very great artist." When this auteurist appeal does not sway Mama Jeanne, Tabard continues, "I do hope you'll forgive me for saying, you are as lovely now as you were in the movies." Mama Jeanne warmly demurs, smiling more widely than ever before and saying, "It was a long time ago, children. It was another time. And I was another person." Tabard replies, "Would you like to meet her again?" and then, emphatically, "We have a film." In short, Tabard alienates Mama Jeanne's past and present selves and articulates the paradigm that still warps much film representation: men command the artist's gaze, women are gazed upon.

This moment upholds Laura Mulvey's diagnosis of "the patriarchal order in which we are caught" and which classical Hollywood film perpetuates, in which the male gaze looks upon the white female subject.[54] Mulvey explains a gendered split between spectacle and narrative, saying, "The man controls the film phantasy and also emerges as the representative of power in a further sense: as the bearer of the look of the spectator, transferring it behind the screen to neutralize the extra-diegetic tendencies represented by woman as spectacle."[55] Tabard appeals to Mama Jeanne as spectacle, persuading her by invoking her power as an image—rather than her husband's authorial status. Though Mama Jeanne contributes a few pedagogical asides, including brief explanation of frame-by-frame tinting and the star system ("We weren't movie stars like they have today"), the screening emphasizes her scopophilic allure. Twice, the screening demonstrates "extra-diegetic tendencies" of "woman as spectacle" by interrupting Méliès's action for two (fabricated) close-ups of Mama Jeanne as a female constellation presiding over the sleeping lunar explorers.[56] The inserted close-ups demonstrate Mulvey's claim that "the presence of woman . . . tends to work against the development of a story line, to freeze the flow of action in moments of erotic contemplation."[57]

The close-ups also highlight Scorsese's addition to Méliès's mise en scene, re-vealing a fused authorship. When Méliès appears in the living room at the end of the screening (much like Tabard, the author magically appearing just after "reading" his text), Méliès answers Isabelle's breathless admiration of Mama Jeanne ("You were beautiful"), saying, "She still is." The auteur treats his star as "spectacle," even in life, enacting the patriarchal, classical cinema gendering that Mulvey describes in prose. No such exchange appears in the novel.

The diegetic *A Trip to the Moon* screening, featuring the newly restored 2011 print, fuses silent and post-classical film aesthetics.[58] The cutaways to Mama Jeanne are only two of Scorsese's many manipulations of the *A Trip to the Moon* quotation. Perhaps ironic for the archivist-auteur, in the restored *Trip* quotation, Martin Bonnard argues, "Martin Scorsese doesn't follow the rules of film preservation, freely altering the archival material in *Hugo*."[59] Scorsese both expands and collapses *Trip*, beginning the quotation with the rocket being loaded into the canon—excising more than five minutes from the film opening, cutting thirty seconds from liftoff—and then expands the synecdochical man-in-the-moon moment by intercutting Hugo's awestruck reaction without losing any screen time from the original. In all, Scorsese condenses an eleven-and-a-half-minute short film into roughly sixty-three seconds of on-screen quotation. In other words, Scorsese performs a metacinematic "translation" of silent cinema for easier "reading" by contem-porary audiences. Scorsese's "translation" follows David Bordwell's claim that visual storytelling "hasn't fundamentally altered since the studio days" and that "new style amounts to an *intensification* of established techniques."[60] This intensification includes "interrelated tactics," including "more rapid editing" and "closer framings," which Scorsese uses liberally on the *Trip* quotation.[61] Bordwell remarks that "the triumph of intensified continuity reminds us that as styles change so do viewing skills."[62] Or as Astruc might say, as (*caméra-stylo* penmanship?) enunciative styles change, so do "reading skills." Scorsese "intensifies" Méliès for contemporary "readers" through selective quota-tion, choosing the flashiest, most fast-paced moments of *A Trip to the Moon*, leaving no room for the exploratory or subjective-input of essayistic film. Rather, Scorsese quotes deliberately and strategically, crafting a moving image argument as forcefully written as any auteurist diatribe in prose.

Scorsese concludes his metacinematic auteur-theory argument by con-ferring the "authority" and canonicity of the "auteur" label: dramatizing the 1929 gala in Méliès's honor. Tabard provides a sound bridge from the male-adoption scene to the gala, saying, "I am proud to welcome you to this gala," addressing a diegetic and extradiegetic "you," over an iris-in on the man-in-the-moon's single eye. The moon-eye image hangs on the stage curtain, dwarfing Tabard and Méliès in enormous reproduction, like a visual proof of auteurist genius. By now, Scorsese's quoting *caméra-stylo* has so exhaustively cataloged the image across description, sketch, and moving image that the man in the moon communicates the authorial signature that previously accompanied it in the automaton scene. Like Peter Wollen's description of the auteur critic's metaphoric task, Scorsese's metacinematic writing "deciphers" authorial signature, modeling the discovery of "a hard core of basic and often recondite motifs."[63] Scorsese's *caméra-stylo* assembles and then strategically, progressively reveals Méliès' auteurism, modelling the auteur-critic's experience of "decipherment" that culminates in this final scene, conferring Méliès's authorial status.

During Méliès's address to the crowd, an extreme long shot catalogs the applauding auditorium and Méliès dwarfed by the enormous man in the moon—evoking the "KANE" and Charles Foster Kane image that dwarf Orson Welles during *Citizen Kane*'s (1941) political rally scene. Further, *Citizen Kane*'s rally marks the heights of Kane's political powers in his quest, as Jedediah Leland (Joseph Cotton) says, to win "love on [his] own terms." Similarly, this auteurist conclusion, whether self-consciously or not, marks Méliès's bid to be loved on his own terms, to appeal to a crowd for recognition, for privilege, for status as auteur. This auteurist echo, stages Méliès in a lineage, not unlike the lineage suggested in the Film Academy Library scene (which included other actor-auteurs Buster Keaton and Charlie Chaplin). Tabard mentions, almost casually, that Méliès is "the newest member of the Film Academy faculty" (an increasingly harrowing gauntlet in contemporary academia, especially for the historically under/un-represented), conferring legitimacy and authority.

A subtle dolly-zoom during Méliès's gala speech shows Méliès grow in relative size while the moon seems to rise up behind him. This visually pairs the ascendance of author and authored image. Backed by his "proof of authorship," Méliès thanks the "auteur critic" for discovering him. As always, authorial masculinity and paternity remain central, as Méliès begins, "I am standing before you tonight because of one very brave young man, who saw a broken machine and against all odds, he fixed it. It was the kindest magic trick that ever I've seen." Shot-reverse shot between Méliès and Hugo solidifies paternalistic fondness, and the mention of magic and machines links adoptive father and son in vocational union. Yet is the "kindest magic trick" auteur-theory enunciation? Writing that transforms a *metteur-en-scène* into an auteur? Historiography that honors one's artistic contribution? Or simply Hugo's help for Méliès to rejoin the film industry? As Joshua Clover pithily points out, "If romances once ended with everybody in the right marriage, now they end with everybody in the right job. Let's call them Comedies of Reemployment."[64] Yet Scorsese secures his own employment here, too. By insistently pairing homage and paternity, tribute and inheritance, Scorsese's metacinematic, quotational writing simultaneously honors a fore*father* auteur while simultaneously co-opting authorial status for *himself* as auteur-critic and historian-preservationist.

During the gala, Scorsese underwrites auteur adoration with a plug for film preservation—which supports his own film scholar-maker status. In Tabard's opening remarks, he triumphantly announces the recovery of "old negatives, boxes of prints, and trunks full of decaying film, which we were able to save. We now have over eighty films by Georges Méliès." These efforts match Scorsese's Film Foundation (TFF), "dedicated to protecting and preserving motion picture history," which he founded in 1990.[65] In extratextual resonance, TFF supported the preservation of two Méliès films housed at the George Eastman Museum: *La danse du feu* (1899) and *Les fromages automobiles* (1907). DeBona argues that *Hugo*'s topic and focus "could not be more coincidental to a director who has made his own life with the movies such a public part of his persona—*A Personal Journey*—as he calls it in his documentary on American cinema. The very social construction of 'Martin Scorsese' as film director/scholar/historian would help grant an aura of authorship to Hugo."[66] The *caméra-stylo* (supporting a "comedy of reemployment") writes on behalf both of Méliès's and Scorsese's own auteur- status, at once championing Méliès's filmmaking and Scorsese's auteurist "magic tricks" and preservation efforts.

Scorsese showcases the fruits of preservationists' labor during the gala's climactic screening in a montage of Méliès's "greatest hits." It culminates, predictably, with the man-in-the-moon image—this time, hand-tinted and rendered in 3D. This high-production "fan-vid" mimics internet-hosted mash-up, compilation, and supercut aesthetics; its quick cuts, widely sourced clips, and overlaid unifying musical track, all in service of a central argument, integrate the videographic form within mainstream filmmaking—the digital *caméra-stylo* on the big, 3D screen. As Scott Higgins summarizes,

> Méliès' moon floats out of the screen-plane, well into the area of negative parallax, but it is ostensibly on a screen located at the far end of a deep shot over the heads of the fictional audience. The result is an impossible dimensional space in which recession and emergence seem to coexist. A fleeting avant-garde exercise, Scorsese's image challenges distinctions; the moon appears in a space outside of diegesis, directly addressing the viewer, while it is resolutely anchored to and placed within the film's world[67]

Méliès's 3D moon visually epitomizes Méliès's and Scorsese's fused autho-rial inscription. Yet the negative parallax, between the screen and the viewers, visually separates the synecdochical image into "a space outside of diegesis, directly addressing the viewer, while it is resolutely anchored" to the die-gesis. Higgins's 3D description here suggestively doubles as a description of metacinematic enunciation. Like Méliès's moon, floating somewhere between diegetic and nondiegetic space, *Hugo*'s metacinematic enunciation, too, sig-nifies diegetically and extradiegetically. Scorsese's metacinematic demon-stration of *caméra-stylo* capabilities places *Hugo* in the negative parallax, somewhere between narrative fiction and videographic criticism, writing with the historiographic eloquence of scholarly prose. In this way, Scorsese is correct to write in the *New York Review of Books* "that verbal literacy is necessary," and that "we have to treat every last moving image as reverently and respectfully as the oldest book in the Library of Congress."[68] However, Scorsese's metacinematic writing is more respectful and reverent of some films than others—which plays out consistently across raced and gendered lines. Yet, ultimately, Scorsese is correct on both counts. We need more inclu-sive film preservation *and* film historiography—in prose and on screen—and we need to continue to teach the "visual literacy" needed to parse the prejudi-cial, exclusionary, and myopic writing of the quotational *caméra-stylo*.

Notes

1. John T. Caldwell, "Authorship below-the-Line," in *A Companion to Media Authorship*, ed. Jonathan Gray and Derek Johnson (Oxford: Wiley-Blackwell, 2013), 351–52.
2. Alexandre Astruc, "The Birth of a New Avant-Garde: *La Caméra-Stylo*," in *Film Manifestos and Global Cinema Cultures: A Critical Anthology*, ed. Scott MacKenzie (Berkeley: University of California Press, 2014), 604.
3. Astruc, "Birth of New Avant-Garde," 854.
4. Jennifer Clement and Christian B. Long, "*Hugo*, Remediation, and the Cinema of Attractions, or, The Adaptation of Hugo Cabret," *Senses of Cinema* 63 (2012), http://sensesofcinema. com/2012/feature-articles/hugo-remediation-and-the-cinema-of-attractions-or-the-adaptation-of-hugo-cabret/.
5. Catherine Russell, *Archiveology: Walter Benjamin and Archival Film Practices* (Durham, NC: Duke University Press, 2018), 12.
6. For an impressive list of the silent film titles and directors quoted in *Hugo*, see Victoria Duckett, "Unwinding the Film Spool: *Hugo*, Méliès, and Our Return to Early Film," *Studies in Documentary Film* 8, no. 1 (2014): 35.
7. Russell, *Archiveology*, 22.
8. Timothy Corrigan, *The Essay Film: From Montaigne, after Marker* (New York: Oxford University Press, 2011), 6.

9. Drew Morton, "'Look. I Know You're Not Following What I'm Saying Anyway.': The Problem of the 'Video Essay' and Scorsese as Cinematic Essayist," *[in]Transition* 1, no. 4 (2014), http://mediacommons.org/intransition/2014/12/12/look-i-know-youre-not-following-what-im-saying-anyway-problem-video-essay-and-scorsese-ci.

10. As when Henry Hill "contemplate[s] his existence in prison...Henry Hill is 'thinking through a public experience'" (Morton, "Look," n.p.).

11. Christian Keathley, "La Camera-Stylo: Notes on Video Criticism and Cinephilia," in *The Language and Style of Film Criticism*, ed. Alex Clayton and Andrew Klevan (New York: Routledge, 2011), 179.

12. Laura Mulvey, *Death 24× a Second: Stillness and the Moving Image* (London: Reaktion Books, 2006), 114.

13. Mulvey, *Death 24×*, 151.

14. For a detailed, feminist analysis of the "man-in-the-moon" image, especially in relation to comedy, satire, and incoherence, see Victoria Duckett, "The Stars Might Be Smiling: A Feminist Forage into a Famous Film," in *Fantastic Voyages of the Cinematic Imagination: Georges Méliès' "Trip to the Moon,"* ed. Matthew Solomon (Albany: State University of New York Press, 2011), 161–81.

15. Sandra Annett, "The Nostalgic Remediation of Cinema in *Hugo* and *Paprika*," *Journal of Adaptation in Film & Performance* 7, no. 2 (2014): 172.

16. Guerric DeBona, "*Hugo* and the (Re-)invention of Martin Scorsese," in *A Companion to Martin Scorsese*, ed. Aaron Baker (Oxford: Wiley-Blackwell, 2015), 478.

17. Duckett, "Unwinding the Film Spool," 37.

18. Janet Staiger, "The Politics of Film Canons," *Cinema Journal* 24, no. 3 (1985): 4.

19. Staiger, "Politics of Film Canons," 18.

20. Astruc, "Birth of New Avant-Garde," 854.

21. Scorsese progressively, repetitively reveals Méliès's works (and attendant early film technologies) like the progressive still images in Hugo's flipbook, such that, when viewed, they in sequence create motion.

22. Patricia White, *Uninvited: Classical Hollywood Cinema and Lesbian Representability* (Bloomington: Indiana University Press, 1999), 197.

23. Duckett, "Stars Might Be Smiling," 166.

24. Brian Selznick, *The Invention of Hugo Cabret* (New York: Scholastic Press, 2007), 173.

25. Selznick, *Invention of Hugo Cabret*, 177.

26. Astruc, "Birth of New Avant-Garde," 854–55.

27. Selznick, *Invention of Hugo Cabret*, 191–93.

28. Georges Méliès, "Cinematographic Views," trans. Stuart Liebman, *October* 29 (1984): 26.

29. Astruc, "Birth of New Avant-Garde," 854–55.

30. The only brief (seemingly belated, half-hearted) respite from white men controlling diegetic pens, authorship, and enunciation comes in the final voice-over. Unlike Selznick's novel, which ends by revealing Hugo as the book's author, in the film, Isabelle writes a book about Hugo, "this singular young man." Isabelle's language perpetuates the auteur-criticism cycle, as though Scorsese will happily include female authorship *if* that authorship is lauding another example of "singular" white masculinity.

31. This line also aligns the automaton with *Hugo*'s larger narrative structure, foreshadowing Hugo's familial abandonment and Méliès's abandonment by audiences and film history. In both cases, male interaction, kinship, and adoption facilitate the happy ending.

32. We glimpse the grim world that awaits Hugo outside adoptive paternity when the station inspector cages young boys and packs them into the paddy wagon. This depiction of caged, rebellious youth invokes Astruc's contemporary and champion of the *politique des auteur*: François Truffaut and his debut film, *The 400 Blows* (1959). Like Hugo, Truffaut's life and films dramatized paternal adoption. In life, Truffaut repeatedly sought an adoptive father, most famously in André Bazin, to whose memory *The 400 Blows* is dedicated. *400 Blows* is an evocative intertext for *Hugo*, both in its depiction of rebellious youth as metaphor for young filmmakers overthrowing the "Cinema du Papa," or the father's cinema, and in its evocation of Truffaut as perhaps the most infamous critic-turned-filmmaker, a writer expressing himself across media, from pen to *caméra-stylo*.

33. Later, a fight among J. R.'s friends leads to a creative re-editing of film stills from *Rio Bravo* (1959, dir. Howard Hawks), using close-ups, jump cuts, and added sound effects to "animate" the image and create the illusion of movement.

34. J. R. quotes Ethan (John Wayne) and Scar's (Henry Brandon) dialogue mocking one another's language skills, Ethan snarling, "You speak good American—for a Comanche. Someone teach you?" and Scar replying, "You speak good Comanche. Someone teach *you*?" This at least obliquely touches on *The Searchers*' ambivalent racial politics. This auteurist obsession with *The Searchers* re-emerges six years later, when Scorsese includes film quotation of *The Searchers* in *Mean Streets* (1973).

35. This intervention is uniquely Scorsese's: the corresponding scene in Selznick's novel features many of the same sketches but forgoes both the *A Trip to the Moon* image and the thaumatrope-like effect (Selznick, *Invention of Hugo Cabret*, 284–87).

36. Selznick, *Invention of Hugo Cabret*, 282.

37. Selznick, *Invention of Hugo Cabret*, 319.

38. Staiger, "Politics of Film Canons," 10.

39. Staiger, "Politics of Film Canons," 10.

40. Selznick, *Invention of Hugo Cabret*, 346.

41. Martin Scorsese, "Introduction to Modern Library: The Movies," in *The Art of the Moving Picture*, by Vachel Lindsay (New York: Modern Library, 2000), v.

42. Deems Taylor, *A Pictorial History of the Movies* (New York: Simon and Schuster, 1943), x.

43. Scorsese, introduction, v–vi.

44. Duckett, "Unwinding the Film Spool," 37.

45. "The May-Irwin Kiss" appears on page 4 of Deems Taylor's *Pictorial History*, and *The Great Train Robbery* appears on page 7.

46. Martin Scorsese, "The Persisting Vision: Reading the Language of Cinema," *New York Review of Books*, August 15, 2013.

47. Staiger, "Politics of Film Canons," 9.

48. Ralph Ellison, *Shadow and Act* (New York: Random House, 1964), 276. Ellison's rhetoric here resonates with both Sam Spade's famous line at the end of *The Maltese Falcon* (1941, dir. John Huston), describing the eponymous MacGuffin as "the stuff that dreams are made of," and a much older (and more classic, reified) source, spoken by Prospero in William Shakespeare's *The Tempest*.

49. Richard Dyer, *White* (New York: Routledge, 1997), 83, 89.

50. Jane Gaines, Radha Vatsal, and Monica Dall'Asta, eds., *Women Film Pioneers Project*, Center for Digital Research and Scholarship (New York: Columbia University Libraries, 2013).

51. Selznick's novel too credits help from film scholars, including Dr. Melinda Barlow, Dr. Claudia Gorbman, and Dr. Tom Gunning, "for advising me on movies to see and what films Hugo and Isabelle would have enjoyed, as well as helping me understand the world of Georges Méliès and his incredible vision." Selznick, *Invention of Hugo Cabret*, 529–30.

52. Kyle Meikle, "Rematerializing Adaptation Theory," *Literature/Film Quarterly* 41, no. 3 (2013): 180.

53. Selznick, *Invention of Hugo Cabret*, 391.

54. Laura Mulvey, "Visual Pleasure and Narrative Cinema," in *Feminism and Film Theory*, ed. Constance Penley (New York: Routledge, 1988), 58.

55. Mulvey, "Visual Pleasure," 63.

56. Duckett points out how these close-ups also register 2011-beauty-standard sensibilities, as "actresses recreate Méliès's scenes but no longer sport visible underarm hair." For more, see Duckett, "Unwinding the Film Spool," 35.

57. Mulvey, "Visual Pleasure," 62.

58. For more on the technological and production backstory on the 2011 restoration, undertaken by the Technicolor Foundation for Cinema Heritage, Groupama Gan Foundation for Cinema, and Lobster films, see Martin Bonnard, "Méliès's *Voyage* Restoration: or, The Risk of Being Stuck in the Digital Reconstruction," *Moving Image* 16, no. 1 (2016): 139–47.

59. Bonnard, "Méliès's *Voyage* Restoration," 143.

60. David Bordwell, "Intensified Continuity: Visual Style in Contemporary American Film," *Film Quarterly* 55, no. 3 (2002): 16.

61. Bordwell, "Intensified Continuity," 21.

62. Bordwell, "Intensified Continuity," 25.

63. Peter Wollen, *Signs and Meaning in the Cinema* (Bloomington: Indiana University Press, 1969), 80.

64. Joshua Clover, "Marx and Coca Cola: Enjoy the Silents," *Film Quarterly* 65, no. 4 (2012): 7.

65. "Mission Statement," Film Foundation, http://www.film-foundation.org/mission-statement.

66. DeBona, "(Re-)invention of Martin Scorsese," 460.

67. Scott Higgins, "3D in Depth: *Coraline, Hugo*, and a Sustainable Aesthetic," *Film History* 24 (2012): 207.

68. Scorsese, "Persisting Vision."

PART II

ILLUMINATION FROM THE DUPLICATIONS AND REPETITIONS OF REFLEXIVE CINEMA

6

8½

Self-Reflexive Fiction and Mental Training

Joshua Landy

Why do films sometimes break the fourth wall, reminding us that what we're seeing is a fiction?[1] Why do they sometimes feature characters who tell us they don't exist, speak directly to the camera, or make a movie suspiciously similar to the one we've been watching? My suggestion here will be that at least some such films—films like Federico Fellini's 8½ (1963)—have a very specific intention: to help us flex a major mental muscle. By periodically interrupting the action to remind us of its unreality, they deliberately give us practice in stepping back from our own attitudes, creating and maintaining a divided mental state, doubting what we believe, believing what we doubt. In what follows I'll try to show, drawing on results from empirical psychology, that divided mental states of that kind are not just possible but desirable; I'll also try to show that it makes sense to think of Fellini-style metacinema as strengthening our capacity to create and maintain them. As long as it includes thematic pointers prompting the right kind of uptake, a self-reflexive fiction like 8½ can help us cultivate enduring habits of mind, allowing us to sustain life-saving illusions even when we know them to be false.

Aesthetic Redemption

Let's start by briefly recalling what happens in 8½. Fellini's protagonist, Guido Anselmi, is a middle-aged filmmaker suffering from writer's block, spiritual emptiness, and crippling self-doubt. Critics call him a has-been and a failure; he himself worries he will never create anything again; his female friends accuse him (not without reason, it should be admitted) of being incapable of love; his life feels devoid of anything that would justify it, lift it up above the merely physical, endow it with some kind of higher significance. What is more, the sequence of events he has experienced fails to hang together, to

Joshua Landy, 8½ In: *Metacinema*. Edited by: David LaRocca, Oxford University Press. © Oxford University Press 2021. DOI: 10.1093/oso/9780190095345.003.0007 produce anything remotely resembling a story: his memories, as presented in the early scenes, constitute what his French collaborator Daumier rightly calls a "series of completely gratuitous episodes," and his present-day experiences are little better. (These two problems may well be related, since—if Jean-Paul Sartre is right—having a "fundamental project" gives every single event a coherent meaning, whether as a step toward the goal, a setback, or a regrettable diversion. Without a fundamental project, our experience shatters into a thousand senseless fragments.)

Over the course of two hours or so, the film presents us with a number of attempted remedies—remedies via the body (pointless spa treatments), remedies via the heart (fruitless encounters with women), remedies via the soul (unhelpful interviews with members of the church)—each of which comes to nothing. What finally changes everything for Guido is a simple realization: instead of shooting the absurd piece of science fiction he had initially planned, he should turn his own life into a movie. Miraculously, all the discordant elements within him now begin to harmonize. Saraghina, the symbol of physical love, trades places with Claudia, the symbol of spiritual love (Saraghina now appears in white, Claudia's trademark color; Claudia now appears on the beach, formerly the domain of Saraghina), as though the division between them no longer makes any sense.[2] And soon the other figures come to join them, as, hand in hand, father, mother, wife, lover, muse, friends, and everyone else of note begin to dance together in a huge circle, in front of the abandoned set.

"Why piece together the tatters of your life, the vague memories, the faces, all the people you never knew how to love?" asks Daumier, in what he takes to be an unanswerable rhetorical question. There is, however, an excellent response available. For the very piecing-together is what allows Guido for once to love all these people; not in the ordinary sense, to be sure, but in the special sense of appreciating them for the place they have in the totality that is his life, one which he now understands as having a certain aesthetic power to it. Is his life a constant frenetic motion turning in circles? Yes; but from a strictly aesthetic standpoint, that's not necessarily a bad thing. Has his life contained its share of disenchantment, on the way to this triumphant re-enchantment? Yes, but that only makes it a better story. The film closes on the figure of young Guido, the black-clad schoolboy whose life was such misery, now dressed in white and leading the band. Noise has given way to music, and music is about to give way to a new, perfect silence.

Thanks to the magic of art, then, suffering has been transfigured into aesthetic bliss; Guido's painful mess of a life turns out to have a beautiful shape to it; and each of its inhabitants turns out to have a necessary place within that shape, like tiles within a mosaic, or daubs of paint on a canvas. It is not that all conflicts can actually be resolved. It is just that all conflicts can be seen as vital contributors to a thing of beauty, and hence given a justification, and hence, in a special sense, redeemed.[3]

A Film about a Film

It should, I hope, already be apparent that *8½* calls attention to its own fictionality in the closing sequences, with Guido on the verge of making a movie suspiciously similar to the one we have been watching. But in fact Fellini has been dropping little hints throughout. Although Guido is officially working on some kind of science-fiction picture, in which survivors of a nuclear holocaust flee to another planet, what he has actually shared with Daumier is the screenplay for a film about his own life. And so when Guido reviews the screen tests of actors hoping to star in his movie, what we see are women playing his wife and mistress, men playing cardinals, and boys playing Guido. Not an alien or spaceman in sight.

This frequently puts us in a rather odd position, unable to decide whether a given event depicted on screen is supposed to belong to Guido's reality—what he is currently seeing, remembering, experiencing—or to his script. Did he really just have a vision of a woman in white, for example, or was he just inventing it for cinematic purposes? When we first see this mysterious figure, we take her to be a hallucination that Guido is actually seeing before him; a few short scenes later, however, we learn that she is merely (or also) a character in the screenplay. "And the capricious appearances of the girl," asks Daumier in his notes to Guido, "what are they supposed to mean? An offer of purity? A tender gesture to the hero? Of all the symbols that abound in your story, this one is the worst."[4]

And what about the scene involving Carla's high fever? Carla has drunk too much of the spa water, and Guido is not impressed. "What do you expect?" retorts Carla. "You leave me alone all the time." Again, this seems for all the world like something that is actually happening to Guido. But when we come to see the screen tests, we find various actresses pronouncing a virtually identical line: "You know it's dangerous to leave me alone [*è pericoloso lasciarmi sola*]." Given that the screen tests have been prerecorded, and that we are watching them a mere day after Carla's high fever, we are once again in a quandary: did we witness something "real"[5]—something actually present, right now within Guido's mind or world, like the spa and the sunglasses and Daumier—or something invented?

What, for that matter, of the truly bizarre conversation between Guido and Carla in which she asks him whether he could "choose one single thing, and . . . make it the one thing that gives your life meaning," and he replies "no, the character I'm thinking of couldn't [*no, questo tipo no, non è capace*]"? Has Guido himself shrunk—in his own mind, if that makes sense—to the status of a fictional character?

In all three of the instances I've mentioned, an event or character suddenly loses its status as something "real" in order to become something fictional. There are also, however, occasions on which things move in the other direction, with figments of imagination oddly making their way into reality. All Guido has to do, for example, is tell his sister-in-law that he's "putting everything in [his movie], even a sailor who does the soft-shoe" and hey presto, a soft-shoeing sailor suddenly appears out of nowhere. And even after Guido is told that it would be the height of absurdity to expect an audience with a cardinal in a spa, that impossible audience with a cardinal is exactly what we see on the screen before us.[6]

Over and over again, then, *8½* reminds us that it is a work of fiction. Over and over again, we are forced to oscillate between engagement and detachment. Just when we become absorbed in the story, we are reminded that it's only a film; just when we become used to treating it as unreal, along comes something emotionally laden, and we return to caring deeply about the characters. Everything we believe is subject to doubt—but everything we doubt can, conversely, become something to believe.

Lucid Illusions

What does this formal feature have to do with the themes of chaos, conflict, and redemption we started with? Many, I am sure, would be tempted to answer that question by invoking some kind of *message*, some kind of deep Truth about the World, the point of all formal features being (they assume) to *mean* something. This, however, would be a big mistake. It is true that any number of film theorists have taken this for granted (I'll come back to them later), and that any number of critics—including their fictional brethren in *8½*![7]— have followed suit, but truly astute fiction-makers have always understood that they have more important things to do than *say* things (which they do, in any case, far less efficiently than writers of nonfictions).[8] Instead, at their best, they *do* things; and what a self-reflexive fiction like *8½* does is to *give us practice in believing what we don't believe*.[9]

We saw a moment ago that *8½* forces us to shuttle continually from engagement to detachment. One moment we are worried about Carla's high fever;

the next moment Carla is just a character in a screenplay. One moment we are laughing at the pretentious device of a woman in white; the next moment we see her again, and have our breath taken away. Now in sending us on this relentless rollercoaster ride, 8½ gives us two hours' worth of practice at doubting what we believe, two hours' worth of practice at believing what we doubt—practice, in other words, in entertaining an illusion and knowing that it is not true.

Why is this so important? Because the kind of redemption Guido achieves— and the kind of redemption available to *us*, too—depends to some degree on illusion. Guido's mother and father are dead, yet here they are alongside the living; Guido's wife and mistress don't exactly get along, yet here they are dancing in a ring together. Living happily, as Nietzsche understood so well, requires a certain degree of self-deception. At the same time, only one kind of self-deception is dignified: the kind that knows itself for what it is. The good life, for Fellini, is not pure escapism (if it were, then the science-fiction movie would be just as good as the fictionalized story of a life). Rather, the good life is as much truth as one can stand, coupled with the illusion one cannot do without, *at the same time as an awareness that the illusion is illusion*.[10] And that is precisely where self-reflexivity begins to do its work.

Informational Encapsulation

There is, as far as I know, no concrete evidence (as yet) that what I have said so far is true. As most cognitive scientists will tell you, their own field is in its infancy; in fact, one of the most delightful features of talking to cognitive scientists is the number of times you will hear the most famous experts saying "I just don't know." (How often have you heard those four words from a literary theorist?) And if cognitive science is in its infancy, cognitive aesthetics is scarcely out of its swaddling clothes. We are sure, at this point, of almost nothing. Do the ideas I have proposed hold water? To borrow the language of cognitive science, I just don't know.

That said, I believe there are a number of findings that make my hypothesis at least plausible, the most important of which is what is sometimes referred to as "informational encapsulation."[11] Many scientists now think of the brain as being organized into a set of functionally specialized systems: a system for seeing, a system for hearing, a system for memory encoding, and so on. This does not mean that each system is confined to a single physical area within the brain; specialization is not the same as localization.[12] It also does not mean that the data are never combined—that the left hand is always in the dark about what the right hand is doing—let alone that there is no central controller.[13] What it does mean, however, is that the brain is capable of performing multiple tasks simultaneously.[14] (The brain, as some like to put it, is a *massive parallel processor*.)[15] And what it also means, most crucially for our purposes, is that the various systems do not have to be in agreement, or even in communication.[16]

Optical illusions are an excellent example of this. When a straight straw looks bent after it's placed in a glass of water, what's happening is that two separate systems are operating on the same sense data and delivering opposite verdicts. Perception is telling you the straw is obviously crooked; inference is telling you it is still as straight as it was five seconds ago. And neither side entirely carries the day. Perception doesn't entirely win, since you don't act as though the straw is bent (by, say, going and getting another straw); inference doesn't entirely win either, since you can't helping seeing the straw as bent, no matter how certain you are that it isn't. (Telling yourself that something is an optical illusion makes no difference to what you perceive. Try it!) At a higher level, it is possible to inspect the deliverances of the two systems—to say to yourself "goodness, I *see* the straw as bent but *infer* it to be straight"—but down in the trenches, the two systems are operating completely autonomously.[17]

What we know about informational encapsulation suggests three things that are relevant for our purposes: first, it is entirely possible to hold two conflicting attitudes toward a single state of affairs (the straw is bent, the straw is straight); second, it is entirely possible to become aware of having those two attitudes (using, presumably, a third subsystem); and such awareness, finally, need not affect our experience (even when we know that the straw is straight, we still continue to see it as crooked).

This ability to entertain competing attitudes simultaneously comes on line remarkably early in life. At the age of three or four, children hosting make-believe tea parties are easily able to keep track of the fact that Susie's cup already has tea in it, whereas Johnny's cup does not—even though, in reality, both cups are empty. (The children, in other words, are simultaneously holding in their mind the proposition "Susie's cup has tea in it" and the proposition "Susie's cup has no tea in it.")[18] It does not take long, either, for the demarcations to become even more sophisticated. In an ingenious experiment designed by Deena Skolnick and Paul Bloom, children aged four to six were just as good at adults in answering the question "Does Batman think that Spongebob is real?"[19] (Similarly, and equally surprisingly, Marjorie Taylor found that children with imaginary friends tended to be perfectly aware that the latter did not exist.)[20] Most significantly for our purposes, children playing make-believe are perfectly capable of renegotiating the rules mid-game ("now *you're* the crocodile"), a fact that surely suggests some kind of double consciousness on their part. All of this is not to say, of course, that children make no mistakes; they do better, however, than we often suspect.

Useful Fictions

The relative autonomy of mental systems—our capacity to compartmentalize, to "quarantine" beliefs from one another[21]—explains, then, how it is *possible* to maintain conflicting attitudes at the same time. In itself, however, that does not explain why it might be *desirable*. This is where the work of Shelley Taylor comes in. Taylor, a psychologist at UCLA, discovered that overly optimistic views of our qualities, circumstances, and prospects actually promote mental health.[22] It is of course possible to go too far—acting on the belief that one is impenetrable to bullets is probably not the best idea, for example, when entering battle—but within certain limits, we are just going to be *happier* if we get it a little bit wrong about how smart we are, how much people like us, and how bright our future is going to be. Researchers have also discovered a correlation between athletic success and propensity for self-deception.[23] Correlation is not causation, but is it not at least possible that William James was right in thinking that the only way to leap across an abyss is to fool ourselves into thinking that there is absolutely no chance of falling?[24]

Perhaps the strongest single piece of evidence, however, is the "mirror box," that wonderful invention designed to provide relief to amputees suffering from phantom pain. A patient who has lost an arm, for example, can place the other arm next to the mirror, giving herself the illusion of still having both; somehow, miraculously, the phantom pain dissipates. From which we can learn, again, two important things. First, illusions can be highly beneficial; second, and counterintuitively, they can *continue* to be beneficial even after we know them to be illusions. The parallel layering of mental activity not only makes genuine self-deception possible (whatever people like Sartre may have said) but also makes *conscious* self-deception possible. And the nature of human existence makes both kinds of self-deception *desirable*, at least under certain conditions.

Mental Rehearsal

Do self-reflexive fictions actually have anything to do with all this, however? As I acknowledged earlier, we don't yet know for sure. But what we do know is that, in a general sense, people get better at what they practice (thanks to the strengthening of neural pathways and more efficient organization of strategies); this can be true, what is more, even when the practice takes place in their imagination. Flight simulators are excellent training for handling real-life airplanes, and video games are sometimes made use of by the military: skills are often "transferable" from imaginary to actual contexts.[25] There is even an example that comes very close indeed to what I take Fellini to have in mind. That example is lucid dreaming.

As its name suggests, a lucid dream is one in which the dreamer knows she is asleep, an awareness that is sometimes accompanied by a degree of control over what she experiences. However strange it may sound to non-lucid dreamers, the phenomenon is a real one, as a growing body of research has corroborated. In one series of studies, for example, subjects agreed in advance to count, draw, or make a fist in their dream; later, with the subjects in REM sleep, researchers detected increased activity in the relevant brain areas and/or parts of the body.[26] Another study found differences in brain activity—in particular, an increase in beta-1 activity in the parietal areas—between lucid and non-lucid dreamers.[27] So here we have another situation, confirmed by experiment, in which (however counterintuitive it may appear) our senses are deceiving us, and we *know* they are deceiving us, yet we continue to let them do so.

Now the fascinating thing is that it is actually possible to *cultivate* this capacity. There are certain techniques we can use, in other words, to make it more likely that we will develop a degree of awareness and control over our dreams, including—most crucially for our purposes—the practice of asking ourselves repeatedly during the day whether we are awake or asleep.[28] What this means is that one can train oneself to enter one state of divided consciousness by deliberately entering another state of divided consciousness; being reminded that everything we are experiencing might be an illusion can carry over into other activities, presumably because different states of divided consciousness work more or less the same way. And this in turn means that engagement with self-reflexive fictions could well strengthen our ability to sustain all those illusions that are so favorable to our flourishing.

Content Primes for Form

It might still, of course, be objected that even if such strengthening is *feasible*, and even if it is *desirable*, I still haven't shown that it is *likely*. After all, isn't it the case that for any formal feature one can mention, there are a variety of effects it can generate, depending on the context?[29] A long, tender, ornate speech between lovers might be designed to produce tears, or it might be designed to produce laughter; free indirect discourse can be used to offer the vision of a world with weaker ego-boundaries (Woolf), but it can also be used to skewer characters more cruelly (Flaubert).[30] Why assume that Fellini's self-reflexivity will be put, so to speak, to good use?

It has to be admitted that there is no guarantee of the intended uptake. (That, of course, is the fate of every aesthetic object.) But again, artists can at least increase the chances of the desired result taking place. And they do so by means of *priming*. What any number of psychological researchers have discovered is that an initial stimulus makes us more sensitive to related stimuli; certain concepts, thoughts, and attitudes become more salient, more accessible, more likely to affect our judgment and action. If, for example, we are hungry (or have just been shown the word "food"), we will be more likely to read the letter sequence SO_P as "soup"; if, on the other hand, we are in need of a shower (or have just been shown the word "wash"), we will be more likely to see it as "soap."[31] That, I think, is precisely how content works in cases like Fellini's 8½. In itself, the formal device of self-reflexivity tells us nothing about it wants us to do with it. But when it is coupled with a plot involving the necessity of life-affirming illusions, everything changes. We have a hard time, I think, *not* connecting the two—not thinking that the happy ending and the repeated breaking of the fourth wall are intimately linked. The content of a literary work primes us, I am claiming, for a particular way of taking up its formal features.

We are left, then, with the following overall picture, consistent with many results from the world of cognitive science. The content of 8½ serves as priming, making thoughts of necessary illusions more accessible and salient to us; this in turn leads us to understand the form—the self-reflexivity—as an opportunity to hone our capacity for conscious self-deception; conscious self-deception is possible because of the modular structure of the mind, involving a number of mutually encapsulated systems; conscious self-deception is desirable because illusions are sometimes good for us; and fictions can be a venue for its training because we get better at what we practice, even when the practice is only in our head.

Eight-and-a-Half Reasons for Reflexivity

This still leaves room, of course, for self-reflexive fictions to have other plausible ambitions, primed by different kinds of content.[32] All that *Verfremdung* in Brecht or Spike Lee, for example, is almost certainly designed to make it easier for us to detach ourselves from our rash assumptions, easier to turn the bright light of critical thought onto what we had previously taken as "natural" and immutable.[33] All that metaleptic craziness in Unamuno's *Mist*, similarly, may be part of what the prologue-writer calls "Don Miguel [Unamuno]'s campaign against public gullibility" (assuming, of course, that this prologue-writer is to be trusted). And again along similar lines, Queneau's *Witch Grass* (*Le chiendent*) may perhaps aim to strengthen our capacity for putting everything in doubt—even what we currently take to be true—as a spur to ever deeper philosophizing. (That, more or less, is Friedrich Schlegel's theory of romantic irony.)[34] In each of these cases, reflexivity still has the function of fine-tuning our capacity to hold two attitudes at once; here, however, the ultimate goal is not to maintain our beneficial illusions but rather to loosen their grip of their malevolent cousins, to make sure *those* ones are never completely in control.

Or again, the divided state that self-reflexivity cultivates may provide a vital protective shield against crippling internal division: when one finds oneself holding two contradictory beliefs or feeling two contradictory feelings, and when it is simply not possible to jettison either of them, the only solution may be to step back from both, identifying oneself with the system that inspects them as though from without. (I take this to be Diderot's ambition in *Jacques le fataliste*.)[35] And then, finally, there are fictions (like Coetzee's *Diary of a Bad Year*, perhaps) whose self-reflexivity is a way of entitling themselves to a little heartfelt emotion, in a world saturated with cynicism; and others (like Gide's *The Counterfeiters*, perhaps) whose self-reflexivity simply serves a way to explore the resources of the medium.

Still, Fellini was not alone in wanting to put reflexivity in the service of conscious self-deception. Stéphane Mallarmé, Paul Valéry, Auguste Villiers de l'Isle-Adam, Marcel Proust, and Luigi Pirandello had preceded him; Milan Kundera and others would follow him.[36] There is, after all, no substitute for the maintenance of necessary illusions, and no substitute for self-reflexive fictions as a venue for their training.

Increasing the Weights

In a way, of course, *all* fictions put us in a divided state of mind. There is always a part of us lurking around to register that what we are reading or watching is not real: as Kendall Walton so memorably pointed out, horror movies cause our pulses to race and our hearts to pound . . . but not our legs to carry us out of the theater, or our fingers to dial our friends to warn them of the impending danger.[37] What is more, while we generally root for the protagonist, we also rather like the idea of him or her getting into trouble (no trouble, no plot!).[38] Finally, our empathetic suffering for Clarissa Dalloway finds itself strangely tempered by our enjoyment of the artistry with which her travails are crafted and rendered by Virginia Woolf. So we believe and do not believe, at once; we want and do not want, at once; we feel and do not feel, at once. This is a truly extraordinary triple fact about the experience of (interesting) fiction, one that lies at the heart of its peculiar power.[39]

What self-reflexive fictions do is to ratchet up, and make blatant, that generalized double-consciousness.[40] In the standard case, our sense of the work's fictionality is a background awareness, the kind of awareness we have, while driving, of the steady hum of the engine. With Fellini, by contrast, we are forced to place it at the center of our conscious attention, while also being invited to maintain somehow the referential illusion, to continue the make-believe game, to keep playing along. By gradually increasing the size of the cognitive weights we have to lift—by putting additional pressure on our simultaneous ability to have and to stand back from a given mental attitude, whether belief, desire, or feeling—reflexive fictions like Fellini's give an intensive workout to our capacity for simultaneous trust and distrust, readying us for the difficult business of life.[41]

Yes, that difficult business often involves knowing the truth; but at times it requires us to be ignorant, or even frankly mistaken. And when that happens, it is generally better for us to maintain an awareness of what is going on. And for that I think it helps if we have watched a little Fellini.

Notes

1. The present chapter offers a modification of an earlier work—"Mental Calisthenics and Self-Reflexive Fiction"—that appeared in The Oxford Companion to Literary Studies, ed. Lisa Zunshine (New York: Oxford University Press, 2015), 559–80. I am grateful to Stephen Kosslyn for a tremendous amount, not least the numerous hours he was so generously willing to devote to conversations about literature and cognitive science. A better interlocutor simply could not be imagined. Thanks, too, to Karen Zumhagen-Yekplé for inviting me to deliver some of this as a talk, and to Neil van Leeuwen for planting, all these years ago, the vital germ of the central idea.
2. Cf. to some extent Marilyn Fabe, Closely Watched Films: An Introduction to the Art of Narrative Film Technique (Berkeley: University of California Press, 2004), 164–65.
3. See R. Lanier Anderson, "Nietzsche on Redemption and Transfiguration," in The Re-Enchantment of the World: Secular Magic in a Rational Age, ed. Joshua Landy and Michael Saler (Stanford, CA: Stanford University Press, 2009), 225–58. I am not suggesting that Guido is exemplary in every way; he owes it to those around him to think of them as heroes of their own story, not just secondary characters in his.

4. Similarly, when we first see Saraghina, we take this to be a memory Guido is having, triggered by having seen a woman who resembles her. But in the very next scene, Daumier discusses this "memory" as though it were actually an episode in the screenplay Guido has given him to read. ("What does it mean?" he asks. "If you want to denounce Catholicism, you need less nostalgia and more logic!")

5. To be more precise, one should say "true within the fiction" (borrowing Kendall Walton's terminology); I'm just trying to keep my vocabulary as untechnical as possible.

6. Fellini also plays with editing and sound to illusion-undermining effect; see Fabe, *Closely Watched Films*, 166–71.

7. Toward the end of the movie, Guido finds himself surrounded by hostile critics. "You has-been," shouts one, "what do think you can teach?" "Do you have anything to say?" asks another. "He is lost. He has nothing to say!" laughs a third, in English. The more astute Daumier, by contrast, realizes that an author's intention can be (among other possibilities) "to make us think" or even "to make us afraid."

8. See Joshua Landy, *How to Do Things with Fictions* (New York: Oxford University Press, 2012), ch. 1.

9. I have made similar arguments with respect to Mallarmé in *How to Do Things with Fictions*, 69–92.

10. I am paraphrasing Nietzsche, who wrote both that "the falsest judgements are the most indispensable to us" (*Beyond Good and Evil*, trans. Walter Kaufmann [New York: Random House, 1966], sec. 4) and also "the real measure of value" is "how much truth . . . a spirit [can] endure" (*Ecce Homo*, trans. Walter Kaufmann [New York: Random House, 1969], Preface, sec. 3). In an important article, R. Lanier Anderson refers to the will to truth and the will to illusion as "mutually regulating ideals" in Nietzsche: see "Nietzsche on Truth, Illusion, and Redemption," *European Journal of Philosophy* 13, no. 2 (2005): 185–225. For a list of pro-illusion passages in Nietzsche (giving the lie, among other things, to Richard Rorty's claim that Nietzsche has a pragmatist theory of truth), see Joshua Landy, *Philosophy as Fiction: Self, Deception, and Knowledge in Proust* (New York: Oxford University Press, 2004), 209 n. 37.

11. The connection between self-deception and informational encapsulation was first suggested to me by Neil van Leeuwen. I subsequently read something like it in Danica Mijović-Prelec and Drazen Prelec, "Self-Deception as Self-Signalling: A Model and Experimental Evidence," *Philosophical Transactions of the Royal Society* 365 (2010): 227–40, and then in Robert Kurzban's *Why Everyone (Else) Is a Hypocrite: Evolution and the Modular Mind* (Princeton, NJ: Princeton University Press, 2012), where the idea is more developed but also accompanied by some rather shady arguments about agency. *Caveat emptor.*

12. On this point, see Kurzban, *Hypocrite*, 47; Paul Ehrlich, *Human Natures: Genes, Cultures, and the Human Prospect* (Washington, DC: Island Press, 2000), 119; Stephen Pinker, *How the Mind Works* (New York: Norton, 2009), 30. On functional specialization, see also Ellen Spolsky, "Making 'Quite Anew': Brain Modularity and Creativity," in *Introduction to Cognitive Cultural Studies*, ed. Lisa Zunshine (Baltimore: Johns Hopkins University Press, 2010), 86–89.

13. For the combination of inputs in a "global conscious workspace," see Stanislas Dehaene, *Reading in the Brain: The New Science of How We Read* (New York: Penguin, 2010), 318–23 and Ellen Spolsky, *Gaps in Nature: Literary Interpretation and the Modular Mind*

(Albany: SUNY Press, 1993), 20. For the confident claim that there is no central controller, see Kurzban, *Hypocrite*, 10, 22, 60–62. When faced with the question of how coordination happens, Kurzban helpfully tells us, "I don't know" (67).

14. Edward E. Smith and Stephen M. Kosslyn, *Cognitive Psychology: Mind and Brain* (New York: Prentice Hall, 2006), 42; Pinker, *How the Mind Works*, 26 and 77; Spolsky, *Gaps in Nature*, 32.

15. On parallel processing, see, e.g., Pinker, *How the Mind Works*, 26.

16. Theorists who have argued for at least some degree of informational encapsulation include Jerry Fodor, *The Modularity of Mind: An Essay on Faculty Psychology* (Cambridge, MA: MIT Press, 1983), e.g., 67–72; Donald Davidson, "Deception and Division," in *The Multiple Self*, ed. Jon Elster (Cambridge: Cambridge University Press, 1985), 79–92; and Marvin Minsky, *Society of Mind* (qtd. Spolsky, *Gaps in Nature*, 24).

17. A variety of additional phenomena, such as blindsight, hemispatial neglect, alien hand syndrome, and self-outwitting, all confirm the independent activity of systems. See Kurzban, *Hypocrite*, 9–18. This is not to say, of course, that "top-down" processes never influence "bottom-up" processes.

18. I am referring to a classic series of experiments by Alan Leslie. See, e.g., Alan M. Leslie, "Pretense and Representation: The Origins of 'Theory of Mind,'" *Psychological Review* 94, no. 4 (1987): 412–26. For discussion, see Shaun Nichols, "Imagining and Believing: The Promise of a Single Code," *JAAC* 62, no. 2 (2004): 129.

19. Deena Skolnick and Paul Bloom, "The Intuitive Cosmology of Fictional Worlds," in *The Architecture of the Imagination: New Essays on Pretence, Possibility, and Fiction*, ed. Shaun Nichols (New York: Oxford University Press, 2006), 73–86.

20. Taylor is very forthright: "Young children," she says, "do not think their imaginary companions are real." (Marjorie Taylor, *Imaginary Companions and the Children Who Create Them* [New York: Oxford University Press, 1999], 90.) She found that when children were interviewed at length about their imaginary companions, they would often end up warning the interviewer, "It's just pretend, you know"! (112)

　　There is of course a great deal of variation here, as Taylor herself admits. In general, children do better (a) the older they are; (b) the more control they have over the imagining; and (c) the less other people are actively trying to convince them that something is real (as in the case of Santa Claus). Most two-year-olds are already able to recognize certain acts as pretense (89); most three-year-olds will be shocked if, during a game involving Playdough "cookies," you actually put one in your mouth ("Yuk, do you always eat that Playdough?") (105); most four-year-olds are agile enough to handle rule changes in mid-game (104); most five-year-olds know that what they see on TV and read in fictional books is not real (96); and by the age of eight, most children know that cultural myths like Santa Claus and the tooth fairy are imaginary (96). Mistakes continue to be made periodically at all levels, but as Taylor points out, adults too are liable to be affected by their dreams (111), to care about fictional characters (113), to conflate an actor with his or her character (97), and to be unwilling to drink from a perfectly harmless bottle that happens to be marked "cyanide" (101). All in all, "children's mastery of fantasy is impressive" (116).

21. The term is Leslie's ("Pretense and Representation," 415).

22. See Shelley E. Taylor, *Positive Illusions: Creative Self-Deception and the Healthy Mind* (New York: Basic Books, 1989); Shelley E. Taylor et al., "Psychological Resources, Positive Illusions, and Health," *American Psychologist* 55 (2000): 99–109; Shelley E. Taylor and

Jonathon D. Brown, "Illusion and Well-Being: A Social-Psychological Perspective on Mental Health," *Psychological Bulletin* 103 (1988): 193–210. See also Kurzban, *Hypocrite*, 101–19.

23. Joanna E. Starek and Caroline F. Keating, "Self-Deception and Its Relationship to Success in Competition," *Basic and Applied Social Psychology* 12, no. 2 (1991): 145–55.

24. "It is only by risking our persons from one hour to another that we live at all. And often enough our faith beforehand in an uncertified result is the only thing that makes the result come true. Suppose, for instance, that you are climbing a mountain and have worked your-self into a position from which the only escape is by a terrible leap. Have faith that you can successfully make it, and your feet are nerved to its accomplishment. But mistrust yourself, and think of all the sweet things you have heard the scientists say of maybes, and you will hesitate so long that, at last, all unstrung and trembling, and launching yourself in a mo-ment of despair, you roll into the abyss. In such a case (and it belongs to an enormous class), the part of wisdom . . . is to believe what is in the line of your needs, for only by such belief is the need fulfilled." William James, "Is Life Worth Living?," in *The Will to Believe and Other Essays in Popular Philosophy* (New York: Dover, 1956 [1897]), 59.

25. More anecdotally, Jim Holt reported that memorizing a series of lyric poems improved his capacity to store information—not just poetry, but other things as well—in working memory. See Laura Miller, "Make Kids Learn Poetry," http://www.salon.com/2012/06/13/make_kids_memorize_poetry/.

26. Morton Schatzman et al., "Correspondence during Lucid Dreams between Dreamed and Actual Events," in *Conscious Mind, Sleeping Brain*, ed. Jayne Gackenbach and Stephen LaBerge (New York: Plenum Press, 1988), 155–79.

27. Brigitte Holzinger et al., "Psychophysiological Correlates of Lucid Dreaming," *Dreaming* 16, no. 2 (2006): 88–95.

28. This was Paul Tholey's discovery. See Stephen LaBerge, *Lucid Dreaming* (Boston: Houghton Mifflin, 1985), 21.

29. This is what Meir Sternberg calls the "Proteus principle." See "Universals of Narrative and Their Cognitivist Fortunes," *Poetics Today* 24, no. 3 (2003): 552.

30. Free indirect discourse, says the inimitable Blakey Vermeule, is "a technique whose main virtue seems to be to slice the character's head off more effectively." *Why Do We Care about Literary Characters?* (Baltimore: Johns Hopkins University Press, 2009), 44.

31. See Daniel Kahneman, *Thinking, Fast and Slow* (New York: Farrar, Straus and Giroux, 2011), 52.

32. For fuller discussion of the following theories, see Landy, *How to Do Things*, 90–92.

33. Before the action gets going in *The Exception and the Rule*, the chorus enjoins us: "Findet es befremdend, wenn auch nicht fremd . . . *damit nichts unveränderlich gelte*" ("find it alienating, albeit not alien . . . *so that nothing should appear immutable*"). *Die Ausnahme und die Regel*, in *Fünf Lehrstücke* (London: Methuen, 1969), 94; my translation and em-phasis. See also *Brecht on Theatre*, trans. John Willett (New York: Hill and Wang, 1964), 136–40. On Brechtian elements in Spike Lee, see Douglas Kellner, "Aesthetics, Ethics, and Politics in the Films of Spike Lee," in *Spike Lee's "Do the Right Thing*," ed. Mark A. Reid and Horton Andrew (New York: Cambridge University Press, 1997), 75–86. It is worth pointing out that this ambition—the ambition of training audience members to step back from their own beliefs—is very different from the ambition to *inform* them of some-thing. Quite a few theorists have, unfortunately, decided that it is entirely reasonable to

use the device of reflexivity to send some kind of message about the constructedness of (social) reality. See, e.g., Astradur Eysteinsson, *The Concept of Modernism* (Ithaca, NY: Cornell University Press, 1990), 115; Christian Quendler, *From Romantic Irony to Postmodernist Metafiction* (Frankfurt am Main: Peter Lang, 2001), 160; and Patricia Waugh, *Metafiction: The Theory and Practice of Self-Conscious Fiction* (London: Methuen, 1984), 18–19. This, it seems to me, is a decidedly strange view to hold. If a novel by Gide is enough to convince us that everything is constructed, might not a novel by Balzac be enough to restore our original opinion? What kind of person would one have to be to allow one's mind to be changed on such a fundamental point by a formal device in a work of fiction?

34. "Étienne . . . plunged into a series of considerations relative to the necessity of prelimi-nary doubt in all philosophical inquiry." Raymond Queneau, *Witch Grass*, trans. Barbara Wright (New York: NYRB Classics, 2003), 233. On Schlegel's position, which is much more complex than I am able to explain here, see D. C. Muecke, *The Compass of Irony* (London: Methuen, 1967), 200.

35. See Landy, *How to Do Things*, 90–91; J. Robert Loy, *Diderot's Determined Fatalist: A Critical Appreciation of "Jacques le Fataliste"* (New York: King's Crown Press, 1950), 151; Lloyd Bishop, *Romantic Irony in French Literature from Diderot to Beckett* (Nashville: Vanderbilt University Press, 1989), 2.

36. For an explanation of how this works in Proust, see Landy, *Philosophy as Fiction*, 143; for Mallarmé, see Landy, *How to Do Things*, 87–89. For Pirandello, key evidence comes from his play *Enrico IV*. Kundera is not an entirely clear-cut case, but there are suggestions (see *Immortality*, trans. Peter Kussi [New York: HarperCollins, 1999], 12, 341, and especially 344) that he is in the Fellini camp.

37. Kendall L. Walton, "Fearing Fictions," *Journal of Philosophy 75* (1978): 25.

38. Compare Gregory Currie, "Narrative Desire," in *The Philosophy of Film: Introductory Text and Readings*, ed. Thomas E. Wartenberg and Angela Curran (Oxford: Blackwell, 2005), 139–44; Amy Coplan, "Empathic Engagement with Narrative Fictions," *Journal of Aesthetics and Art Criticism 62*, no. 2 (2004): 147.

39. By "interesting" I do not mean "canonical." The TV show *Buffy the Vampire Slayer*, which is hardly canonical, contains elements of reflexivity; the crucial distinction is not between "elite" and "popular" but between challenging and facile. To be sure, Fellini, Proust, and Mallarmé are arguably more likely to have the desired effect, since the device is more cen-tral in them and since their readers and viewers tend to arrive expecting to contribute a rel-atively high degree of mental effort. But where a work is sufficiently ambitious, and where its appreciators are sufficiently diligent, its commercial appeal should never be counted as a strike against it.

40. Compare Jean-Marie Schaeffer: "Même si la scène implique une 'transgression paradoxale des frontières,' cette transgression, loin d'être une anomalie, n'est qu'une exemplification particulièrement explicite de ce qui constitue la caractéristique définitionnelle centrale de l'immersion fictionnelle, à savoir le fait qu'elle implique un état mental scindé." "Métalepse et immersion fictionnel," in *Métalepses: Entorses au pacte de la représentation*, ed. John Pier and Jean-Marie Schaeffer (Paris: Editions de l'Ecole des Hautes Etudes en Sciences Sociales, 2005), 325.

41. On fiction as space for "cognitive workout," compare Lisa Zunshine, *Why We Read Fiction: Theory of Mind and the Novel* (Columbus: Ohio State University Press, 2006), 161.

7

Clouds of Sils Maria

True Characters and Fictional Selves in the Construction of Filmic Identities

Laura T. Di Summa

Clouds of Sils Maria, Olivier Assayas's 2014 feature, is a compelling contemporary example of metacinema. In a way that is reminiscent of Luigi Pirandello's oeuvre and, most notably, of his take on character impersonation, the film plays with the history of film, with the layering of performances, crossing theater and film, actors and characters. Set in the stunning landscape of Sils Maria, Switzerland, a location that is as naturally breathtaking as it is dense with cultural, literary, and philosophical references, the movie tells the story of Maria Enders, played by Juliette Binoche, an actress who (like Binoche), having reached the peak of her career, is now contemplating her role as a mature woman and performer. Binoche balances, in her character, a wide array of emotions, emotions that in turn draw the traits of Enders in poignant, allusive ways. In a classic doubling familiar to metacinema, we are quickly faced with the fates of these two women—Enders and Binoche—and thus drawn into the tension these doubleness creates for a cinematic portrayal of character. Afraid of aging, afraid of not being who she once was, loving, jealous, and proud, Enders reminds us, as critics have noted, of the characters in films like Billy Wilder's *Sunset Boulevard* (1950), Ingmar Bergman's *Persona* (1966), Rainer Werner Fassbinder's *The Bitter Tears of Petra von Kant* (1972), and, quite directly, of Margo Channing, one of Bette Davis's most compelling roles, in Joseph Mankiewicz's *All About Eve* (1950).[1] More recently, Annette Bening's embodiment of Gloria Grahame, in *Film Stars Don't Die in Liverpool* (2017, dir. Paul McGuigan, 2017), reveals the durability of the theme for cinematic narrative.

Numerous threads make Enders the contemporary heir of such memorable characters, threads that appeal to themes they largely share—from the overlapping of theater and film to the lesbian subtext to the relation, so pressing for film stars, between fame and aging. These are undoubtedly fascinating features of the movie (or, I should say, of these movies) and contribute to its

Laura T. Di Summa, *Clouds of Sils Maria* In: *Metacinema*. Edited by: David LaRocca, Oxford University Press. © Oxford University Press 2021. DOI: 10.1093/oso/9780190095345.003.0008 charm and aesthetic success. However, in this chapter, I will mostly avoid drawing comparisons with other productions and character roles and focus exclusively on Assayas's film and on the ways Binoche/Enders engages us in a multifaceted reflection on what it means to *be* a character, to create one for ourselves, and to assess the very viability of such a creation.

My goal is to emphasize a connection between such a reflection and the on-going philosophical debate on personal identity, and, more narrowly, on how such an identity may unfold. I will argue that *Clouds of Sils Maria* is capable of adding a significant contribution to the debate, within analytic aesthetics, on the advantages and the dangers of seeing our lives as narratives. For while watching the feature film may prompt an agreement with Peter Lamarque's criticism of the "narrative view,"[2] which highlighted how a "story-like" narration of our lives might transform nonfictional, factual events into fictional works, we are also reminded of how such a crafted and constructed rendition of facts may ultimately be inevitable. In this sense, *Clouds of Sils Maria* does more than introduce or exemplify a philosophical account; it allows us to assess it, thereby opening new vistas for further critical analysis.

I will begin with a brief overview of the narrative view (as we find it expressed in analytic aesthetics). In the second section, I will outline the narrative construction of *Clouds of Sils Maria* and focus, predominantly, on the aesthetic choices that contribute to the "mood" of the feature, and that are in turn essential to its reception. Specifically, I will concentrate on Maria Enders's performance in relation to both her former and present character roles and in relation to the environment that surrounds her, from her attachment to her assistant, Valentine ("Val"), played by Kristen Stewart, to her interaction with the landscape of Sils Maria. I will then consider what I take to be *Clouds of Sils Maria*'s contribution to the debate, and to the project underway in the present volume. The film, I will argue, not only allows us to better understand the contours of the debate on personal identity, but also deepens that understanding by adding a unique philosophical contribution through means that are specific to motion pictures—means, as I will emphasize, and as *Clouds of Sils Maria* makes evident, that are dependent on a hyper-awareness of the self-referential capacities of the medium.

Should the Self Aspire to Narrative Coherence?
On the Risk and Advantages of Narrative Identity

For the most part, we go on living our lives without particularly worrying about the connections among our experiences; we can spend days without wondering what our contribution, as active selves, as agents, might be to the world we inhabit and leave behind; we can easily overlook the link between what it means to live a life and what it means to *act* in our lives, or better, to *enact* the story of our lives. And yet sometimes things change. Sometimes, in other words, we *do* see ourselves as the protagonists of an unfolding story, as the detectives at work on the case of our own lives: searching for connections, clues, linking past events to their effects, lingering on our memories, recollecting and reconstructing a life, the life that belongs to us: our story.

In genre studies, such an activity is often seen as the basis of autobiographical narratives, whether literary, dramatic, filmic, or of other nature. After all, autobiographies, sophisticated as they are, raise issues of identity, of memory recollection, of narrative structure, of authenticity, and many others, but they also, quite frankly, stem from a primary, and likely evolutionary, need to "make sense" of a life that is perhaps just a senseless sequence of events, but that is made much more significant—and valuable—by means of our ability to portray it as the only story that can indeed be said to belong to us. But without entering the topic of autobiographies in the arts—a topic far too vast to be included in the scope of this chapter—it is sufficient to outline the theses and assumptions that are usually at the basis of the connection between narrative and identity.

The so-called narrative view of the self, namely the view according to which identity unfolds as a narrative, and thus follows the narrative structure that characterizes narrative works as, prominently, a series of causal connections that culminate with a sense of closure, is comprised of several positions. Among the most relevant, but also one of the strongest, is Marya Schechtman's "Narrative Self-Constitution View."[3] Her idea, broadly, is that a narrative conception of selves helps with the very "constitution" of what amounts to a sense of identity, a constitution that unfolds across what Schechtman refers to as the four features of identity: moral responsibility, self-interested concern, compensation, and survival.[4]

A person, according to Schechtman, necessarily cares about the moral value and evaluations of her actions, thus adopting a self-judgmental stance. At the same time, the self-interested concern shows an interest in fulfilling personal desires and goals, where, by setting goals, we also imply the feeling of wanting, for instance, to make a difference for others or to foster personal development. These desires are not, in Schechtman's analysis, mere wishes but are instead profoundly related to the past and future expectations we can derive from our histories. In this latter sense, a self-interested concern is balanced by a form of compensation through which we gauge, for instance, what we might or might not be willing to sacrifice. Finally, the combination of moral responsibility and a balanced self-interested concern constitutes a broad sense of survival where the emphasis is on the continuity of the self as a means of psychological survival.

Two aspects of her theory are particularly interesting for our purposes of thinking about personal identity in *Clouds of Sils Maria*: first, the belief that a "person creates his identity by forming an autobiographical narrative—a story of his life"; second, that the analysis of autobiographical narratives can "explain our intuitions about the relationship between personal identity and survival, moral responsibility, self-interested concern, and compensation."[5] There is a sense in which, to put it somewhat crudely, abiding by a narrative conception of the self is not just something we do—one of our cognitive features—but something that we are *better off* doing, for such a notion can help with an improved understanding of who we are as human beings and as agents in this world. This assertion, which is normative, has come under scrutiny.

There are, broadly, two lines of objections that have been raised against the "narrative view." On the one hand, we have a firm rejection of his tenets, as in Galen Strawson's anti-narrative position.[6] On the other hand, we have a series of doubts concerning the extent to which a narrative conception of the self may genuinely depict who we are and, most importantly, help with an honest understanding of our lives. If in the first case, a narrative conception of the self is just not how we routinely see and analyze our lives, in the second case, adopting it may lead to more problems than we may have expected (since, indeed, we did not expect problems, but, just the opposite, their tidy resolution). While I have defended the plausibility of the first objection elsewhere,[7] I am here interested in the second strand of objections, the one pointing at the risks hidden behind the narrative view.

Peter Lamarque has, in this respect, questioned the plausibility of the narrative view in light of fictional narratives. The core of Lamarque's argument is that the life we usually live is dramatically different from the lives of characters in fiction.[8] Literary narratives have aesthetic and moral purposes; they are constructed, that is, *authored* according to specific intentions, causally driven, and so on. Daily life is instead "unstoried," with life events following each other without pre-ordered or preordained causality. We are not characters in our life story; we simply have a life, and it would be wrong, and dangerous, to see ourselves as the protagonist of a story, as fictional characters (the normative tone of these claims should be strikingly evident here). First, the narrative view is, we may say, after Lamarque, aesthetically flawed, for it simplifies literature by wrongly comparing literary works and their characters to everyday people. Second, it misses the mark by providing a skewed analysis of what the understanding of our own identity amounts to—or should mean in terms of offering a coherent, meaningful "story." To see the self as a character in a story is to fictionalize the self, thus dismantling the authenticity, and, more crucially (again recalling the normative stakes of the project), the *moral authenticity* that personal narratives were instead supposed to bring to light.

Several accounts position themselves in between these two poles. An attractive solution, and perhaps a compromise, is what Peter Goldie, in his acute book, *The Mess Inside*, labels "narrative thinking."[9] While not advocating the notion of a narrative self as the privileged route to solving the question of identity, Goldie maintains that to think narratively about our lives, contra Lamarque, may indeed be useful.[10] Whether or not confronted by an audience (say, paying to experience a dramatic story), we often organize our lives according to our perception of the meaningful causal connections linking different events, events that we further analyze by complementing our perspective of ourselves with the hypothetical perspective of an outsider (thus introducing the further notion—crucial to metafiction—that authorship is capable of bifurcating or doubling, so that characters can suddenly become conscious, and conscious of themselves, just as we might become, or insist that we are, characters in the midst of the narratives we have come to call our lives). Narratives can help achieve emotional closure—a sense of an ending that also, and frequently, encompasses moral and emotional evaluation.

Similarly to Lamarque, Goldie is also careful to emphasize possible risks associated with narrative thinking. Once again, the risk of narrative thinking is that we might begin, in our struggle to build a narrative, to *fictionalize* our lives. Finding cohesion and coherence might require altering events, forcing connections, indeed, inventing! It might require us, one may say, to become *characters* and not persons, and thus to jeopardize what, at least initially, was a search for one's own-most personal, authentic identity.

It is precisely this conflict—the one between the "need" or at least the eventual use of narrative thinking and the acknowledgment of the risks it may imply—that is at the center of *Clouds of Sils Maria*. More specifically, the movie is interesting because it shows us both positions (viz., pro-narrative and anti-narrative), motivating the viewer to assess them independently, but also, importantly, in tandem, in conversation. Differently put, what makes the movie philosophically interesting is that it does not simply exemplify the two positions, but undertakes the careful—but also potentially confounding—work uniquely suited to metacinematic portrayal and thus investigation: by presenting the two positions simultaneously, the film invites the viewer to assume a critical stance that in turn leads to a novel and nuanced understanding of the accounts' merits and downfalls. The film, as it were, is already thinking about itself. This is evident in the choices made by Assayas, who is consciously thinking metacinematically in starring Binoche (a point on which I will soon return), but it is also part of what gives the feature, at once, its particular aura and solidity. Characters are presented to us as both persons and actors, they are between theater and film; little distance is established between acting and rehearsing as they live and inhabit different roles and as they weave them together in complex and fascinating ways. It is a tribute to metacinema, and thus particularly suited for this volume. The audience cannot but pause and reflect on its effects, which are aesthetically, cinematically, and philosophically meaningful. More, additionally, will be said about such philosophical advancement that is conveyed through cinematic means, thus by means that, unlike propositional expression and analytic argumentative practices, are usually unorthodox in philosophy—at least until the prominent wave of film-philosophers has made movies a standard, even expected part of our philosophical debates and deliberations.

A Layered Performance: The Narrative Identity of Maria Enders

Sigrid, in Three Characters

As many critics have noticed, and as Assayas has claimed, *Clouds of Sils Maria* is a movie designed for, and in part based upon, the actress Juliette Binoche. In film, she has been the muse of directors such as Krzysztof Kieślowski and Abbas Kiarostami; in theater, she has starred in both Broadway plays and in the work of ambitious and experimental directors, such as Ivo Van Hove.[11] And, of course, she is not unknown to Assayas, who first cast her as a young and still relatively unknown actress in *Rendez-Vous* (1985), a film that is associated with her breakthrough in French cinema, and then proceeded to feature her in *Summer Hours* (2008), *Paris, I Love You* (2006), and *Alice and Martin* (1998). Taking further chances at metacinematic references, he has also, after featuring her in *Clouds of Sils Maria*—the movie I'll be discussing here—given her a critical role in the recent, albeit not particularly critically successful, *Non-Fiction* (2018), where Binoche plays Selena, an actress stuck in a TV role she does not anymore enjoy and who is (not unlike Enders in *Clouds of Sils Maria*) annoyed by the changes introduced by our increasingly technology-driven society.

In *Clouds of Sils Maria*, Binoche plays a character, Maria Enders, who like her has received tremendous critical attention and success, but who is in middle age and trying to navigate how the female aging of cinematic stars interacts with power, prestige, celebrity, and the "kinds of characters" one is invited, indeed, allowed to play. In the diegesis of the film, Enders was brought to notoriety by Wilhelm Melchior, who chose her for his play *The Maloja Snake*, in which she played Sigrid, a young assistant who, thanks to her beauty, but also to a certain cruelty, drives her boss, Helena, an older woman who fell in love with her, to commit suicide.

In the first sequences of Part I (for quick reference, the movie is divided into two parts and includes an epilogue, a clear echo to the theater), Enders and her assistant, Val (Kristen Stewart), are seen traveling to Sils Maria. Enders is to attend a ceremony in honor of Melchior, the director who, as mentioned previously, launched her as an actress when she was only eighteen years old. While still on the train, she hears of his sudden death, by suicide. Now scheduled to receive the award in his stead, while reciting his eulogy, Enders is confronted with her past and with the weight it exercises on her present. However, as we quickly realize, her present is not altogether distinct from her past: soon after attending the ceremony, Enders meets with Klaus Diesterweg (Lars Eidinger), a notorious, emerging director, who wants to cast her in a sequel of Melchior's *The Maloja Snake*. Not surprisingly, after twenty years have passed, Enders is asked to play the role of Helena, that is, the role of the older woman, a woman Enders does not want to *be* and thus does not want to *play*.

In the scenes preceding and following the ceremony (now a memorial), Enders is glamorous, fittingly vain, and sarcastic. Clad in Chanel (the designer donated almost all the clothes to the production and was, not incidentally, crucial in financing the movie), she enjoys being flattered as well as flirting with the men she meets. It is, arguably, these encounters that begin to build a picture of Enders's inner fears and active duplicity. Significant, in this respect, is her interaction with Henryk Wald (Hanns Zischler), an older actor who has starred with her in several productions, and with whom she had a tumultuous affair. When describing him to Val, Enders remarks that Henryk is interesting, as an *actor*, and horrible, as a *person*, thus enforcing the distinction between characters and the actors (i.e., the persons) who impersonate them.

The lucidity of such insights, however, is not to last. The two engage in playful banter when returning to their hotels, and it is clear that Enders is, once again, playing the part of Sigrid, of the young seductress. When she leaves him her room number, Enders's confidence is palpable—it is the confidence of Sigrid, but when it becomes obvious that Henryk will not call her or join her in her room, Enders's dissatisfaction is readily apparent, and it is here, arguably, that we first truly see her as an older woman. This is, in turn, a bow to the metacinematic game of the film, as it is virtually impossible not to think of Juliet Binoche, the actress we have so often encountered and admired, and to wonder whether she, too, has become an "older woman" and whether such a definition is actually appropriate or the sore echo of Hollywood's lust for eternal youth. The unflattering image of Enders in a hotel bathrobe stands in stark contrast to the revealing black cocktail dress she wore at the ceremony; wearing that dress, only hours earlier, she had told Klaus that she was still Sigrid, that playing Helena would have been impossible for her. Now, alone, she looks for pictures of Jo-Ann (played by Chloë Grace Moretz), on her iPad, the actress who has been chosen to play Sigrid. It's a furtive, solitary moment: Enders had already expressed her disdain for technology and is never seen checking the internet when in the company of others. Moreover, her search is a search for images, and, quite naturally, for the image she once was and for the image she has now to confront, as Helena.

In the second part of the movie, Val and Enders retire to Melchior's chalet to rehearse the play. In fact, *we* are, in a sense, in the play. For in these sequences, we are brought incredibly close to the layering of performances by becoming the audience not of a play, or of the movie we are watching, but of the making of both. Val, Enders's assistant, helps her prepare the role of Helena by reading the lines of Sigrid, virtually erasing any distinction between the Val/Enders and the Sigrid/Helena's relationships. One role observes and assesses the other, and, to a large extent, we are asked to do the same: invited to shift our attitude from passive viewership to critical observers. We then come to realize, through these wonderful scenes of deft acting, how Assayas—and his band of talented performers—contests the doubleness that we are so familiarly teased by (e.g., in ways familiar to anyone who has struggled with the Madeleine and Judy characters in Hitchcock's *Vertigo* [1958] by flattening the two "parts" [character/person] so they are collapsed, as if unified).

On the one hand, these rehearsal scenes allow the audience to better understand Enders's relationship with both her former (i.e., younger) role—the dominant role that cannot anymore be assigned to her (by virtue of her age, and thus, by factors beyond her control)—and the fear of the consequences of having lost it. The dramatization is made even more explicit by Enders's possessiveness about and attraction to Val. We see her gazing at Val's body with a vampiristic lust similar to the one Alma casts upon Elisabeth in *Persona*, but we also see a more candid, harmless form of attraction: their interactions are lively, often tinged with a sarcasm at odds with eroticism. There is obvious affection, but an affection that, to Assayas's credit, is nonetheless always at risk, or risky—threatened by the confusion of identity we see unfolding in multiple directions; threatened by Enders's very fragility, by her (internal and external) fight with her own identity.

On the other hand, while the presence of Val reminds and reinforces Enders's inability to be Sigrid, it also alerts us to the perils of such identification. Val, Assayas is careful to emphasize, is not Sigrid and she is not playing a part, since she is skeptical of the movie star's life—and its presumed values; she is thus critically aware of the mistake, and danger, of living (or reliving) one's life as the life of a character. When Val tries to persuade Enders of the power, and richness, of Helena, she reminds Enders that "the text is like an object. It's going to change perspective based on where you are standing." She points out that "thinking about a text is different from living it," thus offering Enders a way out of a character, Sigrid, she cannot, it would seem, stop playing. Before I elaborate on this last point, it is important also to mention the second female character interacting with Enders: the new Sigrid, Jo-Ann.

Jo-Ann's role is, arguably, performed with less nuance than the one played by Val (and in a typical metacinema mode, we are left wondering if this is a function of Chloë Grace Moretz's talent or her lack of it), but is a clear reminder of Enders's aging, of her fear of disappearing, and, more broadly, of the passing of time and of how film and the entertainment industry have changed—or better, that Enders has changed: she has aged, while "the industry" remains steadfast in its commitment to youth and the portrayal of young lives. Chloë Grace Moretz was only seventeen when the movie was filmed and exudes the youthful esprit of her generation: Jo-Ann is a social media star, famous for her role in superhero movies, studiously arrogant, cunningly aware of her status—and, needless to say—of her power over Enders. (Again, it may be Moretz's talent for this vacuity that exhibits her genius as a performer, or it may be that the character/person divide is much narrower than we may think, and Moretz herself is much like the character she plays.) Moretz is the representative of what it is to be Sigrid, but also, and especially, of what it is to be Sigrid twenty years *later*, in a world of internet-based paparazzi, social media scandals, and over-the-top superhero sci-fi movies. As the Sigrid of the first production of *The Maloja Snake*, Jo-Ann is aware of her seductive beauty; as the Sigrid of its sequel, she knows that to shine you cannot just seduce one woman, you have to entice the whole World Wide Web.

Contrasting Jo-Ann and Enders further highlights how Enders's attachment to her role as Sigrid, her desire to *be* her (even though Sigrid is a character), is, ultimately, undoubtedly dangerous. It is, more radically, impossible. Hence, at a certain high point in the film's drama, we see *Clouds of Sils Maria* as a cautionary parable—one that can be readily adapted to a range of delusions that can ruin lives. The world of Enders as Sigrid, like Enders's life as a young woman, is no more and can only be looked at with nostalgia. Additionally, Enders's interaction with Jo-Ann is underscored by a conflict: the compressed, rapid time-scale of the social media world (the world that is the present-day reality, and thus the world in which Val and Jo-Ann live; they spend, after all, quite a bit of time texting and juggling iPads) and the natural surroundings of the chalet: the extended time-scale of the mountains and, of course, the Maloja Snake, a cloud formation that envelops the entire valley, and an obvious but still potent metaphor for the sinuous, very slow, and all too relentless passing of time. The importance of the environment cannot, and should not be underplayed, for, as I will argue in the next section, the environment is an essential vehicle through which the question of Enders's identity and identification with Sigrid is further conveyed. Allow me to turn to this point.

Clouds of Sils Maria's Moods

The cinematic experience is not limited to the experience of images and sounds—or what we might just call the "screen experience." There is something about the patterns created by moving images and accompanying sounds that escapes the reduction to a physiologically minimal perceptual account. We are not just receiving and processing sensorial inputs: we are experiencing them. Traditionally, the complexity of cinematic experience has led to the development of two different approaches. The first, popular in contemporary cognitive analyses of film, defines the nature of cinematic experience as a distinct form of perceptual experience. Scholars such as Murray Smith,[12] Ted Nannicelli,[13] Tim Smith,[14] and others have used the tools of naturalist analysis and neuropsychology to describe the nature of cinematic experience. Following a path opened by Noël Carroll and David Bordwell in their seminal work *Post-theory: Reconstructing Film Studies*,[15] this group of scholars is investigating cinematic experience in light of scientific knowledge pertaining to the function and understanding of everyday physiological and cognitive responses—an approach that, at least when it first emerged, was in stark contrast with the existing work in film studies, which privileged a psychoanalytic approach. The second, which interests me here, looks instead at the phenomenology of cinematic experience, as, to borrow Thomas Nagel's famous expression, the "what it is like" to experience a film.

Phenomenological accounts rely on the quality added by film's unique use of cinematic patterns and on the symbolic and emotional connotations such patterns remind us of. Such considerations, championed by scholars such as Vivian Sobchack, are tremendously important when analyzing a film and its philosophical import, and this for at least three reasons. First, because, as Robert Sinnerbrink, Berys Gaut, and Carl Plantinga have shown,[16] the appreciation of film is strongly affected by the "mood" that it exudes and by the emotional responses it triggers. Feeling for fiction is a nuanced mechanism that relies on a variety of factors such as bodily and physiological reactions, aspectual factors—such as recognizing a specific situation, topos, pattern, and so on—and also, as Jenefer Robinson has argued, on unconscious states.[17] Second, phenomenological accounts are essential for critical analysis of cinema and specifically for the identification of aesthetic and, eventually, artistic features of a film. To put it somewhat crudely, as much as it is possible to provide broad accounts of what the experience, generally construed, of fictional works may be like, we cannot deny that works differ from each other: that they evoke and allow us to entertain diverse and subjective aesthetic experiences, experiences that remain mostly unique (both temporally and personally) and that are fundamental to the aesthetic assessment of each work. Last, phenomenological accounts foster our very ability to learn, to be affected, and to, in a sense, appropriate and carry with us the message of a work. Phenomenological accounts are, in this sense, one of the leading tools of film criticism: there to reveal a message that may not be entirely or immediately apparent. The specific "mood" of *Clouds of Sils Maria* can then be seen as the quintessential cinematic entryway through which the film contributes to the philosophical debate on the importance, but also on the risks, of the narrative conception of the self that I have so far outlined. Such mood is conveyed, primarily, by the natural environment depicted cinematically. And here, by chance, I make my parenthetic point: while most of the mainstream criticism of *Clouds of Sils Maria* has appreciated the doubleness of the film's cast (young/old; actor/character, etc.), very little has addressed the character—indeed, the mood—of the environment, of its special doubleness (e.g., as a real place and as a represented place), and of its role in the metacinematic achievement of the film.

Sils Maria, the location of Assayas's film, is, after all, much more than two words in the film's title. A small town in the Swiss Alps, Sils Maria shines with what seem to be the features of Edmund Burke's romantic sublime, from awe to terror, to the inevitable feeling of our own, so very human, inferiority. Sils Maria was, for a period, a refuge for Friedrich Nietzsche—who spent his summers there—and the closest town to the Hotel Waldhaus (where a few scenes are filmed), which counts in its guest list almost all the names we could find in a syllabus in modern European literature. It is unconditionally spectacular, so spectacular as to make us wonder about its reality or, shall we say, about reality itself. For the breathtaking beauty of the Alps is permeated with mystery: far from lifeless formations, the peaks of Sils Maria are animated, pregnant with energy, engorged with life, the kind of life that, as in the sublime, trumps our own. Then, as the title of the film indicates, it has clouds. The Maloja Snake, a rare phenomenon leading to the formation of a cloud system resembling the shape of a snake, is not only a clear invitation to ponder the majesty and almost mystical power of nature, but it is also, more directly, the very title of the play Enders performed in the past—and is once again asked to perform. The Maloja Snake, to our surprise, is also a double!— a work of theater *and* a natural formation. And both of them are fraught, elusive phenomena that haunt our protagonist (in her own doubleness and self-reference). Clouds, the audience appears to be invited to conclude, are a natural as well as a cultural phenomenon: they stand for nature to the same extent to which they hold for the arts.

Nature, thanks to splendid sinuous camera movements and a series of technically masterful long takes, is shown as wholeheartedly alive as if it were an agent, a character, and an actor. More formally, the film appears to be playing with what Blakey Vermeule, in her work on fictional characters, labels a conceptual primitive.[18] Conceptual primitives are based on the development of identification mechanisms that are essential to the refinement and maturation of our social intelligence. As treated in *Clouds of Sils Maria*, we see Nature as an actor—a presence on its own terms—and this, in turn, supplies us with a better understanding of the web of actions characterizing the entire story, including those of the (other) characters that populate the narrative. As an agent—an "actor" with a role—Nature is capable of providing us with the kind of information we would expect from a dramatic performer, say, from Juliet Binoche or Kristen Stewart; its significance is much more layered, nuanced, and vital to the story than it would have been if Nature were treated merely as the backdrop against (or "upon") that events take place. For Assayas, Nature is not a stage, but a thespian worthy of membership in his troupe. As an active participant in the story, Nature is also inevitably linked to the narrative, to the multiple narratives that lead to the discovery of Enders.

If we follow this line of analysis, then we can see, in the Maloja Snake, some demon, a force that is, at any given time, going to take over the characters. Plato thought that, in order to perform, actors need to be in a state of "madness," possessed: something else, the Muse, talks through them. More than two thousand years later, on screen, the situation appears unchanged. Enders seems poisoned, captured by something stronger than her—and so she acts, reciting the only possible lines: the lines of the character she once was. Nature and the atmospheric phenomenon known as the Maloja Snake alert us, together with narrative twists and with Enders's interaction with other characters, of her duplicity, of her need to see herself as Sigrid, to return to her. Nature, differently put, actively points to the necessity of metacinematic analysis. It underscores Enders's character shifts, and while it obviously also provides a setting for her performance, its look remains hard to capture, diffused: imposing as the mountains of Sils Maria may be, they are also an "in-between" place, one where the multiple levels of this film can ultimately meet.

But, as argued in the previous section, *Clouds of Sils Maria*, in addition to exemplifying the narrative view, is equally effective at portraying its risks—and the environment (Nature) plays a part in this respect as well. The presence and power of Nature cannot be explained and cannot be analyzed in the same way as a causally connected episode within the storyline. Nature, and the effects it has on the characters and on the overall structure of the film, appears abruptly, unexpectedly—with force. Standard narrative conceptions of identity point to the importance of a coherent, causally driven chain of events; Nature shows us how such cohesiveness can be threatened. Nature punctuates the story in an enigmatic manner. This is visible toward the very end of Part II, when Val and Enders are hiking toward the panoramic location from which the Maloja Snake can be observed. While walking they are also quarreling over the interpretation of the play, Val trying, unsuccessfully, to make Enders look at the role of Helena differently. Perhaps, she remarks, Helena does not die in the end; instead, she moves on—a hypothesis that is rejected by Enders. We see Val growing impatient, more impatient than she has ever been during the sojourn in Sils Maria—and then she disappears, without explanation. And while we are rationally to believe that she has simply left the trail, we are also left wondering—indeed, invited to consider—whether something mystical may have happened. The episode remains partly inexplicable, unnervingly hard to decipher, and yet it is essential to the understanding of who Enders is—it provides us with a glimpse into her (complex) identity while also alerting the critic, and philosopher, of new ways of thinking about the constitution of identity—one in which authenticity is at jeopardy and coherence is abandoned. For now, at this juncture of the film, Enders is alone in Nature, as the low-lying clouds are entering the Maloja Pass. Standing there with her, we know that she still has not understood, that she is still clinging to the only identity she can accept: she is Sigrid, but Sigrid as a lie—a young woman who can no longer exist. We know that in this she is both alone and wrong.

Epilogue: On Narrative Identity and Fictional Characters

Maria Enders's life is based on her life as Sigrid. Her narrative began when, at only eighteen, she was scripted to play the part of a young, attractive woman.

That part, we know, she loved, she identified with—indeed, identity is the perfect philosophical word for the phenomenon, since Enders = Sigrid as 1 = 1. Much later in life, when she is confronted with the death of Melchior, her attachment to Sigrid becomes (oddly?) *even more* evident and irresistible. In a way, though, it is justified. Being Sigrid shelters Enders from her fear of aging, from being forgotten, losing her power over others, since characters, unlike human beings, last forever, their lives perfectly plotted, their traits immutable. Enders made Sigrid's traits her own because Enders saw herself as Sigrid; not unlike Pirandello's characters in *Six Characters in Search of an Author*, she can only be Sigrid. As the arrival of ingénues must go on, it is not surprising, then, to see Enders hesitating, dreading the idea of being Helena despite the fact that Helena's story, as we realize throughout the movie, is her story, the narrative that best fits her in her present state—the future that she perhaps believed would never arrive. Maria, as her name has surreptitiously hinted all along, must herself be an ender—must come to an end. And as the film's title too has hidden in plain sight: these are Maria's clouds.

For the preceding reasons, *Clouds of Sils Maria* shows us that while seeing our lives as narratives that unfold diachronically can be tempting, rewarding, and at times the most appealing, soothing way of affirming our own identity, it is also dangerous. Both Lamarque and Goldie warn against the risks of, respectively, the narrative view and narrative thinking, and it is not hard to see those criticisms in Enders's relation to Val and, more broadly, as we have seen, in her relation to what surrounds her. Life does not follow the causal chains we find in fictional works, and while remembering the events of our life may often require reconstructing memories and playing, in a way, our own life story, we should be admonished about the allure of transforming ourselves in fictional characters (again, as if there are two people here: the real person and the character she plays in her life); doubleness follows us out of the movie theater. Along these same lines, we recognize that one's personality does not match the fixed traits of a character, so to force such rigidity upon ourselves (as characters) can only stunt our development and impair our self-understanding. The Enders we leave at the end of Part II is alone, stranded by herself on a trail leading to who knows where. Clouds fill up the frame, and her life. The great fear of oblivion has visited her and may consume her. Enders's narrative, the narrative she had up to that moment appropriated from Sigrid, does not exist or, better, cannot exist. She can't be Sigrid just as she cannot have Val. They are both impossibilities—one for reasons pertaining to the strictures of fiction, the other to the contours of dramatic art.

If the clouds have obscured Maria's view, there are many things that we can clearly observe in Assayas's film, among them a specific and special way for film to do philosophy. For film can, in certain cases, do a lot more than simply exemplify, through audiovisual language, a given philosophical theory; indeed, the exemplification function is one of its weakest attributes—making film little more than a handmaiden to philosophy. When we see film *doing* philosophy, its credentials as a potent art are more fully acknowledged. Philosophers like Aaron Smuts,[19] believe that film can, at times, actively contribute and expand the philosophical discussion. This does not mean that film must necessarily launch a whole new philosophical argument (even though that is not something I would entirely exclude), but simply that it can contribute to a given debate or argument by offering new perspectives and by raising new questions—much like an essay or an article. In the case of *Clouds of Sils Maria*, a philosophical contribution is afforded by making us engage in a reflection on three separate threads of discussion. The first, which we have seen in Enders's need to see her life as the life of a character, provides us with an example, albeit extreme, of how we may make sense of ourselves by relying on a (hoped for) coherent narrative (because we have learned through experience that the narratives of fictional characters are more consistent and more reliable than ours). The second thread, exemplified by Enders's relation to Val and Jo-Ann, shows the downsides and risks of such identification in a manner that is likely to remind us of Peter Lamarque's criticism of the narrative view. Human beings are different from fictional characters, and to enforce a narrative conception of the self would perilously equate life and literature (or, in this case, theater). Last, though, *Clouds of Sils Maria* appears to partly redeem the narrative view. The film seems to tell us that, after all, the narrative view *does* work—if managed. Whether such management yields a happy and satisfying life is another question.

This last thread can be observed, I argue, in the epilogue of the film, which, while ambiguous, can make us reconsider the critical stance against the actor/character identification that dominates Part II. The epilogue moves us to London, where we see Enders in the final stage of a rehearsal. It is not an easy moment for her. Jo-Ann, who in a previous scene, filmed in the notorious Hotel Waldhaus, had opportunistically flattered her, is now at once bratty and tremendously at ease in this new environment that better suits her, her native environment of social media, gossip, and paparazzi. In fact, that very environment is now threatening the debut of the play: the wife of a successful novelist has found out that he and Jo-Ann are having an affair and has tried to kill herself, causing understandable turmoil. Jo-Ann appears barely touched by the gravity of the situation, her claims of distress ringing overtly false. She is, after all, Sigrid, and to this extent, she is free to ignore everyone but herself, for she is the only center of attention—her own.

At the end of the film, the bathos-laden dominance of Jo-Ann, the appropriation of her role of Sigrid, and the storming in of the social media/paparazzi world that had so far waited just outside the frame has a significant effect of Enders. Her first reaction is, not surprisingly, a mix of shyness and stupor. Enders feels left behind when the scandal surrounding Jo-Ann and her lover makes the discussion of any other issue seem unimportant, and her only attempt at reliving the life of Sigrid is confined to a short, much-quoted, exchange between her and Jo-Ann during rehearsal. Enders asks Jo-Ann to alter her performance and to look at her, playing Helena, one more time before closing the door behind her: "You leave without looking at me. . . . The audience follows you out, but instantly forgets about [Helena], so . . ." Jo-Ann responds: "No one really gives a fuck about Helena at this point, do you think? I'm sorry, but I mean it's pretty clear to me this poor woman is all washed up"—and after a sadistic pause—"I mean, your *character*, right, not you." Though the overtness of these lines may mark an infelicitous moment in the film, they nevertheless deliver a compelling message: Enders is now, despite her protestation, Helena, her past as Sigrid has been erased, and "her" role recast (by Jo-Ann). But has Maria Enders, the actress, and woman, also disappeared?

The movie appears, at this point, to have reached an end. But it is a temporary, partial end. What has ended is the Maloja Snake, in its two versions, two versions that both end with the death of Helena and the triumph of Sigrid. Life, instead, moves on and with it the life of Enders. It is only in these final scenes that Enders is not Sigrid or Maria, but an actress, and it fits her stupendously. One of the last sequences of the movie sees her meeting with a young director who is hoping to cast her as a genetically hybrid creature—a sci-fi character who has "no age" and is "outside of time." Enders is now confirmed as a character; she is asked to be one, to keep playing a part that can't be affected by time. And at this point it is time for her to walk on stage to a full house—the camera following her traversal of the screens and windowpanes that compose the theatrical play's scenography, and finally coming to rest on her face, smiling. It is possible here that Enders is smiling at herself. As an actress, her role is to make a character's narrative hers, and I believe she knows that this is in fact her role. Enders may have *played* Sigrid, but her true role, her narrative, in the movie as well as in life—isn't it "La Binoche" that we see here?—is *to play the actress*. She is bound, in this sense, to find a new narrative in every new character, and those narratives will, to some extent, become hers. Perhaps making your life the life of a character is not so bad after all.

Notes

1. William Mooney, "From *All about Eve* (1950) to *Clouds of Sils Maria* (2014): Adapting a Classic Paradigm," *LFQ: Literature / Film Quarterly* (2018), https:// lfq.salisbury.edu/_issues/ 45_3/from_all_about_eve.html.

2. Peter Lamarque, "On the Distinction between Literary Narratives and Real Life Narratives," in *Narrative and Understanding Persons*, ed. Daniel D. Hutto (Cambridge: Cambridge University Press, 2007), 117–32.

3. Marya Schechtman, *The Constitution of Selves* (Ithaca, NY: Cornell University Press, 1996); Marya Schechtman, "Stories, Lives and Basic Survival: A Refinement and Defense of the Narrative View," in Hutto, *Narrative and Understanding Persons*, 155– 78; and Marya Schechtman, "Art Imitating Life Imitating Art: Literary Narrative and Autobiographical Narrative," in *The Philosophy of Autobiography*, ed. Christopher Cowley (Chicago: University of Chicago Press, 2015), 22–38

4. Schechtman, The Constitution of Selves, 93.

5. Schechtman, The Constitution of Selves, 119.

6. Galen Strawson, *The Self?* (Oxford: Blackwell, 2005) and Galen Strawson, "The Unstoried Life," in *On Life Writing*, ed. Zachary Leader (Oxford: Oxford University Press, 2015), 284–301.

7. Laura T. Di Summa-Knoop, "Critical Autobiography: A New Genre?," *Journal of Aesthetics and Culture* 9, no. 1 (2017).

8. Lamarque, "On the Distinction."

9. Peter Goldie, *The Mess Inside: Narrative, Emotion, and the Mind* (Oxford: Oxford University Press, 2012).

10. For further insights on this topic see Schechtman, "Art Imitating Life."

11. A recent production had Binoche play the role of Antigone.

12. Murray Smith, *Engaging Characters: Fiction, Emotion, and the Cinema* (Oxford: Oxford University Press, 1995) and Murray Smith, *Film, Art, and the Third Culture: A Naturalized Aesthetics of Film* (Oxford: Oxford University Press, 2017).

13. Ted Nannicelli, *A Philosophy of the Screenplay* (Abingdon-on-Thames: Routledge, 2013)

14. Tim J. Smith, "Read, Watch, Listen: A Commentary on Eye Tracking and Moving Images," *Refractory* 25, no. 9 (2015) (open access), Video 1, Video 2, Video 3.

15. David Bordwell and Noël Carroll, eds., *Post-theory: Reconstructing Film Studies* (Madison: University of Wisconsin Press, 1996).

16. Robert Sinnerbrink, *New Philosophies of Film: Thinking Images* (New York: Continuum, 2011) and *Cinematic Ethics: Exploring Ethical Experience through Film* (New York: Routledge, 2015); Berys Gaut, *A Philosophy of Cinematic Art* (Cambridge: Cambridge University Press, 2010); and Carl Plantinga, *Moving Viewers: American Film and the Spectator's Experience* (Berkeley: University of California Press, 2009).

17. Jenefer Robinson, *Deeper Than Reason: Emotion and Its Role in Literature, Music, and Art* (Oxford: Oxford University Press, 2005).

18. Blakey Vermuele, *Why Do We Care about Literary Characters?* (Baltimore: Johns Hopkins University Press, 2010), 26.

19. Aaron Smuts, "Film as Philosophy: In Defense of a Bold Thesis," *Journal of Aesthetics and Art Criticism* 67, no. 4 (2009): 409–20.

8

Holy Motors

Metameditation on Digital Cinema's Present and Future

Ohad Landesman

Leos Carax's *Holy Motors* (2012) is a film that opens before film, with the photographic motion experiments of Étienne-Jules Marey. Those early moments of movement captured on screen are among the first proto-cinematic human performances, and they appear at the beginning of a film that is entirely shot on digital. Such a clear duality marks an essential trait in *Holy Motors* right from the outset: here is a film that is celebrating the past in order to envision what is going to happen in the future. As the medium is finalizing its transition into the digital age, Carax takes a hard look at the legacy of 120 years of film history and rethinks the basic constituents of the cinematic experience.

With clearly nostalgic yearning for the early days of celluloid cinema, on the one hand, and concomitantly inciteful optimism about digital possibilities, on the other, *Holy Motors* becomes a metacinematic work about both the death of cinema and its concurrent rebirth. The film represents and complicates, as I will argue in this chapter, cultural and critical anxieties about the impact of new technologies on cinema's development in the twenty-first century, whether such impact entails the omnipresence of small digital cameras without an audience; new media capacities for formulating a fragmented and non-narrative story; the virtual, non-indexical presence of the rapidly changing shape of digital performance; or simply the disappearance of an immersive and contemplative filmgoing experience in a theatrical setting. *Holy Motors* also encapsulates a personal dimension, the creative anxiety of a filmmaker making his first film in thirteen years, not without elegiac feelings about how in that period of time the medium has irrevocably changed.

Holy Motors, in my opinion, looks at the transition to digital from a critically balanced position that *puts the old and the new together*—it treats digital cinema *not* as a historical point of rupture and crisis, but as a necessary and evolutionary stage that is merely extending the past indefinitely into the future rather than altering the present completely. It celebrates the past of celluloid technology and mourns the disappearance of "old" cinema in order to

Ohad Landesman, *Holy Motors* In: *Metacinema*. Edited by: David LaRocca, Oxford University Press. © Oxford University Press 2021. DOI: 10.1093/oso/9780190095345.003.0009 envision how properties of film affect the present and future of digital cinema. In its post-DV (or now nearly all-DV) landscape, digital cameras have become so small and omnipresent that performances are held endlessly in front of what amounts to an invisible audience. Is this really the end of cinema, or a futuristic version of its reincarnation—one that, to our surprise, may have already arrived?

Cinema Is Dead: Long Live Cinema!

Holy Motors begins with short excerpts from Étienne-Jules Marey's late nineteenth-century chrono-photographic experiments, a few seconds of a naked man moving backward and forward. Those brief black-and-white segments of movement dissected into single frames in succession refer immediately to the idea of performance, and foreground cinema "as a site or vehicle of physical movement, of imaginative transport and technological transformation."[1] Immediately after appears an image of a lifeless and faceless audience sitting in a dark movie theater. Since we cannot see the eyes of the viewers, or hear their reactions, we soon wonder whether they are really watching the movie projected in front of them. Are they paralyzed, sleeping, unaware of what is going on, or simply disengaged with the movie? While the nature of the film being shown on the screen remains unlabeled to us (though attentive cinephiles would probably recognize the image of the audience as a clever homage to the final shot of King Vidor's *The Crowd* [1928]), we hear its diegetic sounds that attest to mobility and movement: heavy traffic, a gunshot, and a ship's siren. The first two shots of *Holy Motors* formulate, then, a telling juxtaposition between cinematic kinesis and the theater "as a place of total immobility."[2]

What immediately follows is a meaningful cameo by its maker, Leos Carax, who is revealed to us all curled up in bed. Our *Le Dormeur* (the sleeper), Carax is one of France's most important film auteurs and had not directed any film for more than a decade since his *Pola X* (1999). Carax (or his character?—an ambiguity that will recur elsewhere in the film) awakens from a state of creative hibernation, a long period of passivity in which technological changes have been overtaking the film industry, yet again. Keeping this extratextual knowledge in mind, we may wonder: Why has he been inactive? Was he disillusioned by the presumably disappointing state of cinema at the dawn of the third millennium? Was it difficult for him to get inspired? With a strangely shaped middle-finger key, Carax opens a door into the theater we saw earlier, or into what could be later interpreted as the age of digital cinema. That is, our age. But is it still an age of or for cinema? The absent audience, the hellhound that walks through the theater's corridor, the digitally distorted images of *La Père Lachaise* we will later see, or simply the fact that so many characters in the film would later die (whether assassinated, or simply pass away of old age) are all indications that *Holy Motors* is a film dealing with the death of its own medium, and in a related fact or symptom, the death of the spectator in the traditional filmic space of the theater. Can cinema survive out of doors and without beholders?

Yet inside *Holy Motors* itself—a film that contains films and scenes of filmmakers—is it the content of what is shown to the audience that is putting them to sleep? C. M. Olavarria puts the blame for inattention on contemporary Hollywood cinema and suggests that the audience we see is lobotomized "by the hollow triumph of specta-drivel brain-frying 3D superhero comic book blockbusters, endless bankable sequels, prequels, adaptations, and remakes, palpable pretentious 'indies' and everything in between."[3] Interesting as this suggestion may be to briefly characterize the state of current cinema that has been produced while Carax was "sleeping," I think that the argument here is aimed toward the medium itself. Carax laments a bygone era of theatrical cinema, or at least the experience of it, and suggests that in the digital age the film theater no longer promises a vibrant and engaging experience. If we examine more precisely the reference from *The Crowd*, we will notice that every single member of the audience in Vidor's film is moving in his or her seat while laughing.

In 1975, when Roland Barthes spoke of walking out of a movie theater, he described the act of watching a film as a state of "hypnosis,"[4] characterized by "the relaxation of postures,"[5] in which the image becomes a "lure" with which the spectator is confined. He writes: "The image is there, in front of me, for me . . . the image captivates me, captures me: I am *glued* to the representation."[6] Christian Metz, writing his famous notes on the impression of reality in cinema at around the same time, describes in similar terms how "films release a mechanism of affective and perceptual participation in the spectator (one is almost never totally bored by a movie),"[7] while Gabrielle Pedullà describes the "induced passivity" of the audience in the movie theater as "the enforcement of physical stillness [that] in turn demands not only greater mental action but deeper empathetic reaction."[8] Even Susan Sontag, composing at the end of the previous century a diatribe on film as a decadent art, longs for "the experience of surrender to, of being transported by, what was on the screen." "You wanted to be kidnapped by the movie," she laments, recalling what for her is now a bygone era, "and to be kidnapped was to be overwhelmed by the physical presence of the image."[9]

All of these complex accounts of spectatorship in a traditional movie theater focus on a certain submission to the screen that, instead of leading to a dormant state of disinterestedness, results in an absorbed and affected audience. But film viewing in *Holy Motors* happens elsewhere, outside of the movie theater and without a screen. We soon realize that the film follows a mysterious Parisian character named Monsieur Oscar (Denis Lavant), a businessman-turned-actor who travels in a limousine from one location to another, performing in each stop a different role in a continuous but overtly incoherent life-drama. The structure is fragmented and episodic, and the meetings (each functioning as a specific film genre) gradually become darker, more brutal, and more violent. The viewers watching Oscar's performances, just like the faceless audience in the theater, seem to care less and less about all his acts (more on this later). Even the fact that our cineaste creature lights up a cigarette in between roles may suggest, as Jocelyn Szczepaniak-Gillece brilliantly observes, his own wish to return to an earlier legacy of watching, or "a more reverential, more immersive, and more contemplative filmgoing experience."[10]

The discourse around *Holy Motors* as a melancholic film that laments celluloid and projects the anxieties of its filmmaker in the midst of the digital revolution is both rich and limited, in my opinion. Elena Gorfinkel, for example, claims that the film is about the "ethical melancholy of the digital abyss,"[11] while Sheldon Gaskell, following Gilles Deleuze's idea of the schizophrenic, argues that "*Holy Motors* can be defined as a new cinema of melancholic longing not only for the past memory of film, but also for the past human that once existed tangibly, before the digital revolution, within the cinema like a gear within a motor."[12] We need to remember, though, that while *Holy Motors* celebrates the analog technology of celluloid in melancholia, it is a film that both is shot digitally and also constructs a hard look back at the history of cinema from the perspective of the digital age. During the opening shot of the dormant audience, almost unnoticeable in the frame is a naked baby running toward the screen shortly before the hellhound appears. Carax is insinuating, perhaps, that every death brings with it a rebirth of something else, and that besides the potential threat that digital poses, it also opens up many possibilities. Is digital really an/the end of cinema in *Holy Motors*? And if so, why and in what sense?

Cinema Will Remain the Same but Will Be Utterly Different: Carax and the Prophetic Discourse on Digital Cinema

It is surely tempting to regard *Holy Motors* as merely a requiem for celluloid filmmaking and to align Carax's position in it with the early apocalyptic discourse that welcomed the digital with statements like the "death of cinema"[13] or "film after film."[14] Carax, however, refuses to surrender to any simplistic reduction of the medium to specific technological features or to embrace a narrow definition of medium specificity. His *Holy Motors*, as Rose Wei notes, questions alternatively "whether the meaning of cinema has evolved or deflated with the emergence of new technologies."[15] It delineates cinema in the digital age as a medium that is drastically changing, but nonetheless keeps essential ingredients intact to remain gripping and fascinating. There are not too many movies like *Holy Motors*, as Daniel Morgan notes, that embrace such balanced approach toward technological change and "look at how new technologies of image production and manipulation fit within, and change or sustain, older cinematic appeals."[16] But first, we need to look back briefly at the prophetic discourse that expressed both the promise and the anxiety generated by the so-called digital revolution in film.

The emergence of digital film technologies within the last three decades has transformed existing modes of production and postproduction, exhibition and distribution, and may constitute "the most extensive reworking of the role of images since the inauguration of cinema."[17] At the same time, the often-heard labeling of this ongoing period of transformation as a "digital revolution" suggests a radical change in media technology, which various commentators have interpreted as a paradigmatic shift, "an epistemological rupture between existing ideas and patterns of thinking and the ways in which ideas will be conceptualized and conveyed in the future."[18] While digital tools have been significantly refining filmic strategies and reinvigorating major traditions, writing about digital cinema, at least in the early stages of its development, has been predominantly focused on treating the newness of digital technology as radically disruptive, a threat to film's traditional characteristics, and the digital age as a historical point of rupture and crisis.

In this vein, a striking number of film and photography scholars treat the *indexical* as a problem child in the digital age, a term against which the digital may be defined, and which it presumably surpasses. As Mary Anne Doane makes clear, "Within film theory, confronted with the threat and/or promise of the digital, indexicality as a category has attained a new centrality."[19] Side by side with such accounts, a growing number of utopian voices about the promise of new digital cameras have been expressed by different filmmakers and documentarists. These overly enthusiastic expressions of faith in the potential of digital equipment focused primarily on how digital video can enable radical gestures of intimacy and immediacy, democratize filmmaking to make it accessible to everyone, and capture the ultimate truth by becoming less intrusive or simply invisible. Those accounts also predicted that DV would thoroughly modify the filmmaking experience and were voiced by several canonical filmmakers whose work has been traditionally associated with celluloid practices.[20]

Both types of reactions, essential to our understanding of *Holy Motors*, tend to focus on quite different aesthetic materializations of the technology. Scholars writing in the first years of digital integration were inclined to focus on the anxiety generated by the presumed loss of indexicality during post-production, while filmmakers who have just "converted" to digital looked at the promising contribution of digital cameras to the production of cinema. Those contradictory tones are not too surprising, considering that "all new technologies in our century—film, radio, television, 16mm film, video, and now digital—have been greeted with equal measures of hope and despair, of optimism and pessimism."[21] Even more importantly, though, both approaches characterize a recurring divergence in thinking often accompanying the advent of new technologies in cinema, maintaining that innovations allow us to undertake activities completely different from those we used to take in the past. "This is change when viewed from the fringe, far from the centre," argues Roger Wyatt. "It's a view of the future that contains a future, not just a past."[22]

Any change, though, can also be viewed from the point of view of the status quo, as merely extending the present indefinitely into the future rather than altering the present completely. When digital technologies were starting to take over and change the different stages of filmmaking in the late 1990s, Thomas Elsaesser prophetically declared that cinema "will remain the same but will be utterly different."[23] In other words, even if digital processes have fundamentally transformed the materiality of cinema, they may have not radically changed the production process or the experience of viewing films. *Holy Motors* exemplifies such a claim, in my opinion, showing how digital entails the reproduction and imitation of prior forms, styles, technologies, and models of production and reception, rather than manufactures something completely new and utterly different. The digital in *Holy Motors* is placed within contradictory junctures of idealized promises and concrete actualities. Carax, then, refuses either to accept the dominant discourse of technological rupture or to surrender to what Philip Rosen calls "the strategy of the forecast," an ongoing attempt to treat digital's characteristics as pure futuristic ideals rather than to ground them in tangible actualities.[24] Carax is looking back not only at more than a century of celluloid film, but also at over twenty years of prolific and multifaceted digital production, in order to account for the ways in which the digital is reshaping and refining aesthetic sensibilities.

Appointments All Day: Blurring the Line Between Acting and Being

Holy Motors has a metamorphic quality as it transitions from one episode to another, blurring any clear boundaries between all performances. Our protagonist, Oscar, puts on various outfits in the limousine, the vehicle through which he makes this nonlinear narrative exploration and becomes a different avatar each time. Arguably, all nine appointments that occur through the course of one day stand for different film genres. Those include, among others, a family drama (a father picks up a fight with his adolescent daughter), a science-fiction fantasy (whose making-of we watch in a motion capture studio), a monster horror film (where a grotesque leprechaun is terrorizing the city of Paris), and a musical (in which Oscar, or perhaps his character, meets his old-time lover). The future of digital cinema happens outside of the movie theater, suggests Carax, but still maintains the rigid boundaries of genre classification. The noticeable and puzzling blur that occurs is in fact not between genres, but between role-playing and real life. On the one hand, Oscar is fully incorporating the personas of his acts (his performance as a dying uncle seems to be prolonged way after the unheard "cut" instruction is given), but on the other hand, he also seems to be completely unaffected by the consequences of his actions (Oscar, whether as an actor or a character, dies several times during the film but manages to wake up and keep on).

This situation seems to be the imagined utopia that derives from the miniaturization of digital cameras. The cheap cost of equipment and stock, the ability to shoot many takes easily, and the increased mobility of the apparatus all result in a different kind of tension between fiction and reality. "Digital cinema allows for a different kind of relationship between actor and camera, because the digital video camera looks in a different way," write Adam Ganz and Lina Khatib; "the boundaries between the actor as person and the actor in performance become less clear when all can be recorded and edited into the finished film."[25] While Ganz and Khatib refer in their illuminating analysis of performance in the digital age to early DV productions such as Abbas Kiarostami's *Ten* (2002) and Lars von Trier's *Dogville* (2003), their lucid arguments echo the bizarre situation that happens in the fictive reality of *Holy Motors*: "Since the digital camera is potentially always on, the performers are potentially always performing."[26] If acting was, since cinema's creation, a mode of being in front of the camera, the ubiquity of video surveillance makes us permanent performers: being simply is acting.

The circular nature of Oscar's performances leads to a situation in which he is not capable of doing anything else other than acting. "You look beat, Dad," his daughter notices when he picks her up from a house party during the fourth appointment. "Yes, appointments all day," he replies. We cannot help but wonder: are we watching another performance, or is he out-of-character now, talking to his real daughter? A few appointments ahead, when Eva Grace (Kylie Minogue) will sing about their mutual daughter, this puzzling moment will ring louder. The unquestioned complicity between performing and being becomes more challenging during that appointment, which is performed around the contours of the musical.

Oscar meets his ex-lover Eva Grace by accident while she is waiting to begin her role as Jean, an air hostess living her last night on earth. "We have twenty minutes to catch up on twenty years," she tells Oscar and then warns him: "After that you will not see me anymore." Is she saying this with the knowledge that she is going to end her life as an actress and not as a character? And when she suddenly bursts out singing about her tragic love affair with Oscar, are we watching another appointment, this time a musical, or is it an act outside of performance, a making-of or behind-the-scenes moment? She then decides to commit suicide and falls to her death shortly after removing her clothes to reveal an air hostess outfit. As a character in costume, does she fall "within character," so she can later come back to life? If so, why is Oscar screaming in terror when he suddenly notices her body on the ground (along with her lover's from their future appointment), and why is he rushing in fear straight back to the limousine, as if to be transferred quickly to another genre? These questions are all left unanswered.

Shortly before the film ends, Oscar leaves for his last appointment of the day and meets his chimpanzee family. This is a startling moment, because it blurs the boundaries again: Is it another performative act, or has Oscar's life become a performance in itself? What, therefore, constitutes a cinematic identity in Carax's universe, and does an actor really have any personal life outside of cinema? When the cars begin to talk immediately after, one of them says to the rest, "Men don't want visible machines anymore," to which another car replies, "Yes, no more action." Such an enigmatic exchange has been interpreted by many, but a possible reading of it could be the future disappearance of any making-of places, in-between spaces where acting is separated from reality. Those cars would probably disappear soon, either because the dormant audience is not interested in film action anymore (e.g., an apocalyptic discourse about the death of cinema) or, more reasonably, because life and art would diffuse into each other. When tiny cameras are always on and the actors are aware of the fact that they are constantly being filmed even while changing costumes, there is no need for "behind-the-scenes" moments.

"I Miss the Cameras": *Holy Motors* as Total Cinema

At one point in the film, a man (Michel Piccoli) appears out of nowhere and engages in a cryptic conversation with Oscar. We soon realize that this man is in charge of the grand celebration of performances we are watching, and he inquires with Oscar what is it that makes him carry on and stay in the business. Oscar replies that he continues to act for the same reason that made him start, "the beauty of the act [*La beauté du geste*]." To this cinephilic impulse the man replies with skepticism, "Beauty? They say it's in the eye, the eye of the beholder." But then Oscar proposes a possibility that the film has been suggesting throughout: "What if there's no more beholder?" In other words, Oscar insinuates that we are watching the making of a futuristic cinema, one where the audience disappears entirely or simply becomes irrelevant. The series of performances may be occurring in a post-celluloid world where everyone is performing in front of an invisible audience while it becomes difficult to understand who *is* in fact "holding" the camera. "I miss the cameras," Oscar admits. "They used to be heavier than us. Then they became smaller than our heads, and now you can't see them at all." The cameras in *Holy Motors* are both ubiquitous and unnoticeable, thus epitomizing an evolutionary stage in a deterministic process of miniaturizing technology in film. Their transparency also dictates their shapeless form, so when they presumably engage in a dialogue with each other at the end of the film, they may borrow the shape of cars (this could be an alternative interpretation for what the cars stand for). One of them says to the other worryingly: "You'll soon have loads of time to sleep! Won't be long till they send us to the junkyard. We're becoming . . . inadequate."

Shortly after World War II, André Bazin proclaimed that what inspired the invention of cinema and carried it through with every single technological invention thereafter (sound, color, stereoscopy, and so forth) is the myth of an "integral realism, a recreation of the world in its own image, an image unburdened by the freedom of interpretation of the artist or the irreversibility of time."[27] Bazin not only theorizes the development of a medium that is fifty years old at the time of his writing, but also envisions its future: "Every new development added to the cinema must, paradoxically, take it nearer and nearer to its origins."[28] For Bazin, the notion of "total cinema" is a myth because every development still carries with it an inherent deficiency in its ability to reproduce reality. Cinematic representations are always measured against how people experience the world, and therefore will always remain incomplete: "Inventors conjure up nothing less than a total cinema that is to provide that complete illusion of life *which is still a long way away*," writes Bazin. 'In short, cinema has not yet been invented!"[29]

The future of cinema, as envisioned by Bazin, becomes the present of *Holy Motors*, one where the recording apparatus, along with the audience watching, turn out to be entirely invisible. Once the medium itself disappears, the complete illusion can presumably occur, and the distance between fictional performance and life itself diminishes: actors have no idea where cameras are being placed, at what point a recording begins or ends, or whether cameras exist at all. They are performing for the sake of the act itself, the beauty of the gesture only.[30] However, even this technological utopia leaves viewers craving for more, just like Bazin imagined. "Some don't believe in what they're watching anymore," complains the man in charge of Oscar. Not unlike the disinterested audience inside the movie theater during the opening of the film, those who watch Oscar's bizarre adventures outside also become uninvolved and indifferent to what they are watching. "Some days," Madame Céline (Edith Scob) suggests to Oscar after he leaves one of his assassination appointments all injured and battered, "even one murder is not enough."

Performance or Visual Effect? Motion Capture and the Ease of Transformation

At the outset of the digital cinema era, film theorists have become more and more interested in how new technologies can create a final break between an image and its referent, focusing on the graphical manipulability of digitized images, and privileging the realm of fantasy film and special effects-laden blockbusters to support such a claim.[31] A solid representative of such a dominant wave of scholarship is Lev Manovich, who attempts in 1995, just when cinema celebrates its first centennial, to characterize new options afforded by the plasticity of the digital image. Manovich argues that when cinema, a medium he defines as "the art of the index,"[32] enters the digital age, it becomes difficult to distinguish it from animation: "It is no longer an indexical media technology but rather a subgenre of painting."[33] According to Manovich, cinema was born from animation (with the early films of Stuart Blackton, Émile Cohl, and Georges Méliès), pushed animation to the margins, only to come full circle and become animation again in the digital age.[34] While Manovich should be praised here for reclaiming the stature of animation within the history of early cinema, such a claim is highly reductive. Without much attention given to the significant portion of live-action digital cinema, Manovich goes so far as to suggest that the automatic recording of reality in cinema "was only an exception, an isolated accident in the history of visual representation."[35] Now, with new options for digital image processing, "cinema becomes a particular branch of painting—painting in time. No longer a kino-eye, but a kino-brush."[36]

The motion capture sequence in *Holy Motors* is a case in point, as it illustrates how Carax's practice is antithetical to Manovich's theoretical stance. It shows how postproduction capacities of digital manipulation can nonetheless retain photographic indexicality and remain entirely dependent on old-fashioned physical performance. Oscar enters a gargantuan movie studio, all dressed up in a dark body suit dotted with motion sensors, and commences a session of an intense acrobatic performance: he engages in a martial-arts dance, runs on a treadmill while holding a machine gun in his hand and fighting imaginary assailants, and even performs a simulated sexual act with a woman wearing a similar latex suit. After a long sequence that emphasizes a techno-human synthesis in which "the bodies of the actors perform their various roles through their material enhancements,"[37] the camera pans to the right and briefly exposes the unimpressive result, a fantasy video game that seems much less inventive than what produced it. We never really see the face of the person who is giving Oscar instructions on his performance, nor do we see the face of the woman, thus granting the whole sequence an alienating quality in terms of its production process.

Daniel Morgan notes that this scene negotiates further the inherent tension between actor and character, because the quick transition from live action to fantasy stands in complete contrast to the intensive preparations Oscar makes inside the limousine in order to "get into character" before each of his appointments (whether that entails putting on makeup, trying different wigs, etc.) According to Morgan, Carax's interest lies in showing us "the *ease* of transformation" that the digital allows from a flesh-and-blood performance to a virtual character (a dragon-like figure), in which "the final product is divorced from the process that produced it."[38] While it is true that movement in the digital age can be easily captured, manipulated, and molded, the scene also shows us that the making of motion capture is more important and interesting than the final result, because it allows Oscar to perform multiple possibilities of the human body. Carax is making clear to us that much is obfuscated by the numeric grid that we finally see on-screen, namely the huge contribution of Lavant's physical performance to the success of the scene. We are asked to marvel at the physical capacities of Lavant as an actor, and the sequence functions as a documentary-of-sorts of these skills. It is here that the envisioned future of film relates back not only to the silent era, when actors relied heavily on their physiognomy to compensate for an inability to express words, but also to the proto-cinematic experiments of Marey and the naked man who runs back and forth at the beginning of the film.

The legitimate place of motion capture as an artistic strategy in animation has been the subject of a heated debate recently. Motion capture is pulled in several different directions at once in the industry, as actors often claim it as a method of performance, while animators label it a visual effect. As Yacov Freedman notes, "By capturing live movement as raw computer data, it [motion capture] exists as an unprecedented amalgam of both recorded and synthetic cinema."[39] Carax's position in this debate, in my opinion, is not simply that digital media fails "to intimately engage the viewer as effectively as the human body behind the digital rendering," as Gaskell suggests,[40] but that motion capture retains a significant performative value that is rendered without the need of a film camera. It is here (again) that Carax demonstrates his balanced approach toward digital cinema and shows how the traditional components of cinema will survive and prolong despite (or simply because of) technological modifications.

Conclusion: Continuity Editing for the Metahistory of Cinema

Holy Motors is a film that poses many challenges for the viewer. It proceeds without any narrative logic, embraces a fragmented and disorienting structure, provides unmotivated character behavior, and produces steady epistemological confusion. The only thing that *Holy Motors* makes clear from its early moments is that it is a film about film, and that its unconventional narrative refers both in content and in structure to the medium of cinema. In *Holy Motors* Carax is paying respect to his characters and actors by placing intertextual references throughout: Kylie Minogue's 2001 hit song "Can't Get You Out of My Head" is playing at the party from which Oscar is picking up his daughter during one of his appointments; Lavant revisits his role as Mr. Merde, referring back to Carax's segment *Merde* in the 2008 anthology film *Tokyo!*; Edith Scob is wearing a medical mask similar to the one she wears in Georges Franju's *Eyes without a Face* (*Les yeux sans visage*, 1960); and there are explicit and periodic homages to the works of Eadweard Muybridge, Étienne-Jules Marey, and King Vidor.

Carax, who was part of the *cinéma du look* French film movement of the 1990s, surely has a tendency to cite other films, but his film is much more than simply a tribute to cinema with postmodern or deconstructive intertextuality. *Holy Motors*, as Elena Gorfinkel notes, "conceives the 'cinema situation,' or our contemporary *dispositif* as a series of unexpected instants";[41] it exhibits an abundance of metacinematic traits, referring, as we would expect in such cases, to itself and to the world beyond itself (including the world of other movies). It entails an intermission (entitled "Entr'acte"), for example, that strangely enough, never really provides a break, neither to the viewer nor to the characters. This alone testifies not only to Carax's interest in exploring boundless performance in digital cinema, but also to his reluctance to meditate on cinema in a purely intellectual manner. As Morgan observes, Carax wishes to "think through the various appeals of cinema, and the kinds of philosophical puzzles it raises, while at the same time remaining within its thrall."[42]

Holy Motors was used in this chapter as a rich case study for evaluating the merits and limitations of mourning cinema's passing era in the midst of the technological revolution. The imaginary landscape of the film, as I have shown, is nonetheless grounded on practice, and envisions what digital cinema can afford, given the current manifestations of technology in both film production and exhibition. Carax is offering us a view of correlations and continuities across the historical gamut of film technologies, thus seamlessly changing his (and our) response to the transition from melancholy to wonder. *Holy Motors* is a film that invites us to re-evaluate today the early rhetoric of crisis, death, and rupture, prevalent in the early days of digital cinema, and to trace not only what has been arguably lost in the transition, but also what could be ultimately gained from it.

Notes

1. Saige Walton, "The Beauty of the Act: Figuring Film and the Delirious Baroque in *Holy Motors*," *Necsus* 3, no. 1 (Spring 2014): 251.
2. Johannes Pause, "Cinema's Journey into Homelessness: Leos Carax's *Holy Motors*," *Transfers* 4, no. 1 (Spring 2014): 133.
3. C. M. Olavarria, "The Church of *Holy Motors*: A Transformation in Metafilm," *Bright Lights Film Journal*, October 31, 2013, https://brightlightsfilm.com/church-of-holy-motors-transformation-in-metafilm.
4. Roland Barthes, "Leaving the Movie Theatre," in *The Rustle of Language*, trans. Richard Howard (Oxford: Basil Blackwell, 1986), 345.
5. Barthes, "Leaving the Movie Theatre," 346.
6. Barthes, "Leaving the Movie Theatre," 348. Italics added.
7. Christian Metz, "On the Impression of Reality in the Cinema," in *Film Language: A Semiotics of the Cinema*, trans. Michael Taylor (Chicago: University of Chicago Press, 1974), 4.
8. Gabriele Pedullà, *In Broad Daylight: Movies and Spectators after the Cinema*, trans. Patricia Gaborik (London: Verso, 2012), 105.
9. Susan Sontag, "The Decay of Cinema," *New York Times*, February 25, 1996.
10. Jocelyn Szczepaniak-Gillece, "Cigarettes, Cinephilia, and Reverie in the American Movie Theater," *Film History* 28, no. 3 (2016): 86.

11. Elena Gorfinkel, "Carax's Oneiric Drive," *In Media Res*, December 11, 2013, http://mediacommons.futureofthebook.org/imr/2013/12/11/caraxs-oneiric-drive.

12. Sheldon Gaskell, "Digital Schizophrenia and Technogenesis in Leos Carax's *Holy Motors*" (master's thesis, Western Illinois University, 2017), 55.

13. Paolo Cherchi Usai, *The Death of Cinema: History, Cultural Memory and the Digital Dark Age* (London: BFI, 2001).

14. J. Hoberman, *Film after Film: Or, What Became of 21st Century Cinema?* (New York: Verso, 2012).

15. Rose Wei, "*Holy Motors*: Leos Carax's Island of Cinema" (master's thesis, Swansea University, 2016), 23.

16. Daniel Morgan, "The Curves of a Straight Line: *Holy Motors* and the Powers and Puzzles of Cinematic Forms," published as "Kurverne i den lige linje: *Holy Motors* og den filmiske gådes kraft," trans. Lasse Winther Jensen, *Krystalbilleder: Tidsskrift for filmkritik* 5 (2015): 30–45.

17. Holly Willis, *New Digital Cinema: Reinventing the Moving Image* (London: Wallflower Press, 2005), 4.

18. Keith Beattie, *Documentary Screens: Nonfiction Film and Television* (New York: Palgrave Macmillan, 2004), 205.

19. Mary Ann Doane, "The Indexical and the Concept of Medium Specificity," *Differences* 18, no. 1 (2007): 129.

20. Iranian filmmaker Abbas Kiarostami, e.g., expressed his newly formed devotion to the format in *10 on Ten* (2004), a prescriptive theoretical film lecture about the possibilities of DV. Using these cameras in films such as *ABC Africa* (2001) or *Ten* (2002), as Kiarostami explains, allowed him to display the "absolute truth" rather than to forge one, to eliminate any artifice embedded in the cumbersome old equipment, and to remain faithful to natural settings. With even more unrestrained enthusiasm, Wim Wenders announced in 2001 that "the future of the cinema no longer lies in its past" (quoted in Shari Roman, *Digital Babylon: Hollywood, Indiewood & Dogme 95* [Los Angeles: iFilm Press, 2001], 35). The new digital technologies, Wenders asserts, are not merely extensions incorporated to film, adding a new dimension to it, as sound did; they are about to take over and replace film, changing everything we know about the craft and the industry (Roman, *Digital Babylon*, 36). Spicing things up even further, David Lynch confessed is his book about new technologies (and meditation) that celluloid, the material he has been so accustomed to work with, is probably becoming a thing of the past: "I'm through with film as a medium. For me, film is dead . . . I'm shooting in digital video and I love it" (David Lynch, *Catching the Big Fish: Meditation, Consciousness, and Creativity* [New York: Penguin Group, 2006], 149). Even Agnès Varda opens her *The Gleaners & I* (*Les glaneurs et la glaneuse*, 2000), a ciné-essay about the meeting between DV and documentary filmmaking, with enthusiasm for the early potential of DV to create different effects than those afforded by film. "These new small cameras," Varda notes in metaphorical terms, "they are digital, fantastic. Their effects are stroboscopic, narcissistic, and even hyper-realistic."

21. Erik Barnouw, quoted in Patricia R. Zimmermann and John Hess, "Transnational Digital Imaginaries," *Wide Angle* 21, no. 1 (January 1999): 149.

22. Roger Wyatt, "The Emergence of a Digital Cinema," *Computers and the Humanities* 33 (1999): 375.

23. Thomas Elsaesser, "Digital Cinema: Delivery, Event, Time," in *Cinema Futures: Cain, Abel or Cable? The Screen Arts in the Digital Age*, ed. Thomas Elsaesser and Kay Hoffmann (Amsterdam: Amsterdam University Press, 1998), 204.

24. Philip Rosen, *Change Mummified: Cinema, Historicity, Theory* (Minneapolis: University of Minnesota Press, 2001), 316.

25. Adam Ganz and Lina Khatib, "Digital Cinema: the Transformation of Film Practice and Aesthetics," *New Cinemas* 4, no. 1 (2006): 26.

26. Ganz and Khatib, "Digital Cinema," 26.

27. André Bazin, "The Myth of Total Cinema," in *What Is Cinema?*, trans. Hugh Gray, vol. 1 (Berkeley: University of California Press, 1967), 21.

28. Bazin, "Myth of Total Cinema," 21.

29. Bazin, "Myth of Total Cinema," 20–21. Italics added.

30. The idea of performing repeatedly before omnipresent cameras has somehow materialized in the recent Soviet production *DAU. Natasha* (2020), which won the Silver Bear for an Outstanding Artistic Contribution at the Seventieth Berlin International Film Festival. Already described as the "Stalinist Truman Show" and blacklisted as pornographic propaganda in Russia, Ilya Khrzhanovsky's harrowing film experiment consisted of creating a closed Stalinist society in the Ukranian city Kharkov, where participants were required to spend three years of their lives cut off from the outside world, living in a thirteen-thousand-square-meter reproduction of a Soviet-era totalitarian regime.

31. See, on this topic, to name only a few central examples, the writings of Lev Manovich, "What Is Digital Cinema?," in *Post-Cinema: Theorizing 21st-Century Film*, ed. Shane Denson and Julia Leyda (Falmer: Reframe Books, 2016), 20–50; Stephen Prince, "The Emergence of Filmic Artifacts: Cinema and Cinematography in the Digital Era," *Film Quarterly* 57, no. 3 (Spring 2004): 24–33; and "True Lies: Perceptual Realism, Digital Images, and Film Theory," *Film Quarterly* 49, no. 3 (Spring 1996): 27–38.

32. Manovich, "What Is Digital Cinema?," 21.

33. Manovich, "What Is Digital Cinema?," 22.

34. Manovich, "What Is Digital Cinema?," 29.

35. Manovich, "What Is Digital Cinema?," 41.

36. Manovich, "What Is Digital Cinema?," 42.

37. Felicity Colman, *Film Theory: Creating a Cinematic Grammar* (New York: Columbia University Press, 2014), 62.

38. Morgan, "Curves of a Straight Line." Italics in original.

39. Yacov Freedman, "Is It Real . . . or Is It Motion Capture? The Battle to Redefine Animation in the Age of Digital Performance," *The Velvet Light Trap* 69 (Spring 2012): 38.

40. Gaskell, "Digital Schizophrenia and Technogenesis," 81.

41. Gorfinkel, "Carax's Oneiric Drive."

42. Morgan, "Curves of a Straight Line."

PART III
AFFECTIVITY AND EMBODIMENT
IN METANARRATIVES

9

Fight Club

Enlivenment, Love, and the Aesthetics of Violence in
the Age of Trump

J. M. Bernstein

Introduction

When reading *The Republic* now it is impossible not to see the prisoners in the
allegory of the cave who accept as real the shadows reflected onto the wall as
actually being in thrall to the silver screen, with the original ascent into daylight as the routine business of leaving the cinema to join the sunlit world.
After that exit from the movies, the philosophical critique of the arts in Book
X reads as just the fuller explanation of an exit we have already undergone
time and again, as if the attraction of the movies and leaving them is part of
what now counts as becoming adult. With scattered exceptions, and they
without wide cultural weight, the razing of the arts in Book X has never been
quite withdrawn; official culture still deposits the arts where Plato left them or,
at best, ignores the Platonic story for a short time, goes to the movies (theater,
museum, concert hall, fictional world), only to be forced out of the darkness
and into the sunlight after an interlude of regression from the demands of
reason and reality.

But this concern for escaping from appearances does not belong to philosophy alone. Near the beginning of David Fincher's *Fight Club* (1999), the
Platonic critique of art and everyday life is echoed when the nameless protagonist, played by Edward Norton, says that with insomnia "nothing's real.
Everything's far away. Everything's a copy of a copy of a copy." "Far away" is
meant to echo Plato's having his prisoners chained to their seats; "far away"
thus signifies that what appears cannot be meaningfully touched or appropriated, that is, what is cannot be brought into a fully satisfying relation to human
needs and desires. Whatever the actual standing of such an item—a couch,
table, or luxury car—it is as if *only* an image, *only* an appearance without a corresponding reality. If we assume that Fincher harbors no commitments to a
world of Forms or Ideas, it follows this he weighs and comprehends the "copy

J. M. Bernstein, *Fight Club* In: *Metacinema*. Edited by: David LaRocca, Oxford University Press. © Oxford University Press 2021.
DOI: 10.1093/oso/9780190095345.003.0010

of a copy of a copy" conundrum differently than Plato: what Plato claims about the ontological deficiency of art, Fincher is claiming about consumer culture; even when the advertised item becomes a material object in the home, it remains an illusory appearance in principle incapable of providing abiding human satisfaction.[1] And this in turn sets up Fincher's defiant critique of Plato: for now, the most potent escape from the life-draining emptiness of consumer culture—an actual world of appearances more enveloping and dangerous than anything Plato could have imagined—is through the passionate and painful enlivenment provided by art. In the movie, the fight clubs where the nameless protagonist and his alter ego, Tyler Durden (played by Brad Pitt), go to escape the everyday are, I will argue, also a metaphor for art and the experience of art; and the movie itself thus a reflection on the meaning of movies in a time of cultural crisis, again echoing an orienting theme of the *Republic*.

At the very least, *Fight Club* screens a sometimes plaintive, sometimes savage, sometimes comic response to Platonic skepticism about the arts. Because either plaintive, or savage, or comic, the response is an *aesthetic* challenge to Platonic anti-aesthetics, hence still exposed to the scalpel of Platonic critique. In this setting, philosophical criticism is the underlaborer to such art, offering back to it the truth content of its aesthetic demonstration.

Fight Club is, however, more than a simple aesthetic critique of modern life; Plato's critical lessons were not totally wrong: art can be dangerous. While the ontological deficiency of the arts is Plato's lead argument (*Republic* 595–602c), his deeper concern is that poetry, especially tragedies, appeals to the wrong parts of our soul (*Republic* 602c–606d), leading us to lament out of season; and thereby, in separating the capacity for feeling and emotion from the control of the reasoning part of the soul, disorienting the soul generally. Heightened affect belongs to the impetus and nisus of the arts; but the conditions that allow for the emancipation of affect from the reality principle equally encourage a search for affect at the expense of reason and the reality principle. Fincher is not naive about the dangers of art forms as sources of critique, escape, and satisfaction; art's *intrinsic* promise of happiness can lead art into the streets, and in extremis, to political excess. In *Fight Club* this excess takes the form of the aesthetic community evolving into paramilitary band of black-shirted fascists set upon very real destruction. The formation and operation of this fascist aestheticizing of politics, with the hopeful anarchist title of "Project Mayhem," now appears to be an all-too-accurate anticipation of the authoritarian tendencies of the Trump presidency.

My argument will fall into two parts. In the first, after providing an outline of *Fight Club*'s aesthetic structure as an allegorical reflection on the meaning and fate of autonomous art in general, I will analyze the central terms of that allegory: fights clubs as metaphors for autonomous art. Of course, that analysis must be put into conversation with the continuing but suppressed shadow narrative, namely, the blocked romance between the nameless protagonist (to whom I shall refer from now on as Jack)[2] and Marla Singer (played by Helena Bonham Carter); at one level, *Fight Club* is a romantic comedy under erasure, a romantic comedy in the time of its disavowal by men, which perhaps, sotto voce, is what romantic comedy is always about. In the second part, I shall use Freud's *Group Psychology and the Analysis of the Ego* with Theodor W. Adorno's essay "Freudian Theory and the Pattern of Fascist Propaganda" (1951) to help analyze Tyler Durden / Brad Pitt and Donald Trump as ego ideals for their fascist followers. I understand such an analysis as equivalent to trying to answer the question, how is fascist politics possible? The surprising answer Freud and Adorno offer is that fascism is one of the forms of love. But this form of love has everything to do with movies and hence the arts generally; in coming to see Donald Trump as a Tyler Durden figure—as the leveling transfiguration of Hollywood charisma in the age of reality television—we not only learn something about the aesthetic deformation of politics, but at the same time and thereby about one of the true dangers intrinsic to the arts.

"Our Great Depression Is Our Lives": Art Among the Ruins

The primary plot of *Fight Club* concerns the developing relation between Jack and Tyler Durden, from their meeting on a plane flight, to Jack asking to move in with Tyler after his apartment mysteriously blows up, to their forming Fight Club, to Fight Club becoming the center of their lives, to Fight Club first spreading throughout the city, then into other cities until it morphs into a fascist paramilitary group whose project is to blow up the downtown city buildings that store our national credit card debt. With everyone's debt erased, society can have a new beginning. This is a utopian thought that has become ever more needful since its being proposed twenty years ago.

Fincher's narrative arc can strike one as opaque: how do we get from the formation of fights clubs to blowing up buildings? And a related query that is also a continuing hermeneutical puzzle about the movie, why does the movie appeal to those who are not drawn by the claim being made for fighting and fight clubs? I understand *Fight Club*'s narrative thread as having a logic and a claim that is other than the immediate appeal of men regaining their manhood through violence, and it is this quasi-allegorical thread, a thread about seeing the fight clubs as themselves metaphors that enable a simultaneous, differentiated response to the movie's narrative progression. My hypothesis is that *Fight Club* presents what might be termed either the natural history (diachronically) or structural anatomy (synchronically) of autonomous art as a form of social critique. Presented narratively in the movie, there is reason to think that what unfolds there is the deep structure of autonomous art in capitalist modernity, that *Fight Club* means to return modernism's critical relation to modernity to the precincts of representational art. And it is *Fight Club*'s insistent allegorical patterning and self-conscious metaphoricity that enables its soldering of filmic representation to modernist social critique.

Let me first outline the seven stages or moments of this structure that, I am claiming, underlie the movie's narrative progression, before elaborating on some central features and episodes.

1. *Insomnia.* In response to socially produced feelings of emptiness and meaninglessness—the dominant metaphor for which throughout the movie is the liminal half-awake, half-asleep state of insomnia—there emerges a need for feeling and expression, a yearning for something through which one could awaken from the insomnia of everyday life. Awaking from insomnia is then the image of reconnecting one's representation of the world with the feelings and emotions appropriate to those representations that have mysteriously evaporated. Insomnia is hence the figure of an appearing world without the affective orientations attaching to it that would make it meaningful. Jack first acquires a sense of the need to reconnect representation and feeling from his participation in support groups for those suffering debilitating or life-threatening illnesses. His addiction to those clubs—where addiction to the affective charge of what removes the "pain" of emptiness is a subtheme in the movie—is to experiences in which the line separating being alive from being dead can be meaningfully drawn because fully *felt* as actual.

2. *Expressive action and the origins of art.* Art begins in everyday expressive gestures, movements, and speaking; these expressive gestures are abstracted from their everyday setting, and then recontextualized into an autonomous form.[3] In *Fight Club* this arc moves from an everyday feeling of a need to be hit to a rule-governed formation of expressive gestures consequent on those feelings: from casual fighting to the formation of fight clubs as wholly autonomous forms of behavior wholly outside the demands and structures of everyday life, wholly outside any practical purpose. The random or sporadic feeling-gesture (the original trading of being hit and hitting outside the bar) and its continuation

into an autonomous form provides in an emphatic manner the essential feeling of aliveness that had been absent from ordinary life. In this mode, art can appear as an extraordinary mode of salvation from the destitution of everyday living, and *therefore* as a critique of that from which it stands apart; art as escape and as answer to a need have never been far apart. As the meaning of this art is clarified through its continuing practice, its role as a mode of critique becomes increasingly evident and significant for its practitioners.

3. *A structural ambiguity in modernist art.* Like all modernist arts, fight clubs suffer from what can become a debilitating ambiguity, an ambiguity that first became manifest in modern dance as it underwent the transition from ballet to modern dance proper as mediated by, say, Isadora Duncan. While Duncan is often credited with critiquing ballet's abstract formalism in relation to natural and spontaneous bodily movement, underlying that critique is a deeper one: between first-person participation (dancing, fighting) and third-person spectatorship (watching dancing or fighting). For Duncan, the dancing body is bodily movement for its own sake, hence the revelation of a suppressed stratum of human embodiment in general. Her dancing not only was a democratization of the dancing body, but invited the transition from spectatorship to participation. Because that division echoes a central feature of consumerism as a form of life that turns participant-feeling into numbed spectatorship, overcoming that separation is central to a critique and an overcoming of this form of life. Part of the seductive success of the fight club is that its founding rules prevent the scission between first and third person, so preventing participant and spectator positions from coming apart. On the contrary, the rules keep them joined—when you first attend fight club, you must fight.[4]

4. *Aesthetic community.* The productive side of the ambiguity between participation and spectatorship—spectatorship promises participation and the satisfaction of participation—is the formation of a highly charged aesthetic community, that is, a community bound together by the affects released in the experiences of participating and spectating. Art experiences in modernity always solicit aesthetic community, a community joined by the binding power of the experience undergone. The undergoing specific to art is that it is experienced as emphatically shareable, and at its height, shared, the establishing of a *sensus communis*; art experiences thus invoke the sharing of a heightened feeling state in relation to a sensuous particular prompt. Not only, then, does art enjoin an affective enlivenment absent from everyday experience, but the precise

aesthetic form of that experience solicits and brings into being an aesthetic community of the living among the lifeless community of everyday life. Art, by reconnecting representation with feeling, is one of the solders through which affect becomes fused with and into community. Throughout *Fight Club*, the members seeing one another on the outside, each identifiable through his bruised and battered face, provides a continuing reaffirmation of their membership in the community of the living.

5. *Transition: the paradox of autonomous art.* Consider stages 1–4 as equivalent to the formation of an autonomous aesthetic practice and community on the model of high-modernist art. Given the intensity of the experience this art provides, the natural question is: why should this art remain *autonomous*, sheltered in a basement or a museum or movie theater? Recall that the social function of this art form is to critique the emptiness of consumer society. The authority of aesthetic experience contains the promise of happiness, the promise that life can have persisting and assertive forms of satisfaction. Art cannot avoid making that promise because here and now, in *Fight Club*, in the movies, we are undergoing an experience of aliveness, and hence we know that aliveness is a real human possibility. Yet, as autonomous, art must at each moment break the promise it makes: you can have the experience of aliveness just so long as it remains without practical reach or significance, just so long as it remains bound within these special locales with these wholly formal rules of making and undergoing; only in those locales and not outside them can the bond between representation and affect be sustained. Think of this as the paradox of autonomous art: art can provide the experience that everyday life evacuates only on the condition that it remains autonomous, its practice sheltered from the exigencies of everyday living, as long it remains without practical purpose.

6. *Avant-garde.* One posited resolution to the paradox of autonomous art is the development of an avant-garde art that contends that art's distance from everyday experience, art's autonomy, is self-imposed, and hence that art practices can and should become connected to everyday life— as happenings, as installation art, as street art, as public art, as graffiti, as pranks, as interventions.[5] *Fight Club* expands into the world, testing whether its form of expression can hold its place amid the very structures it was designed to be averting and subverting. Some of the guerilla activity undertaken is meant to recall Tyler's days as a projectionist splicing a pornographic frame into a family movie, as a waiter placing human

waste in the dishes of the elite, and so on. Such guerilla art involves art connecting to everyday experience by directly intervening in it.

7. *Aestheticizing Politics*: If avant-garde art has as one of its forms the making actual of the aesthetic critique of modernity through direct aesthetic intervention in the world, a natural consequence of this is the thought that modern life needs aesthetic reformation as such and throughout; only an aestheticizing of politics can fulfill the original promise of happiness made by autonomous art. In this way we can trace the natural history that leads from the avant-garde effort of joining art with life to art becoming politics, to the aestheticizing of politics in the manner of fascism. In *Fight Club*, this is represented as the transformation of Fight Club into Project Mayhem. As we shall see, the causal mechanism that allows this final step—the ideology of the leader—diverges from the natural history underlying it, namely, the actualizing of the aesthetic fusion of representation and affect with community.

I take the ease with which we accept the abrupt narrative transitions in *Fight Club* as evidence for this seven-part structure, for the idea that the narrative is tapping into a certain logic of alienation, critique, and overcoming that is bound up with our experience of modernist art. The movie gives form to the claim that the authority of modern art derives, at least in part, from its being experienced as a form of enlivenment in response to the stultifying mechanisms of everyday life. The further structural features follow from the thesis that the experience of aesthetic enlivenment has as its primary characteristic the issuing of a promissory note about the possibility of true living, which in its turn either directly or indirectly leads to the desire to subvert the very autonomy through which art derives its power of critique and enlivenment, with avant-garde art and fascist aestheticizing of politics not merely plausible but historically actual upshots of the desire for subversion.

Although the theme of fighting has been interpreted, for good reason, literally—the need for modern men to rediscover their manhood through violence, which is without question a central thematic element in the movie—that literal interpretation is too narrow to bear the weight of all that Fincher attempts to accomplish: it ignores the setting of those fight clubs in a movie whose fable-like and allegorical dimensions are pervasive. It would be difficult to locate a single moment in the represented world of *Fight Club* that could not bear interpretation in allegorical, metaphorical, or symbolic terms; but if that principle holds for the movie as a whole, then it had better be especially true of it organizing metaphor: fight clubs.

Before addressing the interpretation of fights clubs as allegories of art, a brief canvas of their setting is necessary. Both Plato and Fincher, for different reasons, think everyday life is composed of deceptive and seductive appearances that we need to escape from if true living is going to be possible. I understand the state of insomnia to be an image of a state in which the difference between waking and sleeping has disappeared, and that is because the difference between being truly awake, alive, and truly asleep, dead, has disappeared. For Marla the slippage between sleep and wakefulness occurs with an overdose of sleeping pills. Everything about this movie concerns wakefulness, the need to wake up, the need to be kept awake in order to *live*. Death is of course the Big Sleep. The insomniac is thus a modality of the walking dead, a zombie. Being the living dead is the image that we are offered of a life in consumer society, a life without reality, a life composed of images that mean nothing while remaining nonetheless compelling, all but irresistible. So compelling are the images of consumer goods that acquiring them comes to feel like the satisfying of a true need or necessity; while the reality of this image world is that it drives out all life, all vitality, everything that might count as being awake and alive. Above all, consumer culture obliterates any conception of truly caring, of caring about what deserves to be cared about.

Fight Club's critique of modern life radiates out from the critique of consumer culture, from the ways in which consumer items have become literal fetishes for Jack, items whose appearance in a catalog are sufficient to generate a need and desire not only to possess the item, but to inhabit the image world defined by their presence and arrangement. During the following speech, as Jack mentions a catalog item, it appears in his living room:

> I had become a slave to the IKEA nesting instinct. If I saw something like the clever coffee table in the shape of a Yin Yang—I had to have it. The Klipsk personal office unit, the Hovetrekke home exerbike, The Johanneshov sofa with the Strinne green stripe pattern . . . I would flip through the catalog and wonder, "What kind of dining room set defines me as a person? . . . We used to read pornography. Now it was the Horchow Collection.

Fincher is seeking here to articulate the thesis of consumer culture as the displacing of true living with the illusions of designer goods whose radiance seems to demand possession, pressing the idea to its absurd fulfillment: being defined by one's dining room set—by one's Air Jordans or one's iPhone.

The underside of consumer culture is the vicious side of capitalism, instanced in the movie by Jack's own profession as a recall specialist for a large automobile manufacturer. His job is to investigate accidents, deciding whether it would be cheaper to issue a recall to repair the model in question, or to pay the likely out-of-court settlements for the injuries and deaths caused by the fault. The hollow consumer world of mere appearances is undergirded by the cold calculations of capitalist accounting in which broken bodies and lost lives are variables in a formula. Jack states that he deploys a simple mathematical calculation:

> Take the number of vehicles in the field, *A*, multiply by the probable rate of failure, *B*, multiply by the average out-of-court settlement, *C*. *A* times *B* times *C* equals *X*. If *X* is less than the cost of a recall, we don't do one.

Patently the critique of consumer culture and capital's equal cruelty form the motivation for everything that happens in *Fight Club*. Does *Fight Club*'s brief summation of consumer capitalism's enchantment and viciousness succeed as a critique of capital? Is consumer culture too narrow an object of critique?[6] Narrative film necessarily engages social reality through its impact on particular individuals. *Fight Club*'s driving premise is that even the ordinary inhabitants of the capitalist form of life, that is, even those who *can* benefit from the cornucopia of goods produced, do not in fact benefit but rather are drawn into a dehumanizing half-life—one for which the idea of being in a permanent state of insomnia appears a powerful because easily recognizable metaphor. Whatever else is wrong with liberal capitalism, that it invites and can yield a humanly vacuous form of life is essential to the overall critique one makes of it, quite apart from its cruelty and indifference—a point I shall return to directly.

Jack's mention of his generation as one for whom pornography is replaced by the Horchow Collection in the structuring of their desire insinuates a second thematic axis in the world of *Fight Club*, namely, the withering of erotic desire, and the waning of sexual difference, which jointly are taken as involving a feminizing of culture and a loss of the ideal of masculinity. This theme is introduced when Jack's doctor suggests he go visit a support group for men with testicular cancer if he wants to see real suffering; those really suffering are men who have lost their balls. And if there is hesitancy about how literal to take this literalism, our first glance of Jack in the support group Remaining Men Together is of him pressed into the breasts of Bob Paulsen (played by Meat Loaf Aday): "Bob had bitch tits" is the lead line. Bob, a former gym owner and bodybuilder, whose muscular bulk had enabled him to do product endorsements on TV, had been ruined by steroids. The image of the former ideal male physical specimen now not only feminized but womanized is constructed as the exemplary product, the literal embodiment of capital's joining of seduction through the image with modern science.

Although working through what at the time remained a roiling cultural marker,[7] namely, the idea of a generation of men who had lost a robust conception of manhood,[8] *Fight Club* interprets this cultural trope as *continuous* with the image-character of consumer culture's deformation of eros, and the consequent depletion of the possibilities of human meaningfulness. One hears all these themes rhyming and coming together in Tyler's "middle children of history speech," where the emphasis is on the need and necessity for spiritual renewal. Tyler gives the monologue at the commencement of a Fight Club meeting where a host of new recruits have appeared.

> Man, I see in Fight Club the strongest and smartest men who've ever lived. I see all this potential, and I see it squandered. God damn it, an entire generation pumping gas, waiting tables; slaves with white collars. Advertising has us chasing cars and clothes, working jobs we hate so we can buy shit we don't need. We're the middle children of history, man. No purpose or place. We have no Great War. No Great Depression. Our great war is a spiritual war. Our great depression is our lives. We've all been raised on television to believe that one day we'd all be millionaires, and movie gods, and rock stars, but we won't. And we're slowly learning that fact. And we're very, very pissed off.

That this speech is given by a beautiful movie god matters to the movie's argument; put this aside for the moment. Even if Fincher gives the Iron John, emasculation-and-recovery theme a full-on portrait, he also pointedly locates it within the wider diagnosis of consumer capitalism. One would not know from Tyler's eloquent monologue that this was a movie about fight clubs; rather, it places *Fight Club* in a wider cultural context that is said to be a defining moment in human history whose significance, because spiritual, would be all too easy to overlook. I take the "no purpose or place" as the crux: lives without meaningful direction through time or meaningful location in space.[9]

If the crisis of modernity operates through the suppression of sexual difference and a diluting of erotic desire, then what would be worth desiring? How could desire become meaningful again? Throughout, the image of what deserves to be cared about but which is refused, disavowed, feared, and ignored is Marla. In the world of *Fight Club*, caring finally means caring about Marla, loving Marla, rather than being IKEA boy absorbed in plates with bubbles and imperfections showing they were truly handmade. Jack says in the opening scene, "Suddenly I realized that all this—the guns, the bombs, the revolution—has got something to do with a girl named Marla Singer." We should hear that claim not only in simple narrative terms, or in terms of movie genres (as if male-oriented genres were really about the avoidance and suppression woman-oriented genres), but in human ones. Marla is the point and purpose of it all; she is not a girl, but The Girl. She is the catalyst for the events that follow.[10] Marla is Jack's spiritual twin, since she too exists in a reality drained of meaning and significance in which the gap between life and death is marginal. In her case, it is because she has internalized the truth that death is certain and indefinite, not forever in the future but something that could happen at any moment. In Marla's ironic existentialist ethic, because death could happen now, there is no purpose to asserting or securing the difference between life and death; hence Marla's casual insouciance when crossing the street in the midst of traffic. As a consequence, it is at first unclear why Marla does go to support groups—which is where she and Jack meet; she too is "tourist," just visiting, there for the group uplift rather than because she has the malady the support group aids. Marla's official line is that going to support groups is like going to the movies, only cheaper; and they serve free coffee. (The rhythms of old-fashioned, one-liner stand-up comedy are scattered throughout the movie.) Both her insistence on going to support groups— she too is addicted—and her call for help after taking a sleeping pill overdose indicate an unconscious desire for life. It is Tyler who saves Marla from her overdose, keeping her awake and alive through a night of sexual passion—at least here making literal the "sleeping beauty" myth of the man *awakening* the woman to sexual desire and so life itself.[11] If Tyler embodies what Freud terms the "sensual" as opposed to the "affectionate" form of love, sexual love as opposed to "unsensual, heavenly love,"[12] and if we now remind ourselves that Tyler is a split-off and projected portion of Jack's psyche, then we can say that Tyler is that portion of Jack's psyche which is awakening to desire and life, but only in a mode separated from the bonds of romantic love proper, the great civilizational synthesis of sensual and affectionate love.

Hence, even as *Fight Club* symbolizes a rebellion against feminization and resistance to consumer society, it also explicitly performs an avoidance of love; for most of the movie Jack thinks of Marla as obstacle, annoyance, and competition for Tyler's attention. Nonetheless, the true purpose of Jack's life, would that he realized it, is Marla—which is how the movie concludes, with he and Marla holding hands, watching through the screen-size window, as if at the movies, the buildings of downtown Wilmington, Delaware explode, signaling the possibility of a new beginning. But if the movie ends with Jack and Marla at the movies ready to begin their lives, finally, then given the diagnosis of desire's deformation and depletion, it is evident that there can be no love, no passion, no erotic bonding until the possibility of desire is reignited.

If *Fight Club* has something to do with manhood, it equally has something to do with the reigniting of bodily sensuality, with refinding the path of desire, with acknowledging the need for love—probably in that order. *Fight Club* is, I am arguing, a dark, even savage romantic comedy, a romantic comedy for men about the avoidance of love and the repudiation of romance. Fincher is at least testing the hypothesis that just as male genre movies desperately enact through the auspices of "guns, bombs, and revolution" the refusal of love as the condition of civil order (rather than "marshal" law), romantic comedy interrogates the depth and character of men's refusal of romantic comedy, their refusal of absolute dependence on women; and their refusal of a conception of civilization as defined in accordance with the structures of mutuality and reciprocity that constitute modern love.[13] How can Fincher's movie house these opposing—fighting (guy flick) versus loving (chick flick)—orientations?

Escaping the copy world of appearances requires a recharging of desire, of the demand for satisfaction, and hence an awakening as if to life itself. Fincher's cinematic claim is that in the first instance only more appearances can provide an exit route to the real—appearances that know they are appearances, fictions that know they are fictions and hence do not mistake themselves for reality. This movie is, finally, not about fighting or fight clubs; rather it is a movie about the saving power and necessity of art and fantasy more broadly; this is a movie about the meaning of movies; how, perhaps, only through movies can we be guided back to and so (re)discover reality. I understand the retreat into the unreality of fight clubs as the movie's image of the retreat into art, that fight clubs are the images or allegories of art in that they are set apart from the everyday life of work, friends, and family; hence, fight clubs belong to a space that is not reality; but, although out of the world, they are somehow more intense than the real world; Fight Club provides its participants with the feeling of reality, or, more precisely, it takes intensity of feeling, of corporeal sensibility, as the emergence of reality and as how reality demonstrates its presence and authority. The most immediate feeling of reality is thus pain; hence Fight Club provides a world of meaningless pain, pain without any practical purpose, that is, useless feeling, *feeling for the sake of feeling.*[14] Fight clubs are not life, but they do provide those involved with an *image or semblance* of life, feeling alive, and thus what a life lived with feeling and intensity would be like as opposed to the emptiness of consumer society.

Fight clubs sternly follow the modern idea that works of art are practically useless, purposeless in terms of worldly practice, but nonetheless purposeful in themselves: purposive but without purpose. Such is fighting where there is no reason to fight, no winners or losers, no monetary reward, no worldly result or value apart from the *experience* they provide. Aesthetic experience provides real feelings detached from the real objects normally associated with those feelings (emotions and sensations). Generally, games, play, sport have the same purposive but without practical purpose structure as art, and enable intense feelings and emotions detached from the usual occasions of such feelings and emotions. My suggestion is that rather than this fact providing a good reason for considering fight clubs as a deformed version of a sports club, a boxing gym, say, the shared pattern of separation from empirical reality joined with a structure of purposiveness without purpose is precisely what enables the easy transition from the literal business of purposeless fighting to the metaphorical use of fight clubs in the movie. Sport is the wrong kind of analogy not only because *Fight Club* is indifferent to the sporting ideals of virtuosity and winning, but also because of the way that *Fight Club* connects the return of affect (also available in sport) to the critique of modern life, and how that critique obsesses over a version of the problem of appearance and reality. What is even more surprising is that *Fight Club* enacts the avant-garde critique of autonomous art, coming to see the *inevitable* extension of Fight Club practice as first social disruption, and then aestheticized radical politics. This has never been the trajectory of sport in the modern world, but it has been a repeated gesture within the modern art-world beginning with German romanticism.

In part Fincher is thus reminding us that fundamental to the experience of art is feeling, and one of the functions of the kind of feeling that artworks provide is the feeling of life, of being alive, as if before encountering the work of art we are mortified, dead to the world, insomniacs and zombies one and all. Art criticizes somnolence, and seduces us into an unreal world that feels, because of its affective charge, more real than reality. Fincher might even be construed as arguing that enlivening in this way is the essence of art; and further, that so difficult is it to provide that right kind of feeling, a feeling *for* life in an empty world without feeling, that often pain is the only feeling available. If masochism is a routine of object of film, film violence, representations of brutality and cruelty, is often nothing but masochistic desire projected outward.

Each fight for the fighter is like a mini-tragedy: in a safe setting, they are forced to confront their deepest fears of pain, suffering, and mortality; and each time they have the catharsis of surviving, again. Deep pain is the truest sign of life and wakefulness. Pain has always been the surest sign of sentience, of being alive as such, and the deepest reminder of our mortality. In *Fight Club* useless pain is its own reward. But if the lesson of pain is to succeed, then pain must yield more than momentary aliveness; it must teach the value of life. If Fight Club *seems* to teach Jack some lesson or version of manhood, it mostly *fails* to teach him the value of life, fails to teach him that there is a connection between pain, sacrifice, and value: "Without pain, without sacrifice, we would have nothing." This is why Tyler must continue to press Jack beyond the safety of Fight Club, to bring pain itself into focus, to bring the connection between pain and mortality into focus: first the lye burn; then the threat to kill the innocent store clerk, Raymond K. Hessel ("Tomorrow will be the most beautiful day of Raymond K. Hessel's life. His breakfast will taste better than any meal you and I have ever tasted"); and finally, the "near-life experience" where Tyler intentionally crashes the car. Being fearless can be another way of not caring about the difference between life and death. Hence, at some point Jack must be brought to the possibility of fiercely affirming life; but what would such an affirmation look like?

A Tyler Durden for Everyone: The Divagations of Love

I have argued that the narrative path of *Fight Club* tracks the natural history of art from autonomous art through avant-garde art to its diversion into fascist politics, where the impetus is provided by art's promise of happiness, which is also a promise of community. I have now argued that the anchoring theme of *Fight Club* concerns the avoidances of love, a trajectory that has its culmination in the community of black-shirt fascists. Those two themes come neatly together once we recognize that fascist community is also a work of love. That thesis becomes less surprising when we remind ourselves that aesthetic satisfaction involves and helps secure aesthetic community, such that love of art and love of community are grammatically joined; hence if fascist community belongs to the natural history of autonomous art, then the fascist formation of community must in some manner inherit the logic of aesthetic community. Still, seeing fascist community, or any of its mass-community progenitors, as a work of love is surprising; detaching the question from aesthetics, in *Group Psychology and the Analysis of the Ego*, Freud argues that love is required simply to *explain* the phenomena of mass psychology.

After providing an approving survey of Gustav Le Bon's *Psychologie des foules* (1885), Freud argues that what is missing from Le Bon is an account of the bond holding a mass crowd together. Reminding us that sexual love in the form of "Eros" as depicted by Plato "coincides exactly with the love-force, the libido of psychoanalysis," Freud argues that "love relationships . . . also constitute the essence of the group mind."[15] Freud thinks that only love, only Eros has the force to *bind* individuals together in the manner of a group having the characteristics Le Bon outlines. Although this formula oversimplifies, Freud's

driving idea can be recognized as claiming that the shift from aesthetic subli-
mation to social pathology occurs through a shift in emphasis: aesthetic community is joined by sharing the (erotic) *experience* of the loved object ("We
each experience this"), while aesthetic fascist community is joined by the
(erotic) experience of sharing the loved *object* ("We each experience *this* [*the
leader*]"). Fascism thus becomes one of the forms of love.

Freud summarizes the authoritarian features of the mass group in chapter 2:

> Since a group is in no doubt as to what constitutes truth or error, and is conscious,
> moreover, of its own great strength, it is as intolerant as it is obedient to authority.
> It respects force and can only be slightly influenced by kindness, which it regards
> merely as a form of weakness. What it demands of its heroes is strength, or even vi-
> olence. It wants to be ruled and oppressed and to fear its masters. Fundamentally it
> is entirely conservative, and it has a deep aversion to all innovations and advances
> and an unbounded respect for tradition.[16]

Certainly this description of the (fascist) mass group strikes a series of familiar notes; but, again, Freud's thought is that without a psychodynamic accounting, we have a description without an explanation. What binds such a
community? How are those distinctive features of it to be explained? Only
Eros has the power to (freely) bind a group in this manner. Some formation of
love must be at stake, but one in which the bond holding the group together is
somehow connected to the leader, the master.

This returns us to what at first looks like a typically suppressed representation of homoerotic bonding between Jack and Tyler until we discover, toward the end of the movie—although there have been clues throughout—that
Jack and Tyler are one. Only by the time we reach this juncture, the puzzle
about Tyler has deepened since he is not only Jack's idealized other, but also
the charismatic leader of Fight Club who has guided the club first through its
avant-garde experiments, and then into the formation of a paramilitary group
preparing for mass destruction. In the language of psychoanalysis, charisma
has something to do with the leader as an ego ideal. In *Group Psychology*,
Freud distinguishes the ego ideal in its ordinary existence and manifestations
from the devolved ego ideal of the mass group. Behind this thesis is the
thought that the ego ideal has two distinct sets of functional orientations. First
is the familiar idea that usually goes under the heading of "superego"; these
include the functions of "self-observation, the moral conscience, the censorship of dreams, and the chief influence in repression."[17] In describing the opposing functional orientation of the ego ideal—the one usually considered
under that head—he emphasizes that it "is the heir to the original narcissism

in which the childish ego enjoyed self-sufficiency; it gradually gathers up from the influences of the environment the demands which that environment makes upon the ego and which the ego cannot always rise to; so that a man, when he cannot be satisfied with his ego itself, may nevertheless be able to find satisfaction in the ego ideal which has been differentiated out of the ego."[18] The ego ideal is both the self one wants to be, should be, ought to be, but also, in is narcissistic inheritance, who one most emphatically is or must be. Under the conditions in which the pathology of mass psychology comes into effect, the repressive, conscientious functions of the ego ideal disappear in the face of its function as the heir of narcissistic self-love that, in coming to represent one's ideal self, can preserve one's sense of self-worth in moments of duress.

In the world of *Fight Club* duress has become the norm in part because in the genial consumer culture, in the world without fathers, no viable dual-functioned ego ideal was ever formed—only a weak ego ideal in the absence of superego functions. As a consequence, in this world even the difference between self-love and self-contempt is hard to sustain—as our original encounters with Jack and Marla demonstrate; they are simultaneously self-absorbed, self-pitying, self-loathing, and without a meaningful self. The obvious question to ask here is *how* in a world so devoid of effective ideality can the protagonist find an ego ideal; where in the desert of American consumer culture are viable ego ideals to be found? Since no ordinary ego ideal is sufficient for the critical purposes to hand (that is just what has disappeared from the developmental landscape), only a heavily idealized ego ideal will do. As Jack plumbs the memory bank of his unconscious, the only image of a better self available is that of a Hollywood star: the charismatic beauty of Brad Pitt. Although the alter ego figure has a proper name (unlike nameless Jack), Tyler Durden, everything in the movie turns on his being Brad Pitt, that no viewer of the movie can fully separate Tyler Durden the character from the truly ripped and beautiful movie star. Movie stars were, precisely, the literally larger-than-life beautiful figures who were always identifiable as themselves in each of their roles; as stars their function was to erotically shine, their charismatic beauty soliciting like love (= I want to be "like" you, be you) just as emphatically and urgently as object love (= I want to sexually have you, possess you). Hollywood stardom was, throughout the heyday of the movie era, the safe space for the production of narcissistic ego ideals. Male Hollywood stars could be ideals of power, masculinity, sexiness, courage, freedom, whose distance from their audience generated the space for idealization and whose narcissistic indifference to their audience enabled adoration without the possibility of the failure of reciprocity to become an issue. Hence the soft pathology of fan love: rapture for the larger-than-life screen *image*, where the separation of the "star" from each role she or he inhabits allows a sufficient tincture of reality to enter into the work of idealization and attachment. Hollywood stardom operates through and as the formation of (like love) ego ideals.

How can this identification with an ego ideal function to organize a group? Freud's punctual answer is this:

> A primary group of this kind [which has a leader and has not been able by means of too much "organization" to acquire secondarily the characteristics of an individual] is a number of individuals who have put one and the same object in place of their ego ideal and have consequently identified themselves with one another in their ego.[19]

Each of the members of Fight Club make Tyler their ego ideal; that is, they each substitute him for their own ego ideal, each identifying with this beautiful being who loves only himself—who need love only himself since he is nothing but a narcissistically enjoined ego ideal. It is then the business of each *substituting* the figure of Tyler for their ego ideal rather than merely having him as a partial love object that joins them into a community. In making Tyler their ego ideal, each member of the group can surrender his ego to the ideal, surrender separateness, surrender authority over what is to be done, surrender needing a voice of his own, surrender his very self to the leader: "You are not a beautiful and unique snowflake" is the Project Mayhem mantra.

In our American present, it was not a Hollywood star, but an *equally imaginary figure* from reality television who took up the surplus of societal duress and disappointment. Reality television recognized something about the medium of television that had not previously been adequately recognized, namely, picking up on the implication of Andy Warhol's quip, "In the future, everyone will be world-famous for fifteen minutes." It would seem to be possible that *any man or woman*, hence someone without any natural charisma but appropriately packaged, given some grandiosity of character, could become a "star," an ego ideal. Reality television is a mechanism for making "stars" out of everyman/everywoman figures—Snooki from *Jersey Shore* or Omarosa from *The Apprentice*. Donald Trump was and is a reality television star generated by a culture industry whose precise mechanism in this instance involved deleting the difference between larger-than-life Hollywood stardom and reality, letting the star mantle fall on a common-man caricature. Reality television is the effort of deleting the difference between Hollywood stars and everyman/everywoman stars. Without the hybrid mixture of fantasy and reality of reality television, there is no Donald Trump, that is no figure of narcissistic idealization who could cross over into political space. For his followers, there is no crossover: Trump is a fantasy figure installed in a fantasy reality that was indistinguishable from reality. *Donald Trump is Tyler Durden for everyone (for everyman)*, or more accurately, since both are ego ideals for everyone, *Donald Trump is the everyman Tyler Durden for everyone.*[20] There is no "fascist propaganda," that is, there can be no empty messages that are nonetheless capable of forging an affectively charged social unity without the dynamics of narcissistic identification. That is the source and character of Trump's power.

The social bond through which Trump is connected to his followers is exorbitant. In "Freudian Theory and the Pattern of Fascist Propaganda," Adorno adopts Freud's analysis of the mass group to reveal its precise fit with fascism—a fit that spills over uncannily onto the American present. The Adorno-Freud analysis of this kind of exorbitant bond between leader and follower requires, again, a particular formation of the most powerful forms of human bonding available: love and hate, where the formation of social love lives off and depends on social hatred. What makes this formation authoritarian is that *both* the love and the hate, both the identification with the leader *and* the negative integration through hatred of some out-group, are empty. Adorno begins pacing out the argument this way: because the leader is, above all, an *image*, and further because there are so few positive contents available with which to hold the authority of the leader in place, then a negative integrating force needs to be found. As he recognizes, Freud had already come upon the idea of negative integration: "The leader or the leading idea might also, so to speak, be negative; hatred against a particular person or institution might operate in just the same unifying way, and might call up the same kind of emotional ties as positive attachment."[21] But because the bonds of love connecting leader and followers (and followers with themselves) is without substantive content, receiving all its authority from what it repudiates—blacks, Muslims, migrants, women, Jews, fact-based news, and so on—then "negative integration feeds on the instinct of destructiveness."[22] Said differently, because there is no content to the collective bond, where the stakes of the collective bond are self-love itself, where the capacity to have a conception of oneself as worthy and lovable that is conferred through group membership, any criticism of the group or the leader is intolerable: dogmatic rigidity is a consequence of a value vacuum that has only violence with which to respond to criticism. Because the criticism cannot be rationally rebutted, the critic must be destroyed. Hence, when Trump claims that nothing can detach his followers from him, he is recognizing that the circuit of mutual dependence is a matter of ego survival for each: to become separated from one's like-love object of love would mean losing the capacity for that minimal form of self-love required in order to care about oneself at all.

While the broad outlines of this analysis are compelling, what is unnerving and uncanny about Adorno's essay is how accurately it point-by-point accounts for the Trump phenomenon as a particular development of the Tyler Durden paradigm. Among the characteristics of the Trump phenomenon that Adorno's analysis highlights are:

- Because of the ordinariness of the ego ideal, it follows that there is only a small gap between ego and ego ideal. Because there is only a small gap between ego and ego ideal in the group, then the superego functions, the usual functions of self-observation, scrutinizing, and moral conscience, lapse when one joins the group by identifying with the leader. Because there is thus nothing left to separate oneself from the group, "individuals are made to undergo regressions which reduce them to mere members of a group" (119). Black shirts for everyone or MAGA hats are mechanisms for acknowledging that this regression has occurred.
- Thereby, "In a group the individual is brought under conditions which allow him to throw off the repressions of his unconscious instincts" (117).
- This is equally why "the potential short-cut from violent emotions to violent actions" (118) belongs to the logic of group psychology.
- "While appearing as a superman, the leader must at the same time work the miracle of appearing as an average person . . . as a composite of King Kong and the suburban barber" (122), a composite of a powerful billionaire and an uncensored, politically incorrect, louche womanizer. What struck Adorno as working a "miracle" is precisely what reality television made possible for Trump.
- Adorno highlights "the leader's startling symptoms of inferiority, his resemblance to ham actors" (122).
- "The leader can guess the psychological wants and needs of those susceptible to his propaganda because he resembles them psychologically" (127); it is this that explains how an apparent lack of intellect is compatible with a kind of political brilliance, a remarkable capacity to dominate the political conversation and every news cycle, keeping his followers in thrall. (Something of instinctively knowing how to use new media like Twitter is also but centrally involved here.)
- "The famous spell they exercise over their followers seems largely to depend on their orality: language itself, devoid of its rational significance, functions in a magical way" (127).
- "The objective aims of fascism are largely irrational in so far as they contradict the material interests of great numbers of those whom they try to embrace" (129).

- "The category of 'phoniness' applies to the leaders as well as to the act of identification on the part of the masses and their supposed frenzy and hysteria." The followers do not "completely believe their leader. They do not really identify themselves with him but act this identification, perform their own enthusiasm, and thus participate in the leader's performance" (131).
- "The continuous danger of war inherent in fascism spells destruction and the masses are at least preconsciously aware of it" (129).

I could go on. In general, however, it would appear that these distinguishing characteristics all derive from or are otherwise symptoms of the specific erotic intensity and value emptiness of the social bond between leader and followers. Hence, when during the 2016 election Trump bragged, "I could stand in the middle of Fifth Avenue and shoot someone and I wouldn't lose any voters" (January 23, 2016), he was grasping something about the social-psychological bond between his core supporters and himself that his critics have noted but ignored. The signature threat of the Trump presidency lay in the specific character of his bond with his followers since it is this bond that marks the arrival of a new form of authoritarian nationalism into American politics. Trump intuitively understands that it is the specific character of the bond with his followers that is the source of his political authority, which is why he continued throughout his presidency to address his attention primarily to them, while ignoring the rest of the American populace. Reaching beyond his base was irrelevant for the kind of power he possessed and sought to maintain, namely, the continuous circuit of narcissistic love between him and his followers devoid of any content apart from the erotic bond itself.

Fight Club pointedly underlines the dangers in this constellation; this is part of this movie's intelligence: it knows better than its audience that aesthetic pleasure is not innocent, and that fantasies are dangerous. Tyler's charismatic fearlessness is his not caring much about individual lives; thus his invulnerability—even if you shoot him he does not die. But then being a fantasy hero, he exemplifies the dangers of fantasy: Tyler's own fantasy of a black-shirted fascist army of nameless members dreaming of an anarchic future. Fight clubs are, again, also *a substitute for reality*, a place of avoidance, above all avoiding Marla by fighting instead of loving; only Tyler, the fantasy hero, can risk making love to Marla. Loving is far more threatening and dangerous than fighting since in sexual love as opposed to fight clubs there are no frames, no rules, no way to tap out. Of course, you must risk something in order to fight, just as you must be willing to risk something in order to truly engage with artworks. But the risk of Fight Club is minor compared to the risk of love—bodily pain is frightening, but once suffered you realize you can survive it; the pain of love and loss almost always appears as if it cannot be survived; and the loss of love always appears as a form of dying.

Fight Club can morph into a neo-fascist community because it is itself a small, rule-governed and *nearly* neofascist community, that is, a community determined, like an artwork, by strict rules that have no meaning outside it—"The first rule of Fight Club is you do not talk about Fight Club"—a community in which one can participate anonymously, joined with others through participation in its simultaneously complete and empty practice. I take Fincher to be arguing that art in a consumer society can barely avoid becoming an image of what it means to resist—fight clubs become another consumer item, a new fashion and a new franchise, again the small but an emphatic transition from community in *sharing* the object of passion to community in sharing the *object* of that passion as one's ego ideal. Tyler Durden is a brand; Donald Trump has always wanted more than anything to be the brand: Donald Trump.[23] The movie's humor both supports and undermines its fantasy myth-making. And when art and politics are confused with one another, when politics is aestheticized, and aesthetics made into politics, then one deeply plausible result is nihilistic destruction—which Fincher appears to be both enchanted and disgusted by (a fantasy of a left politics in which no one suffers). The very moment that Jack finally kills his fantasy double, Marla appears, and they both return to being spectators at the movies. Here it is enough to say that fight clubs stand for art and formalism; but art is, again, *only the promise of happiness*. Dissatisfaction with that promise can lead to the avant-garde desire to break down the wall or window or screen separating art and life, to turn art into politics and politics into art, so confusing art and life, whose only result here is destruction. This is the temptation that Tyler insists upon and Jack finally learns to resist.

And that is why the movie ends with Jack and Marla at the movies. Being at the movies is, of course, still being in the dark, and thus a very different business from living happily ever after. We still do not know if true life is possible in this culture. But the scene of Jack and Marla together is the picture of the knowledge that a beginning can be made, and that knowing the movies for what they are—which is knowing also the terrible dangers of both disappointment and fanaticism that belong to the logic of aesthetic pleasure—is knowing the difference between appearance and reality that only the appearance world of movies makes both possible and satisfying.[24]

Postscript (April 1, 2021)

Donald Trump lost the 2020 Presidential Election to Joseph Biden by over 7 million votes, and he lost the Electoral College by 74 votes, 306 to 232. To this day, Trump has not conceded that he lost the election. On the contrary, even before the election, Trump was arguing that the election was rigged; and afterwards, he continued to insist that the election was fraudulent, that it had been stolen from him. Somewhere between half and three-quarters of all Republicans continue to believe Trump's baseless claims that the election was invalid.

On January 6, 2021, the day in which the Congress of the United States had gathered to validate the Electoral College votes and officially declare Biden the victor, Trump organized a rally at the Washington D.C. Ellipse. Before some 30,000 followers, Trump repeated his allegations that the election was stolen, criticizing Vice President Mike Pence by name a half-dozen times, accusing fellow Republicans of not doing enough to back up his allegations, and stating that he would walk with the crowd to the Capitol. At that point a huge tranche of supporters descended on the Capitol, and slightly before 2:00 pm broke through the barricades and entered the building through smashed windows. At no time in the history of the United States has the Capitol building been successfully invaded. What occurred on January 6th was a failed coup. The following day, in the vote to confirm the Electoral College results, over one hundred members of Congress and eight members of the United States Senate continued to support Trump's blatantly false claims about the election.

Two far-right extremist groups, supporting ultra-nationalist, white supremacist and patriarchal sexist beliefs, the Proud Boys and the Oath Keepers (an anti-government militia organization), were involved in planning and carrying out the insurrection and attempted overthrow of the election. Even before the riot, the Southern Poverty Law Center (SPLC) had identified the Proud Boys as a new "alt-right fight club."[25] This identification is not happenstance: the events of January 6th—from the propagandist libeling of the election to the insurrectional violence—followed the pattern of charismatic bonding becoming political fascism becoming political violence, as proposed in this chapter. While the claim that Trump is a charismatic personality is widespread, the fierce loyalty his followers have evinced throughout the post-election period, and their clear willingness to risk their lives for him require the recognition that fascism is a form of love. At the Republican nominating convention in 2020, Trump did not even bother to propose a platform of policy goals and value commitments for the upcoming 2020 election; from the beginning, loyalty to him, and hence to the ego ideal displayed by him that bound his followers into a community of the disaffected and betrayed, was what the election was about. In his 1967 lecture "Aspects of the New Right-Wing Extremism," Adorno argued that propaganda—authoritative baseless beliefs—was the mechanism of fascism, and what mattered was primarily "power, conceptless praxis and, ultimately, unconditional domination."[26]

As Timothy Snyder has persuasively argued, what turned the already dangerous Trump phenomena into an authentic fascist irruption was the extraordinary breadth and size of "the big lie" that, contrary to all evidence, the election had been stolen. Love of the charismatic leader allowed, continues to allow millions of American to embrace wild fiction in place of ordinary reality: "The force of a big lie," Snyder argues, "resides in its demand that many other things must be believed or disbelieved. To make sense of a world in which the 2020 presidential election was stolen requires distrust not only of reporters and of experts but also of local, state and federal government institutions, from poll workers to elected officials, Homeland Security and all the way to the Supreme Court. It brings with it, of necessity, a conspiracy theory: Imagine all the people who must have been in on such a plot and all the people who would have had to work on the cover-up." But this big lie, like the original Nazi one about the Jews, has a lining of unqualified racism: "At bottom, the fantasy of fraud is that of a crime committed by Black people against white people."[27] The Capitol riot intended a new beginning for the republic as fully as the blowing up of the credit card companies in Wilmington, Delaware (the home of President Biden) that concludes *Fight Club*. The fiction of a new beginning is what movies have always offered their sleepless Marlas and Jacks. Whether the events of January 6th betoken only an eruption of fiction into reality or the beginning of fiction overtaking reality is undecided. In these circumstances, Adorno's own concluding words are apt: "How these things will continue, and the responsibility for how they will continue, that ultimately lies in our hands."[28]

Notes

1. Throughout, I will employ the convention of ascribing the words, thoughts, and claims made by a movie to the director. In this case, as Fincher would be the first to acknowledge, credit must be shared by Chuck Palahniuk's novel, *Fight Club* (New York: Norton, 2005 [original 1996]); the script by Jim Uhls; together with later input by Fincher and the two male leads. The fundamental conceit that I am crediting to the movie of being an allegory about the meaning of art is patently not a part of the Palahnuik's novel—it really is about

fight clubs where Gen X men go to recover their manhood. That said, some of the best lines in the movie are taken straight from the novel.

2. While the namelessness is necessary to keep Jack's and Tyler's actual identity hidden, there is also the metaphorical thought of Jack being a nameless function of consumer culture. "Jack" is how he is referred to in the script and how he refers to himself in his role as narrator when he imitates the language of a magazine that introduces the parts of the body in an intimate first-person manner to express his feelings: "I am Jack's raging bile duct."

3. For this account of the origins of art, see Suzanne Langer, *The Problems of Art* (New York: Charles Scribner's Sons, 1957), ch. 1. It might be noted here that sports have an analogous origin, namely, taking effortful human actions of running, jumping, throwing, fighting (wrestling) and separating them from their practical setting in order that they can be elaborated in their own right. The natural interpretation of this placing of human abilities into a purposive setting (competition) without a practical purpose is that they allow the celebration of the types of (antigravity) virtuosities of which the human body is capable. Something of the celebration of the virtuosity of the human body is shared by sport and the arts, especially dance as the "first" art. Why not then say, as the Press's reader urged in criticism of this essay, that fight clubs are just some version of sport? Is it not more natural to connect fighting with sport than with art? As I will say more about later, a central reason why fight clubs are not primitive forms of sport is because they are antipathetic to virtuosity. Fights clubs do not recover the origins of boxing or mixed martial arts in street fighting, but rather seek, in a set-apart, purposeless form of fighting, a formation of enlivenment usually associated with the arts. For an unvarnished defense of the claim that art, especially in the form of beauty, is for the sake of enlivenment see Elaine Scarry, *On Beauty and Being Just* (Princeton, NJ: Princeton University Press, 1999): "Beauty is lifesaving. . . . Beauty quickens. It adrenalizes. It makes the heart beat faster. It makes life more vivid, animated, living, worth living" (24–25). Scarry says too little in her account about why life should need to be living; that life can systemically stop living and require enlivenment is Fincher's starting place. That fighting becomes recognizable as an indirect form of social critique *to its practitioners*—which becomes the dominant theme of the movie—is another good reason for thinking that fighting here is an art metaphor rather than a literal instantiation of the value of sport: sport may provide a form of enlivenment too, but it does not do so as an explicit form of social critique. Finally, it is a dominant motif of modernist art that beauty is no longer available, that art beauty is now pacification, not enlivenment, and hence that the work of enlivenment has been passed to the artistic sublime in which the experience of pain is the necessary prelude to aesthetic satisfaction.

4. Sport too, I should concede, suffers from and sometimes works against the dualism between spectator and participant. However, while overcoming that dualism is essential to *Fight Club*, its function is to overcome the dualism between spectator-representation and participant-feeling, which belongs to the critical/therapeutic function of the practice.

5. The best statement of the critique of autonomous art by avant-garde art is Peter Bürger, *Theory of the Avant-Garde*, trans. Michael Shaw (Minneapolis: University of Minnesota Press, 1984).

6. Henry A. Giroux and Imre Szeman, "Ikea Boy Fights Back: Fight Club, Consumerism, and the Political Limits of Nineties Cinema," in *The End of Cinema as We Know It: American Film in the Nineties*, ed. Jon Lewis (New York: NYU Press, 2001), 96: "*Fight Club* has nothing substantive to say about the structural violence of unemployment, job insecurity,

cuts in public spending, and the destruction of institutions capable of defending social provisions and the public good."

7. Poet Robert Bly's *Iron John: A Book about Men* was published in 1990, and spent over a year on the bestseller list. In contemporary culture, the same idea of a crisis in masculinity is pursued with the same cultural fervor by the Canadian psychologist Jordan Peterson.

8. Reasons given for this change include transformations in culture generally, its becoming more civil and caring, less competitive (in the decades before the onset of neoliberalism), etc., or the waning of the Oedipus complex, a thesis supported by critical theory (see Theodor W. Adorno, *Minima Moralia: Reflections from Damaged Life*, trans. E. F. N. Jephcott [London: Verso, 2006], fragment 2), or because of the increasing literal absence of fathers in the home.

9. It would take another essay to give a full genealogy of the fear that bourgeois society is constitutively empty, incapable of housing defensible forms of human practice that could yield value-saturated, non-transient forms of satisfaction. It is there in the romantic criticism of science and industrial society; it is present in the emergence of the aesthetic of the sublime in the eighteenth century. Most obviously, the trend begins properly with Kierkegaard's clarion call: "A revolutionary age is an age of action; ours is the age of advertisement and publicity. Nothing ever happens but there is immediate publicity everywhere," in *The Present Age: On the Death of Rebellion*, trans. Alexander Dru (New York: Harper & Row, 1962), 6. The same thought is there in Nietzsche's last man who is tired of life, or in *On Liberty*, John Stuart Mill's everyman who lives "as under the eye of a hostile and dreaded censorship. Not only in what concerns others, but in what concerns only themselves, the individual, or the family, do not ask themselves—what do I prefer? or, what would suit my character and disposition? or, what would allow the best and highest in me to have fair-play, and enable it to grow and thrive? They ask themselves, what is suitable to my position? what is usually done by persons of my station and pecuniary circumstances? or (worse still) what is usually done by persons of a station and circumstances superior to mine? I do not mean that they choose what is customary, in preference to what suits their own inclination. It does not occur to them to have any inclination, except for what is customary" (Harmondsworth: Penguin Books, 1986, 125–26). A similar thought is there in chapter 1 of *Walden* where Thoreau states: "The mass of men lead lives of quiet desperation. What is called resignation is confirmed desperation. From the desperate city you go into the desperate country, and have to console yourself with the bravery of minks and muskrats. A stereotyped but unconscious despair is concealed even under what are called the games and amusements of mankind. There is no play in them, for this comes after work. But it is a characteristic of wisdom not to do desperate things" (New York: The Library of America, 1991, 9). The destitutions of late capital's consumer culture are a recognizable apotheosis of this series.

10. I am assuming that Fincher is here wholly self-conscious in making Marla the instigation for the movie's action but not a participant; that he has absorbed and is commenting on Laura Mulvey's thesis of the Hollywood female figure as "image" or "spectacle," as connoted by "to-be-looked-at-ness" that inspires "him" to feel and act. Laura Mulvey, "Visual Pleasure and Narrative Cinema," in her *Visual and Other Pleasures* (London: Palgrave Macmillan, 2009), 19–20.

11. It is a further declension of the sleeping beauty myth that it elides utterly the difference between rape and consensual sex. The fullest interrogation of this aspect of patriarchy is

Pedro Almodóvar's *Talk to Her* (2002). In this movie, Almodóvar places both female lead characters in a coma, thus making Mulvey's "to-be-looked-at-ness" thesis so literal as to be unavoidable.

12. Sigmund Freud, *Group Psychology and the Analysis of the Ego*, trans. James Strachey (New York: Bantam Books, 1960). Given there is no edition whose pagination is standard, I will provide chapter followed by page number. Here: VIII.55.

13. Fincher has said *Fight Club* is *The Graduate* (1967) for Gen X, a thought he acknowledges with the final scene, echoing the image of Benjamin (Dustin Hoffman) and Elaine (Katherine Ross) fleeing her wedding, sitting together at the back of the bus as they escape the snares of the vapid middle-class life their parents had designed for them. *Film Club's* scriptwriter, Jim Uhls, has said he thinks of it as a romantic comedy. On the reading I am offering, Fincher is critically interrogating the duality between the male movie genres that express the value of social order (westerns, war, noir) versus the female genres that celebrate the values of social integration (melodramas and romantic comedies), where the first concerns the policing of contested space, while the latter concern the habitation of always already civilized space—following Thomas Schatz's schema in *Hollywood Genres: Formulas, Filmmaking, and the Studio System* (New York: McGraw-Hill, 1981). *Fight Club*, I am tempted to say, operates as a form of nostalgia for the genre of social order—where violence was necessary, and men were the protectors of a threatened world—in the time of its disappearance. Because the disappearance is real, the nostalgic reading of the film, embracing the Iron John mythos, tends to eclipse Fincher's considered verdict about its disappearance. To rehearse a serious conversation between these deep genre orientations is central to *Fight Club's* achievement.

14. The idea of pain, especially masochistic pain, as a saving gesture is almost a film genre of its own. Horror movies are premised on the pleasure of being terrified; but explicit masochism is there in *Belle de jour* (1967), *Last Tango in Paris* (1972), *Crash* (1996), *The Piano Teacher* (2001), and on. The direct need for masochistic pain is there in *Black Swan* (2010) and *The Wrestler* (2008).

15. Freud, *Group Psychology*, IV.30–31.

16. Freud, *Group Psychology*, II.14.

17. Freud, *Group Psychology*, VII.52.

18. Freud, *Group Psychology*, VII.52.

19. Freud, *Group Psychology*, VIII.61. I have removed the italics from the original.

20. I owe this phrase to Katie Kelly. A reader for the press objected here that I fail to account for the disanalogies between Tyler Durden and Trump, above all that Durden possesses integrity, attractiveness, and intelligence. I certainly want to agree that the movie for the viewer would fail if Durden did not have these characteristics; there is something of a classical ego ideal about Tyler Durden. But, and it is this Fincher is depending on, it is not those features that account for the charismatic authority of the Durden-Pitt figure, of all those moments when it is the beautiful, ripped, and roguish Brad Pitt as Tyler Durden that is the object of the shared gaze of Fight Club members and the movie viewers. This is most explicit and self-conscious in the bus scene where Durden mocks the image of the advert of the ripped guy in Gucci underwear. On the other side, it is important to see Trump as his adorers see him: as successful, powerful, roguish, against etiquette, capable of attracting beautiful women, etc.; he is *their* Durden-Pitt figure. Finally, in understanding how alike and how different Durden and Trump are, it is important to grasp the meaning of the

transition from Hollywood charisma to reality television charisma. Since Trump is closer to the model sketched by Adorno than Durden is, it also needs saying that Fincher plainly thinks that *we*, you and I, require something of the force of Hollywood charisma in order to undergo and find plausible the experience of charismatic authority had by the members of Fight Club. Durden-Pitt is the form of charisma we can experience even as we continue to find the charismatic authority of Trump experientially baffling.

21. Freud, *Group Psychology*, VI.41.

22. Theodor W. Adorno, "Freudian Theory and the Pattern of Fascist Propaganda," in *The Culture Industry: Selected Essays on Mass Culture*, ed. J. M. Bernstein (London: Routledge, 1991), 125. Further references to this essay in the body of the text will be referenced as Adorno, followed by the page number in this edition. This stretch of the essay is borrowed from my "Reading Adorno's Essay on Fascist Propaganda in the Age of Trump," *Public Seminar*, October 5, 2017, http://www.publicseminar.org/2017/10/adornos-uncanny-analysis-of-trumps-authoritarian-personality/. At the same place, one can find a like-minded essay by Vladimir Pinheiro Safatle, "Adorno's Freud in the Age of Trump." And, again applying the Adorno essay to Trump, see Claudia Leeb, "Mass Hypnoses: The Rise of the Far Right from an Adornian and Freudian Perspective," *Berlin Journal of Critical Theory* 2, no. 2 (July 2018): 59–81.

23. On this aspect of *Fight Club*, see James Haggestrom, "*Fight Club* and the IKEA Personality," *Reel 3*, July 30, 2011, http://reel3.com/fight-club-and-the-ikea-personality/.

24. I want to thank Katie Kelly for reading the penultimate draft of this essay and suggesting numerous ways in which the argument could be improved. I am also grateful to the Oxford University Press reader for urging me to clarify the argument at central points. I have been teaching *Fight Club* for over a decade; doubtless ideas about the movie in this essay are borrowed from the fabulous teaching assistants for my university lecture courses Philosophy and Film, and Aesthetics; they know my gratitude. I also recall, when I first started teaching *Fight Club*, reading the draft of a wonderful essay by Nancy Bauer. This essay has since appeared as "Cogito Ergo Film: Plato, Descartes, and *Film Club*," in *Film and Philosophy: Essays on Cinema After Wittgenstein and Cavell*, ed. Rupert Read and Jerry Goodenough (Florence, KY: Palgrave Macmillan, 2005), and revised as "The First Rule of Fight Club: On Plato, Descartes, and *Fight Club*," in *Fight Club*, ed. Thomas Wartenberg (London: Routledge, 2011), 112–31. In Wartenberg's reader are helpful essays by Charles Guignon on the masculine identity theme in *Fight Club*, and a different reading of the movie as a romantic comedy by Ben Caplan. Cynthia Stark attempts to figure out the relation of Marla to the movie's dominant masculine appeal. Wartenberg frames his collection by *Fight Club's* anticipation of 9/11; the Trump presidency demands a different frame for analysis and discussion.

25. For this see: https://www.splcenter.org/hatewatch/2017/04/25/new-fight-club-ready-street-violence. For the SPLC general report on the Proud Boys, see https://www.splcenter.org/fighting-hate/extremist-files/group/proud-boys).

26. Theodor W. Adorno, *Aspects of the New Right-Wing Extremism*, trans. Wieland Hoban (Medford, MA: Polity Press, 2020), 28. The lecture to Austrian Socialist Students' Association had been tape recorded; it was finally transcribed and published in 2019.

27. Timothy Snyder, "The American Abyss," *New York Times Magazine*, January 9, 2021; nytimes.com.

28. Adorno, *Aspects of the New Right-Wing Extremism*, 40.

10

Funny Games

Film, Imagination, and Moral Complicity

Paul Schofield

> In many contexts we take ourselves, our real, non-fictional selves,
> to be implicated in what we're feeling and how we're feeling it in the
> movie theater... When we are appalled, or gratified, or vengeful, or
> aroused, or indignant, we are responding as the very people we are.[1]
>
> —**Richard Moran**

A well-off family of three is paid a visit by two young men purporting to seek a favor. Within minutes, the men have incapacitated them all. Over the course of the night, the men torture and humiliate their captives, forcing them to play sadistic games in hopes of having their lives spared. A few attempts at escape are made, but each ultimately fails. One by one, the entire family is murdered, and the perpetrators prepare to repeat the exercise with another set of victims.

That audiences would respond with outrage to a film that can be summarized in this way is unsurprising. But Michael Haneke's *Funny Games* (1997 and 2007) is as likely to perplex as it is to provoke. While subjecting its audience to appallingly gruesome displays of torture and torment, it nevertheless seems intent upon saying *something* about violence in the movies. For the film contains multiple Brechtian moments in which a character on screen nods knowingly at the viewer, addresses questions to her, refers explicitly to the events portrayed as fictitious, and so forth. Such moments signal a metacinematic interest in the film's horrific goings-on. But what exactly is being said, and whether what's being said is particularly interesting, subtle, or deep, has been a source of controversy since the film's release.

In interviews, Haneke tends to express a dim view of cinematic violence, and so this film's metacinematic commentary is typically read as a critique of violence in the movies.[2] But whether it has any genuine insight to share seems

Paul Schofield, *Funny Games* In: *Metacinema*. Edited by: David LaRocca, Oxford University Press. © Oxford University Press 2021. DOI: 10.1093/oso/9780190095345.003.0011 open for debate. Critics are divided on the film's merit, with many judging it to be crude, blunt, and obvious. Dana Stevens, in her 2007 review, gives expression to the sentiment most common among the film's detractors: "The direct-address interludes come off as fatuous and hectoring. . . . *Funny Games* is 110 minutes of pure reptile-brain jolts (fear, mostly), with a couple of metanarrative finger wags thrown in."[3] Film scholars have tended to treat the film less dismissively, but my view is that there's more interpretive work left to do if we're to understand fully the film's thinking on these matters.

My hope, in this chapter, is to demonstrate that *Funny Games* develops certain themes found in Richard Moran's 1994 paper, "The Expression of Feeling in Imagination." While the bulk of Moran's article is devoted to attacking a particular trend in the philosophical aesthetics literature, wherein film viewing is understood as an exercise in make-believe, Moran ends on a constructive note, recommending additional ways that imagination might be deployed for the purpose of appreciating art. His remarks on this subject are intended to be cursory, and there have been, to my knowledge, few attempts to develop them further. But my suggestion is that *Funny Games* uses the resources of its medium to investigate the role of imagination in our engagement with film in ways first suggested by Moran, thereby engaging philosophically with questions about aesthetics, art, and the philosophy of film.[4]

The Film

Funny Games is a German-language Austrian film released in 1997, which Haneke remade for English-speaking audiences a decade later in hopes of finding an American audience. Though the 2007 version departs from its predecessor in small ways, it is in essence a shot-for-shot remake. I'll be referring to the remake, unless otherwise noted, but most of what I say applies equally well to either version.

The film begins with a bourgeois family driving to their lake house. George (Tim Roth), Ann (Naomi Watts), and their young son Georgie (Devon Gearhart) play a game in which they attempt to identify operas playing on the car stereo. At home, Ann prepares dinner as two men arrive at the door. The two introduce themselves as Paul (Michael Pitt) and Peter (Brady Corbet). Their stated reason for visiting is that they've been sent by the neighbor to borrow eggs. While Paul goes outside, supposedly to hit a golf ball with George's designer club, Peter repeatedly drops "on accident" the eggs that are given to him. Eventually Ann becomes agitated and makes a scene while ordering the company gone. Paul, who has come in from outside, expresses bemusement, while George and Georgie arrive on the scene. George sides with his wife and requests that the visitors depart, at which point Paul picks up a golf club and strikes him with it, breaking his leg. Sadistically toying with Ann, Paul sends her outside on a hunt for the family dog, which she eventually discovers dead in the back of their car, having been killed, apparently, by Paul with the golf club. Now the whole family is placed in the living room, where they're told they will be forced to play "games" in order to earn the right to live. Paul bets the family that they will not survive until 9:00 the following morning.

What follows is a night of horror, with "games" involving not only physical abuse, but sexual humiliation, as Ann is forced to strip while Peter and Paul evaluate her body. At one point, young Georgie manages to escape, but is recaptured in short order and then is killed by Peter with a shotgun. When Peter and Paul exit the house, the victimized pair devise a plan wherein Ann will walk to town to fetch help, leaving George with his broken leg. But when Ann exits the property, she is soon retrieved by Peter and Paul, who return her to the house. In the living room, Peter and Paul force the pair to play another game, and George is killed with a shotgun. Peter and Paul then take Ann, bound and gagged, onto a sailboat. With an hour remaining before the 9:00 a.m. deadline, they casually throw her off the side of the boat, leaving her to drown. They move on to their next family, whom they'll presumably victimize in a similar fashion, and the film ends.

Funny Games, I've said, distinguishes itself from typical thrillers or horror pictures with its inclusion of several metacinematic moments. For instance, just before Ann is about to discover the murdered family dog, Paul cranes his neck 180 degrees to offer a knowing look directly to the audience—and in the 1997 version, he actually winks. Later, at a moment in which it appears that Ann will simply give up on the games and therefore be killed, Paul pauses to ask the audience whether they're hoping for a "real ending." Closer to the conclusion, Paul uses a remote control to rewind the film, undoing an attack that George has carried out against Peter—acknowledging explicitly, I take it, that the events taking place in a filmic universe are a contrivance. And at the film's conclusion, Paul enters the house of the family he's preparing to victimize next and makes direct eye contact with the audience as the credits begin to roll.

It's these moments that render the film distinctive. It's these moments that suggest the film is up to something more than merely supplying cheap thrills, or satisfying audience appetite for brutality. Nevertheless, questions remain about what, precisely, the film is saying about cinema, how these moments manage to say it, and whether what is said is genuinely insightful.

Audience Complicity

Haneke, we've said, intends *Funny Games* as a critique of violence in the movies, or, more precisely, as a critique of finding entertainment in it. However, anyone aiming to advance such a critique must face a familiar defense of such enjoyments. The defense is that the violence depicted onscreen occurs in a fictional universe. That universe, being fictional, contains no actual violence, as it contains no actual *anything*. A murder depicted in a film is no actual murder, torture in a film is not actual torture, and suffering in film is not actual suffering. The audience attends a film with full knowledge of this, and so when they cheer on the violence, all that they cheer, and all that they intend to cheer, is non-actual violence, which isn't violence at all. And why think there is anything morally illicit about *that*?

This defense presumes a sharp divide between the fictional universe of the film and the real world inhabited by moviegoers. Were a murder to occur inside the theater itself during a screening of *Funny Games*, all admit that it would be abominable to treat it as entertainment. That the world onscreen is fictional, according to the argument, makes all the difference. This all-important divide is breeched, however, when the audience is acknowledged by characters in the film. As Marc Vernet says in his well-known paper "The Look at the Camera," such moments put "the space of the film and the space of the movie theater in direct contact."[5] Viewers are thus understood *not* simply to be peering voyeuristically into a hermetically sealed world, but to occupy a universe in common with fictional persons who possess the capability of addressing them. So when Paul looks into the camera and says, "You want a real ending, right?" our response isn't, "Why is he talking to himself?" or, "Perhaps he's addressing someone situated directly behind the camera." We experience the words as addressing us, qua audience members.

It is significant, I believe, that when the line between the filmic universe and the real world is breeched, it is always the assailant who addresses the camera, giving knowing glances to the audience, asking its opinion, seeking its approval, and attending to their preferences. This all suggests that the acknowledgment emanating from the film is serving to put us into communion with the perpetrators. Indeed, in an interview contained on the DVD for *Caché* (2005), Haneke himself says as much: "The killer communicates with the viewer," he explains. "That means he makes him his accomplice." That the character onscreen makes the viewer an accomplice simply by communicating with them is, perhaps, an overly hasty inference. Can a person really implicate another in one's deeds simply by addressing them? Though it seems dubious to suggest that they can, it's worth noting a weaker sense in which such address might connect its recipient to the wrongful action of the person who issues it. Imagine that someone carries out a bad deed in my presence, and then addresses me in a way that presumes we are allies. Even if I've not previously thought of myself as an accomplice, being addressed in this way implicates me. For at the very least, I might wonder what I've done to earn the presumption that I am an ally, and I might further wonder about how I'm required to respond to the presumption now that it's been made explicit. To be addressed as a fellow perpetrator alters the normative circumstances whether I like it or not.

This assertion that we are placed on the side of the killers requires some further attention. The victims, after all, are not themselves monsters, constructed in such a way as to make us think they deserve the torment coming their way. Yet our alliances are ambiguous. In his essay written for the Criterion Collection release of the Austrian version of the film, Bilge Ebiri writes:

> As much as we may imagine that we're aligned with the victims, *Funny Games* dares to suggest that the opposite is true. . . . After all, we have come to watch a thriller, and the villains of *Funny Games* are our shock troops, there to do the audience's bidding with just enough plausible deniability to let us continue with the fantasy that we have nothing to do with the horrors on-screen. . . . [V]iolent thrillers always go through the motions of putting us on the side of their protagonists, even as they ultimately deliver on our not-so-secret desire to see those same people victimized, sometimes even killed.[6]

Whether any particular audience members do in fact find themselves on the side of the villains will hinge upon their individual experience of the film. However, the film *does* seem interested in inspiring viewers to self-reflect about their reasons for finding entertainment in movies such as this. Consider, for instance, the scene in which Ann is forced to strip naked, while Peter and Paul comment on her body. She sobs and begs for mercy while the camera lingers on her, leering much in the way the villains do. However, the camera denies the viewer any glimpse of nudity, which consumers of horror films and thrillers presumably expect, given the conventions of the genre. In having them frustrated, viewers have their expectations themselves called to their attention. And surely this signals to viewers that their expectations to be entertained in this way put them into community with the villains.

Insofar as the film indeed allies the audience with the perpetrators, what is being suggested, exactly? One possibility, I suppose, would be that the film is accusing the audience of being complicit in actual murder. Support for this reading could be drawn from a bit a dialogue between Peter and Paul late in the film, in which Peter says, "Isn't fiction real? . . . You can see it in the movie, right? . . . Well then it's just as real as reality." Taken at face value, however, this suggestion is pretty dubious. Peter Brunette writes:

> To what extent *could* any self-reflective gesture, an address directly to the audience, ever imply a collaboration between audience and killer? . . . [T]he self-reflexivity, by definition, immediately indicates that what is going on is *playacting*, not real violence, so what exactly can the audience ever be guilty of if it knows that everything is fake?[7]

We've returned, it seems, to the defense of cinematic violence with which we began, which is that the violence depicted on-screen occurs in a fictional universe without any actual violence. Characters who address the audience may breech the supposed divide between the fictional universe and ours. But when they do so, they also underscore that the events depicted in the film *are a fiction*. That is, when Peter and Paul address the audience, they address us not as co-conspirators in an actual murder, but *as members of a film audience*. All of this would seem to work against the possibility of being implicated in anything at all. Thus, Ebiri suggests that Haneke, by including these metacinematic moments, "pulls us out of the film at precisely the moments when it threatens to become too disturbing to bear." By doing this, "He seems to reassure us that it's all just a movie."[8] We're left, then, with a puzzle. If the film is indeed intended as an indictment of the audience—an attempt to reveal our moral complicity in film's events—how could placing us on the side of the villains manage to do this when its way of attempting to do so straightforwardly acknowledges that the audience is watching a fiction in which no one is actually tortured or killed?

Moran on Feeling and Imagination

This is the place where the film's preoccupations come into contact with themes from Richard Moran's "The Expression of Feeling in Imagination."[9] Much of this paper concerns itself with the view, advocated famously by Kendall Walton, that engagement with the mimetic arts involves imagining oneself in the art's universe, using the artistic artifact as a prop in a complicated game of make-believe.[10] So, for instance, watching *Funny Games* might on such a view be analogized to sophisticated child's play, wherein audiences imagine themselves to be present as the atrocities are carried out. Moran argues that this restricts too narrowly the role of imagination, ultimately recommending the possibility of imaginative engagement of a different sort. It's this other sort of imagining that is relevant to our discussion here, and so I will begin by explaining it.

Hume's "Of the Standard of Taste" serves as Moran's point of departure, and so I will commence by quoting a lengthy passage from it:

> But where the ideas of morality and decency alter from one age to another, and where vicious manners are described, without being marked with the proper characters of blame and disapprobation; this must be allowed to disfigure, and to be a real deformity. I cannot, nor is it proper that I should, enter into such sentiments; and the poet, on account of the manners of his age, I can never relish the composition....
>
> The case is not the same with moral principles, as with speculative opinions of any kind. These are in constant flux and revolution. The son embraces a different system from the father. Nay, there scarcely is any man, who can boast of great constancy and uniformity in this particular. Whatever speculative errors may be found in the polite writings of any age or country, they detract but little from the value of those compositions. There needs but a certain turn of thought or imagination to make us enter into all the opinions, which then prevailed, and relish the sentiments or conclusions derived from them. But a very violent effort is requisite to change our judgment of manners, and excite sentiments of approbation or blame, love or hatred, different from those to which the mind from long custom has been familiarized.[11]

A work of art can easily prompt us to imagine that states of affairs obtain that do not obtain in the real world. So if we're shown Ann and George living in a handsome lake house, then for the purpose of following and engaging with the narrative, we simply hold as true the proposition "Ann and George live in a handsome lake house," or if we're told that Ann and George have a young son, we reason from the premise "Ann and George have a son" for the purposes of engaging the film. Things are different when it comes to morality, however, and this is what Hume is struggling with in the quoted passages. For a work of narrative fiction *cannot* simply stipulate that for the purposes of the narrative, certain acts are good, right, moral, or worthy of sympathy. That is, it cannot, in the way it stipulates that Ann and George live in a handsome lake house, stipulate that Peter and Paul are on the side of the right when they sexually humiliate Ann, or that Peter is worthy of our admiration when he murders young Georgie, or that the family's bourgeois demeanor renders them deserving of dehumanization. Whereas accepting the former set of stipulations requires "but a turn of mind," accepting the latter would require a "very violent effort" indeed.

It can seem a bit mysterious, though, why there would exist this divide between that which can be imagined so unproblematically, and that which should never be imagined and could only be imagined with a very violent effort. Hume's brief attempts to solve the mystery are relatively feeble, and so I'll pass over them without comment. Moran, however, points us in a helpful direction, suggesting that there are different *kinds* of imagination at play here:

> I think we have to distinguish hypothetical and dramatic imagination and the types of resistance appropriate to them. It seems, then, that understanding these passages in Hume requires us to distinguish between two quite different activities, which we may call hypothetical and dramatic imagining. Strictly speaking, neither one of them necessarily involves a genuine alteration of judgment, but in the case of dramatic imaginative rehearsal it's easy to lose track of the difference between supposition and conclusion, between fantasy and acting out.[12]

While hypothetical imagination consists in holding particular propositions as true, dramatic imagining involves immersion of oneself in a worldview. I can, through an act of imagination, hold fixed all of my other beliefs and hypothetically hold as true a proposition about the existence of a particular family and about the type of home they own. But this is an activity very different in character from, say, imagining oneself into a perspective from which the prospect of torturing an innocent person appears choiceworthy. And it's not difficult to see why the latter would necessitate a violent effort, requiring as it does that one *work* to see the world and the people in it in a radically different light. Moran continues to develop the thought:

> Imaginatively adopting a perspective on something involves something different from the sort of imagination involved in ordinary counterfactual reasoning. Hypothetical reasoning involves seeing what would follow from the truth of some proposition. . . . By contrast, imagination with respect to emotional attitudes may require such things as dramatic rehearsal, the right mood, the right experiences, a sympathetic nature. It thus says more about a person that he is either able or unable to imagine something in this way, and he bears a different responsibility for it. . . . [I]magination with respect to the cruel, the embarrassing, or the arousing involves something more like a point of view, a total perspective on the situation, rather than just the truth of a specifiable proposition. And imagining along these lines involves something more like genuine rehearsal, "trying on" the point of view,

trying to determine what it is like to inhabit it. It is something I may not be able to do if my heart is not in it.[13]

Imagination of the dramatic sort, then, involves "trying on a point of view." And this, it would seem, *does* morally implicate the person doing the imagining. To begin to see this, think of someone who relishes a racist joke contained in a film. Here it's no defense for her to say that for purposes of the film, it's been stipulated that this sort of thing is a lark, just as it's stipulated that some characters own a lake house. Finding such a joke funny requires not just holding a particular proposition true for the purpose of further reasoning, but sympathizing with the sentiment underlying it. That is, it requires seeing the target race in a hateful or condescending light, and directing certain derogatory feelings toward its members. To do this, one must already occupy a problematic stance toward the racial group or be prepared to do some work in an effort to take it up. Either way, it "says a good deal about someone" (to put it as Moran does) that she's able to enjoy the joke, which is why we might begin to think this person is morally implicated.

In this insight, we can see the beginnings of an answer to the question with which we ended in the previous section—the question about how it's possible for a film that is a mere fiction, depicting wholly unreal events, to morally implicate a viewer. My task in the rest of the chapter is to bring Moran's insights to bear on *Funny Games* itself, specifically in regard to this idea that the audience might be made into "accomplices."

Trying on a Point of View in *Funny Games*

Funny Games, I wish to suggest, isn't simply an exercise in moralistic finger-wagging, but an invitation to reflect on the way narrative films prompt us to "try on" points of view, and on how we in the audience become implicated when abiding the prompt. For the film itself does attempt to get us to try on a specific point of view, even as it criticizes us for doing so. In attempting to specify the content of this point of view, we find nothing particularly sophisticated, however. The film goes out of its way to deny that the atrocities carried out onscreen have any deep ideological underpinning—when offering reasons for their deeds, Peter and Paul glibly offer conflicting explanations such as, "The truth is he's white trash. He comes from a filthy, deprived family. Raised poorly, drugs, etc.," and then, "He's a spoiled little brat. He's jaded and disgusted by the emptiness of existence," and then, "You want another version? . . . He's a drug addict." The causal background here—whatever we might be inclined to blame the behavior on—is a nonfactor, irrelevant to the film's interests. Indeed, Haneke confirms this reading in his press conference at the 1997 Cannes Film Festival, where he denies that the villains harbor deep ideological or political thoughts, of which their actions are outward expressions.[14] The pair are making an existential choice, engaging in an act of self-definition, deciding to torment and torture people for no reason other than to make themselves into torturers. It is this point of view that the film invites us to try on. It invites us, that is, to join the killers in the degradation of others, and to turn away from their humanity. It invites us to feel excitement at the thought of causing anguish and inflicting suffering. It invites us to leave behind societal and moral norms. It invites us to feel satisfaction at withholding sympathy from the victims.

Viewers of *Funny Games* are not likely to assent wholeheartedly to Peter and Paul's amoralist and sadistic perspective, nor are they likely to continue to engage sympathetically with Peter and Paul for the duration. Insofar as one "tries on" the relevant point of view, they are likely to do so only partially and sporadically. As Brunette says, "Haneke puts audience identification into play, as it were . . . oscillating between various poles of empathy and attachment that are being offered."[15] For instance, at an emotional turning point in the film, we're presented with an extended shot in which we're left to watch a wounded George and Ann alone in a room with their murdered son. There's no doubt that we're expected here to be distressed and disgusted. But this reaction is solicited only at the end of a progression in which the audience has presumably become increasingly immersed in the goings-on in the film, and in which the allegiance of the audience has been increasingly called into question. So the sympathy one is inclined to feel for the victims serves as a contrast to whatever enjoyment and approval one experienced in the preceding moments. Indeed, the contrast calls attention to this enjoyment and approval, affording the audience an opportunity to reflect on the attitude they took toward the events that led to this atrocity as those events were unfolding. It calls attention to the extent to which the audience had entered into community with the killers.

The moments in which Paul addresses the audience are similarly likely to alert the viewer of the extent to which they're trying on the perpetrators' point of view. For I take it that we are, in these moments, expected to feel disconcerted and exposed, as if we've been caught and "called out." To the extent that a viewer reacts in this way, it says a considerable amount about her relationship to the action on screen, as these feelings of having been exposed are only comprehensible if she's engaged with the events onscreen in a way that morally implicates her—it only makes sense to feel "called out" if she's managed to get herself morally implicated in one way or another. It's tempting, we've said, to suggest that a fiction film is "just a movie," depicting events that never occurred, and therefore incapable of implicating anyone. But as Moran insists, it *says something about the viewer* that she's able to "try on" a view presented in a film. And whereas Moran can only report on his own experience of engagement with film, *Funny Games* actually gives the viewer the experience of trying on a point of view, while at the same time forcing us to confront our own complicity on the spot. In other words, the hope is that our own experience of watching the film tells against the "It's just a film" defense, or, at the very least, complicates the issue considerably.

The preceding has focused on the possibility that something is *revealed* about a person when she tries on a point of view. However, entering into a point of view is something that a person *does*. And so it seems possible for a film to *entice us to do something wrongful*, in addition to revealing our bad character, when it solicits our imaginative engagement. *Funny Games* suggests that we might be so enticed. So, halfway through the film, Paul turns to the audience and says, "You're on *their* side, aren't you?" In asking this question, we might introspect and attempt to discover whom we're actually rooting for—we can imagine someone reacting to the question with disturbed surprise as she notices that her allegiances are divided, or perhaps that they have drifted toward Peter and Paul. But putting this question explicitly to the audience member can also highlight the choice she has in determining her allegiances. Imaginative engagement is, or can be, *active*, after all. Beginning with the moment she decides which film to see in the first place, and moving on to the moment when she chooses whether to avert her eyes or instead to relish the violence onscreen, a person is exercising agency. As with someone who seeks out a racist comedian and allows herself to marinate in the bigotry, someone who goes to a film advertised as torture porn and then empathetically engages with Paul and Peter is acting in her capacity as an agent. Thus, the concern is not simply what is *revealed* about her, but with what she is *doing*.

The moral wrong inhering in the audience's action is not, of course, one committed against a specific person. It's not as if an audience member is linked to Georgie through an ethical nexus, and acts immorally by committing a wrong against this specific fictitious person. Instead, the moral trouble consists in the audience member's attempt to assume a posture of mind that eschews concerns about wronging altogether. For the point of view that one is invited to "try on" here is one from which no other person registers as an object of moral concern at all. When we become accomplices with Peter and Paul, others become nothing to us—others are removed from our moral radar, and the question about what we owe to each other does not arise. Thus, we eschew altogether the standpoint from which duties to others grip us in the first place. It would seem that doing this would indeed require a "very violent effort." But it also seems like an effort the film requires us to take if we're to consume it as entertainment. And making such an effort doesn't just reveal something about a person. It is also a troubling thing to *do*, for it is a significant step toward removing oneself from the moral community altogether.

While *Funny Games* most obviously concerns itself with thrillers and horror, and with the ways they invite audiences to take a dehumanizing perspective on the characters, its concerns about moral complicity generalize. Think, for instance, of a film like D. W. Griffith's *The Birth of a Nation* (1915), which tells of the Ku Klux Klan "defending" the nation from black persons after the end of the Civil War. The film is notorious for its racism, but also universally lauded for its artistic merits. So it's often argued that we might condemn the bigotry embedded in it while appreciating its beauty.[16] But armed with the insight supplied to us by *Funny Games*, we might begin to link the film's moral trouble more closely with its artistic merits. For the film arguably invites the viewer to try on a viewpoint from which Klansmen are heroes, and from which blacks are the subhuman enemy to be defeated. Griffith uses, with great skill, the various tools of the medium to inspire audiences to see black persons as a threat and to feel sympathy toward those who wish to drive them out. So full engagement with the film's artistry requires working to occupy a perspective that is wholly repugnant. To try on the point of view encouraged by the film is, in other words, to try on a point of view from which members of a particular race are seen as lacking humanity. The implications of this line of thought expand when we contemplate ways in which a film might invite us to try on a point of view that is *not* obviously sinister. Consider, for instance, how Ridley Scott's *Blade Runner* (1982) might be thought to encourage us to see humanity in beings in which we hadn't seen it in before—to try on a view from which the concern for humanity isn't so narrowly applied, or so specifically tied to biology. At any rate, the possibilities for use of imagination in one's interaction with film appear to be broad, and so we ought to acknowledge that the line of thinking pursued by *Funny Games* seems to have application far beyond considerations about violence in the movies.

The Social Aspect of Moral Complicity

I will conclude by considering society's complicity in what happens in the movies. During Paul's asides in *Funny Games*, he sometimes alludes to the fact that the film is created in order to satisfy preexisting preferences of the audience. For instance, there is a moment when Paul acknowledges that the audience is looking for a particular sort of ending, and implies that he might tailor his actions to make possible such an ending. And in the Austrian version, he makes it clear that he is extending the games so as to ensure that the film has the running time that the audience expects. As Catherine Wheatley puts it, "Paul does not merely acknowledge the audience as spectators, but he also accuses them of being his very raison d'être."[17] Thus, the film highlights the fact that it is not simply asking its audience to try on a particular moral point of view, but is responding to pre-existing demand. As a general matter, the films that exist are the result of choices that we make collectively. We decide what to patronize. We decide what to praise and what to recommend. We decide which points of view will be offered for the public to "try on."

One could imagine a film that tried to diagnose the societal ills that inspire our demand for these sadistic sorts of films—blaming capitalism, or the breakdown of the family, or secularism. But *Funny Games* offers no such diagnosis, as far as I can tell. What, then, is it trying to say? Recall how the film refuses to supply us with a plausible causal explanation for Peter's and Paul's behavior, and how it instead presents their choices as existential acts of self-definition. Here I believe the film is similarly focused on the existential choice we're making as a society or as a culture when we demand certain sorts of art. *Funny Games* is not interested in blaming a sociological factor. It is interested in calling to mind the fact that the very artifact we are consuming is the product of our collective free will, and it is interested in encouraging us to reflect upon this. And insofar as we ultimately find Peter and Paul to be objectionable—and by the end, we're certainly supposed to, our complicity not withstanding—we might begin to wonder what our negative judgment of them implies about *us*. For it's their point of view that we demand the opportunity to try on.

Notes

1. From an interview published at *3:am* magazine. https://316am.site123.me/articles/keeping-sartre-and-other-passions.
2. Michael Haneke, "Violence and the Media," in *A Companion to Michael Haneke*, ed. Roy Grundmann (Chichester: Wiley-Blackwell, 2010), 575–79.
3. From her review of the film, see http://www.slate.com/articles/arts/movies/2008/03/michael_hanekes_funny_games.html.
4. Another way to put this point is that *Funny Games* "does philosophy" in the way that Stephen Mulhall and Thomas Wartenberg have argued that films can. See Mulhall, *On*

Film (New York: Routledge, 2001) and Wartenberg, *Thinking on Screen: Film as Philosophy* (New York: Routledge, 2007).

5. Marc Vernet, "The Look at the Camera," *Cinema Journal* 28 (1989): 48.

6. Bilge Ebiri, "Don't You Want to See How It Ends?," https://www.criterion.com/current/posts/6347-funny-games-don-t-you-want-to-see-how-it-ends.

7. Peter Brunette, *Michael Haneke* (Urbana: University of Illinois Press, 2010), 58.

8. Ebiri, "Don't You Want to See."

9. Richard Moran, "The Expression of Feeling in Imagination," *Philosophical Review* 103 (1994): 75–106.

10. Kendall Walton, *Memesis as Make-Believe: On the Foundation of the Representational Arts* (Cambridge, MA: Harvard University Press, 1993).

11. David Hume, "Of the Standard of Taste," in *Essays: Moral, Political, and Literary, Revised Edition*, ed. E. Miller (Indianapolis: Liberty Fund, 1987), 246–47.

12. Moran, "Expression of Feeling," 104.

13. Moran, "Expression of Feeling," 104.

14. The press conference is included as a supplement in the Criterion Collection's release of the film.

15. Brunette, *Michael Haneke*, 56.

16. See Richard Brody, "The Worst Thing about 'Birth of a Nation' Is How Good It Is," *New Yorker*, February 1, 2013. https://www.newyorker.com/culture/richard-brody/the-worst-thing-about-birth-of-a-nation-is-how-good-it-is.

17. Catherine Wheatley, *Michael Haneke and Cinema: The Ethics of the Image* (New York: Berghan Books, 2009), 46.

11

Shoah

Art as Visualizing What Cannot Be Grasped

Shoshana Felman

History and Witness, or the Story of an Oath

"If someone else could have written my stories," writes Elie Wiesel, "I would not have written them. I have written them in order to testify.[1] My role is the role of the witness. . . . Not to tell, or to tell another story, is . . . to commit perjury."[2]

To bear witness is to take responsibility for truth: to speak, implicitly, from within the legal pledge and the juridical imperative of the witness's oath.[3] To testify—before a court of law or before the court of history and of the future; to testify, likewise, before an audience of readers or spectators—is more than simply to report a fact or an event or to relate what has been lived, recorded, and remembered. Memory is conjured here essentially in order to *address* another, to impress upon a listener, to *appeal* to a community. To testify is always, metaphorically, to take the witness's stand, or to take the position of the witness insofar as the narrative account of the witness is at once engaged in an appeal and bound by an oath. To testify is thus not merely to narrate but to commit oneself, and to commit the narrative, to others: to take *responsibility*—in speech—for history or for the truth of an occurrence, for something that, by definition, goes beyond the personal, in having general (nonpersonal) validity and consequences.

But if the essence of the testimony is impersonal (to enable a decision by a judge or jury—metaphorical or literal—about the true nature of the facts of an occurrence; to enable an objective reconstruction of what history was like, irrespective of the witness), why is it that the witness's speech is so uniquely, literally irreplaceable? "If someone else could have written my stories, I would not have written them." What does it mean that the testimony cannot be simply reported, or narrated by another in its role as testimony? What does it mean that a story—or a history—cannot be told by someone else?

Shoshana Felman, *Shoah* In: *Metacinema*. Edited by: David LaRocca, Oxford University Press. © Oxford University Press 2021. DOI: 10.1093/oso/9780190095345.003.0012

It is this question, I would suggest, that guides the groundbreaking work of Claude Lanzmann in his film *Shoah* (1985), and constitutes at once the profound subject and the shocking power of originality of the film.

A Vision of Reality

Shoah is a film made exclusively of testimonies: firsthand testimonies of participants in the historical experience of the Holocaust, interviewed and filmed by Lanzmann during the eleven years that preceded the production of the film (1974–85). In effect, *Shoah* revives the Holocaust with such a power (a power that no previous film on the subject could attain) that it radically displaces and shakes up not only any common notion we might have entertained about it, but our very vision of reality as such, our very sense of what the world, culture, history, and our life within it, are all about.

But the film is not simply, nor is it primarily, a historical document on the Holocaust. That is why, in contrast to its cinematic predecessors on the subject, it refuses systematically to use any historical, archival footage. It conducts its interviews, and takes its pictures, in the present. Rather than a simple view about the past, the film offers a disorienting vision of the present, a compellingly profound and surprising insight into the complexity of the relation between history and witnessing.

It is a film about witnessing: about the witnessing of a catastrophe. What is testified to is limit-experiences whose overwhelming impact constantly puts to the test the limits of the witnesses and of the witnessing, at the same time that it constantly unsettles and puts into question the very limits of reality.

Art as Witness

Secondly, *Shoah* is a film about the *relation between art and witnessing*, about film as a medium that *expands* the capacity for witnessing. To understand *Shoah*, we must explore the question: what are *we* as spectators made to witness? This expansion of what we in turn can witness is, however, due not simply to the reproduction of events, but to the power of the film as a work of art, to the subtlety of its philosophical and artistic structure and to the complexity of the creative process it engages. "The truth kills the possibility of fiction," said Lanzmann in a journalistic interview.[4] But the truth does not kill the possibility of art—on the contrary, it requires it for its transmission, for its realization in our consciousness as witnesses.

Finally, *Shoah* embodies the capacity of art not simply to witness, but to take the witness's stand: the film takes responsibility for its times by enacting the significance of our era as an age of testimony, an age in which witnessing itself has undergone a major trauma. *Shoah* gives us to witness a historical crisis of witnessing, and shows us how, out of this crisis, witnessing becomes, in all the senses of the word, a critical activity.

On all these different levels, Claude Lanzmann persistently asks the same relentless question: What does it mean to be a witness? What does it mean to be a witness to the Holocaust? What does it mean to be a witness to the process of the film? What does testimony mean, if it is not simply (as we commonly perceive it) the observing, the recording, the remembering of an event, but an utterly unique and irreplaceable topographical position with respect to an occurrence? What does testimony mean, if it is the uniqueness of the performance of a story that is constituted by the fact that, like the oath, it cannot be carried out by anybody else?

The Western Law of Evidence

The uniqueness of the narrative performance of the testimony in effect proceeds from the witness's irreplaceable performance of the act of seeing—from the uniqueness of the witness's "seeing with his/her own eyes." "Mr. Vitold," says the Jewish Bund leader to the Polish courier Jan Karski, who reports it in his cinematic testimony thirty-five years later, in narrating how the Jewish leader urged him—and persuaded him—to become a crucial visual witness: "I know the Western world. You will be speaking to the English. . . . It will strengthen your report if you will be able to say: '*I saw it myself.*'"[5]

In the legal, philosophical, and epistemological tradition of the Western world, witnessing is based on, and is formally defined by, firsthand seeing. "Eyewitness testimony" is what constitutes the most decisive law of evidence in courtrooms. "Lawyers have innumerable rules involving hearsay, the character of the defendant or of the witness, opinions given by the witness, and the like, which are in one way or another meant to improve the fact-finding process. But more crucial than any one of these—and possibly more crucial than all put together—is the evidence of eyewitness testimony."[6]

Film, on the other hand, is the art par excellence that, like the courtroom (although for different purposes), calls upon a witnessing by seeing. How does the film use its visual medium to reflect upon eyewitness testimony, both as the law of evidence of its own art and as the law of evidence of history?

Victims, Perpetrators, and Bystanders: About Seeing

Because the testimony is unique and irreplaceable, the film is an exploration of the *differences* between heterogeneous points of view, between testimonial stances that can neither be assimilated into, nor subsumed by, one another. There is, first of all, the difference of perspective between three groups of witnesses, or three series of interviewees; the real characters of history who, in response to Lanzmann's inquiry, play their own role as the singularly real actors of the movie, fall into three basic categories:[7] those who witnessed the disaster as its *victims* (the surviving Jews); those who witnessed the disaster as its *perpetrators* (the ex-Nazis); those who witnessed the disaster as *bystanders* (the Poles). What is at stake in this division is not simply a diversity of points of view or of degrees of implication and emotional involvement, but the *incommensurability* of different topographical and cognitive positions, between which the discrepancy cannot be breached. More concretely, what the categories in the film give us to see is *three different performances of the act of seeing.*

In effect, the victims, the bystanders, and the perpetrators are here differentiated not so much by what they actually see (what they all see, although discontinuous, does in fact follow a logic of corroboration), as by what and how they *do not see*, by what and how they *fail to witness*. The Jews see, but they do not understand the purpose and the destination of what they see; overwhelmed by loss and by deception, they are blind to the significance of what they witness. Richard Glazar strikingly narrates a moment of perception coupled with incomprehension, an exemplary moment in which the Jews fail to read, or to decipher, the visual signs and the visible significance they nonetheless see with their own eyes:

> Then very slowly, the train turned off of the main track and rolled . . . through a wood. While he looked out—we'd been able to open a window—the old man in our compartment saw a boy . . . and he asked the boy in signs, "Where are we?" And the kid made a funny gesture. This: (draws a finger across his throat) . . .
>
> *And one of you questioned him?*
>
> Not in words, but in signs, we asked: "what's going on here? And he made that gesture. Like this. We didn't really pay much attention to him. We couldn't figure out what he meant. (34)

The Poles, unlike the Jews, *do* see but, as bystanders, they do not quite *look*, they avoid looking directly, and thus they *overlook* at once their responsibility and their complicity as witnesses:

> You couldn't look there. You couldn't talk to a Jew. Even going by on the road, you couldn't look there.
>
> *Did they look anyway?*
>
> Yes, vans came and the Jews were moved farther off. You could see them, but on the sly. In sidelong glances. (97–98)

The Nazis, on the other hand, see to it that both the Jews and the extermination will remain unseen, invisible; the death camps are surrounded, for that purpose, with a screen of trees. Franz Suchomel, an ex-guard of Treblinka, testifies:

> Woven into the barbed wire were branches of pine trees. . . . It was known as "camouflage.". . . So everything was screened. People couldn't see anything to the left or right. Nothing. You couldn't see through it. Impossible. (110)

It is not a coincidence that as this testimony is unfolding it is hard for us as viewers of the film to see the witness, who is filmed secretly: as is the case for most of the ex-Nazis, Franz Suchomel agreed to answer Lanzmann's questions, but not to be filmed; he agreed, in other words, to give a testimony, but on the condition that, as witness, he should not be seen:

> *Mr. Suchomel, we're not discussing you, only Treblinka. You are a very important eyewitness, and you can explain what Treblinka was.*
>
> But don't use my name.
>
> *No, I promised.* (54)

In the blurry images of faces taken by a secret camera that has to shoot through a variety of walls and screens, the film makes us see concretely, by the compromise it unavoidably inflicts upon *our* act of seeing (which, of necessity, becomes materially an act of *seeing through*), how the Holocaust was a historical assault on seeing and how, even today, the perpetrators are still by and large invisible: "Everything was screened. You couldn't see anything to the left or right. You couldn't see through it."

Figuren

The essence of the Nazi scheme is to make itself—and to make the Jews—essentially invisible. To make the Jews invisible not merely by killing them, not merely by confining them to "camouflaged," invisible death camps, but by reducing even the materiality of the dead bodies to smoke and ashes, and by reducing, furthermore, the radical opacity of the *sight* of the dead bodies, as well as the linguistic referentiality and literality of the word "corpse," to the transparency of a pure form and to the pure rhetorical metaphoricity of a mere *figure*: a disembodied verbal substitute that signified abstractly the linguistic law of infinite exchangeability and substitutability. The dead bodies are thus verbally rendered invisible, and voided both of substance and of specificity, by being treated, in the Nazi jargon, as *Figuren*: that which, all at once, *cannot be seen* and can be *seen through*.

> The Germans even forbade us to use the words "corpse" or "victim." The dead were blocks of wood, shit. The Germans made us refer to the bodies as *Figuren*, that is, as puppets, as dolls, or as *Schmattes*, which means "rags." (13)

But it is not only the dead bodies of the Jews that the Nazis, paradoxically, do not "see." It is also, in some striking cases, the living Jews transported to their death that remain invisible to the chief architects of their final transportation. Walter Stier, head of Reich Railways Department 33 of the Nazi Party, chief traffic planner of the death-trains ("special trains," in Nazi euphemism), testifies:

> *But you knew that the trains to Treblinka or Auschwitz were—*
>
> Of course we knew. I was the last district. Without me the trains couldn't reach their destination. . . .
>
> *Did you know that Treblinka meant extermination?*
>
> Of course not. . . . How could we know? I never went to Treblinka. (135)
>
> *You never saw a train?*
>
> No, never. . . . I never left my desk. We worked day and night. (132)

In the same way, Mrs. Michelshon, wife of a Nazi schoolteacher in Chelmno, answers Lanzmann's questions:

> *Did you see the gas vans?*
>
> No. . . . Yes, from the outside. They shuttled back and forth. I never looked inside; I didn't see Jews in them. I only saw things from outside. (82)

The Occurrence as Unwitnessed

Thus, in their diversity the testimonial stances of the victims, the bystanders, and the perpetrators have in common, paradoxically, the incommensurability of their different and particular positions of not seeing, the radical divergence of their topographical, emotional, and epistemological positions not simply as witnesses, but as witnesses who do not witness, who let the Holocaust occur as an event essentially unwitnessed. Through the testimonies of its visual witnesses the film makes us *see* concretely—makes us *witness*—how the Holocaust occurs as the unprecedented, inconceivable historical advent of *an event without a witness*, an event that historically consists in the scheme of the literal *erasure of its witnesses* but which, moreover, philosophically consists in an accidenting of perception, in a *splitting of eyewitnessing* as such; an event, thus, not empirically, but cognitively and perceptually without a witness both because it precludes seeing and because it precludes the possibility of a *community of seeing*; an event that radically annihilates the recourse (the appeal) to visual corroboration (to the commensurability between two different seeings) and thus dissolves the possibility of any *community of witnessing*.

Shoah enables us to see—and gives us insight into—the occurrence of the Holocaust as an absolute historical event whose literally *overwhelming evidence* makes it, paradoxically, into an *utterly proofless event*; the age of testimony is the age of prooflessness, the age of an event whose magnitude of reference is at once below and beyond proof.

The Multiplicity of Languages

The incommensurability between different testimonial stances, and the heterogeneous multiplicity of specific cognitive positions of seeing and not seeing, is amplified and duplicated in the film by the multiplicity of languages in which the testimonies are delivered (French, German, Sicilian, English, Hebrew, Yiddish, Polish), a multiplicity that necessarily encompasses some foreign tongues and which necessitates the presence of a professional translator as an intermediary between the witnesses and Lanzmann as their interviewer. The technique of dubbing is not used, and the character of the translator is deliberately not edited out of the film—on the contrary, she is quite often present on the screen, at the side of Lanzmann, as another one of the real actors of the film, because the process of translation is itself an integral part of the process of the film, partaking both of its scenario and of its own performance of *its* cinematic testimony. Through the multiplicity of foreign tongues and the prolonged *delay* incurred by the translation, the splitting of eyewitnessing that the historical event seems to consist of, the incapacity of seeing to translate itself spontaneously and simultaneously into a meaning, is recapitulated on the level of the viewers of the film. The film places us in the position of the witness who *sees* and *hears*, but *cannot understand* the significance of what is going on until the later intervention, the delayed processing and rendering of the significance of the visual/acoustic information by the translator, who also in some ways distorts and screens it, because (as is testified to by those viewers who are native speakers of the foreign tongues that the translator is translating, and as the film itself points out by some of Lanzmann's interventions and corrections) the translation is not always absolutely accurate.

The palpable foreignness of the film's tongues is emblematic of the radical foreignness of the experience of the Holocaust, not merely to us, but even to its own participants. Asked whether he had invited the participants to see the film, Lanzmann answered in the negative: "In what language would the participants have seen the film?" The original was a French print: "They don't speak French."[8] French, the native language of the filmmaker, the common denominator into which the testimonies (and the original subtitles) are translated and in which the film is thought out and gives, in turn, its own testimony happens (not by chance, I would suggest) not to be the language of any of the witnesses. It is a metaphor of the film that its language is a language of translation, and, as such, is doubly foreign: that the occurrence, on the one hand, happens in a language foreign to the language of the film, but also, that the significance of the occurrence can only be articulated in a language foreign to the language(s) of the occurrence.

The title of the film is, however, not in French and embodies thus, once more, a linguistic strangeness, an estrangement, whose significance is enigmatic and whose meaning cannot be immediately accessible even to the native audience of the original French print: *Shoah*, the Hebrew word that, with the definite article (here missing), designates "The Holocaust" but which, without the article, enigmatically and indefinitely means "catastrophe," here names the very foreignness of languages, the very namelessness of a catastrophe that cannot be possessed by any native tongue and which, within the language of translation, can only be named as the *untranslatable*: that which language cannot witness; that which cannot be articulated in *one* language; that which language, in its turn, cannot witness without *splitting*.

The Historian as a Witness

The task of the deciphering of signs and of the processing of intelligibility—what might be called *the task of the translator*[9]—is, however, carried out within the film not merely by the character of the professional interpreter, but also by two other real actors—the historian (Raul Hilberg) and the filmmaker (Claude Lanzmann)—who, like the witnesses, in turn *play themselves* and who, unlike the witnesses and like the translator, constitute *second-degree witnesses* (witnesses of witnesses, witnesses of the testimonies). Like the professional interpreter, although in very different ways, the filmmaker in the film and the historian on the screen are in turn catalysts—or agents—of the process of *reception*, agents whose reflective witnessing and whose testimonial stances aid our own reception and assist us both in the effort toward comprehension and in the unending struggle with the foreignness of signs, in processing not merely (as does the professional interpreter) the literal meaning of the testimonies, but also some perspectives on their philosophical and historical significance.

The historian is, thus, in the film, neither the last word of knowledge nor the ultimate authority on history, but rather, one more topographical and cognitive position of *yet another witness*. The statement of the filmmaker—and the testimony of the film—is by no means *subsumed* by the statement (or the testimony) of the historian. Though the filmmaker does embrace the historical insights of Hilberg, which he obviously holds in utter respect and from which he gets both inspiration and instruction, the film also places in perspective—and puts in context—the discipline of history as such, in stumbling on (and giving us to see) the very limits of historiography. "*Shoah*," said Claude Lanzmann at Yale, "is certainly not a historical film. . . . The purpose of *Shoah* is not to transmit knowledge, in spite of the fact that there is knowledge in the film. . . . Hilberg's book, *The Destruction of the European Jews*, was really my Bible for many years. . . . But in spite of this, *Shoah* is not a historical film, it is something else. . . . To condense in one word what the film is for me, I would say that the film is an incarnation, a resurrection, and that the whole process of the film is a philosophical one."[10] Hilberg is the spokesman for a unique and impressive knowledge of the Holocaust. Knowledge is shown by the film to be absolutely necessary in the ongoing struggle to resist the blinding impact of the event, to counteract the splitting of eyewitnessing. But knowledge is not, in and of itself, a sufficiently active and sufficiently effective act of seeing. The newness of the film's vision, on the other hand, consists precisely in the surprising insight it conveys into the radical ignorance in which we are unknowingly all plunged with respect to the actual historical occurrence. This ignorance is not simply dispelled by history—on the contrary, it *encompasses* history as such. The film shows how history is used for the purpose of a historical (ongoing) *process of forgetting* that, ironically enough, *includes* the gestures of historiography. Historiography is as much the product of the passion of forgetting as it is the product of the passion of remembering.

Walter Stier, former head of Reich railways and chief planner of the transports of the Jews to death camps, can thus testify:

What was Treblinka for you? . . . A destination?

Yes, that's all.

But not death.

No, no . . .

Extermination came to you as a big surprise?

Completely . . .

You had no idea.

Not the slightest. Like that camp—what was its name? It was in the Oppeln district. . . . I've got it: Auschwitz.

Yes, Auschwitz was in the Oppeln district. . . . Auschwitz to Krakow is forty miles.

That's not very far. And we knew nothing. Not a clue.

But you knew that the Nazis—that Hitler didn't like the Jews?

That we did. It was well known. . . . But as to their extermination, that was news to us. I mean, even today people deny it. They say there couldn't have been so many Jews. Is it true? I don't know. That's what they say. (136–38)

To substantiate his own amnesia (of the name of Auschwitz) and his own claim of essentially *not knowing*, Stier implicitly refers here to the *claim of knowledge*—the historical authority—of "revisionist historiographies," recent works published in a variety of countries by historians who prefer to argue that the *number* of the dead cannot be *proven* and that, since there is no scientific, scholarly hard evidence of the *exact extent* of the mass murder, the genocide is merely an invention, an exaggeration of the Jews and the Holocaust, in fact, never existed.[11] "But as to their extermination, that was news to us. I mean, even today, people deny it. They say there could not have been so many Jews. Is it true? I don't know. That's what they say." "I am not the one who knows, but there are those who know who say that what I did not know did not exist." "Is it true? I don't know."

Dr. Franz Grassler, on the other hand (formerly Nazi commissioner of the Warsaw Ghetto), comes himself to mimic, in front of the camera, the very gesture of historiography as an alibi to his forgetting.

You don't remember those days?

Not much. . . . It's a fact: we tend to forget, thank God, the bad times. . . .

I'll help you to remember. In Warsaw you were Dr. Auerswald's deputy.

Yes...

Dr. Grassler, this is Czerniakow's diary. You're mentioned in it.

It's been printed. It exists?

He kept a diary that was recently published. He wrote on 7 July 1941...

7 July 1941? That's the first time I've relearned a date. May I take notes? After all, it interests me too. So in July I was already there! (175–76)

In line with the denial of responsibility and memory, the very gesture of historiography comes to embody nothing other than the blankness of the page on which the "notes" are taken.

The next section of the film focuses on the historian Hilberg holding, and discussing, Czerniakow's diary. The cinematic editing that follows shifts back and forth, in a sort of shuttle movement, between the face of Grassler (who continues to articulate his own view of the ghetto) and the face of Hilberg (who continues to articulate the content of the diary and the perspective that the author of the diary—Czerniakow—gives of the ghetto). The Nazi commissioner of the ghetto is thus confronted structurally, not so much with the counter-statement of the historian, but with the firsthand witness of the (now dead) author of the diary, the Jewish leader of the ghetto whom the ineluctability of the ghetto's destiny led to end his leadership—and sign his diary—with suicide.

The main role of the historian is, thus, less to narrate history than to *reverse the suicide*, to take part in a cinematic vision that Lanzmann has defined as crucially an "incarnation" and a "resurrection." "I have taken a historian," Lanzmann enigmatically remarked, "so that he will incarnate a dead man, even though I had someone alive who had been a director of the ghetto."[12] The historian is there to embody, to give flesh and blood to, the dead author of the diary. Unlike the Christian resurrection, though, the vision of the film is to make Czerniakow *come alive precisely as a dead man*. His "resurrection" does not cancel out his death. The vision of the film is at once to make the dead writer come alive as a historian, and to make, in turn, history and the historian come alive in the uniqueness of the living voice of a dead man, and in the silence of his suicide.

The Filmmaker as a Witness

At the side of the historian, *Shoah* finally includes among its list of characters (its list of witnesses) the very figure of the filmmaker in the process of the making—or of the creation—of the film. Traveling between the living and the dead and moving to and fro between the different places and the different voices in the film, the filmmaker is continuously—though discreetly—present in the margin of the screen, perhaps as the most silently articulate and as the most articulately silent witness. The creator of the film speaks and testifies, however, in his own voice, in his triple role as the *narrator* of the film (and the signatory—the first person—of the script), as the *interviewer* of the witnesses (the solicitor and the receiver of the testimonies), and as the *inquirer* (the artist as the subject of a quest concerning what the testimonies testify to; the figure of the witness as a questioner, and of the asker not merely as the factual investigator but as the bearer of the film's philosophical address and inquiry).

The three roles of the filmmaker intermix and in effect exist only in their relation to each other. Since the narrator is, as such, strictly a witness, his story is restricted to the story of the interviewing: the narrative consists of what the interviewer hears. Lanzmann's rigor as narrator is precisely to speak strictly as an interviewer (and as an inquirer), to abstain, that is, from narrating anything directly in his own voice, except for the beginning—the only moment that refers the film explicitly to the first person of the filmmaker as narrator:

> The story begins in the present at Chelmno. . . . Chelmno was the place in Poland where Jews were first exterminated by gas. . . . Of the four hundred thousand men, women, and children who went there, only two came out alive. . . . Srebnik, survivor of the last period, was a boy of thirteen when he was sent to Chelmno. . . . I found him in Israel and persuaded that one-time boy singer to return with me to Chelmno. (3–4)

The opening, narrated in the filmmaker's own voice, at once situates the story in the present and sums up a past that is presented not yet as the story but rather as a prehistory, or a pre-story: the story proper is contemporaneous with the film's speech, which begins, in fact, subsequent to the narrator's written preface, by the actual song of Srebnik re-sung (re-enacted) in the present. The narrator is the "I" who "found" Srebnik and "persuaded" him to "return with me to Chelmno." The narrator, therefore, is the one who *opens*, or reopens, the story of the past in the present of the telling. But the "I" of the narrator, of the signatory of the film, has no voice; the opening is projected on the screen as the silent text of a mute script, as the narrative voice-over of a *writing* with no voice.

On the one hand, then, the narrator has no voice. On the other hand, the continuity of the narrative is ensured by nothing other than Lanzmann's voice, which runs through the film and whose sound constitutes the continuous, connective thread between the different voices and the different testimonial episodes. But Lanzmann's voice—the active voice in which we hear the filmmaker speak—is strictly, once again, the voice of the inquirer and of the interviewer, not of the narrator. As narrator, Lanzmann does not speak but rather vocally recites the words of others, *lends his voice* (on two occasions) to read aloud two written documents whose authors cannot speak in their own voice: the letter of the rabbi of Grabow, warning the Jews of Lodz of the extermination taking place at Chelmno, a letter whose signatory was himself consequently gassed at Chelmno with his whole community ("Do not think"—Lanzmann recites—"that this is written by a madman. Alas, it is the horrible, tragic truth," 83–84), and the Nazi document entitled "Secret Reich Business" and concerning technical improvements of the gas vans ("Changes to special vehicles . . . shown by use and experience to be necessary," 103–5), an extraordinary document that might be said to formalize Nazism as such (the way in which the most perverse and most concrete extermination is abstracted into a pure question of technique and function). We witness Lanzmann's voice modulating evenly—with no emotion and no comment—the perverse diction of this document punctuated by the unintentional, coincidental irony embodied by the signatory's name: "signed: Just."

Besides this recitation of the written documents, and besides his own mute reference to his own voice on the written cinematic preface of the silent opening, Lanzmann speaks as interviewer and as inquirer, but as narrator, he keeps silent. The narrator lets the narrative be carried on by others—by the live voices of the various witnesses he interviews, whose stories must be able to *speak for themselves*, if they are to testify, that is, to perform their unique and irreplaceable firsthand witness. It is only in this way, by this abstinence of the narrator, that the film can in fact be a narrative of testimony, a narrative of that, precisely, which can neither be reported, nor narrated, by another. The narrative is thus essentially a narrative of silence, the story of the filmmaker's *listening*; the narrator is the teller of the film only insofar as he is the bearer of the film's silence.

In his other roles, however, that of interviewer and of inquirer, the filmmaker, on the contrary, is by definition a transgressor, and a breaker, of the silence. Of his own transgression of the silence, the interviewer says to the interviewee whose voice cannot be given up and whose silence must be broken: "I know it's very hard. I know and I apologize" (117).

As an interviewer, Lanzmann asks not for great explanations of the Holocaust, but for concrete descriptions of minute particular details and of apparently trivial specifics. "Was the weather very cold?" (11). "From the station to the unloading ramp in the camp is how many miles? . . . How long did the trip last?" (33). "Exactly where did the camp begin?" (34). "It was the silence that tipped them off? . . . Can he describe that silence?" (67). "What were the [gas] vans like? . . . What color?" (80). It is not the big generalizations but the concrete particulars that translate into a vision and thus help both to dispel the blinding impact of the event and to transgress the silence to which the splitting of eyewitnessing reduced the witness. It is only through the trivial, by small steps—and not by huge strides or big leaps—that the barrier of silence can be in effect displaced, and somewhat lifted. The pointed and specific questioning resists, above all, any possible canonization of the experience of the Holocaust. Insofar as the interviewer challenges at once the sacredness (the unspeakability) of death and the sacredness of the deadness (of the silence) of the witness, Lanzmann's questions are essentially desacralizing.

> How did it happen when the women came into the gas chamber? . . . What did you feel the first time you saw all these naked women? . . .
>
> But I asked and you didn't answer: What was your impression the first time you saw these naked women arriving with children? How did you feel?
>
> I tell you something. To have a feeling about that . . . it was very hard to feel anything, because working there day and night between dead people, between bodies, your feeling disappeared, you were dead. You had no feeling at all. (114–16)

Shoah is the story of the liberation of the testimony through its desacralization; the story of the decanonization of the Holocaust for the sake of its previously impossible historicization. What the interviewer above all avoids is an alliance with the silence of the witness, the kind of empathic and benevolent alliance through which interviewer and interviewee often implicitly concur, and work together, for the mutual comfort of an avoidance of the truth.

It is the silence of the witness's death that Lanzmann must historically challenge here, in order to revive the Holocaust and to rewrite the *event-without-a-witness* into witnessing, and into history. It is the silence of the witness's death and of the witness's deadness that precisely must be broken and transgressed.

> We have to do it. You know it.
>
> I won't be able to do it.
>
> You have to do it. I know it's very hard. I know and I apologize.
>
> Don't make me go on please.
>
> Please. We must go on. (117)

What does *going on* mean? The predicament of having to continue to bear witness at all costs parallels, for Abraham Bomba, the predicament faced in the past of having to continue to *live on*, to survive in spite of the gas chambers, in the face of the surrounding death. But to have to *go on* now, to have to keep on bearing witness, is more than simply to be faced with the imperative to replicate the past and thus to replicate his own *survival*. Lanzmann paradoxically now urges Bomba to break out of the very deadness that enabled the survival. The narrator calls the witness to come back from the mere mode of surviving into that of living—and of living pain. If the interviewer's role is thus to break the silence, the narrator's role is to ensure that the story (be it that of silence) will go on.

But it is the inquirer whose philosophical interrogation and interpellation constantly reopen what might otherwise be seen as the story's closure.

Mrs. Pietrya, you live in Auschwitz?

Yes, I was born there . . .

Were there Jews in Auschwitz before the war?

They made up eighty percent of the population. They even had a synagogue here . . .

Was there a Jewish cemetery in Auschwitz?

It still exists. It's closed now.

Closed? What does that mean?

They don't bury there now. (17–18)

The inquirer thus inquires into the very meaning of *closure* and of narrative, political, and philosophical *enclosure*. Of Dr. Grassler, the ex-assistant to the Nazi "commissar" of the Jewish ghetto, Lanzmann asks: "My question is philosophical. What does a ghetto mean, in your opinion?" (182)

Differences

Grassler of course evades the question. "History is full of ghettos," he replies, once more using erudition, "knowledge," and the very discipline of history to avoid the cutting edge of the interpellation: "Persecution of the Jews wasn't a German invention, and didn't start with World War II" (182). Everybody knows, in other words, what a ghetto is, and the meaning of the ghetto does not warrant a specifically *philosophical* attention: "History is full of ghettos." Because "history" knows only too well what a ghetto is, this knowledge might as well be left to history, and does not need in turn to be probed by us. "History" is thus used both to deny the *philosophical* thrust of the question and to forget the specificity—the *difference*—of the Nazi past. Insofar as the reply denies precisely the inquirer's refusal to *take for granted* the conception—let alone the preconception—of the ghetto, the stereotypical, preconceived answer in effect *forgets* the asking power of the question. Grassler essentially forgets the difference, forgets the *meaning* of the ghetto as the first step in the Nazi overall design precisely of the framing—and of the enclosure—of a difference, a difference that will consequently be assigned to the ultimate enclosure of the death camp and to the "final solution" of eradication. Grassler's answer *does not meet* the question and attempts, moreover, to *reduce* the question's difference. But the question of the ghetto—that of the attempt at the containment (the reduction) of a difference—perseveres both in the speech and in the silence of the inquirer-narrator. The narrator is precisely there to ensure that the question, in its turn, will *go on* (will continue in the viewer). The inquirer, in other words, is not merely the agency that asks the questions, but the force that takes apart all previous answers. Throughout the interviewing process the inquirer-narrator, at the side of Grassler as of others, is at once the witness of the question and the witness of the gap—or of the difference—between the question and the answer.

Often, the inquirer bears witness to the question (and the narrator silently bears witness to the story) by merely recapitulating word by word a fragment of the answer, by literally repeating—like an echo—the last sentence, the last words just uttered by the interlocutor. But the function of the echo—in the very resonance of its amplification—is itself inquisitive, and not simply repetitive. "The gas vans came in here," Srebnik narrates: "There were two huge ovens, and afterwards the bodies were thrown into these ovens, and the flames reached to the sky" (6). "To the sky [*zum Himmel*]," mutters silently the interviewer, opening at once a philosophical abyss in the simple words of the narrative description and a black hole in the very blueness of the image of the sky. When later on, the Poles around the church narrate how they listened to the gassed Jews' screams, Lanzmann's repetitive echoes register the unintended irony of the narration:

> *They heard the screams at night?*
>
> The Jews moaned.... They were hungry. They were shut in and starved.
>
> *What kinds of cries and moans were heard at night?*
>
> They called on Jesus and Mary and God, sometimes in German . . .
>
> *The Jews called on Jesus, Mary, and God!* (97–98)

Lanzmann's function as an echo is another means by which the voicelessness of the narrator and the voice of the inquirer produce a *question* in the very answer, and enact a *difference* through the very verbal repetition. In the narrator as the bearer of the film's silence, the *question* of the screams persists. And so does the *difference* of what the screams in fact call out to. Here as elsewhere in the film, the narrator is, as such, both the guardian of the question and the guardian of the difference.

The inquirer's investigation is precisely into (both the philosophical and the concrete) particularity of difference. "*What's the difference* between a special and a regular train?" the inquirer asks of the Nazi traffic planner Walter Stier (133). And to the Nazi teacher's wife, who in a Freudian slip confuses Jews and Poles (both "the others" or "the foreigners" in relation to the Germans), Lanzmann addresses the following meticulous query:

Since World War I the castle had been in ruins. . . . That's where the Jews were taken. This ruined castle was used for housing and delousing the Poles, and so on.

The Jews!

Yes, the Jews.

Why do you call them Poles and not Jews?

Sometimes I get them mixed up.

There's a difference between Poles and Jews?

Oh yes!

What difference?

The Poles weren't exterminated, and the Jews were. That's the difference. An external difference.

And the inner difference?

I can't assess that. I don't know enough about psychology and anthropology. The difference between the Poles and the Jews? Anyway, they couldn't stand each other. (82–83).

As a philosophical inquiry into the ungraspability of difference and as a narrative of the specific differences between the various witnesses, *Shoah* implies a fragmentation of the testimonies—a fragmentation both of tongues and of perspectives—that cannot ultimately be surpassed. It is because the film goes from singular to singular, because there is no possible *representation* of one witness by another, that Lanzmann needs us to sit through ten hours of the film to begin to witness—to begin to have a concrete sense—both of our own ignorance and of the incommensurability of the occurrence. The occurrence is conveyed precisely by this fragmentation of the testimonies, which enacts the fragmentation of the witnessing. The film is a gathering of the fragments of the witnessing. But the collection of the fragments does not yield, even after ten hours of the movie, any possible totality or any possible totalization; the gathering of testimonial incommensurates does not amount either to a generalizable theoretical statement or to a narrative monologic sum. Asked what was his concept of the Holocaust, Lanzmann answered: "I had no concept; I had obsessions, which is different. . . . The obsession of the cold. . . . The obsession of the first time. The first shock. The first hour of the Jews in the camp, in Treblinka, the first minutes. I will always ask the question of the first time. . . . The obsession of the last moments, the waiting, the fear. *Shoah* is a film full of fear, and of energy too. You cannot do such a film theoretically. Every theoretical attempt I tried was a failure, but these failures were necessary. . . . You build such a film in your head, in your heart, in your belly, in your guts, everywhere."[13] This "everywhere" that, paradoxically, cannot be totalized and which resists theory as such, this corporeal fragmentation and enumeration that describes the "building"—or the process of the generation—of the film while it resists any attempt at conceptualization, is itself an emblem of the specificity—of the uniqueness—of the mode of testimony of the film. The film testifies not merely by collecting and by gathering fragments of witnessing, but by actively exploding any possible enclosure—any conceptual frame—that might claim to *contain* the fragments and to fit them into one coherent whole. *Shoah* bears witness to the fragmentation of the testimonies as the radical invalidation of all definitions, of all parameters of reference, of all known answers, in the very midst of its relentless affirmation—of its materially creative validation—of the absolute necessity of speaking. The film puts in motion its surprising testimony by performing the historical and contradictory double task of the breaking of the silence and of the simultaneous shattering of any given discourse, of the breaking—or the bursting open—of all frames.

Notes

1. The present chapter is drawn from the first section of my "In an Era of Testimony: Claude Lanzmann's *Shoah*," *Yale French Studies*, no. 97 (1991), 103–23. The analysis included here constitutes the starting point of a longer reading of the film *Shoah*, developed as the concluding chapter of my later book, *Testimony: Crises of Witnessing in Literature, Psychoanalysis, and History* (New York: Routledge, 1992), with Dori Laub, pp. 204–83.
2. "The Loneliness of God," published in the journal *Dvar Hashavu'a* (magazine of the newspaper *Davar*): Tel-Aviv (1984). My translation from the Hebrew.

3. "To tell the truth, the whole truth, and nothing but the truth"; an oath, however, which is always, by its nature, susceptible to perjury.

4. An interview with Deborah Jerome ("Resurrecting Horror: The Man behind *Shoah*"), *The Record*, October 25, 1985.

5. *Shoah*, the complete text of the film by Claude Lanzmann (New York: Pantheon Books, 1985), 171. Quotations from the text of the film will refer to this edition, and will be indicated henceforth only by page number (in the parentheses following the citation).

6. John Kaplan, foreword to Elizabeth R. Loftus, *Eyewitness Testimony* (Cambridge, MA: Harvard University Press, 1979), vii.

7. Categories that Lanzmann borrows from Hilberg's historical analysis, but which the film strikingly embodies and rethinks. Cf. Raul Hilberg, *The Destruction of the European Jews* (New York: Holmse and Meier, 1985).

8. Interview given by Lanzmann on the occasion of his visit to Yale University, and filmed at the Video Archive for Holocaust Testimonies at Yale (interviewers: Dr. Dori Laub and Laurel Vloch), on May 5, 1986. Transcript, 24–25.

9. Cf. Walter Benjamin, "The Task of the Translator," in *Illuminations*, trans. Harry Zohn, ed. Hannah Arendt (New York: Schocken Books, 1969), 69–82.

10. "An Evening with Claude Lanzmann," May 4, 1986, first part of Lanzmann's visit to Yale, videotaped and copyrighted by Yale University. Transcript of the first videotape, 2.

11. Cf., for instance, Robert Faurisson: "I have analyzed thousands of documents. I have tirelessly pursued specialists and historians with my questions. I have in vain tried to find a single former deportee capable of proving to me that he had really seen, with his own eyes, a gas chamber" (*Le Monde*, January 16, 1979). We have "a selective view of history," comments Bill Moyers. "We live within a mythology of benign and benevolent experience. . . . It is hard to believe that there exist about a hundred books all devoted to teaching the idea that the Holocaust was a fiction, that it did not happen, that it has been made up by Jews for a lot of diverse reasons." Interview with Margot Strom, in *Facing History and Ourselves*, Fall 1986) 6 and 7.

12. Statement made in a private conversation that took place in Paris, on January 18, 1987: "J'ai pris un historien pour qu'il incarne un mort, alors que j'avais un vivant qui était directeur du ghetto."

13. Lanzmann, interview, 22–23.

PART IV

METADOCUMENTARY, EXPERIMENTAL FILM, AND ANIMATION

12

The Act of Killing

Empathy, Morality, and Re-Enactment

Thomas E. Wartenberg

The Act of Killing (2012, dir. Joshua Oppenheimer, Christine Cynn, and Anonymous) is a complex film that intentionally makes it difficult for an audience to know how it should respond.[1] If one begins watching the film expecting a traditional documentary about its apparent subject, the Indonesian genocide of 1965–66 in which upward of one million so-called Communists were killed, one will be disappointed. Instead of, say, a soundtrack explaining the carnage enacted by Suharto and his deputies to support the coup that overthrew the democratically elected government of President Sukarno, paralleled by newsreel footage documenting the atrocities that were committed, one encounters a phantasmagoria of images made by the filmmakers in the years prior to the release of the film that include what appears to be scenes from a Bollywood-style musical, nightmarish re-enactments of the genocide orchestrated by the perpetrators themselves, bizarre fantasy scenes with one of the male perpetrators in drag,[2] and seemingly straight documentary footage of the perpetrators both talking among themselves and responding to interview questions posed by Oppenheimer. There are only three, relatively short intertitles early in the film to help its audience members grasp its subject matter and approach. It's not surprising to find even reviewers of the film puzzled by how to make sense of what they have seen, including what the film's actual subject is.[3] More relevant to the topic of this chapter is the disagreement about what the film shows about its central character, Anwar Congo, one of the perpetrators of the Indonesian genocide of 1965–66.

This chapter focuses on one aspect of this film: its use of re-enactments featuring the perpetrators of the crimes being re-enacted.[4] Although re-enactments are often employed in documentary films, *The Act of Killing*'s use of this technique is unusual, for the re-enactments are orchestrated by the gangsters who are the central characters in the film. Because of this, the film doesn't simply *use* re-enactments, but *reflects* metacinematically on what re-enactments can tell us about the horrific actions that are being re-enacted.

Thomas E. Wartenberg, *The Act of Killing* In: *Metacinema*. Edited by: David LaRocca, Oxford University Press. © Oxford University Press 2021. DOI: 10.1093/oso/9780190095345.003.0013

As we shall see, the mixture of garish scenes reminiscent of Bollywood musicals, nightmarish re-enactments, bizarre fantasies, and more or less straight documentary footage all aid our understanding of the mindset of Anwar Congo, the central character in the film. What the film uncovers is the emotional deficiency—I will call it "empathy deficit"—that allowed Congo to brutally murder hundreds of people without fully understanding the moral and psychological terror of his actions. As a result, we gain a better grasp of what allows a person to perform unspeakable evil and to accommodate himself to the knowledge of what he has done.

The Structure of Re-Enactment and the Nature of Evil

I have claimed that the re-enactments in *The Act of Killing* are innovative. What we now have to investigate is what makes these re-enactments so groundbreaking.

The most fundamental departure from the typical use of re-enactment in documentary films is that the filmmakers allow the perpetrators of the Indonesian genocide to control the creation and recording of the re-enactments featured in the film.[5] Giving control of the filming of the re-enactments of torture and killing to the very people who performed those actions seems odd and ill-advised, since it gives the perpetrators of genocide and their comrades a public forum in which to present their own, self-justifying version of the events that form the subject of the re-enactments. It thus appears to violate the documentary commitment to being a truthful portrayal of events.

We immediately need to reject the notion that the film's allowing the perpetrators control of the filming of the re-enactments is ill-considered. Although the killers do get to film scenes that they intend as self-glorifications, we do not interpret them that way, for the filmmakers did not create a film whose shots are completely directed by the perpetrators.[6] Instead, they have created a film that *includes* such scenes but also others, and this results in an *ironic overall structure* that allows the perpetrators to reveal to us who they are in a way that cuts against the image of themselves they would like to present. Being aware of how the film creates this ironic structure is crucial to understanding its message.

One important feature that is responsible for the film's ironic nature is the inclusion of footage other than that shot by the perpetrators. For example, the film includes a number of scenes in which we see the gangsters discussing how to film a scene that we then see filmed. We can capture the difference between shots such as those and the ones directed by the gangsters by speaking of two cameras doing the filming: the first, which is the camera filming the re-enactments, can be thought of as *the gangsters' camera*; but there is also a second camera, *the filmmakers' camera*, that records the filming of the re-enactments by the gangsters' camera. Let me be clear that this distinction is not a literal rendering of how the film was composed, although there are some shots that explicitly involve a recording by the filmmakers' camera of the gangsters' camera recording a scene. Rather, it is a theoretical distinction to aid us in interpreting the films, one that conceptualizes the means the film employs to present an ironic narrative.

This doubling of cameras is central to the particular mode of re-enactment used in the film, for the filmmakers' camera also records interviews with the gangsters as they watch rushes of their re-enactments on a television as well as in various other contexts. This is an important aspect of the film's unique, self-reflexive re-enactment style. Not only does it allow the film to provide access to the emotional experience of the gangsters during and after the re-enactments, an aspect of the film that will provide the key to its analysis of evil, but it emphasizes the role of what has been called "the cinematic gaze" in the perpetrators experience and self-understanding.

There are at least four different types of shots included in *The Act of Killing*. The first two are fairly typical of documentaries: recordings of a re-enactment taking place and recordings of interviews with the participants and of actions they perform during the time period of the making of the film. More unusual are shots recording the playing back of the recording of a re-enactment to one or more of the participants in it and recordings of the participants' reactions as they watch themselves acting in the re-enactment. This use of cinema's ability to record and project profilmic events in distinct types of shots differentiates this film from one that simply records events taking place before a camera in the style of direct cinema. The doubling of the cameras, multiple style of shots, and the complex editing resulting from integrating these different types of shots constitute the film as making a substantive use of the film medium[7] that allows it to embody an ironic structure conveying a point of view other than that of the perpetrators.

The analysis of the structure of *The Act of Killing* that I have just presented allows us to understand what the subject of the film actually is. Despite appearances, the subject of the film is not really the Indonesian genocide, for it shows us very little about those actual events but only their re-enactment. So the subject of the film must be something quite different.

The film has two general concerns. First, the film contains a great deal of information about the current state of Indonesia, especially Medan. What we learn is that the democratic institutions of the country are undermined by rampant vote buying and that the gangsters enjoy free rein to extort payments from merchants in exchange for "protection," for the politicians who are interviewed explicitly state that the gangsters play an important role in maintaining the political status quo. Indeed, how contemporary Indonesia is affected by the presence of the unpunished and unrepentant perpetrators of genocide is an important subject of the film.

Important as this topic is, I will not discuss it farther here, for the subject upon which I want to concentrate is the film's depiction of the perpetrators of the original genocide and their "mentality." This is because, as I shall argue, this aspect of the film is the most significant philosophically.[8]

The Act of Killing's Hybridization of Re-Enactment

In what follows, I am going to concentrate on a single re-enactment, although the film contains a number of others.[9] I call this *the torture scene*, though it is not the only re-enactment of torture contained in the film. In this scene, four gangsters re-enact their brutal torturing of a victim. Since Congo later specifies the victim's name, we should take this re-enactment to be of the torture of a specific individual, though it also illustrates the type of torture that Congo and his associates engaged in. The only gangster in this scene who is one of the actual killers is Congo, and interestingly he is not doing the torturing in the re-enactment but playing the victim. The three other gangsters are younger, including Herman Koto, who does most of the torturing. Given their ages, they could not have participated in the original torture.

The fact that Congo was a participant in those tortures takes on great significance, for although he acts in the role of a victim rather than his actual role of perpetrator, the fact remains that he was a participant in the torture that the re-enactment intends to recreate. Because Congo is an actor playing a role in the dramatic re-enactment of the torture he also participated in, he can direct the scene in a way that arguably allows for an accurate recreation of the actual events of 1965–66.[10] For my purposes here, I will simply ignore distortions that might have resulted from the perpetrators' desire to present themselves in a positive light to the public.

Since my analysis of the torture re-enactment scene focuses on the impact that playing a victim has on Congo's consciousness, it will be useful to consider his initial self-presentation in the film, for it shows us how significantly acting in the re-enactment affects him. The scene in which we first get a sense of Congo is clearly shot with what I have called the filmmaker's camera, for we hear Congo directly addressing Oppenheimer, who is doing the shooting. The Congo captured in this scene is an unrepentant murderer who is bragging about having solved a problem that occurred during the murders, even as he admits to having been troubled by what he did. Standing on the roof of a building that was the actual site of many of the killings, Congo explains the problem he and his fellow killers faced. The fastidiously attired Congo tells us that when you simply cut someone's throat, although that is an effective way to kill them, blood spills everywhere, resulting in a mess whose smell cannot be eradicated even after all the blood was cleaned up. What was needed was a more efficient way to dispatch his victims, one that would leave no traces of the killings that had occurred.

In a very simple demonstration of the technique he developed, Congo uses one of his fellow gangsters—later, we learn that he is actually the stepson of one of Congo's victims—to demonstrate with evident pride the more effective killing method he developed. He takes a wire that has one end attached to a pipe and the other tied to a piece of wood that can be held in the killer's hand and places it around the neck of his "victim" and pulls it tight. The actual result is a quick and tidy death. This method of "garroting" one's victims was derived by Congo, we later learn, from its depiction in Hollywood gangster films.

Dressed in white pants and a bright green shirt, Congo seems attired for a country club, not a demonstration of a technique for mass murder. The scene ends with Congo admitting that what he did troubled him, but he says that he overcame his qualms with drugs and alcohol, supporting the claim by dancing about—ironically, with the very wire with which he demonstrated his method of dispatching his victims wrapped around his neck. As the scene concludes his co-conspirator intones, "He is a happy man," a pronouncement that will later be seen to be supremely ironic given the nightmares from which Congo suffers.

The connection between Hollywood films and the Medan killers is quite important and underscores the film's metacinematic concerns. The gangsters actually modeled themselves on the film heroes they saw in Hollywood films made from the 1930s onward. They were colloquially referred to as "the movie theater gangsters" because, when they were recruited to participate in the genocide, they were working as ticket scalpers at the local cinemas in Medan. More shocking and surprising than the fact that they modeled themselves on the characters they saw portrayed on the screen is their application of the methods of killing taken from different genres of Hollywood films for their horrific deeds.

Their interest in American films helps explain why the gangsters want to participate in the making of this film and, more specifically, why the film takes the peculiar form that it does. These gangsters believe they have not received their due—they see themselves as having played a crucial role in supporting the Suharto regime that has not been officially acknowledged—and the opportunity to star in a film offers them the chance to show their story to the public and thus to immortalize themselves. That is why they want to make a film that is beautiful and that shows them in a positive light. And this explains why the film includes elements from popular film genres, including the musical, the western, the horror film, and, most significantly for my purposes, film noir.[11]

From Acting to Being

We are now in a position to examine how the film presents Congo's recognition of the true dimensions of the evil he perpetrated. This will require us to consider two scenes: The first is the torture scene in which Congo acts as a victim in a re-enactment of the tortures he perpetrated. The second is *the viewing scene*. It presents Congo watching himself re-enact the torture and then discussing with Oppenheimer, who has been filming Congo's reactions with the filmmakers' camera, his understanding of what transpired. While the torture scene results in Congo's experiencing the terror of victimization, it is only during the viewing scene that he links his own experience during the re-enactment to that of his victims. And it is this latter realization that brings home to him the true nature of his crimes and to us, the audience watching/listening to him, the emotional deficit that made his crimes possible.

The torture scene is one of the most brutal in a film filled with brutality. As Congo acts in the role of one of the victims, this remarkable scene depicts his inability to maintain the stance of an actor playing the role of a victim. Instead, he comes to experience what he takes to be the very emotions that a victim of his crimes actually experienced.

To understand what transpires in this scene, we need to understand the ontological structure of this re-enactment. Congo is both a perpetrator of torture and an actor in its re-enactment, though playing the role of one of his own victims. There is thus a distinction between Congo the real human being who was a perpetrator of torture and the character he plays in the re-enactment, namely a victim of that torture. Congo himself enters into the re-enactment with an awareness of both aspects of his situation, something that is characteristic of being an actor.

During the re-enactment there is an *ontological collapse* of this structure, for Congo, who is playing a character, actually comes to fully inhabit the being of the character, at least imaginatively, so that a perpetrator of torture and murder becomes his own victim.[12] As a result of this double collapse of role and reality—in which the "actor" becomes the character he is supposed to simply be acting as, experiencing himself fictionally as a victim of his own re-enacted crime—Congo himself has a *real experience of victimization.*

This re-enactment takes place with the four "actors" arranged around a table. Congo is seated behind the table with the camera recording the scene located slightly to Congo's left and in front of the table. One of the "interrogators" sits in front of the table with part of his front side revealed to the camera. The two "muscles" stand on either side of Congo, with Safit Paradede, a local paramilitary leader, on his left, and Koto on his right, carrying a knife that he will place on Congo's throat, threatening to slit it.

As the re-enactment begins, Paradede hits Congo's chair loudly with a board and then the table before yelling loudly at him and pushing him. Congo winces, as we would expect an actor to do, but his reaction is so authentic that it seems pretty clear that he has been startled by the loud noise and is reacting naturally, not simply acting, a reaction many audience members share.

The actual interrogation begins when the interrogator asks Congo his name, to which he replies, "I'm Jaludin Yusuf," the leader of the local communists in Medan. The two muscles harass Congo/Yusuf by making noise, pushing him around, putting a knife to his neck, and screaming loud questions at him. Congo, acting in the role of victim, begs, "Please, sir." Koto responds to this request violently, pulling Congo's hair and forcing his head back, telling him not to attempt to get friendly with him, and slamming a board onto the desk, causing a loud sound. After Koto threatens to break his legs if he doesn't answer, Dana, the interrogator, asks, "Besides Titi Kuning, where else are you active?" After Congo responds, "Hamparen Perak," Koto again threatens him. Then, while threatening him with a knife, he gets Congo to take off his watch and all his jewelry. Soon Koto stops the torture—though the camera (the filmmakers'?) keeps rolling, allowing us to see what transpires—because, he says, Congo has gotten makeup in his eyes. After it has been wiped off, Congo takes some deep breaths. They resume the re-enactment and Koto places a knife at Congo's throat. Congo has to turn his head to avoid being cut. He is now accused of "trying to ban American films in Indonesia." One of the rationales the gangsters give for their slaughter is that the communists were hurting their business as ticket scalpers by attempting to ban American films, so they here want the victim to confess to doing this. Soon we hear Oppenheimer say, "Cut!" Congo takes some more deep breaths as he attempts to recover.

After the break, Koto blindfolds him. At this point, the camera, which had been stationary, shifts perspectives, at one point giving us a close-up of the blindfolded Congo. With the camera back in its original position, Koto places the metal wire around Congo's neck in exactly the manner that Congo had done when he demonstrated this method of killing for Oppenheimer and the film's audience. As Koto pretends to strangle Congo, we suddenly see Congo's body go rigid and he appears to faint. The concerned Koto comes to Congo, touches him, and removes the blindfold. Congo says that he felt like he was dead for a moment. Koto tells him not to think too much and gives Congo water. Congo now seems recovered, saying, "Let's do it." Koto again prepares to garotte Congo. As he does, Congo's right hand suddenly flops about, as if to call everything off. As he removes the blindfold, Congo says, "I can't do that again" and seems to pass out, so Koto gets some water for him. End of scene.

The power of this scene derives most centrally from what happens to Congo. The contrast between his breakdown and the bravado he demonstrated earlier is startling, for we witness a transformation in Congo's psychology we could not have anticipated. For what happens is that the experience of playing a torture victim becomes so intense that it overwhelms him, whose emotional state becomes that of a torture victim. I have referred to the result as an ontological collapse, for Congo is unable to separate himself and his emotional state from that of the victim he is portraying.

But what precisely causes Congo to break down? Isn't he aware that he is just playing a role in a re-enactment of the torture that he participated in nearly half a decade previously? Why should taking part in a dramatic recreation of a torture scene whose structure he has devised cause him to have such a visceral reaction?

As a first step in determining what has taken place, we might reflect on the experience of an actual victim placed in the situation recreated in the re-enactment. Clearly, an actual victim would realize that he was in a very dangerous situation. The fact that he was being brought in for interrogation by gangsters who were involved in killing of many so-called communists is something he would be aware of, so it is reasonable that a victim would fear for his life. Even if he were not sure that he would be killed, he would be incredibly fearful and this would affect his perception of everything that happened to him, making him more likely to see everything that took place as threatening, giving him a reason to be even more fearful.

This fear would be accentuated by a number of things that the torturers did. For example, especially if the victim were blindfolded, a loud noise caused by one of the torturers hitting a table or chair with a large board would certainly startle the victim. Such a response is well documented by psychologists, who tell us that "the startle reflex occurs in response to intense and abrupt auditory, visual or tactile stimuli."[13] The startle reflex includes a group of involuntary (autonomic) responses to certain stimuli, including sudden loud noises and quick, unexpected movements toward one's eyes.

Given the victim's already primed state of fear, the sudden loud noise would amplify his fear, as he worried what that noise signified. We can imagine him wondering if he was going to be hit or stabbed. The fear would be augmented and might even develop into abject terror at his prospects: Would he be physically harmed? Would he be killed? Would the gangsters use the knife at his throat to slit it? His abject state would induce blind terror and might result in his sobbing and loss of control over his bowels. Whatever dignity he might have had would be destroyed. This is, in a nutshell, what I will call "the process of victimization."[14]

At first blush, it would appear that Congo is insulated from such a response. After all, he is only acting in the role of a torture victim. In order to act in a convincing manner, he does have to imagine what a torture victim would feel so that he can react and behave in a convincing manner during the re-enactment. But imagining that a victim would be scared so that he could himself act as if he were scared is not the same as actually being scared, for an actor's consciousness is not generally completely determined by the emotional state of the person whom he is trying to portray, involving, as it does, a type of double consciousness. On the one hand, one has to be aware of the state of mind of the person one is portraying. Here that would entail being aware of the fear and even terror that a victim experiences. On the other hand, the actor has to *act*, that is, perform having an emotion in a manner that conveys to the audience what the character is supposed to be feeling.[15]

What can we say about what happens to Congo when he acts as a torture victim during the re-enactment? Despite acting in a role, *Congo actually experiences victimization*. Although he knows the general situation of the re-enactment, he cannot anticipate exactly what actions his "torturers" will perform nor when. Because his torturers are standing behind him and make very loud and sudden noises with their sticks hitting his chair, Congo reacts much as we in the audience do, only much more intensely. As we watch the scene, we are also startled by the loud noises and may feel our body jerk in response to them. We are only watching the scene, while Congo is directly in it. That he would react even more strongly is obvious, and we can see evidence of that in the way that his body jerks in response to the loud noises he experiences. This is part and parcel of the "flight-or-fight response" that also includes bodily changes such as an increase in the breathing and heart rates, increased muscle tension, sweating, and so on. We can actually see Congo flinch in response to the first loud noise he experiences. The collaborators also scream at and push Congo, all of which increase his growing fear.

So Congo loses his grip on his actual situation as an actor playing a torture victim. The emotions he experiences as a torture victim come so to dominate his consciousness that it is as if he were actually being tortured rather than merely acting as if he were. Particularly important here are the automatic responses that are generated by the loud noises with which his fellow gangsters bombard him and the way they also violate his control of his own body by putting a knife to his neck and grabbing and pulling his hair. All of these violations of his personal integrity cause Congo to undergo the ontological collapse in which he loses awareness of the fictitiousness of his victimhood and comes to experience the emotional responses characteristic of victimization. Indeed, I am tempted to say that the re-enacted scene of torture becomes an actual instance of torture, though, of course, it does not involve the physical harm to the victim that took place in 1965–66.

The ontological collapse I have just described is something that we also experience at other points in the film. The most prominent example is while watching the re-enactment of the burning of the village of Kampung Kolan that took place in 1965. Viewers of the scene report that the graphic manner in which that scene is shot, with images of flames both obscuring the devastation and allowing us to see through them to the conflagration, causes them to forget that they are watching a re-enactment. During this scene, it is as if we are seeing an actual documentary of the burning of the village, something also encouraged by the reactions of many of the participants in the re-enactment, who themselves are truly terrorized and not just acting as if they were. Christine Cynn's admission to me that this was the only scene that got out of their control helps explain why viewers might take this scene to be more than a re-enactment.[16]

From Being to Screening

The Act of Killing illuminates what transpired in Congo's consciousness during the torture scene through a scene in which Congo watches some of the rushes from the film and then reflects on what he has seen and heard, "the viewing scene."

After a couple of short vignettes, the film returns to the waterfall scene that was the second one in the film, only this time the scene is fully edited and is accompanied on the soundtrack by the song "Born Free" rather than the voice of the scene's director.[17] The symbolism of the song has already been explained to us, for the perpetrators repeatedly tell us that *preman*, an Indonesian word for "gangster," derives from the English words "free man." Although this is not true, *preman* does stem from the Dutch term for free man, *vritman*. It turns out that what we are seeing, although we are not at first aware of it, is the film that Congo is watching on a small television screen in his home. The content of the scene is a musical number filled with dancing girls, Koto in drag, and Congo in an old-style black robe. Soon two men representing victims of Congo's crimes place wire loops over their necks, symbolizing the method of their killing, and one of them places a medal around Congo's neck, thanking him for killing him and sending him to heaven, all the while as the strains of "Born Free" continue to sound. Clearly this represents Congo's fantasy, not a re-enactment.

After a cut to Congo watching this scene, the film shows us the TV screen with the scene on it, allowing us to understand that Congo has been watching the very scene we have just ourselves observed. Congo is thrilled by what he has seen, telling Oppenheimer—now clearly established as filming this scene—how pleased he is with what he has produced, for he couldn't imagine creating "something so great."

So both the audience and Oppenheimer are surprised when Congo asks Oppenheimer to see the scene where he is "strangled with a wire." Even more startling, to both viewers and Oppenheimer, is Congo's desire to have his two grandsons watch the clips with him. Twice brushing off Oppenheimer's suggestion that the scene is too violent for the young children, Congo proudly discusses his acting with the two young boys who have come to sit on his lap and watch their grandfather on television.

Once they have left, Congo suddenly squints, as if he now sees something more on the screen. "Did the people I tortured feel the way I do here?" a puzzled Congo asks Oppenheimer. "I can feel the way the people I tortured felt because my dignity has been destroyed. My pride has gone and then fear comes right then and there," he continues, as he looks at his own image on the screen, explaining his understanding of what transpired during the re-enactment. "All the terror possessed my body. It surrounded me and possessed me," he admits.

Congo here explains his dawning recognition of the emotional process that his victims underwent during the torture to which they were subjected. Although the basis for his new awareness is his experience of victimization during the re-enactment, it also results from his watching that very scene on a screen along with his two grandsons. His awareness requires his observing himself on the screen, something that places him in the position of a viewer of the re-enactment in which he participated.

Congo now realizes that the brutal interrogation to which his victims were subjected destroyed their dignity and pride, leaving nothing in their wake but brute terror. Even though he was "just" acting as a victim in the re-enactment, Congo actually experienced these feelings. Indeed, an element in the compelling nature of this film is its repeated demonstration that re-enacting brutality is itself a brutalizing process that creates its own victims, who cannot maintain their ontological distance from the experience of the real victims of the mass murders.[18] Congo claims that he has felt the very same emotions that the actual victims of his torture felt, a claim that we can conceptualize by concluding that the process of victimization undergone by Congo is identical in many respects, though not all, to that experienced by his real torture victims.

Oppenheimer's reaction to the apparently naive question Congo asks him—"Did the people I tortured really feel the way I do here?"—reveals that, at least at the time of the filming, he did not fully realize the significance of what he had captured on film. Rather than helping Congo explore the significance of his reaction, Oppenheimer cruelly rejects Congo's acknowledgment of what he had experienced by telling him, "Actually, the people you tortured felt far worse because *you* know it's only a film. They knew they were being killed." Whether Congo did or did not feel the very same emotions as his victims is a red herring that fails to acknowledge his experience of victimization. Even if Congo does not characterize his own experience in a completely accurate manner, Oppenheimer's brusque response brushes off his realization.

Congo is puzzled by Oppenheimer's reaction, as he cocks his head slightly to the side. He then looks down, as if he's considering the truth of Oppenheimer's words. "But I can feel it, Josh. Really, I can feel it," he responds. Slowly, as if a light is dawning, he says plaintively, "I did this to so many people, Josh." He then cries. "Is it all coming back to me? I really hope it won't. I don't want it to, Josh," he says, as he wipes tears from his eyes with his right hand. He shakes his head as if to dispel the horror of his realization. The scene ends with a cut to a still of Congo in his role as torture victim displayed on the television.

This is the first time we have seen Congo fully acknowledge the suffering of his victims and the immorality of his own actions.[19] Gone is the bravado of the mass killer demonstrating his clever technical innovation. In its place, a shaken, vulnerable human being emerges who realizes, for the first time nearly fifty years after the events in question, the actual nature of what took place. Sure, he had always known that he killed many, many people, and this had given him nightmares. But taking part in the re-enactment of the torture provides Congo with an experience of victimization, and this provides a connection to his actual torture victims. Having labeled them communists who were threatening his livelihood and the stability of the new regime in

Indonesia, Congo previously was able to dehumanize them. By providing him with an experience of victimization, taking part in the re-enactment produces a more than empathetic connection to his victims.

Congo himself provides a basic phenomenological account of this experience. First, his pride disappears and is replaced by fear. Sitting in a chair surrounded by people who are threatening him, albeit in a "fictional" re-enactment, causes this reaction in the manner I have analyzed earlier, where occupying the position of a victim of torture results in an emotional experience that undermines his ability to separate his playacting from the reality of his situation. Congo's mention of dignity is quite informative. The actions of the torturers—making loud, threatening sounds; pressing a knife against his throat as if to slit it; screaming at him; removing all the valuables from his body—all of these actions work to take away from Congo the psychological resources that provide him with a sense of his own dignity. The result, he tells us, is that terror "possessed" his body and "surrounded" him, a visceral image of what his experience was like.

As we watch Congo's realization of the horrific experience to which his victims were subjected, we modify our assessment of him. Earlier, as we saw and heard him brag about developing a method for coping with the mess caused by the killings, we could not but be horrified by the pride that occluded the horrific nature of the acts he performed. But as we watch the film, our attitude toward Congo becomes more complex, for we see him in different contexts—from teaching his grandsons not to be cruel to young chicks to exhibiting great cruelty himself while re-enacting the murder of a baby before its parent's eyes. What the viewing scene contributes is the insight that Congo was previously unable to empathize with his victims, an inability that is only overcome when he reflects on his own experience of victimization during the re-enactment of his crimes.[20]

Conclusion

In this chapter, I have only been able to scratch the surface of this intriguing and puzzling film. Most importantly, I have not been able to discuss how the use of re-enactment allows the film to address the question of how people can perform acts they know to be horrific and live with themselves. Addressing this question would allow us to see that *The Act of Killing*, in addition to be an innovative metacinematic documentary film, makes an important contribution to our understanding of the nature of evil. Addressing that topic will have to wait for another occasion.

Notes

1. There are two versions of the film. The original and longer version is now generally referred to as "the director's cut," despite its being the original form in which the film was released. The shorter version was developed to assist in theatrical release in the United States, among other places. There are significant differences in the editing of the two versions. I shall be discussing the original release.

   Versions of this paper were presented at Bates College in May 2018, the Docusophia conference in Tel Aviv in May 2018, the Society for the Cognitive Study of the Moving Image conference in June 2018, and the Society for the Philosophical Study of the Visual Arts in January 2019. It has benefited in substantial ways from the comments made by audience members at those occasions as well as from very helpful comments on drafts by Cynthia Freeland and Paul Schofield.

2. One confusing scene takes place in front of a giant fish that is located near a lake. The now decrepit structure was formerly a restaurant, and the lake is the crater of a volcano that caused massive destruction when it erupted seventy-five thousand years ago, giving this scene great symbolic weight for those who understand its elements.

3. For this claim, see, e.g., Benedict Anderson, "Impunity and Reenactment: Reflections on the 1965 Massacre in Indonesia and Its Legacy," *Asia-Pacific Journal* 11, Issue 15, no. 4 (April 15, 2013), http://apjjf.org/2013/11/15/Benedict-Anderson/3929/article.html. Robert Sinnerbrink discusses the objections lodged against the film in an attempt to defend it in "Gangster Film: Cinematic Ethics in *The Act of Killing*," in *Cinematic Ethics: Exploring Ethical Experience through Film* (New York: Routledge, 2016), 165–84.

4. Although many gangsters participate in the re-enactments, only a few of them actually committed the genocides of 1965–66. Others are simply too young, though they clearly identify with the perpetrators.

5. *The Act of Killing* is not the first film to feature perpetrators of genocide. Rithy Panh's *S21: The Khmer Rouge Killing Machine* (2003) made this innovation. However, it doesn't appear that Panh gave the perpetrators control of the filming of the very schematic re-enactments presented in the film.

6. Oppenheimer has been criticized for deceiving the perpetrators about the nature of the film he was shooting. He denies having deceived them in any way. On this, see Sinnerbrink, "Gangster Film."

7. Philosophers and film theorists have generally claimed that only films that make central use of the cinematic medium can actually do philosophy. I think *The Act of Killing* does so, as should be evident here.

8. This allows us to see why so much of the negative criticism of the film for not being an accurate portrayal of the Indonesian genocide is off-base. The film is not attempting to present a more accurate version of the events of that time period than is generally known, at least outside of Indonesia. Rather, it focuses on the situation in present-day Indonesia as well as the consciousnesses of the perpetrators some forty-five years after the coup and killings it inspired.

9. The most prominent of these are other re-enactments of interrogation and torture, and a truly horrifying re-enactment of the burning of a village.

10. In the theatrical release, Congo is shown actually telling the other gangsters how to begin his interrogation. For some reason, Oppenheimer edited this out of the director's cut of the film.

11. Koto appears in drag because they are mobilizing an anticommunist myth involving the two characters they portray. For details see Saskia E. Wieringa, "Sexual Politics as a Justification of Mass Murder in *The Act of Killing*," *Critical Asian Studies* 46, no. 1 (2014): 195–99.

12. Bill Nichols calls this the "fantasmatic." See his *Introduction to Documentary* (Bloomington: Indiana University Press, 2001).

13. Ramirez-Moreno, David Fernando, and Terrence Joseph Sejnowski, "A Computational Model for the Modulation of the Prepulse Inhibition of the Acoustic Startle Reflex." *Biological Cybernetics* 106, no. 3 (2012): 169–76.

14. In another scene in the film, Congo's neighbor, Suryono, exhibits such fear when he acts as his stepfather, a victim in 1965. At one point, Congo comments to Zulkadry, "It's sadistic, Adi."

15. In discussing "Bad Faith" in *Being and Nothingness*, trans. Hazel Barnes (New York: Washington Square Press, 1963), Sartre writes as if the situation of the actor were indicative of all human consciousness, in which there is a division between having an emotion and being aware that one is having that emotion. Only someone living in bad faith, such as Sartre's waiter who fully inhabits his role of being a waiter, fails to exhibit this dualistic structure. Congo's collapse can be seen to be related to the phenomenon of bad faith.

16. All the participants in this scene were either perpetrators or their families. Some of them directly re-experienced the horror of the event.

17. Once again, the theatrical cut eliminates the intervening scenes, moving directly from the torture to the viewing scene.

18. There are other scenes in which we see people engaged in the re-enactments suddenly overcome, e.g., a woman witnessing the restaged burning of Kampung Kolan is overcome, and the stepson of a victim breaks down completely as he re-enacts his stepfather's torture. I am suggesting that Congo's experience provides the key to understanding what has happened during these re-enactments that makes them so powerful as a cinematic tool for the exploration of evil.

19. Earlier, Congo did express some empathy for the victims. During the burning of the village, he remarks that the children who had witnessed it would be traumatized. He also seems upset by Suryono's breakdown.

20. One of the most controversial scenes in the film is the one in which Congo returns to the roof where many of the killings took place and dry heaves before descending the staircase on which he ascended. Many audience members contend that Congo is here acting. I disagree. What transpires is Congo's realization that there is no way that he can expunge his memory of the horrific acts he performed—hence his inability to bring up anything when he retches—so that he realizes that the attempt to use cinematic re-enactment to put an end to his torment is a failure, leaving him a more tragic figure than the boastful killer we encountered on the roof early in the film.

13

Waltz with Bashir's Animated Traces

Troubled Indexicality in Contemporary Documentary Rhetorics

Yotam Shibolet

Recent developments in the affordances of digital media problematize the rhetorics and spectatorial experience of "truth" in video representation, perhaps now more than ever before. Waning faith in indexical evidence (evidence providing tangible traces that point toward past occurrences) provided by photography and historical archives may be cited as a key cause of this trouble, which has been a central point of inquiry in media research long before terms such as "alternative facts" and "fake news" took central stage in public debate. The contemporary state of affairs is particularly challenging for the practice of documentary filmmaking, whose foundational aim, we are told, is to meaningfully capture something "true" about reality.

In this chapter, I aim to reflect on the meaning of this challenge and on documentary strategies of adapting to it. In this context, I suggest an analysis of the animated documentary *Waltz with Bashir* (2008, dir. Ari Folman). By employing animation to represent traumatic war memories, *Waltz with Bashir* constructs a system of documentary rhetorics that rely on spectatorial trust in the authenticity of creatively depicted experiences, rather than faith in indexical, observational evidence. My reading focuses on the film's final sequence, which concludes and presumably substantiates the animated narrative via appropriation of archival footage. In the context of the film's representational rhetorics, this transition from animation to archival footage may be understood as a reversal of the aforementioned strategy of animated documentaries—a return to reliance on captured indexical photographic truth. I will explore *Waltz with Bashir*'s critical approach to truth claims in both personal memory and photography in order to lay the ground for an alternative, somewhat subversive reading of this final sequence.

Yotam Shibolet, Waltz with Bashir's *Animated Traces* In: *Metacinema*. Edited by: David LaRocca, Oxford University Press.

Documentary Rhetorics in the Age of Suspect Indexicality

In a 2018 article in *The Atlantic*, "The Era of Fake Video Begins," Franklin Foer addresses deepfake videos, a video manipulation technology aided by deep-learning AI, which allows a near-seamless synthesis of different videos and/or images in a new integrated video—effectively masking the superimposition. This technology allows video manipulators, for example, to convincingly plant a person's face on another's body. In combination with voice-mimicking tools, it is already theoretically possible to produce convincing video representation of public figures saying things they have never said in situations they have never been in. Such extreme manipulations are expected to become increasingly commonplace as the technology proliferates (and already have to an extent since the publishing of Foer's piece).

Foer's argument leads to a very grim and hyperbolic conclusion: "The digital manipulation of video may make the current era of 'fake news' seem quaint. Fabricated videos will create new and understandable suspicions about everything we watch . . . [and] ultimately destroy faith in our strongest remaining tether to the idea of common reality."[1] While deepfake technology is indeed concerning, such "understandable suspicions," are hardly a unique problem of the digital age—as Tom Gunning asserts: "The claim that the digital media alone transforms its data into an intermediary form fosters the myth that photography involves a transparent process." Gunning reminds us that photography has always been a deeply mediated process, involving multiple layers of framing and filtering of imagery, rather than a transparent capturing of "a direct imprint of reality."[2] This position is substantiated by "The Voice of Documentary," a pivotal text on the documentary form written two decades earlier, where Bill Nichols states that "documentaries always were forms of representation, never clear windows onto 'reality'; the film-maker was always a participant-witness and an active fabricator of meaning."[3]

If we take a broader historical view, the exceptional state is not the precarious truth-value of visual imagery in the new age of seamless digital manipulation—the exception, rather, is the era in which the moving images of documentary footage were culturally acceptable as "naked evidence" of what took place in the past. In no other era did humanity have access to this sort of "cutting proof" of moments gone by. To paraphrase Google scientist Ian Goodfellow, quoted in Foer's piece, it has been quite a historical fluke that we were able to treat video representation as "evidence that something really happened" to begin with. If the era of video evidence was just a temporary fluke, though, Foer's treatment of its presumed reliability as our "only thread of common reality" should be dismissed as hyperbole. Our notion of "common reality" hinges first and foremost on far more sustained and fundamental factors (such us a shared sense of being in the world). Representational media have always been about doing something *with*, or expressing something *about*, this underlying experience of shared reality—rather than about producing it afresh.

The preceding sentiments are evident in Nichols's definition of the essential documentary practice, which can be paraphrased as "making powerful truth claims about reality" through "creative treatment of actuality" (a claim that can be traced back to John Grierson).[4] This definition, largely, still holds in light of the contemporary situation. The only meaningful caveat imposed on it by the aforementioned issues is an increased doubt that the *source* of cinematic material can be considered a piece of "actuality."

According to the canonical semiotic analysis of cinema via Charles Sanders Peirce's typology of signs, cinematic footage is, simultaneously, an iconic sign—it looks and sounds *like* reality (like a realistic painting)—and an indexical sign, a captured tangible trace *of* reality (like a footprint).[5] This duality can be described as the key axiom behind the concept of cinematic "actualities": the footage captures a trace of a real event by resembling it, and resembles the past event by capturing it. Cinematic actualities can therefore be said to *look* like what they *are* (or were), as pieces of events detached from delimitation to occurring at a particular space and time. One could even argue that footage is, in a sense, a piece of actuality even when the source event is fictionalized: as Roland Barthes asserts in his concept of *punctum*,[6] even a staged photo inevitably captures a material occurrence (actors perform real actions, scenery is composed of real objects), and contains tangible traces of that past that are partially beyond the authors' control. Even accepting that a piece of actuality is never the full transparent truth of the event, but a perspective on it, and suspecting the ways in which captured actualities were pieced together into a film, the actuality itself remains, in a partial but crucial sense of tangible *thereness*, beyond doubt. Truth is, literally, in (the mechanism of) representation.

The potential for seamless, ubiquitous digital rendering and manipulation of cinematic material casts a skeptical shadow upon this axiom of cinema's grounding in indexicality. Given a sufficiently advanced toolbox, the filmmaker can control not only the extent to which footage resembles reality, but also the extent to which it hinges on reality at all. As the affordances of computer-generated imagery expand, images that could once only be represented via animation may now be rendered in highly realistic aesthetics (as the new "live" versions of classic Disney films testify). Computer-generated imagery is therefore becoming indistinguishable from live footage, and the days when it will be feasible to treat any video imagery as computer-generated animation until proven otherwise are fast approaching.

If we are indeed entering an age where tangible cinematic presence can be digitally manufactured from start to finish, spectatorial skepticism must go beyond questioning the ways in which events are creatively treated, and begin to also question whether events were ever *there* to begin with. The dominant understanding of "real" footage could be in the process of turning from an encounter with actuality to an encounter with *quasi-actuality*, that is: in doubt until we feel sufficiently justified to trust it—much as our trust of written reportage is determined on per-case, context-dependent basis.

Crucially, though, this potential paradigm shift in the treatment of cinematic indexicality does not seem to involve any substantial change in immediate spectatorial experience: footage continues to *feel* like reality, even when we know it does not necessarily bear any tangible trace of it. The degradation of validity in conflating iconicity and indexicality may be urging us to face the full scope of an uncomfortable realization: the degree to which an image is experienced as realistic is not necessarily correlated with the degree to which it captures reality. The sense of immersive, "reality-like" experience the cinematic medium can produce is ever on the rise, but audiences should, in parallel, become more hesitant to conflate this experienced sense of hyper-realness with a judgment that the representation constitutes a transparent capturing of reality. Such hesitancy to accept "real" footage as transparent capture poses a severe issue for traditional documentary rhetorics, which implicitly demand unmitigated faith in precisely this notion.

In summary, the new media landscape, with its ever-expanding arsenal of manipulation affordances and skeptical discourse, accentuates both the severity of shortcomings in the cinematic claim to capturing reality, and our cultural awareness of these shortcomings. Nonetheless, relinquishing the documentary aim of representing reality altogether as a result of this justified suspicion of indexicality would be a costly and hasty conclusion. Experienced reality has not ceased to exist, nor has the cultural and artistic value of human attempts to portray it and to access the traces of times gone by. If the need to represent reality through film remains persistent as ever, the newfound reasons to suspect the classical strategies through which it was addressed call for a new set of strategies, also relating, perhaps, to a new or more refined notion of what "reality" consists of.

In short, then, the challenging task of the contemporary documentary film is to continue telling us something meaningful about *actuality*, despite acknowledging that we cannot take for granted that it is composed out of *actualities.* In other words, if indexical connection to past reality can no longer be validated by photography's iconic resemblance alone, we must inquire after additional means of substantiating a meaningful representation of the traces of the past. I will now turn to analyze *Waltz with Bashir*, in an attempt to develop a reading of the film's documentary rhetorics as a unique and exemplary strategy for meeting the challenges posed by this contemporary state.

Reflexive Narrative Framing Through Exposition Sequence

"Isn't filmmaking also a form of therapy?" *Waltz with Bashir*'s opening sequence raises this question and effectively frames the narrative as an answer in the affirmative. First, we witness a harrowing dream haunting the character of Boaz, featuring specters of the dogs he was commanded to kill during his Israeli Defense Force (IDF) service in the First Lebanon War (1982). Next, Boaz meets his army friend, the main protagonist, Ari, in a bar for consultation and explains his dream. In reply, Ari blatantly denies being affected by his own war memories and recommends his friend see a psychotherapist. Boaz, in turn, poses to him the question I have quoted. In the very next scene, Ari begins to experience a harrowing, recurring dream of his own, where he emerges naked from the sea near the bombarded city of Beirut. The film frames its own making process as Ari's attempt to cure himself from this haunting dream.

In the final expositional scene, Ari spontaneously visits his "therapist friend," Ori Sivan, for consultation. Sivan tells him of an experiment in memory planting: a group of subjects were shown nine real photographs from their childhood, alongside one contrived photo depicting them in a theme park they never visited. The majority of subjects "recognized" the false photo as a childhood memory instantly, and the 20 percent who did not came back for a follow-up interview convinced they had recovered an authentic memory of the event in the interim.[7] Ori tells Ari (and more importantly, the spectator) that this experiment demonstrates something fundamental about the structure and functionality of memory: "Memory is a dynamic, living thing, capable of filling gaps and black holes it encounters to the point of full 'recollection' of something that never even occurred." Ori then encourages Ari to try to learn more about his missing memories from others so he can come to terms with them; assuring him that there is a mental mechanism that will make sure his process of memory recovery will take him "exactly where he needs to go."

This expositional sequence efficiently packages Ari's process of remembering as a catharsis narrative: the recovery of Ari's repressed memory, embalmed and triggered by his dream, ultimately places Ari as an early witness at the site of the Sabra and Shatila massacre (September 18, 1982)—a ruthless butchering of defenseless Palestinian refugees by Phalange militia, committed as retaliation for the assassination of newly elected Lebanese president Bachir Gemayel, enabled by the passive support and willful blindness of the IDF. The dream specters of the first act thus travel full circle, eventually leading into Ari's "waking up" to the repressed horror of his proximity to the atrocity in the final act. The narrative is thus essentially organized in a "predetermined acceptance of traumatic foreclosure":[8] every event sets up the stage for, and seems edited in keen awareness of, Ari's ultimate recovery of traumatic memory. As Paul Atkinson and Simon Cooper argue, this cleanly knit narrative framing makes it safe to assume that *Waltz with Bashir*'s authorial position is reflexively distant from the dissociative mind-state of the depicted director-protagonist. That is to say, we should perceive a degree of distance between Ari, the film's protagonist, and the authorial position of Ari Folman, the director, who consciously employs his own avatar and orchestrates his personal story as the central arc of his film's memory puzzle, carefully constructed to address a larger theme. We might say that while Ari the animated protagonist is shown making something closer to a traditional documentary, Folman's overlying directorial approach to the documentary process is more reflexive and meta. The film, then, is not a raw or transparent portrayal of recovery from post-traumatic repression, but rather a utilization of the post-traumatic recovery narrative for the purpose of exploring the ways by which the troubled war past is actively remembered and actively forgotten.

An Approach to Memory, History, and Cinema

I propose distinguishing three closely related points—already evident in *Waltz with Bashir*'s exposition—that define the film's approach to memory, historical fact, and photographic representation. These points form the basis for the reading I later develop:

(1) *Waltz with Bashir* primarily aims to authentically represent memories and cares relatively little about representing facts through them. Its perspective on the past focuses on its echoes in present lived experience rather than on fidelity to historical precision or political contextualization. This defining choice is addressed to some extent by all academic writing on the film, but its implications tend to become blurred in discussions of the film's message: the

shortness of historical and political contextualization is often taken as a failure to provide the audience with substantial political revelations[9] rather than a direct result of having a different aim than a "classic" antiwar documentary.

While Raz Yosef is correct to point out that the experience and trauma of the Lebanon war was somewhat repressed from the collective memory of Israeli society and that *Waltz with Bashir*'s political ambition revolves around this issue,[10] Ari (like any educated Israeli of his generation) still goes into his research already aware of general facts surrounding the film's culminating event, the Sabra and Shatila massacre. Hence, while there is clear political significance in (re-)exposing audiences inside and outside of Israel to this event—and the film provides sufficient explanation for the "uninformed" spectator— *Waltz with Bashir* makes no claims to any groundbreaking revelations regarding the historical facts of the massacre. As Ohad Landesman and Roy Bendor reiterate, the film's political message is "not intellectualized but experienced."[11]

(2) *Waltz with Bashir* approaches memory as an intermingling of past reality and creative narration. As portrayed by the psychological experiment scene, the film is skeptical in advance about the extent of objective truth value that the recovery of distant memories can produce. "So tell me, Frenkel, was I there?" Ari asks later in the film when a comrade depicts a surreal story of shooting down a young teen as he assaults their unit with a rocket launcher (portrayed to the contrasting tune of harmonic classical music). "Oh, good to know. Of course I was there," he quickly concludes—and while recovering from post-traumatic dissociation is one explanation *Waltz with Bashir* provides for this kind of statement, I believe the similarity to the memory-planting scenario cannot be accidental. While there is no reason to assume the core experience to be false, we can detect quite some creative liberty in Ari's attempt to absorb Frenkel's interpretation of it into his own memory.

The memory of the past, in other words, is addressed as an open, writable—and thus revisable—text, inherently related to both past lived experience and present narrative needs, rather than something like a site of archaeological excavation that guarantees the precision and exactness of its findings (as in the classic psychoanalytical model of post-traumatic recall). As stated by Landesman and Bendor, *Waltz with Bashir* "is as much about memory itself as it is about the retrieval of specific memories,"[12] and its exposition sets the tone for an approach to memory that "straddles the boundaries between past and present, dreams and reality, recollection and hallucination."[13]

(3) *Waltz with Bashir* is a highly reflexive film, which parallels its exploration of memory with a more implicit critical examination of narrated truth in documentary filmmaking and photography. Despite the clear differences

between photographic capture and human memory, both mechanisms are treated as indexical representation systems that simultaneously record and interpret, and whose meaning is to a large extent constituted by framing and subjective experience rather than "objective data." Tellingly, after suggesting filmmaking as a form of therapy related to dreams and memories, *Waltz with Bashir* proceeds to cast a filmmaker in the role of a therapist: Ori Sivan is not actually a psychologist, but rather a colleague, who co-wrote and co-directed Ari Folman's first feature film, *Saint Clara* (1996). His closest connection to psychology is being the executive producer of the Israeli series *In Treatment* (*Betipul*, 2005–8). It is thus fitting that his described experiment deals with personal recollection triggered by *photography*, and reveals the ambivalent truth value of both: photography too is inherently malleable and hence capable of taking advantage of memory's own inherent manipulability, for example by triggering the creation of false or inaccurate recollections. Photography is a crucial component of the way contemporary individuals and societies store and produce memories, but our tendency to perceive it as a "higher source" of indexical evidence of the true reality can be problematic, particularly when this evidence often fails to corroborate lived experience or confirm a single, fixed interpretation of historical events.

This skeptical position is implied in several scenes, perhaps most explicitly when Professor Zahava Solomon, an expert in post-trauma, tells Ari of an amateur photographer recruited to the war who used his camera as a sort of dissociative defense mechanism: documenting the horrors of war as if they were special effects in an action flick or an achievement of his photojournalistic prowess, allowing him to perceive events from a distant, professionally uninvolved perspective that denies much of the sting of their reality.[14]

When the camera finally breaks, the sudden necessity to face the truth of the situation—namely, his presence and active involvement in the scene he was ("just") photographing—makes his experience all the more traumatic. The scene displays the soldier's act of "factual" documentation as a performative fashioning of reality into a work of fiction, which enables a repressive detachment from his subjective experience, even in the present of living it.

In essence, *Waltz with Bashir* depicts two opposed reflexive paradigms of positioning the act of photographic documentation: the uninvolved observer, who collects photographic "evidence" to affectively enable a reporting of events from the position of supposed objective detachment, and the involved maker, who employs representations in a therapeutic attempt to reclaim a meaningful relation to the past (his own past, the past of the interviewees, and the collective historic past). The film can be read as suggesting the second paradigm as means of absolution for having once chosen the first. This choice is particularly meaningful, of course, in the context of witnessing violent acts. At one point, Ari describes his role during the night of the massacre—shooting flares into the sky from the outskirts of the refugee camp, ignorant of what is going on inside—with a Hebrew term (*heramti teourot*) more commonly employed in the jargon of his filmmaking profession as setting up cinematic lightning. This position of cinematically setting the scenery—passively yet directly enabling the atrocity, while in denial of fully "being there"—is the strongest source of individual and collective traumatic guilt portrayed in the film.

Rhetorics of Reality's Representation

Taken together, the three points—paragraphs (1), (2), and (3)—explain something of *Waltz with Bashir*'s idiosyncratic documentary strategy, and the unique approach through which it channels the animated representation of personal war experiences into meaningful truth claims (in Grierson's and Nichols's term) on the reality of the Lebanon war and its afterlife in Israeli memory. The foundational element of this documentary strategy is the choice to use animation. As also expressed by Folman himself, this decision was meant to do much more than merely translate the real: indeed, it was animation's capacity for the surreal, for personally stylized representations, that made it a suitable choice. Many of the film's key moments—such as the absurd, waltz-like dance performed by an IDF soldier in a "duet" with his rifle amid raining enemy fire (and along the way giving the film its name)—could only have been animated.[15]

This defining choice was not the only instance of the film opting for a significantly decreased reliance on the indexical or "real source": many spectators assume, for example, that the interview scenes are rotoscoped, when in fact the entire film was made by digital animation of cutouts based on handmade drawings.[16] Crucially, some of the interviews were never photographed at all.[17] Moreover, all of the dialogue is studio recorded—as well as scripted—based on an earlier version of the interview process. Still more, two of the eight interviews were dubbed by voice actors.[18] Thus, *Waltz with Bashir* reflexively restages not only its depicted memories and sequence of exposition,[19] but in fact, to some extent, nearly every part of the film. Since both the structure of memory and the cinematic restaging of it transform the "source material," the entire film becomes a reflection upon reflection—a model for *mise en abîme* in metadocumentary.

Despite this slew of meta strategies, *Waltz with Bashir* does not merely "dress up" as a documentary to critique and comment on the form, the way a docufiction[20] film would—as the text makes zero attempts at intentional misleading, or at epistemological supplementation (or confusion) for its own sake. It is very much a documentary not only in form—as it appropriates many of the genre's rhetorical and aesthetic tropes,[21] such as intercutting between talking head interviews and enactments of the memories described in them—but even more distinctly in its aim: for a film that treats photographic representation with explicit suspicion,[22] it is highly ambitious in its dedication to authentically represent memory. Its central aim of capturing the lived experience of subjective, traumatic memories is in significant affinity with its suspicion of indexical, objective truth claims. Animation, as argued earlier, allows the film's truth claims to revolve around authentically representing creative re-enactments of the past freed from the pretense of objectively capturing or witnessing it.[23]

Though there is always a prior, missing source event at the root of the creative interpretations provided by *Waltz with Bashir*, the film never intends nor pretends to fully capture that source or act as its replica. Rather, the film aims to capture the core of how the memory of that source event is truly experienced—that is, what about that experience authentically matters to the subjects who had it, rather than how the events would have "really" appeared. It then creatively interprets this core set of insights and the tone of their narration, to make it available for the spectator. Jeanne-Marie Viljoen defines a similar view of the foundation of the film's truth value as a reclamation of "the invisible of the visible" (in Merleau-Ponty's term) in representation of experience[24]—or even more precisely perhaps, a reclamation of the liminal territory in which memory operates. From this perspective, the challenge to distinguish between facts and interpretations in documentary film spectatorship, which haunts canonical documentary strategies, transforms from a curse into an asset. The utilization of this challenge also shapes *Waltz with Bashir*'s unique temporality, as analyzed by Atkinson and Cooper: the film's present is inseparable from the past it reflects upon, and its past is inseparable from the living present perspective through which it is unfolded and restaged.[25]

There is substantial support for the assertion that despite its ambivalent and complex structure, the film succeeds in being experienced as a trustworthy representation by the majority of its spectators: regardless of how it is critiqued in other senses, *Waltz with Bashir*'s capacity to reflect the Israeli experience of the war is highly praised in the vast majority of academic writing on it. It is also one of the best-reviewed, most commercially successful (a rare achievement for any documentary), and prize-winning Israeli films of all time—both inside Israel and outside of it. Perhaps most tellingly, Landesman and Bendor provide several testimonies of Lebanon war veterans touched to their core by the film who cite it—likely precisely (also) because of its disjointed structure and anti-indexical inventions—as the most authentic depiction of the war they have ever seen.[26]

Waltz with Bashir's success in generating such positive spectatorial experiences substantiates the claim that the film manages to effectively tap into some vital aspect of the Israeli collective "lived memory"[27] of the Lebanon War. These stories, however, do not integrate or coalesce into a coherent whole but rather form an assemblage of hallucinatory and fragmented individual experiences. The relation of this disjointed corpus we call *Waltz with Bashir* to collective Israeli memory thus functions similarly to what Ann Rigney calls "counter-memories"[28]—a recovery of memories that have been lost or hidden from the canonical narrative of collective memory (essentially the collective-memory equivalent of the process Ari is depicted as going through). The majority of depicted memories are not explicitly critical of the mainstream Israeli political narrative, but function as counter-memories because they are out of touch with the heroic canonical narrative of what being an IDF soldier participating in a war is supposed to feel and look like. Yosef defines them as "disremembered memories . . . constructed through forgetting and marked with traces of fantasy . . . [thus] allowing soldiers to represent events that are too threatening to be experienced directly."[29] In other words, *Waltz with Bashir* fashions a trustworthy animated archive that taps into Israeli soldiers' traumatic memory of what being in the war *felt* like, and what having been there feels like now, precisely by relinquishing the claim to indexical fact, and seeking instead to "document"—by these alternative means—the surreal state of dissonance between reality and experience.

Indexicality Strikes Back?

Having established a reading of *Waltz with Bashir*'s unique approach to truth in representation, I now turn to address the film's final sequence—perhaps its most powerful, haunting, and commented-upon part—which appears to function as a complete breach of that approach.

Waltz with Bashir culminates in a juxtaposition of its animated aesthetics with appropriated archival footage from the Sabra and Shatila massacre. As Ari finally recovers a memory that places him among the first to witness the aftermath of the massacre during the following morning, the film transitions from the animated universe into the realm of archival footage, and of far stronger indexical claim to truth. At this point, the film spatially links an animated close-up of past-Ari's dissociative expression to footage of a wailing, grief-stricken Palestinian woman situated to fit his point-of-view perspective, that is, as a proxy shot-reverse-shot cut that transitions between the animated and archival.[30] After bringing across this metaphorical engagement in "shared space" between the photo-archived atrocity and animation, the film cuts to footage of brutalized dead bodies, and then fades to black.

Most academic writing on *Waltz with Bashir* analyzes its political message and the degree to which it is pertinent and effective, leaning to a large extent on assessing the statement of this final scene. The "optimistic" readings (e.g., Landesman and Bendor; Garrett Stewart;[31] and to a lesser degree Viljoen) celebrate *Waltz with Bashir*'s success in making the experience of the Lebanon war accessible to the spectators and leading them, along with the protagonist, to go through "an eye opening rude awakening"[32] regarding Israel's collective moral responsibility for the heinous massacre. In this final scene, it follows, "Any layer of shielding distanciation that may have persisted due to the animated form's beauty . . . is peeled off to disclose the naked, visible evidence."[33]

Atkinson and Cooper provide a strong refutation to this reading: Given *Waltz with Bashir*'s suspicion of indexical footage and emphasis on creative restaging of the past over objective evidence, it seems naive to treat the ending of the film as capable of "carrying the burden of genuine historical recognition."[34] Their own account ultimately concurs with Yosef's political criticism, according to which Ari's struggles with his post-traumatic state allow him to cast himself as a victim, thereby forced to become a bystander to historical horrors,[35] while the actual Palestinian victims are left out of the picture.[36] Ari's helplessness and loss of agency is thus a downplaying of Israeli responsibility,[37] and rather than relating to the experience of the Palestinian Others, *Waltz with Bashir* appropriates their suffering to provide a catharsis for its protagonist's process of personal healing.[38]

However, if we support Atkinson and Cooper's own previous argument that *Waltz with Bashir* utilizes trauma and the tropes related to it as "a storytelling device"[39] to enable reflexively staged re-enactments, it is quite strange that *Waltz with Bashir* would end with a reclamation, through indexical "naked visible" evidence, of the absolute truth of Ari's restored memories—rather than with another such (animated) re-enactment. Much like the opening sequence, the cleanly knit and masterfully crafted narrative structure of this final part can be read as another reflexive restaging of the post-traumatic recovery process, cleverly employed to bring the narrative to a unique, carefully sutured closure. The emotional tone of *Waltz with Bashir*'s final fade to black, which refrains from offering closure back in the animated world of the shocked Ari, leaves further space to question this interpretation that the film intended to frame its endings as a perfect catharsis to Ari's process.

It is entirely possible to maintain that *Waltz with Bashir* employs the archival imagery as representing a rude awakening of the buried (suppressed or forgotten) truth of Ari's memory of the atrocity—a cinematic choice that certainly offered a powerful, spectatorial experience, and appeared to substantiate the horror of the Sabra and Shatila massacre by an imposed contrast with non-indexical animation. This result certainly appears to be what the final sequence is telling us (as reflected, for instance, in my own experience upon first viewing), and it is also the consensus reading of *Waltz with Bashir* in previous academic writing. But if we accept this reading of the ending, it should be understood, in the context my earlier discussion, as a somewhat disappointing de-radicalization of the film's treatment of documentary representation and indexical truth: the main narrative conflict is cathartically solved by reclamation of the facts of buried memories via photographic documentation, whose truth value appears superior to the ambivalence of animation and of subjective experience—a notion that previous parts of the film are keenly suspicious of.

Upon reflection, the canonical reading of Ari's remembrance is entirely feasible, but should come attached with the concession that it somewhat weakens the film's aesthetic message and philosophical underpinnings. Additionally, a contemporary reading of the film in these times of indexical suspicion must not allow us to forget the immense ontological gap being skipped over in this "solution" of the plot through the cut from animation to archival footage. As a compensation, I would therefore like to suggest an alternative subversive reading, according to which *Waltz with Bashir* maintains its skeptical approach to facts and indexicality up to and including its ending.

The setup of the final sequence provides some evidence for this suggestion. In the beginning of the final sequence, Ari declares that he regained—via his process of self-inquiry through conversations with others—all of his memories except for the most pivotal one, relating to both his recurring hallucinatory dream and his whereabouts at the time of the massacre. Despite having no factual knowledge of his whereabouts and no leads on whom to reclaim this memory through or from, Ari is assured by Ori Sivan—in a second appearance as a narrative instigator—that his hallucination is real "because it reflects his real emotional concern with the massacre." We are reminded of Ori's earlier promise that the journey will take Ari "exactly where he needs to go." Ori then advises Ari to seek out the true, specific details of the event so that he can position his personal memory in relation to them. Once again, Ori's choice of words to describe the therapeutic/cinematic process he suggests that Ari undertake differs from the classical Freudian psychoanalytic portrayal of recovering traumatically repressed truths by excavating buried memories: Ori seems far less concerned with Ari's memories being factual than with his experience of remembrance being true to his narrative needs. He is never enthusiastic about "organic" recollection, but rather treats memory as fluid and malleable. His only promise is that Ari's search would eventually recover a more cohesive story.

After hearing some reports of the willful blindness of Israeli leadership about the severity of events at Sabra and Shatila as the massacre was taking place, Ari finally restores his crucial memory by relating to the perspective of Ron Ben-Ishay, a charismatic news reporter who was among the first Israelis to witnesses the scene. Ron was already portrayed earlier in the film (from a soldier's perspective) as he confidently toured an active battleground—as if protected from any danger by an invisible, protective shield imposed merely by press membership. Thus it is notable that by giving Ron the final interview, the film appropriates the classical documentary approach: the switch to Ron's perspective emblematizes the classical, more journalistic documentary rhetoric of witnessing truth through observational experience—and along with it creating indexical footage/evidence.

The film's aforementioned last animated shot that cuts into the archival massacre footage—which we can safely assume was taken by Ron's crew—begins from a point of view depicting Ron's perspective, then dollies in, through faceless Palestinian women, into Ari's close-up that cuts into the archival footage. The audio track[40] facilitates the appearance of almost-seamless continuity between the two radically different cinematic materialities and character perspectives. Based on all of the preceding, I contend that it is quite conceivable that Ari plants (implants) himself in the scene of the massacre's aftermath by means of Ron's footage and subsequent story about the events. As further explored in what follows, the film provides us with all the necessary elements to support this reading.

Let us compare the depiction of Ari's cathartic scene of remembrance to the film's aforementioned depiction of the memory-planting experiment: every single person who did not recognize themselves in the theme park photo has "restored" that memory within a week, when provided relatively slight motivation to do so. Ari has a much stronger narrative need to "restore" his memory, and just as in the experiment, "objective" footage that documents the events he needs to relate that memory to (in his case, delivered by the authoritative journalistic figure of Ron Ben-Ishay rather than the lab psychologist). While his character is not planted in the footage as some clever manipulation designed by another, planted memories are in fact most often self-planted, and Ari has an extremely strong circumstantial desire to plant himself in the scene of the massacre: he has reclaimed the knowledge that he actually was somewhere within the general vicinity of Sabra and Shatila that morning, suffers from a recurring, haunting dream urging him to trace back his exact deeds and whereabouts, and begins his questioning of others following his filmmaker/psychologist friend's advice to inquire after the details of where he was in order to arrive "where he needs" to go. It therefore makes sense that Ari, by means of almost the exact same memory-planting mechanism the exposition goes out of its way to explain, would unconsciously utilize the documentary footage he finds to fill the gap in his own organic memory, culminating in his experience of sudden "authentic" remembrance that he was right there, at the very scene of the (indexical) traces captured by the journalistic cameras. This cathartic realization of having been *right there*, and the position of moral responsibility entailed in directly witnessing, and therefore passively enabling, the atrocity, is where Ari needed to go. But we, the spectators, are not in a position to confidently conclude that this is where he actually was.

Whether or not this ambiguity was intended by the filmmaker, I argue that the strong epistemological doubt that hides behind the affective ontological shift invites a skeptical reading of *Waltz with Bashir*'s reflexively staged ending, and thus of the truth value of Ari's remembrance. The revelation of truth occurs through a suspicious mechanism—the planting of archival data in animation, and by proxy, the mechanism of self-planted memory—and therefore should be understood as uncertain. Furthermore, I do not mean to substantiate this as a new privileged reading: it is sufficient to accept my reading as one possibility, in order to have cause to reinterpret the meaning of the film's end: even if the protagonist experiences a perfect catharsis, keeping this doubt in mind should prevent us from exiting the film with one. The film gives us no cause, of course, to doubt the horrifying truth of the Sabra and Shatila massacre, but it provides us with ample tools to doubt the "recovery" of Ari's whereabouts during the massacre, and its narrative role as the clean and clear ending of Ari's inner search.

Examination from my proposed perspective opens the door to an awareness of a more radical knowledge gap in the ending: Yosef is correct to point out the film's distance from the lived experience of the Palestinian Other. The sight of the mutilated bodies and weeping women is undeniably horrific, but we are given no narrative tools to see from their point of view, to meaningfully treat them as characters in the story. The sudden burst into the (animated) scene of the archival footage of inconceivable violence initially leaves us in the same state as young Ari: under dissociative shock, unable to fully contextualize or process the relationship between the two realms.

That conflict, I believe, is exactly the point of the archival appropriation: to flood the immense gap between facts and their meaningful comprehension, between a "merely factual" experience of horrific footage and an authentically meaningful one. While audiences are likely to experience the image as far more poignant and affective than if they had viewed it in isolation, even that experience remains removed from an ability to fully comprehend the "true" victim's perspective. Such a judgment is part of a politically troubling situation, and at the heart of the Israeli-Palestinian conflict: the vast majority of people on both sides lack the capacity to meaningfully engage with the experience and suffering of the other, as "the enemy's" lived experience and perspective are constantly banished and repressed from collective memory. In other words, rather than downplaying Israeli responsibility, I view the ending as authentically portraying the difficulty in meaningfully perceiving it when focalized through an Israeli perspective—most particularly when that responsibility is indirect or grounded in fleeting genuine contact. The presence of Palestinian refugees—including the millions who were not killed in Sabra and Shatila, and therefore must remain unseen—is far removed and constantly repressed from Israeli lives. The vast majority of Israelis therefore fail to experience a direct, embodied proximity to, and therefore a more tangible sense of complicity in, the suffering of Palestinians. Even the minority who view themselves as largely responsible for the occupation and the past and present suffering of Palestinians it entails, struggle to grasp such direct relationality to the struggles of a people they largely cannot truly know and never truly encounter.

Ari's supposed remembrance of "having been there," of personally witnessing the atrocities depicted in the footage, bridges over a significant portion of this distance: he gains the ability to "dolly in" on his presence in the traumatic moment, from his re-focalized present perspective. He can now feel ethically driven to contemplate his involvement, rather than remain in a dissociative limbo or paralyzed by memory gaps. Ari certainly has not gained the ability to fully grasp the Palestinian experience of the atrocity, yet the reframing of his memory may nonetheless be a personally and politically substantial shift in his (inevitably Israeli) perspective—constituting a capacity to more directly and meaningfully acknowledge the Palestinian suffering, and thereby potentially pursue further understanding and action.

Conclusion: *Waltz with Bashir* as a Call for Involved Spectatorship

Waltz with Bashir ends with a moment of powerful transition, where horrifying historical footage literally cuts into the film's unique animated world of muddled and creative personal recollection. While Folman's original intention with this transition was likely to achieve narrative closure through the powerful truth claim of the documentary archive (even at the cost of weakening the film's stylistic message), rewatching the film in this age of suspect indexicality draws our attention to the stitches in this masterfully crafted yet far from seamless transition. From this perspective, my subversive reading argues that the film's broader approach to memory, authenticity, and documentation provides us with ample reason to doubt the factuality of Ari's final reclamation of memory.

Considering what Ari gains from this experience of reclamation, however, how much does it truly matter (in terms of assessing the film's message and effect) whether or not the "recovered" memory is factual or, as it were, merely filmic? Given unavoidable doubt in determining even this memory's truth value, we could view it as an imaginative act of remembrance—one that transforms Ari's spectatorship of the atrocity footage from a passively distant to an actively engaged experience, and thus allows him to develop an authentic relation to the event and the people involved. The character of Ari, who spends most of the film "spectating" memories (including those of others) and attempting to relate himself to them, essentially goes through the spectatorial paradigm shift that Folman's film ideally seeks to invoke in its own spectators.

By revolving its narrative around the unfolding structure of how the traumatic past is narrated in both footage and memory, *Waltz with Bashir* requires both its protagonist and spectators to actively attempt to form a reading of this past, to ponder their experience of the film and its meanings. The film's own creative representations are received as trustworthy largely because they restage and demystify truth in representation, forming a tertiary space in which the depicted hallucinatory scenes can be experienced as authentically representing the intensely personal structure of lived traumatic memory.

Indexical proof is thus not presented as inherently deceitful, but rather as inherently partial and dependent on the context of its creation and interpretation. The film's strongest critique, in my opinion, is not of the indexical goal of relating to an objective (and therefore true) past—it does not dispute or deny the existence of objective facts about the past—but rather of the pacified perception that automatic, naive acceptance of this kind of truth claim can evoke.

Waltz with Bashir expresses a strong performative opposition to the stance of passive, detached spectatorship—of war atrocities, of personal and collective memories, of cinema, and of present experience.

As argued by Atkinson and Cooper, "the realism of the photo is a lifeless process":[41] documentary and archival footage can only produce meaningful knowledge through authentically relating to a narrative that resonates in lived experience in some form or another, and *Waltz with Bashir* shows us how this statement holds even for the documentary representation of significant and horrifying historical facts. In that sense, the film's approach to archival practices can be said to be in line with Eric Ketelaar, who views them first and foremost as storytelling devices, mechanisms for making images seen through tacit narrative framing.[42] *Waltz with Bashir* can thus be considered as a reassertion of Vivian Sobchack's claim that "the documentary film is "less a 'thing' than an experience,"[43] as well Paul Ward's assertion that animated documentaries "create the real."[44]

Similar to Tom Gunning's assertion that "a photograph can only tell the truth if it is also capable of telling a lie,"[45] *Waltz with Bashir*'s message on the documentary medium, in my reading, is that documentary film and photographic documentation at large can only forge meaningful relationalities to the traces of our past because they are equally capable of denying these relationalities by claiming a position of objective detachment (much like the amateur photographer/soldier described by Zahava Solomon). Within this scope, the film can be understood as a call to switch between the two reflexive paradigms mentioned in this chapter's second part: namely, a call to "break the camera" through which we protect ourselves from an experience of active involvement in the world we are depicting or recording, and instead wield a more "animated" camera, through which this involvement—and the constant entanglement between the world we inhabit and our creative acts of interpreting and remembering it—can be actively acknowledged. It is only through the wielding of this "animated" camera, and the new authorial position of creatively processing traces of the past despite relinquishing the premise of transparent indexical documentary truth, that filmmaking can indeed (as Boaz ponders in the opening sequence) act as a form of therapy.

We may no longer be—in the near future of ubiquitous and seamless video manipulation technologies, and likely already in present times—able to interpret cinematic footage as "naked evidence" of the past. But should this loss be taken to mean that the capturing and relating to traces of the past is now any less of a crucial or valid pursuit? *Waltz with Bashir* provides us with a fitting case study to argue for the opposite. The film's patchwork of post-traumatic memories draws its truth value and significance first and foremost from its insightful exploration of active and creative relation to the past. *Waltz with Bashir* marks an inevitable gap between present and past, between "the way things were" and memories or photographic representations of these "things," between historical events and subjective attempts to relate to them. Yet it finds great value in the search to partially bridge or fill these gaps, despite the foregone conclusion that any such connection is prone to skepticism.

Therefore, as traditional documentary rhetorics are losing their sway over contemporary spectators, *Waltz with Bashir*'s alternative strategies for making powerful (though troubled) truth claims about reality can be viewed as a valuable source of inspiration for future documentary works—whether animated, filmed, or digitalized.

Notes

1. Franklin Foer, "The Era of Fake Video Begins," *The Atlantic*, May 2018 (atlantic.com).
2. Tom Gunning, "What's the Point of an Index? or, Faking Photographs," *Nordicom Review* 1–2 (2004): 40.
3. Bill Nichols, "The Voice of Documentary," *Film Quarterly* 36, no. 3 (1983): 18.
4. John Grierson and Forsyth Hardy, *Grierson on Documentary* (Berkeley: University of California Press, 1971).
5. Johannes Ehrat, *Cinema and Semiotic: Peirce and Film Aesthetics, Narration, and Representation* (Toronto: University of Toronto Press, 2005).
6. Roland Barthes, *Camera Lucida: Reflections on Photography*, trans. Richard Howard (New York: Macmillan, 1981).
7. While I was not able to find academic citation of this precise experiment, I strongly suspect it to be a synthesis of very similar experiments run by Elizabeth Loftus and her laboratory at the University of California, one of which involves planting a memory of meeting Bugs Bunny (a Warner Brothers character) in Disneyland. See Elizabeth F. Loftus, "Planting Misinformation in the Human Mind: A 30-Year Investigation of the Malleability of Memory," *Learning & Memory* 12, no. 4 (2005): 361–66.
8. Paul Atkinson and Simon Cooper, "Untimely Animations: *Waltz with Bashir* and the Incorporation of Historical Difference," *Screening the Past* 34 (2012): 269.
9. Nicholas Hetrick, "Ari Folman's *Waltz with Bashir* and the Limits of Abstract Tragedy," *Image & Narrative* vol. 11, no. 2 (2010): 79. Raz Yosef, "War Fantasies: Memory, Trauma and Ethics in Ari Folman's *Waltz with Bashir*," *Journal of Modern Jewish Studies* 9, no. 3 (2010): 315.
10. Yosef, "War Fantasies," 312–13.
11. Ohad Landesman and Roy Bendor, "Animated Recollection and Spectatorial Experience in *Waltz with Bashir*," *Animation* 6 (2011): 15.
12. Landesman and Bendor, "Animated Recollection," 4.
13. Landesman and Bendor, "Animated Recollection," 4.
14. Atkinson and Cooper, "Untimely Animations," 273.
15. Atkinson and Cooper, "Untimely Animations," 261.

16. Landesman and Bendor, "Animated Recollection," 4.
17. In one instance, a friend of Ari agrees to tell his story only as long as it is sketched rather than filmed—but the animated sketches seem able to cut deeper into their subject's psyche than direct photographic representation could hope to.
18. Landesman and Bendor, "Animated Recollection," 5.
19. Atkinson and Cooper, "Untimely Animations," 269.
20. Ohad Landesman, "Lying to be Real: the Aesthetics of ambiguity in Docufictions," *Contemporary Documentary*, eds. Daniel Marcus and Selmin Kara, Routledge (2015), 9.
21. Landseman and Bendor, "Animated Recollection," 7.
22. Atkinson and Cooper, "Untimely Animations," 260.
23. Atkinson and Cooper, "Untimely Animations," 262.
24. Jeanne-Marie Viljoen, "*Waltz with Bashir*: Between Representation and Experience," *Critical Arts* 28, no. 1 (2014): 45.
25. Atkinson and Cooper, "Untimely Animations," 261.
26. Landesman and Bendor, "Animated Recollection," 9–10.
27. Ann Rigney, "Plenitude, Scarcity and the Circulation of Cultural Memory," *Journal of European Studies* 35, no. 1 (2005): 12.
28. Rigney, "Circulation of Cultural Memory," 13.
29. Yosef, "War Fantasies," 318.
30. Landesman and Bendor, "Animated Recollection," 14.
31. Garrett Stewart, "Screen Memory in *Waltz with Bashir*," *Film Quarterly* 63, no. 3 (2010): 58–62.
32. Landesman and Bendor, "Animated Recollection," 14.
33. Landesman and Bendor, "Animated Recollection," 14.
34. Atkinson and Cooper, "Untimely Animations," 267.
35. Yosef, "War Fantasies," 323.
36. See Holger Pötzsch, "The Ubiquitous Absence of the Enemy in Contemporary Israeli War Films," in *The Philosophy of War Films*, ed. David LaRocca (Lexington: University Press of Kentucky, 2014), 313–33.
37. Atkinson and Cooper, "Untimely Animations," 268.
38. Yosef, "War Fantasies," 324.
39. Atkinson and Cooper, "Untimely Animations," 258.
40. The diegetic sound of the post-massacre footage that is assumed by many (e.g., Landesman and Bendor, "Animated Recollection," 14) to substantiate Ari's vicinity to the footage, in fact, first appears earlier in the shot, that is, from Ron's point of view.
41. Atkinson and Cooper, "Untimely Animations," 260.
42. Eric Ketelaar, "Tacit Narratives: The Meanings of Archives," *Archival Science* 1 (2001): 133–40.
43. Vivian Sobchack, "Toward a Phenomenology of Nonfictional Film Experience," in *Collecting Visible Evidence*, vol. 6, ed. Jane M. Gaines and Michael Renov (Berkeley: University of California Press, 1999), 241. See also Landesman and Bendor, "Animated Recollection," 2.
44. Paul Ward, "Animated Realities: The Animated Film, Documentary, Realism," *Reconstruction* 8, no. 2 (2008): 1–28.
45. Tom Gunning, "What's the Point of an Index?," 42.

14

Alone., Again

On Martin Arnold's Metaformal Invention by Intervention

David LaRocca

> I am not a film theorist and I did not try to filmically translate any
> theory of gender politics. . . . Theories that film artists themselves at-
> tribute to their work are to be taken with a grain of salt.[1]
>
> —Martin Arnold

As a final chapter in this series of dispatches on metacinema, consider the
way cinematic form can itself be or become content of an engaging and illuminating sort—yet perhaps not in the way one might think upon a first encounter. Indeed, it is repetition in making and repetition in viewing (and
hearing) film that sits at the crux of our inquiry. For a case study and arresting
instance, we look and listen to Martin Arnold (b. 1959), an Austrian experimental filmmaker who has created media artifacts of special sophistication
and nuance. In the process of developing his body of work, he has become a
fitting heir to several inventive legacies, including the productions of fellow-
Austrian avant-garde filmmakers such as Gustav Deutsch, Kurt Kren, Valie
Export, Mara Mattuschka, Peter Tscherkassky,[2] and especially Peter Kubelka
(*Arnulf Rainer*, 1960); the found-footage tradition, including Craig Baldwin,
Bruce Conner, Ken Jacobs, Barbara Hammer, Matthias Müller, Raphael
Montañez Ortiz, Jay Rosenblatt, Paul Sharits, Luther Price, and Naomi
Uman; structural filmmakers, such as Stan Brakhage, Ernie Gehr, Larry
Gottheim, and Michael Snow; the single-frame editing or flicker-film tradi-
tion, as found in work by Tony Conrad (*The Flicker*, 1965) and Paul Sharits
(*T,O,U,C,H,I,N,G*, 1969); and, last, and not to be overlooked, the cine-sound
experiments of Hollis Frampton, especially *Critical Mass* (1971).[3] In this final
chapter—situated as an invitation to further, future investigations—we approach anew the necessary and complicated relationship between form and

David LaRocca, Alone., Again In: *Metacinema*. Edited by: David LaRocca, Oxford University Press. © Oxford University Press
2021. DOI: 10.1093/oso/9780190095345.003.0015

content in metacinematic works and contemplate reasons why that tender plait in specific films by Arnold is significant more generally for the study of media and metamedia. For instance, something will be said about the mechanics and thematics of form, and indeed, how those realms muddle and fructify our sensibility for metaform. To make such a general query more situated in response to a discrete set of film texts, we turn to Arnold's mechanical, photo-optical transformation of found footage, and closely track how the meanings afforded by his subsequent, surplus work of art may differ, perhaps radically, from the archival media's original thematics.

From the first frames of encounter with Arnold's audiovisual offerings—in work that comprises *The Cineseizure* (1989, 1993, 1998)—otherwise distinct categories rapidly coalesce, and at times radically collapse: Hollywood star, movie director, experimental filmmaker, and audience as well as familiar phenomenological traits, such as playback rate, playback direction, and the nature of the diegetic sound environment. In the generative semantic field of Arnold's late-twentieth century experimental films, a viewer can wonder where meaning is located—in the found footage, in the mode of display, in oneself, in all of them at once? The selections from Arnold's oeuvre here gathered for critical consideration not only deepen in the wake of the savvy studies collected in this volume, they also—with some interpretative assistance—contribute to the discourse on the form and content of filmic reference and reflexivity.

Medium-Specific Metacinema

Nicholas Ray, director of *Johnny Guitar* (1954) and *Rebel Without a Cause* (1955) and the experimental feature film *We Can't Go Home Again* (1973), once remarked that Hollis Frampton's avant-garde classic *Critical Mass* is "the funniest film since Lubitsch."[4] If one is familiar with Frampton's looping meditation on love, (mis)communication, alienation, and the general spatiotemporal separation between humans—what Scott MacDonald calls, after and in antagonism with Stanley Cavell, a "cinema of de-marriage"[5]—one will appreciate the ways MacDonald's ascription and assessment may apply equally well to Martin Arnold's avant-garde classic *Alone. Life Wastes Andy Hardy* (1998). What unites these two works—*Critical Mass* made by an American in the heyday of experimental film in America and the other, *Alone.*, by an Austrian at the dawn of the digital age—is more than the fact that both taught for a time in the Cinema Department at Binghamton University.[6] Rather, what also draws out their connection in the context of this chapter is precisely the ways in which these cinematic experimentalists generate theoretical intrigue by means of manipulations of the film medium itself.

If, as noted in the introduction, "film exists in a state of philosophy: it is inherently self-reflexive," let us dwell on Cavell's claim for its doubleness, or double status.[7] As Frampton and Arnold demonstrate for us, in these and related works, diegetic content is inherently reflexive; so too is the medium of film. Indeed, in the repetitions and recursions of Arnold's *Alone.* (titular period firmly in place—a full stop that stands as an invitation to begin again, and as my title intimates, to repeat again and again, if, as it were, on one's own, all alone), we are granted what appears to be rare experiential access to the fecundity of somatic encounters with film's otherwise and usually hidden—or unconsciously veiled—attributes. As with a first viewing of *Critical Mass*, if one doesn't smile *and then* laugh at (or with) *Alone.*, the film has not broken through. But once one *does* smile and laugh, the discoveries are there to be made: why are we smiling, laughing as well as nervous and ashamed? What is this hypnotic creation coaxing from our casual, even dare I say lazy, or at least passive reliance on the givenness of the film's projection? The smile and the laugh may indicate, first, that one is watching and listening anew; and only second that one may be engaged or troubled by what can be said about the "content" of the film. Given these effects and the ambiguities inherent in their announcement, hence the hope to contextualize and clarify Arnold's achievement within the ongoing conversation in this volume about metacinema—and also in the coursing flow of film theoretical accounts of his work beyond it. What, in effect, does *Alone.*—though not alone in its power to do so—activate in our sense of the meaning and possibilities of the film medium, not least, its inherent reflexivity?

In Martin Arnold's remarkable suite of films exploring (and exploiting) experimental cinematic techniques—commonly referred to by the name *The Cineseizure*—we find *Pièce touchée* (1989, 16 mins.), *Passage à l'acte* (1993, 12 mins.) and *Alone. Life Wastes Andy Hardy* (1998), a fifteen-minute film whose ostensible content is coextensive with a 1940 movie entitled *Andy Hardy Meets Debutante* (dir. George B. Seitz) starring a young Judy Garland and Mickey Rooney, and a 1939 Busby Berkeley movie, *Babe in Arms*.[8] Working from original clips, Arnold offers us a distinctive, now indelible, hyperkinetically paced paratactic visual and sonic style. With each frame side by side, with each sound juxtaposed, Arnold's mechanical, metaformal strategy of insistent, staccato rhythms creates the conditions for thinking through cause and effect, chronology, and naturally, the comparison of states of being. As my title and initial notes rightly suggest, in the pages that follow, I focus mainly on *Alone.*, though I assume the near presence and steady relevance of its two predecessor films, not just because the three films share a methodology, but because (for that reason and unsurprisingly) some of the critical commentary on the 1989 and 1993 works remains valid for thinking about the 1998 project.

Arnold's *Alone.* only contains selected "found footage" from *Andy Hardy Meets Debutante* and *Babe in Arms*, yet, as my remarks in this chapter aim to show, Arnold's conspicuous manipulation of the found footage is transformative not just for the content (for instance, how it is "replayed"—and then, at nonstandard speeds, in two directions, looped, and otherwise mechanically distorted, etc.), but also, more profoundly, for how that manipulation alters—and expands—the possible meanings we might be said to "find" in the 1939 and 1940 originals. Among other things, Arnold troubles our sense of what an "original film"—for example, as a print, say—means; indeed, we are reminded anew that *how* a film is played (played back, replayed) is also part of its ontology as a medium as well as the phenomenology of its reception (as re-viewed). The manner of exhibiting the moving image, and its associated sounds, proves highly consequential for any thinking about the "content" of those sequential audiovisual representations.

While many incisive commentaries exist on Arnold's *The Cineseizure* (which I delightedly hasten to acknowledge and which necessarily inform these proceedings), none, so far as I can tell, explicitly connect his methodologies and results to the notion of metacinema (nor its articulation or practice as a discourse in the study of cinema). My purpose in reviewing, recounting, repeating, and otherwise engaging with some of the excellent literature on Arnold is to explicate how *Alone.*, though not alone among the trilogy of works in *The Cineseizure*, may serve as a useful point of reference when trying to account for the medium-specific qualities of metacinema. Thus, as many of the contributors to the present collection have expertly and convincingly communicated how filmic *content* is metacinematic (quickly, the way the diegesis and mise en scène of a given screen moment may make reference to another work, or to itself), my intention in this final chapter is to re-emphasize a promise contained in the subtitle of the book itself, namely, the extent to which film *form* is also (always already) metacinematic. Arnold's *Alone.* remains, more than two decades on, a salient clinic for coming to consciousness of, as Cavell called attention to, the inherent reflexivity of film. If we have become used to alluding to film's "state" (as philosophical), that prevalence typically addresses elements of content, leaving aside, ignoring, and arguably, most often, simply not perceiving the ways in which film form is metacinematic. Some of our labors in film criticism must be sensible to (and have a sense of humor about), as Ludwig Wittgenstein wryly reported long ago, the way that certain phenomena "escaped remark only because they are always before our eyes."[9] The present chapter is not meant to be a comprehensive statement or proof of film's metacinematic nature as form, but instead a brief reminder that our experience of metacinema will be enlarged and enriched if we retain some vigilance in noting the traits and attributes of its undeniable, if sometimes indiscernible, occasionally overlooked and underheard, form.

Revelation versus Inscription

For good reason, there is a tendency among accomplished film theorists and culture critics to get caught up by, and therefore intently focused upon, the metacontent of *Alone. Life Wastes Andy Hardy* as well as its predecessors *Pièce touchée* and *Passage à l'acte*.[10] If they are understandably diverted, even forgivably tricked, by what they see and hear, we find them not only earnestly studying the halting motions of the human figures on the screen and the clipped sounds they emit, but eagerly rushing to apply—and repeat—savvy psychoanalytic readings of those movements and cacophonies. Indeed, Martin Arnold's own substantive training in psychoanalysis and his candid psychoanalytic accounts of his own films could be cited as a reason critics, having been prompted by his example, feel such license and, indeed, enthusiasm to proceed in his company. While accepting that much of the lavished attention is legitimate and sincere, and the results on offer from these many talented readers gratifying (my work in what follows, to be sure, is predicated on their theoretical formulations), the effort here marks something of a shift of emphasis—or in an Arnoldian spirit, a reversal. Thus, while acknowledging representative portions of what has been said, I also heed a call to the potency of Arnold's achievement in metaform that may, perhaps should, take us in a different direction. Such a correction can be characterized, in part, as an allowance for film content to cede the spotlight momentarily for a glimpse of its form.

As a consequence of this modest recalibration—tacking from awareness of metacontent to metaform—something striking happens, almost inadvertently, and almost at once: one can more easily see that many, if not most, of the (mostly) adoring critics of Arnold's work speak in remarkably uniform, nearly unanimous ways, of how he "reveals" "hidden" "layers" and makes otherwise "latent" content apparent.[11] And if one is attuned only or mostly to content, then such results seem logical; once the trope of revelation is in place, the feeling of cinema's past being suddenly available creates a tremendous satisfaction—like the finding of a secret code for an otherwise inscrutable puzzle. Yet, despite the overwhelming consensus that Arnold "reveals" what is already "in" or "under" the image—somehow until now as it were unseen because we have been watching movies at regular speed (twenty-four frames per second) and thus missed it—dwelling on Arnold's practice with the form (his metaformal intervention), a viewer/listener rather quickly stumbles upon the fact that, well, the deep psychoanalytic readings and the capable gender critiques are not "in" the content of the original after all. Rather, they are—as Arnold himself puts it, and in a metaphor at odds with revelation—"inscribed" in the film, that is, added by the artist, not offered by the originators.[12] To be clear, Arnold is speaking metaphorically: his labors in *Alone.*—as in *Pièce touchée* and *Passage à l'acte*—are not inscribed into the film literally, say, in the way Naomi Uman makes contact with film emulsion in her scratch-and-bleach work (e.g., *Removed*, 1999), but rather "inscribed" figuratively in the mode of selecting and ordering optically printed 16 mm frames and thereafter augmenting their variable frame-rate and direction of playback. He is working *with* the medium, not "on" it; such a method is additive of meaning rather than illuminative of some signification presumed to be "in" the found footage. Doubtless the cumulative effect of works in *The Cineseizure* suggests a mode of "writing upon" or "writing into" the originals (or, in a similar spirit of medial intervention, defacing or deforming). Yet, unlike Uman's direct interference with the emulsion, Arnold does not manipulate the content per se but instead the mode of its presentation. Call this Arnold's photo-mechanical legerdemain: a trick of the hands in which form becomes content.

While most interpreters of Arnold's *Alone.* have rushed to (first) assess the psychoanalytical "content" of *Andy Hardy Meets Debutante* and *Babe in Arms*, perhaps a too-tempting catnip for theorists, it is not the cinematic *content* that demands our initial analysis, but Arnold's formal techniques. In other words, as Scott MacDonald has pointed out, Arnold has not just labored in an experimental and avant-garde cinematic tradition, but, intentionally or not, recuperated certain traits and tricks of *early* cinema, namely, magic. A theorist—film theorist or otherwise—coming to *Alone. Life Wastes Andy Hardy* for the first time, or even many, many times (after repeated viewings, or re-viewings), may be so distracted, so hypnotized, so put under a spell by the density of psychosexual provocations accosting the eye and ear (and other sensitive body parts) that the formal aspects of his achievement become an afterthought, or not thought about much at all.

Most commonly, it appears to me, critics seem to conflate two things: one that is true and one that is not true (or at least misleading): put tersely, that Arnold "transforms" the footage he has selected (true) and thereby "reveals" "hidden" meanings—such as psychoanalytic notions that were always there but were missed (untrue or misleading). If the first (true) point has been made in the critical literature to wonderful effect, the second point has created something of a false or confused/confusing/contradictory reading of Arnold's special contribution to experimental and avant-garde cinema and, I would argue, to the inheritance and appreciation of metacinema more particularly.

Many critics would have it that Arnold—in the position of a (cinematic) psychoanalyst, and again he is professionally trained in psychology—performs something like psychoanalysis on the films he has chosen to extract from; thus, the character Andy Hardy, and his parents, come in for "treatment." At this point, we are told that there are Oedipal urges—"suppressed" erotic feelings for the mother, and "boiling" rage toward the father (Judge James Hardy played by Lewis Stone).[13] Or, for some, better with archetypal capitalization, as seen and here preserved in Martin J. Zeilinger's close reading:

> The meanings we discern in [*Alone.*] are vastly complicated, as the scene now probes the power relations at play between the two characters and homes in on the trauma that is perhaps being inflicted on Son's psyche. Father's stern look stretches into an intense stare of disappointment, accusation, and reprehension, from which Son recoils, with tear-clouded eyes, in a response that gradually changes from an acknowledgment of paternal power to barely contained anger.[14]

Or in another representative scene, when Andy (played by Mickey Rooney) approaches his mother (played by Fay Holden), we hear David Bering-Porter describe Arnold's effect as turning an "innocent squeeze" into an "incestuous grope," thereby echoing Erika Balsom's claim that Arnold "transforms the encounter to maximize its oedipal resonances and imbue it with an incestuous indecency."[15] And still more, another disquieting conclusion—and consensus—as Bering-Porter summarizes: "One does get the impression that Arnold is not so much adding to or changing the existing film, but rather revealing something that existed all along—trapped, as [Michael] Zyrd puts it, in between the 24 frames per second of the film itself."[16]

Now, it is true that in *Alone.* such things as Zeilinger et al. describe can be seen (the slapping, the stroking) and heard (the panting, the hissing). So what's the problem?—That these are not part of the content of *Andy Hardy Meets Debutante* and *Babe in Arms* in the way we have been told they are; rather, those remarkable—dazzling, entrancing, terrifying, arousing, hilarious—attributes that *do* appear to ratify certain strains of psychoanalytic "reading" of film are, instead, created by Arnold. He has put these characters under analysis—but not psychoanalysis, rather cinema analysis: thinking etymologically, he "unloosens" or "takes apart" images and sounds such that the mechanics available to Arnold provide a chance for *him* to create. To use Balsom's word, the original works are "imbued," but the agency of such inspiration is Arnold's. Where Seitz and Berkeley were providing scenes of everyday domestic life and decorous romances, Arnold physically agitates—inscribes, imbues—the film to give up and give over *more* than it contains (or better, something it did not contain until he contrived it) and in the process Arnold creates something of the darker, troubling existential and erotic impasse that lies *not in the film* but at the heart of our familiar, but ever so vexing, attempts at human communion and communication.

That is to say, because of *Arnold's* manipulation of found footage, characters behave in ways that are out of keeping with their behavior as we have come to know it since the 1940s—that is, with more than eighty years to study the originals. In a word, by means of media manipulation, Arnold has generated alternate behavior—indeed, deviant behavior. This effect is evident at the level of the moving image (even with the sound muted); and when sound is added, a pathos is supplied that makes the physical movements even more charged with incongruous qualities—feelings of erotic longing, of misplaced anger, of failed intimacy (a person can barely enter a room, much less manage to walk ably across it), or transformed intimacy (as when two young lovers hiss at one another, like adrenalized animals). Compellingly illustrative of Arnold's contribution—yet a credit often strangely given back to the original directors, actors, and editors—is the cross-cutting frenzy we enter (in what Michael Zyrd calls the "fourth tableau"), namely, between Andy's mom (Fay Holden) and Betsy Booth (Judy Garland) that occurs when Andy tells his mom, upon leaving her: "You know where I'm going."[17] With Arnold as provocateur, we are very far from the sober stylistics and chaste thematics of mid-century domestic melodramas of Americana, such as the iconic and representative Andy Hardy series. Which is to say, Arnold is not, in Patricia R. Zimmermann's useful trope from another context, "mining" found footage, but, as Arnold says, "inscribing" it with meaning by technical, mechanical operations. In this way, after Arnold's intervention, new content emerges from an old, now significantly augmented form. By Arnold's hand, *Andy Hardy Meets Debutante* and *Babe in Arms* become a new work: *Alone. Life Wastes Andy Hardy.*

As a point of reference, consider how it is one thing to say that Douglas Sirk's films offer a representation of a culture *and* a critique of that culture (e.g., as her children wheel a television set into the living room to keep their mom busy, the widower sees her reflection in the glass screen—as if being made the star of her own television melodrama—while she is told: "Here's all the company you need");[18] of course, notes on framing, color, mise en scène are all pertinent. But Arnold is not Sirk—and he isn't George Seitz or Busby Berkeley either. Arnold is not, in sum, a director of the profilmic scene (in which we can "look more closely 'into' the frame . . . to see tracks of the people and the objects that were in front of the camera at the time of the recording"),[19] but rather an after-market scavenger-enthusiast and deft technician of mostly forgotten machines, who picks through found content to set about making his own mark upon it—inscribing it, imposing his will and imagination on the findings. He is akin to the collage artist who uses found photographs, or some version of a different Andy—Warhol—who appropriates material culture to serve his own aims and ends, or none at all. In a different but related valence, as we will explore subsequently, Arnold is a hip-hop artist making an indelible—and clearly audible—"scratch" onto/into the medium. (Note again the literal/figurative tension of the "small" words—into, onto—where it is easy to lose track of the claim's extent. If Arnold is not (literally) "scratching" the medium like Uman, he is—with a hip-hop inflection—figuratively "scratching" it.) From the familiar sound "mix" of standard cinema production, we shift to the hip-hop "remix"—with its distinctive mash-up of (content) appropriation and (formal) generation.

In this sense, this new work, *Alone.* stands alone: it calls out for interpretation as an independent creation—a work of art all its own—worthy of assessment on its own terms. Arnold did not "illuminate" obscured or "hidden" content; he did not liberate meanings that were "contained" or "trapped" in the original movies. Just the opposite: Arnold added meaning by means of adding content. But, perhaps unintuitively, because this new content arrives by way of *form*, it is harder to see, harder to hear. In Arnold's metacinematic adjustments of film form—in particular, the manipulation of medium selection, sequencing, and playback—we are less likely to notice his authorial influence. Arnold's agency somehow recedes (again as if we were caught under a spell) and the *prior* agents and actors were given credit for his effects, and somehow also granted *avant la lettre* the psychoanalytic and postmodern meanings of those effects. Even so, given the conspicuousness of Arnold's remarkably aggressive alteration of the original films, we should be left to wonder how this happened, how, in effect, we have still, despite the visual flair and sonic vociferation of *Alone.*, remained prone to "look through" the medium, through the screen ("into" the scene), to the stuttering, trembling figures—and in so doing bypassed Arnold's artful, alarming, and utterly transformative intervention at the level of form.

Turning to familiar categories of form, what Arnold does in *Alone.* is akin to colorizing film or adding vocal dubbing. Of course, in this case, he does neither. But the change of category may help show that Arnold is not in the business of revealing latent content but adding visible and often volatile new "inscriptions." Yet even this metaphor, borrowed from Arnold's own self-description of his work, needs defining or refining, and it would seem expansion so it can account for the alien phenomenology of the sonic landscape. Arnold has noted certain stylistics of American hip-hop music as a prominent and direct influence on his cinematic methodology, and it is a frame of reference worth taking seriously as an analogue (hence the appeal, just above, to "remix" as a term of art imported from music production that is in better keeping with Arnold's sense of "inscription"). Indeed, despite drawing his source material from the history of American cinema, attributions of that tradition serving as the primary conceptual and methodological inspiration to his craft may be misplaced—and therefore, misleading:

> I think I have been influenced not so much by American film as by contemporary American music. Hip-hop, for example, is full of sampled phrases that are being repeated for longer or shorter durations. Often, turn-tables are used to move records forward and backward. Such techniques are also used in more complex forms of contemporary American music—John Zorn, for example, Christian Marclay cuts up old records and puts the parts together in new ways. He also employs obstacles which make the needle jump forward and backward.[20]

Akin to a hip-hop artist, Arnold "samples" from existing media; film scholars often call that type of media "found footage," or the art of using it "recycled cinema" (a domain that may include practitioners such as Craig Baldwin, Bruce Conner, Ken Jacobs, Barbara Hammer, Matthias Müller, Raphael Montañez Ortiz, Jay Rosenblatt, Paul Sharits, and Naomi Uman).[21] *Andy Hardy Meets Debutante* and *Babe in Arms* are part of the Hollywood archive and thus can be found, extracted from, and then acted upon (where "recycling" has to be parsed in relation to an artist's specific methods). Like the hip-hop artist, Arnold's extraction is not merely vampiric or parasitic, but is a-moment-of-citation-on-the-way-to-a-new-life-as-art. Thus, as sampled drum beats or song phrases become the backbeat or breakbeat of a new rap song, so sampled clips from *Andy Hardy Meets Debutante* and *Babe in Arms* become the conditions for the possibility of a new film called *Alone*.

Notice along the way how many of the techniques Arnold mentions in his accounting for American hip-hop music are also found in his work: not just sampled phrases (what literary types will call citations, extracts, quotations), but repetition for longer or shorter durations ("beats," "loops," "hooks"); movement forward and backward; cutting up and putting back together in new ways (and when the ways are not sufficiently novel, rappers are accused of "biting"—a trope for plagiarism); the imposition of obstacles that frustrate progress and make the material "jump" or "skip" (in the discourse around Arnold, this tends to be called "stuttering").[22] As Arnold puts it: "Every minimal movement was transformed into a small concussion"—a concussion being something that involves both movement and sound, and is often perceived in the immediate wake of an impact (say, an "inscription").[23] But even more crucially, we hear Arnold describe his work as that which transforms; in this respect, there is a vast distance between the found footage (originals) and the processed or digested product, *Alone.* For one thing, thousands of distinct optical prints are created, arranged, and played back in a highly choreographed, captivatingly rhythmic manner. As with hip-hop, we are not speaking of copy-and-paste, but copy-and-transform. Take this reflection by Arnold as an indication, indeed an allegory, of his artistic practice:

> I myself began to put together a tape of "scratched dreams" two months ago. A friend of mine let me use her teenage record collection. Back then she had listened to her favorite passages over and over again lifting the needle and putting it back within the same song. In doing so she had scratched those passages so severely that now the needle gets stuck, endlessly repeating certain grooves: "Dream lo-lo-lo-lo-ver where are you-u-u-u. . . ." Thus the psyche of a young girl has engraved its desires into the record—now a document situated somewhere between the unconscious of a single person and popular culture. This is a good example of how an individual can inscribe herself into popular culture and shift its messages toward collapse.[24]

Arnold's brief reminiscence provides a veritable clinic on how to think about his filmic interventions into *Andy Hardy Meets Debutante* and *Babe in Arms*, and thus, the pathway to accounting for his inventions in the work of art he calls *Alone. Life Wastes Andy Hardy.* The vinyl has been changed by repeated playing so much so that the needle is obstructed from making progress: consequently, the sound stutters and only later finds release (or freedom to move on). The player of the record (or hip-hop artist who "scratches" to make sounds) inscribes marks; in effect, material damage becomes the condition for specific sonic effects ("Dream lo-lo-lo-lo-ver . . ."). Arnold's (figurative) "scratch" is here a metonym for his optical printing (or re-photographing of film frames or film strips) and the variable playback of those images (forward/back/forward/back/forward), along with his imposition of repetition that creates a perceived "stutter" in the movements of the figures and also in the sounds of what was/is their speech; not to be missed, the stutter is real, but it is one among many epiphenomena of Arnold's manipulation of form, and thus not a feature of diegesis in the found footage. While Arnold knows this arrangement, and we are privy to it, slippages—playful and profound— nevertheless emerge. Thus, Arnold-as-psychoanalyst affirms, still speaking of how a person impacts the medium, that by playing the record, "the psyche . . . has engraved its desires into" the record. Here a bit of metaphysics has tottered into photo-optical mechanics. So if we are keen to see psychoanalytic potential in *Alone.*, we are better off looking to the artist who "engraved" his preferences (whatever they may be) into the medium *rather than* ascribe psychoanalytic content to the actors, directors, and editors involved in the narrative films from 1939 and 1940. (And even then, with the genetic fallacy at the ready, and Arnold's own admonition in hand [see again the epigraph], it may sound suspect and unappealing to look for an artist's intentions vis-à-vis his creations.)

Still, keeping with Arnold's account, and looking at the work of art known as *Alone.*, we find a "a good example of how an individual can inscribe [him]self into popular culture and shift its messages toward collapse." After we pause to appreciate the canny way in which the personal can become public (and thus political, philosophical, and psychological) through modes of "playing," it is the very last point of analogical relation that may be the most fascinating and devastating of all—since it is Arnold's intervention in the medium (the engraving/inscription of his psyche) that forestalls the stable or resolute reading of "hidden," "latent" content in *Andy Hardy Meets Debutante* and *Babe in Arms*, or even *Alone.* for that matter. Arnold's creative labors push the earlier (found) work into competition with Arnold's cinematic manipulations to the point where "messages" and meanings are "shifted . . . toward collapse." We critics, at last, are not in a position to confidently and summarily attribute "readings" of, say, Oedipal urges, rages, and erotic longing to Mickey Rooney's character, since those assessments are made possible, it turns out, only by Arnoldian epiphenomena.

If we remain, after such an author/artist-led reframing, committed to speaking of "latent" content and the "revelation" of "hidden" meanings (with respect to the Hollywood originals), then we can at least be sure to make similar types of artistic craft coincident, in this case: treat Arnold's experiment with film as the application (or importation? appropriation? expropriation? translation?) of hip-hop strategies—rather than, say, anoint Arnold as a kind of psychoanalyst of ciné-cultural products. Just as we fête the hip-hop artist for creating a "new sound" by means of "old records," so we can think of Arnold as using old films to generate new representations (and new connotations to go with them, but *not* with the source material); that is, he does not disseminate new meanings for the older, original works (*Andy Hardy Meets Debutante*, etc.), but new meanings by means of the new work (e.g., *Alone.*). A particularly strong backbeat can function (for the hip-hop artist) like the discovery of a new kind of azure paint (for the painter)—but, again, these are moments of medium equivalency. Arnold's optical printing coupled with variations in selection, ordering, and playback timing and direction is his mode of "scratching"—inscribing, imbuing, engraving—*Andy Hardy Meets Debutante* and *Babe in Arms*. And so, in *Alone.*, we have a new song—and new ideas to go with it.

Metaphilosophy of Reception

In a preamble to an interview with Martin Arnold, Scott MacDonald has observed that "the determination to critique industry filmmaking has been related to a fascination"—especially by experimentalists—"with those 'primitive' approaches to cinema 'left behind' as the industry developed."[25] For Arnold and his experiments in recycled cinema, MacDonald underscores that "motion study and magic have been central tactics for deconstructing and refashioning conventional Hollywood visual and auditory gestures."[26] Thus, MacDonald describes how Arnold's films "transform the gesture . . . into a phantasmagoria of visual effects that would make any trick-film director proud."[27] Consequently, we are faced with Arnold "transforming the original scene into a breathtaking mechanical ballet accompanied by a soundtrack that hovers somewhere between rap music sampling and stuttering. . . [and] limping, its visual counterpart."[28] For his take on this portrayal of his work, Arnold responds to MacDonald's promptings: "The structure of space in conventional narrative cinema is as much at a deadlock as the structure of gender, and because of that I felt a great pleasure in thoroughly shaking up that space."[29] Arnold's chosen verb phrase—"shaking up"—feels as pertinent to our experience of his sequence of films as does the admission that pleasure was his dominant emotion in making them. Indeed, in watching these films we are shaken up—disrupted, disturbed, disoriented—and our emotional response to that phenomenology (is it pleasurable?) appears to be very much at the core of how we come to read the achievements of *The Cineseizure*.

In Arnold's pleasure-filled disruption (and subsequent reconstruction, rewriting, re-picting, inscribing, etc.), as MacDonald rightly tells him (with a third use of "transform" in as many sentences), "You do more than discover what's in that shot [of original, found, selected film material], you transform it."[30] Arnold replies in kind, and with his own emphasis in place, that it was "fascinating to see . . . where certain events are *created* just by the forward and backward movement."[31] No doubt, Arnold's italics afford their own pleasure (for us) because they underwrite our thinking about the nature of his artistic input or impact, yet it is also his characterization of that creation as an "event" (or series of events) that also aids our appreciation of his work, since it is precisely in the felt sense of the surplus of activity—at the formal level—that makes old things new, and familiar things strange—estranged. It is not as accurate to say that Arnold quotes or cites an original—the way, for example, I place Arnold's text in display formatting—but that Arnold runs his source material through a kind of mechanical grinder or processor or (as the musician would, an analog or digital) mixer. We may recognize the footage from the Hollywood archive ("Oh, this is a shot from *Andy Hardy Meets Debutante*") but then catch ourselves: "But, of course, not as Seitz shot it or Rooney or Garland acted in it." How far, then, in its effect on us is the burger from the steak? Echoing MacDonald, we viewers of Arnold's films do not "discover" what was "hidden" in, say, *Andy Hardy Meets Debutante* but attend an entirely new event that Arnold places under the name *Alone*.

According to Arnold: "A shot from a movie is an artifact."[32] MacDonald replies with an interpretation of Arnold's claim: "You do a 'motion study' of a social artifact."[33] "While Méliès, and the approaches he inspired, was later incorporated into the history of conventional narrative, you transform"—that word again—"conventional narrative back into magic." MacDonald concludes, "It's like a revenge on film history."[34] (David Clark will sustain the notion by calling Arnold's work "animation's zombie revenge on live cinema"[35]—hence Arnold's act/art of *reanimation*. *The Cineseizure*, on this register, becomes revenge by revenant.) Notice again the strongly psychological/psychoanalytical reading, which Arnold enthusiastically picks up: "I like the expression 'revenge' in this context," adding, "The revenge on one's own history is called psychoanalysis and touches upon the early enemies in one's own head."[36] So it would seem that Arnold explores revenge, as it were, not on film history (as MacDonald suggests) but on his own personal history with film (as Arnold redirects). Such a distinction is lost in the obfuscation and thus regular conflation of source-film-or-its-culture-on-the-couch versus artist-artwork-or-audience-on-the-couch. Indeed, who would (want to) imagine that such experimental works would amount to an attempted revenge on the broad sweep of film history, much less its fulfilment? To take such a swipe seriously, we would have to be mindful of movie magic and its spells. Arnold replies: "As an independent filmmaker, you fight in a very small army; lonely and badly armed, you compete against the star wars systems of Warners and Metro."[37] Such is an asymmetry fit for a mythic undertaking.

Though he speaks here in reference to *Pièce touchée*, Arnold's work in *Passage à l'acte* and *Alone.* is in the same vein. Whether we are looking at the eighteen-second shot from *The Human Jungle* (1954, dir. Joseph M. Newman) used in *Pièce touchée*; the shots from *To Kill a Mockingbird* (1962, dir. Robert

Mulligan) deployed in *Passage à l'acte*; or the clips from *Andy Hardy Meets Debutante* and *Babe in Arms* recycled in *Alone.*, we can ratify Arnold's sense that "the society of the fifties had inscribed some of its codes of representation and a lot of its social norms (above all, concerning gender). And all this was and is apparent in a couple of frames: it is not necessary to watch the complete movie to recognize the obvious and not-so-obvious messages inscribed in it."[38] Notice, then, even by Arnold's own candid admission, we do not need his work—his artistic, metamedial intervention—in order to see and study the social norms of the 1950s "inscribed" in the film; they are apparent in the profilmic scene (as earlier suggested in assessing the culture critique inherent to Douglas Sirk's *All That Heaven Allows*). Thus, any film or media theorist, any cultural or gender theorist, can simply watch *The Human Jungle*, *To Kill a Mockingbird*, *Andy Hardy Meets Debutante*, or *Babe in Arms* (and quite scandalously, Arnold insists, not even the entirety of the films, just a few scenes here and there—"a couple of frames"—will do) and proceed therefrom with critical readings on any number of pertinent topics. In these cases, we seem to recognize acts of "ordinary" criticism, which is to say, criticism of content and metacontent.

Yet we know that Arnold "shaking up that space" through image selection, optical printing, playback direction, variable speed, looping, and related mechanical methods is happening at the level of form and metaform. So we want to be on guard for the conceptual slippage that would allow, or even encourage, us to assert that his techniques, which for example produce a "strong sensual effect"—"created by running the film forward and backward," imitating, no doubt, the familiar and literal motion of sensuality (caressing), sexuality (coitus)—are somehow always already in the profilmic scene with which he began. We know they are not; we have watched the original films for generations. In order to appreciate Arnold's contribution—in his trinity of films—we need to appreciate what he does, in fact, contribute. As Arnold says:

> Many people experience *Pièce Touchée* as erotic; I've been asked again and again why it's so sexual. I think that this impression originates on a formal level, as the product of that irregular vibration. . . . In the beginning, I was surprised myself about the multiplicity of possible ways to influence meaning. . . . It was fascinating to see that miniscule shifts of movement could cause major shifts of meaning.[39]

A midrashic reading of this passage, for our purposes here, would aim to underscore Arnold's awareness of his work's effect on its audience (as "erotic," as "sexual"), and Arnold's implicit rejection of the idea that this effect is happening because the original/source content prompted such reactions. When

Arnold alludes to "all [that] is apparent in a couple of frames," he must be taken to mean on the terms of the found material, not his own uses of it and the works of art that follow. Thus, it is the transformation at the "formal level"—and this is crucial—that becomes the new (or supplemental, surplus, or supervenient) content that has so captivated our attention, especially the critics'. As Quentin Tarantino made genre pictures, grindhouse, B-movies, and Blaxploitation movies au courant, so Arnold has given mild-mannered mid-century works, largely obscured or left behind, new credence and credibility.[40] As Tarantino "remade" earlier films and commercial ephemera in line with his auteurist and metacinematic sensibilities, Arnold discovered that his manipulation of medium was resulting in unexpected "shifts of meaning" and that such movements (even "miniscule" ones) could be at odds with the scale of their conceptual and emotional impact. Small changes yielded massive impacts.

For those first arriving at works in *The Cineseizure*, there is a reasonable allowance that the projector has malfunctioned (again a matter of form, in this case projection). Such a perceived disruption can stimulate its own kind of response—for instance, when we are reminded how our tools and instruments recurrently fail and thus repeatedly embarrass us. Technical snafus are now de rigueur, indeed, an often-expected part of the performance of in-person public presentations (disobedient screens, cords, networks, logging in and password protocols, etc.); the condition has its virtual correlates, of course, ones that have reached new modes of expression during the hyper-mediation of the coronavirus pandemic (frozen screens, masticated audio, etc.). Yet when in the case of *The Cineseizure* the film "goes on"—and goes on like this, with stutters and tics, with jitters and suggestive gestures—we have to recalibrate. If we laugh or are embarrassed, having at last accepted the intentionality and orchestration of the glitchy frames, of the clipped voices, we are called upon to look again and hear anew: if the work is suddenly art (and not the victim of technical or mechanical accident), we join the company of an artist who— taking for granted our intact, well-hewn habits of attunement to montage, cuts, linearity, and so on—manipulates the mise en scène to tell *another* story, one that for all its apparent intimacy (indeed, isomorphic identity) with films made by Busby Berkeley, Robert Mulligan, Joseph M. Newman, and George B. Seitz is distinctly different. Admittedly, the radical repurposing of the old material can be cause for alarm (as well as laughter). Yet, for most viewers, Arnold's results are evident of another degree of subversiveness; it is to his art of metamedial recontextualizing that we are startled into responsiveness.

As could be expected, then, we find continual attention paid in the critical literature to audience responses to Arnold's films. The apparently widespread tendency to laugh is a conspicuous feature of these analyses, for example, as emphasized in Bering-Porter's account.[41] Laughing at *The Cineseizure* is striking, after all, since Arnold has put on offer varied moments of grave emotional intensity: shame, lust, rage, melancholy. Is ours a nervous, involuntary laugh and not a mean or mocking one? In everyday life, when our bodies betray us—stumble, fall, stutter, inadvertently make a rude gesture—as well as when our use of language misfires (e.g., by slips of the tongue, aphasia, etc.), do we wish to be met with the laughter of others? Given that so many critics of this catalog of Arnold's films ("virtually all commentary"), including Arnold himself, dwell on the "stuttering" and "limping" and similar paroxysms of body and speech, our collective assessment of such metaphors may stand in need of focus on how disability is represented in these films, and as crucially, responded to by audiences, including urbane critics. Indeed, as noted, a shorthand way of referring to all three films is *The Cineseizure*. Is this funny?

Fittingly, as a coda to Arnold's handy analysis of his own work (grain of salt firmly in hand), Arnold favors psychological explanations for results such as laughter and its correlate, seemingly involuntary responses: "The representation of genders adds to this [sense of the erotic and sexual] and channels this instinctive mood"; "Forms . . . and rhythms don't affect the spectator in the realm of language and logic; they communicate on deeper levels: I would situate the discourse they take part in in the unconscious."[42] Therefore, again, and against the readings of his films that say we are affected by content—by the skips and slips of speech, by the gyrations of bodies, by the obsessive and repetitive movements that denote sexual intensity or emotional frustration— Arnold directs us first to cinematic form and to the way its metafilmic alteration activates something other than an analytical registration of effects.

The foregoing notes made in the company of Arnold and his cycle of films may come to provide a lesson in repetition of another sort—not just instruction in the adjacencies of the hip-hop loop and the cinematic forward-reverse-forward, but of certain theoretical accounts of phenomena. In the particular case of our many encounters with *The Cineseizure* (from 1989 to the present day, more than thirty years and counting), the repetition—like the well-worn grooves in the well-loved record of "scratched dreams"—has made a mark that has directed and thereby inspired a lot of subsequent criticism. My variation on how we read Arnold's work—with implications not just for the interpretation of his films but for the offerings of others as well (retrospectively and prospectively)—should be reinforced, first, by some of Arnold's own assessments of his compositions, duly noted, but perhaps more so by refreshed attention to the audience experience of them. Apart from the degree of critical recalibration that may follow, I am, in this case of inheriting the history of film, as intrigued by the metaphilosophy of reception as I am by the metacinema of these specific works of film art. The nub is how our methods of reading or responding to extant criticism may get in the way of—obstruct, obscure, constrain, hijack, blind, deafen, dismount, or defeat—our capacity to account for our own, first-person experience. We are in the company not just of ordinary language philosophy's keen attentiveness to "what we say when" but of what might be called ordinary film criticism's "what we sense when."

Metaformal Metamorphosis

As a final gesture, in trying to bring the range of temporal references in this chapter up to the present, it may be productive to think of the increasing prevalence and persuasiveness of deepfakes as an heir to Martin Arnold and his particular contribution to the motion-study-as-magic tradition (that we can trace back to George Méliès et al.). Through the formal manipulation of found footage and sound (or, as in deepfakes, the computational creation of ersatz media that pass for the same), we are faced with or subjected to something new, a representation that ceases to offer content of "presumptive assertion."[43] With the deepfake analogy at hand, for instance, it may be easier to see the way that theorists loyal to the secondary literature (and its invitation to take its lessons at secondhand, and yet with principal authority) can regard Arnold's *Alone.* and its companion pieces as deepfakes of a metacinematic sort.[44] Yet, given the shifts in media—how they are constituted, manipulated, and subsequently presented—let us hold off momentarily on such a conclusion.

While we learn so much by revisiting Arnold's late twentieth-century suite on its own terms—as well as in relation to the history of film—we can also learn a lot by leaping to the present and situating *The Cineseizure* in proximity to a range of emerging technologies that impact the nature of art. As we assess what his actual achievements and the particular revelations of his methods are, correcting and clarifying where need be, his work remains uncannily relevant for thinking about the present and future of metaformal experiments across media types, including the frontiers of deepfakes, general adversarial networks (GANs), and non-fungible tokens (NFTs).[45] Though far from the photo-mechanical context of Arnold's experiments, these dawning technologies—and applications—hint at the to-be-determined near-future of the meta, including metacinema. If any media can become an NFT—a modest op-ed has made the leap[46]—cinema seems poised for adoption and experimentation. How will that migration (or transfiguration?) affect our sense of cinema—its ontology, representations, intertextuality, and so on? As it happens, an NFT's abstraction is highly suited to metacinema, in particular, since blockchain technology also trades in reflexivity, hyper-mediation, recursion, and related challenges to inherited categories of art and commerce.[47] We are obviously well-launched into the next phase of the evolution of meta. Even when the digital art at issue appears to be a self-contained representation—recognizable by existing categories (figurative, abstract, written prose, moving images, animation, etc.)—the algorithm is reflexive; and so metaformal art, familiar to avant-garde and experimental cinema, including the many artists mentioned in this chapter, is succeeded by metaformal innovation in the realm of the computational blockchain and reflexive algorithm.

The sudden and stratospheric rise of non-fungible tokens in the art world—such as the sale at auction of Mike Winkelmann's *Everydays: The First 5,000 Days* for $69.3 million dollars—underscores the monetary "valued-added" portion made possible by technological (in the case of NFTs, computational) manipulation and algorithmic commodification of existing material—putting aside whatever this NFT's aesthetic worth might be. *Everydays* offers a maximalist collage of five-thousand discrete art works produced consecutively over as many days; thus, ordinariness, repetition, and collection of prior content coalesce to suggest an idiom for the (assembled) piece. The winning bidder seems to have arrived at the auction with a fever for referential and reflexive commodities as his pseudonym is MetaKovan, his company is Metapurse, and he subsequently displayed his new acquisition in a digital museum called Metaverse. Despite being the third highest sale for an art work by a living artist (after David Hockney and Jeff Koons), MetaKovan neither owns the original nor the copyright; while financial valuation becomes an epiphenomenon of art, ownership of intellectual property remains with the artist. Befitting the new logic of NFTs, the work of art possesses metadata (data about data) that are processed through a cryptographic hash function. All this to say that where we have been familiar with meta traits in representation since Plato experienced a moral panic over the implications of mimesis in Homer, Caravaggio painted *Narcissus*, and Dziga Vertov became a *Man with a Movie Camera*, the ontology and phenomenology on offer in NFTs puts art at a remove from art, ownership at a distance from objects, and fractures value into an array of potentially irreconcilable (or perpetually competing) commitments.

If dominant culture is more accustomed to creating and looking out for meta content, Arnold reminds us of the richness of the formal and metaformal terrain familiar to avant-gardists. Part of his ongoing legacy as an experimentalist may be in providing a transitional space in which to consider what comes next for metacinema, especially in a metaformal sense. As

Arnold's *The Cineseizure* was informed more by American hip-hop music than by American film, looking ahead, metacinema may be increasingly beholden to computation—artificial intelligence as the separate or surrogate agent of metaformal innovation—than to an individual artist's contingent, biographical nest of influences. At the same time, our immersion in the computational nature of digital art helps us see anew how much of Arnold's labors in *The Cineseizure* were ruled by computational mechanisms of his own design—for example, specific, assigned rhythms for frame rates, patterns for image sequencing, and so on. And as we are courted to recall Arnold's personal agency—his "inscription" on the material conditions of found artifacts—the presence of GANs and NFTs, now on the art market, add yet further dimensions to consider; such computational creations "made without hands" unsettle even as they enchant.[48] While cinema—especially the celluloid of Arnold's studio—may seem old enough to be entirely eclipsed by present-day media, the medium is nevertheless young enough that we can use it to remember that all such traits evolve—from ontology to praxis, distribution to reception, nomenclature to grammar. Befitting such development, we concomitantly face many anachronisms even as we invent new acronyms, algorithms, and accommodations to account for emergent, disruptive technologies.

The manipulation of digital moving images in ways recognizably affiliated with Arnold's analog practice at once extends the pertinence of *The Cineseizure* and provides orientation to the onslaught of novel variations that follow. Consider the arresting, reverberating case of a GIF depicting a rage-filled President Obama kicking open a door as he leaves a press conference. The clip spawned its own political readings, especially as a false positive treated as veritable, and thus as politically viable propaganda. Though the increasing sophistication of digital representations may make us credulous of their reality credentials when we should be dubious, we are by turns becoming more savvy about what I have elsewhere called the phenomenon of hoax *vérité*.[49] Once the GIF was revealed to be a fabrication based on found footage, however, we would not be inclined to claim that the GIF "reveals" some kind of "latent" truth in the original content that was previously unappreciated. In the context of the reception of *Alone.* by critics, we encounter a variant of hoax *vérité*: Arnold's manipulation leads audiences to draw false conclusions (e.g., that these characters felt things that were hidden until Arnold revealed them). Given Arnold's expertise in psychoanalysis, critics made a reasonable connection between such training in psychology and the thematics that emerge from his film practice—yet, they went too far in ascribing credit for the motifs. *The Cineseizure* as a whole, then, catalyzed an unintentional or accidental hoax—in so far as critics were lured by theoretical connections (e.g., psycho-analysis) to exceed the bounds explanation; and yet, as our sustained fascination with *The Cineseizure* underscores, the trinity very much achieved *vérité*, since the work manifestly produces genuine effects in viewers (including not a few learned critics).

In another prominent (and more standard) case of hoax *vérité*, recall that people were scandalized by the live action "documentary" known as *I'm Still Here* (2010, dir. Casey Affleck); a "performance art" stunt was pulled, then revealed: a cardinal tenet of the documentary tradition—defined in large measure by issuing films of presumptive assertion—had been tested and undermined. Now we continue into an era of proliferating digitally animated instances. Yet Arnold's trick is apparent in the squarely analog—from the mechanical effects of the zoopraxiscope to the narrative interventions that Werner Herzog calls "ecstatic truth."[50] With Herzog, like Arnold, we are invited to see and make meaning in/for things that do not originate in the world (either the historical world or the world of the diegesis), but only in the film's constructedness (as a work of art). Herzog is known to manipulate the characters in some of his "documentaries" (e.g., coach their behavior, script lines for them to say, rewrite their histories, etc.), while Arnold uses found footage—and his considerable artistic resources—to (metaphorically) do the same. After this very terse imbrication of early cinema, deepfakes, GANs, GIFs, and NFTs, along with works of hoax *vérité* and ecstatic truth, our return to Arnold's *The Cineseizure* may make for quick analysis: *Alone.* and its filmic companions are not deepfakes, but are boldly, proudly shallow fakes—works of art that wear their manipulation of form as their primary claim to artistic credentialing (and thereafter, fame). Metaformal transformation is "inscribed" on the surface of every jerking, jittery frame, in each attempted kiss and attendant hiss.

Metacinema as Modality and as Symptom

Knowing and acknowledging that I am drawing to a close a book on metacinema—pitched as a general phenomenon of culture, and increasingly with its traits evident across media types—perhaps it is fitting to conclude with something of a plea for cultivating our attunement to the objects that draw our genuine attention and thereby would demand our honest response. Reading or criticizing "through the secondary literature" is part of the business of academic life; one's thoughts about a thing are, as the standards of scholarship go, recurrently forced to stand beside—or stand up to—what has been said by others (and often, variously with chagrin and/or admiration, said better by them). Indeed, Cavell has written of the stacking of interpretation in a "hierarchy of texts" as itself an illustration of metaphilosophy, thereby putting pressure of the very act of reading: "Suppose that an interpretation just is of a text and that to be a text just is to be subject to interpretation; and suppose this means that a text constitutes interpretation."[51] Suppositions worthy of our consideration primarily because they renew our investigations into the films and media that present themselves to and for our critical attention. As Cavell continues:

> Say that my readings, my secondary texts, arise from processes of analysis. Then I would like to say that what I am doing in reading a film is performing it (if you wish, performing it inside myself). (I welcome here the sense in the idea of performance that it is the meeting of a responsibility.)[52]

An aesthetic reading of a film is coupled with an invitation to ethical consideration, apt indeed for raising the stakes of interpretation—perhaps especially for metacinema—since we are now aware that it may be occasionally dismissed as too playful, occupying an impossible category for art: the unserious. But then, what is more serious than taking one's experience seriously?[53] And the very shape of such a posture, such an attention is reflexive and referential. Hence, the way to prove the gravity of metacinema is to offer criticism of it that makes interpretation beholden to one's experience.

At the conclusion of the introduction, I presented the notion that metacinema may be an ally to metacognition. And thus while metacinema could be treated as a symptom of decadence, of decay, of cultural exhaustion and laziness, it may also (and at the same time) be an uncanny accomplice for charting the contours of our thoughts across media types. Metacinema, one among several varieties of the usefully alienating arts, helps us better recognize the commingling of form and content—perhaps especially metaform and metacontent—and no doubt, also adjudicate their necessary and thus complicated interaction. As metacinema increasingly amalgamates with metatheatre and metatelevision and, indeed, it would seem, with the pervasive "metaness" of nearly every cultural or created object (as we enter a permanent state of the hypermeta), perhaps we can take special heed of our direct sensations— feel more immediately, attend to the world as we find it. And then, only then, make a move to theorize, and to metatheorize.

Going forward, as metacinema looks for allies in explanation, it may be advantageous to link such investigations to the way Thomas Elsaesser conceived of media archaeology as a "symptom" of a series of contemporary crises. So, as we speak of decadence and the like, it is worth drawing in Elsaesser's schema with his italics intact:

> Flowing from this loss of faith in progress (but also philosophically distinct from it) is the *crisis in history and causality*, which has amplified into a *crisis in memory and recall*, reflected in turn in the *crisis of narrative and storytelling*. More specifically related to the cinema and to the question I posed in the introduction, namely that film history as media archaeology also challenges me to ask: "what is cinema (good) for[?]" is another crisis—the *crisis of representation and the image*.[54]

With metacinema and media archaeology figured as parallel or kindred phenomena, we can appreciate their complementarity, in particular, as modes of discourse. Elsaesser was familiar with the "complaint . . . that media archaeology does not have a proper method, or has not yet identified clearly enough the problems it is meant to be an answer to," and something similar can be said of metacinema. If it too is a symptom of a crisis—or set of them, including, for instance, D. N. Rodowick's "naming crisis" around "questions of movement, image, time, and history"[55]—what is our claim for critical practice? Perhaps quite appropriately, it is inherent to the very structure of the symptom: metacinema and its attendant criticism should be reassured by the very act of looking with one's own eyes, hearing with one's own ears, and in those embodied encounters celebrate the way referential and reflexive films turn us back upon our experience of them—including the discipline of criticism itself. Hence, reference and reflexiveness coalesce as a methodology for the metacinematician—a mode of metacognition that meets the art at its own demanding level of high expectation.[56]

"As so often in the humanities," Elsaesser persuasively observes, "it is the inherent reflexivity and self-reference—what we used to understand by the term 'critique'—that justifies certain procedures and approaches, not the problem-solving routines of the hard sciences."[57] Complementing Elsaesser's claim, Wolfgang Ernst says that "media archaeology, which is concerned with techno-cultural processes, is both a self-reflexive method and an archival object of research."[58] In reply to complaints from elsewhere, Elsaesser advises that from his "perspective, media archaeology is only one among several parallel developments, where a discipline becomes reflexive in order to redefine its object of study, which in this instance includes revisionist film history, counter-factual history, memory studies and trauma theory, as well as 'the archive' as a distinct area of inquiry and study in the humanities and philosophy."[59] We should consider adding metacinema and meta studies more generally to these "parallel developments."

For among other salient and sustaining attributes, metacinema embodies a theory of form's relationship with content, a theory that stands in need of continual inheritance and interpretation. Critique is at once disguised and out in the open. Metacinematic artists, for instance, show how they "essay" on the work of others—incorporating and digesting in the process of art-making and in pursuit of new works of art (all the while admitting sources through citationality; and trying to progress beyond mere repetition, rehearsal, derivation, quotation, and paraphrase). Metacinema may be a sign of the "crisis of storytelling" (along with the other abiding crises) while also offering a model for how disciplines—say, cinematic practice *and* the practice of theorizing cinema—can themselves become reflexive in order to perpetually define and refine their arts as well as reanimate their objects of study.

Notes

1. Scott MacDonald, *A Critical Cinema 3: Interviews with Independent Filmmakers* (Berkeley: University of California Press, 1998), 350, 354. MacDonald's *Critical Cinema* interview with Martin Arnold (347–62) is a version of an earlier engagement: "Sp . . . Sp . . . Spaces of Inscription: An Interview with Martin Arnold," *Film Quarterly* 48, no. 1 (Autumn 1994): 2–11.
2. See "The Audiovisual Unconscious: Martin Arnold and Peter Tscherkassky," June 9, 2016, a program curated by Arnau Horta and produced in collaboration with LOOP Festival. https://loop-barcelona.com/activity/the-audiovisual-unconscious-iv/.
3. See MacDonald, *A Critical Cinema 3*, 352, 358; Erika Balsom, "A Cinephilic Avant-Garde: The Films of Peter Tscherkassky, Martin Arnold, and Gustav Deutsch," in *New Austrian Film*, ed. Robert von Dassanowsky and Oliver C. Speck (New York: Berghahn Books, 2011), 264; and Akira Mizuta Lippit, *Ex-Cinema: From a Theory of Experimental Film and Video* (Berkeley: University of California Press, 2012), esp. ch. 3, "Cinemnesis" and ch. 7, "Digesture."
4. See Scott MacDonald, "My Troubled Relationship with Stanley Cavell: In Search of a Truly Cinematic Conversation," in *The Thought of Stanley Cavell and Cinema: Turning Anew to the Ontology of Film a Half-Century after "The World Viewed"*, ed. David LaRocca (New York: Bloomsbury, 2020), 113. See also Scott MacDonald, *Binghamton Babylon: Voices from the Cinema Department, 1967–1977; a Non-Fiction Novel* (Albany: State University of New York Press, 2015), 95.
5. MacDonald, "My Troubled Relationship," 116.
6. See MacDonald, *Binghamton Babylon*. See also *Buffalo Heads: Media Study, Media Practice, Media Pioneers, 1973–1990*, ed. Woody Vasulka and Peter Weibel (Cambridge, MA: MIT Press, 2008).
7. Stanley Cavell, *Pursuits of Happiness: The Hollywood Comedy of Remarriage* (Cambridge, MA: Harvard University Press, 1981), 14. Earlier, in the foreword to the Enlarged Edition of *The World Viewed* (1979), Cavell wrote: "Objects projected on a screen are inherently

reflexive, they occur as self-referential, reflecting upon their physical origins" (xvi). For more on material and thematic doubles, see also *The Philosophy of Charlie Kaufman,* ed. David LaRocca (Lexington: University Press of Kentucky, 2011; updated with a new preface, 2019).

8. See details at The Film-Makers' Coop: http://film-makerscoop.com/filmmakers/martin-arnold. For selected texts on Arnold's work from 1992 to 2018, visit https://www.martinarnold.info/texts/. For more on Andy Hardy films, though predating (and arguably anticipating) Arnold's *Alone.*, see Robert B. Ray, *The Avant-Garde Finds Andy Hardy* (Cambridge, MA: Harvard University Press, 1995) and "How to Start an Avant-Garde," in *How a Film Theory Got Lost and Other Mysteries in Cultural Studies* (Bloomington: Indiana University Press, 2001), ch. 5.

9. Ludwig Wittgenstein, *Philosophical Investigations,* trans. G. E. M. Anscombe (New York: The MacMillan Company, 1953), §415.

10. See, e.g., Balsom, "A Cinephilic Avant-Garde"; David Bering-Porter, "The Automaton in All of Us: GIFs, Cinemagraphs, and the Films of Martin Arnold," *Moving Image Review and Art Journal* 3, no. 2 (December 2014): 179–92; "Time Frames and Frames of Mind," in David Clark, "The Discrete Charm of the Digital Image: Animation and New Media," in *The Sharpest Point: Animation at the End of Cinema,* ed. Chris Gehman and Steve Reinke (Ottawa: YYZ Books / Ottawa International Animation Festival and the Images Festival, 2005). Also available at http://chemicalpictures.net/writing/the-discrete-charm-of-the-digital-image/; Martin J. Zeilinger, "Sampling as Analysis, Sampling as Symptom: Found Footage and Repetition in Martin Arnold's *Alone. Life Wastes Andy Hardy*," in *Sampling Media,* ed. David Laderman and Laurel Westrup (New York: Oxford University Press, 2014), 155–67; Michael Zyrd, "*Alone: Life Wastes Andy Hardy,*" *Senses of Cinema,* issue 32 (July 2004), http://sensesofcinema.com/2004/cteq/alone_life_wastes_andy_hardy/.

11. See, e.g., Bering-Porter, "Automaton," "reveal," 179–82; "hidden,"180; "layers," 179; "latent," 180, 183.

12. MacDonald, *A Critical Cinema 3,* 351–52.

13. Zeilinger, "Sampling as Analysis," 156.

14. Zeilinger, "Sampling as Analysis," 155–56.

15. Bering-Porter, "Automaton," 180; Balsom, "A Cinephilic Avant-Garde," 271.

16. Bering-Porter, "Automaton," 180. See also Zyrd, "*Alone.*"

17. See Zyrd, "*Alone.*"

18. I am referencing a scene in *All That Heaven Allows* (1955, dir. Douglas Sirk) when Cary Scott (Jane Wyman) is presented by her children with a television set as part of a compensation package for her newfound widowhood. See Robert B. Pippin's essential work on Sirk, including *Filmed Thought: Cinema as Reflective Form* (Chicago: University of Chicago Press, 2019) and "Love and Class in Douglas Sirk's *All That Heaven Allows,*" in *Movies with Stanley Cavell in Mind,* ed. David LaRocca (New York: Bloomsbury, 2021), 33–56. See also my "A Desperate Education: Reading *Walden* in *All That Heaven Allows,*" *Film and Philosophy* 8 (2004): 1–16.

19. MacDonald, *A Critical Cinema 3,* 351.

20. MacDonald, *A Critical Cinema 3,* 358.

21. See Lippit, "Cinemnesis," *Ex-Cinema,* ch. 3.

22. MacDonald, *A Critical Cinema 3,* 361–62.

23. MacDonald, *A Critical Cinema 3,* 349.

24. MacDonald, *A Critical Cinema 3,* 358–60.

25. MacDonald, *A Critical Cinema 3*, 347.

26. MacDonald, *A Critical Cinema 3*, 347.

27. MacDonald, *A Critical Cinema 3*, 348.

28. MacDonald, *A Critical Cinema 3*, 348.

29. MacDonald, *A Critical Cinema 3*, 350.

30. MacDonald, *A Critical Cinema 3*, 352.

31. MacDonald, *A Critical Cinema 3*, 352.

32. MacDonald, *A Critical Cinema 3*, 351.

33. MacDonald, *A Critical Cinema 3*, 351.

34. MacDonald, *A Critical Cinema 3*, 351.

35. See Clark, "Discrete Charm," n.p. For more on animation and Arnold's work after *The Cineseizure*, see Martin Arnold, *Gross Anatomies* (Vienna: Verlag für moderne Kunst, VfmK, 2015).

36. MacDonald, *A Critical Cinema 3*, 351.

37. MacDonald, *A Critical Cinema 3*, 351.

38. MacDonald, *A Critical Cinema 3*, 351–52.

39. MacDonald, *A Critical Cinema 3*, 352.

40. See *Quentin Tarantino's "Inglourious Basterds": A Manipulation of Metacinema*, ed. Robert von Dassanowsky (New York: Continuum, 2012); *Quentin Tarantino's "Django Unchained": The Continuation of Metacinema*, ed. Oliver C. Speck (New York: Bloomsbury, 2014); and David Roche, *Quentin Tarantino: Poetics and Politics of Cinematic Metafiction* (Jackson: University of Mississippi Press, 2018).

41. Bering-Porter, "Automaton," 182ff.

42. MacDonald, *A Critical Cinema 3*, 352.

43. See Noël Carroll, "Cinematic Representation and Spatial Realism: Reflections After/Upon André Bazin," in *The Philosophy of Documentary Film: Image, Sound, Fiction, Truth*, ed. David LaRocca (Lanham, MD: Lexington Books, 2017), 75–94, and "Fiction, Non-Fiction, and the Film of Presumptive Assertion: A Conceptual Analysis," in *Film and Philosophy*, ed. Richard Allen and Murray Smith (New York: Oxford University Press, 1997).

44. See Cavell, *Pursuits of Happiness*, 36–37, where he articulates ideas about primary, secondary, and tertiary texts. A tertiary text may appear, e.g., when Cavell writes about *his own* secondary text—and in this way such work is (necessarily) self-referential. Let us call metacriticism an incarnation of a tertiary text, thereby making it a subgenre of metaphilosophy.

45. See Introduction, n13.

46. Kevin Roose, "Buy This Column on the Blockchain!" *New York Times*, March 24, 2021. Using a browser extension called MetaMask, and in a distinctly reflexive move, the author turned his article about NFTs into an NFT.

47. See Jonathan Zittrain and Will Marks, "NFTs Show the Value of Owning the Unknowable," *The Atlantic*, April 7, 2021. The authors begin with a consideration of Banksy's high-profile piece of meta-art, *Morons* (2006).

48. See Introduction, n13.

49. See footage: https://youtu.be/SKRuyjJxqv8. See also my "A Reality Rescinded: The Transformative Effects of Fraud in *I'm Still Here*," *The Philosophy of Documentary Film*, 537–76.

50. See my "'Profoundly Unreconciled to Nature': Ecstatic Truth and the Humanistic Sublime in Werner Herzog's War Films," in *The Philosophy of War Films*, ed. David LaRocca (Lexington: University Press of Kentucky, 2014), 437–82.

51. Cavell, *Pursuits of Happiness*, 37.

52. Cavell, *Pursuits of Happiness*, 37–38.

53. See my introduction, "The Seriousness of Film Sustained," in *Movies with Stanley Cavell in Mind*, 1–30.

54. Thomas Elsaesser, "Media Archaeology as Symptom," *New Review of Film and Television Studies* vol. 14, no. 2 (2016): 188.

55. D. N. Rodowick, "The Memory of Cinema," in *What Philosophy Wants from Images* (Chicago: University of Chicago Press, 2017), 3 n3, 4, 7, 17, 21, 25, 48, 57, 74, 88.

56. See my "Autophilosophy," in *Inheriting Stanley Cavell: Memories, Dreams, Reflections*, ed. David LaRocca (New York: Bloomsbury, 2020), 275–320.

57. Rodowick, "The Memory of Cinema," 192.

58. Wolfgang Ernst, *Digital Memory and the Archive* (Minneapolis: University of Minnesota Press, 2013), 41.

59. Elsaesser, "Media Archaeology as Symptom," 192.

Acknowledgments

My first thanks are directed to the remarkably gifted and generous contributors to this collection. Thank you for sharing your incisive and stimulating thoughts on metacinema, thereby endowing a novel discourse while also creating one—yet another meta move to study and savor.

At Oxford University Press, I have Norman Hirschy to thank for welcoming the project and seeing it through the review process with masterful good sense and good cheer. Throughout, Lauralee Yeary guided the endeavor and was a stalwart accomplice while navigating production. I am so grateful to both of them for their care and attention with the manuscript.

I extend sincere thanks to anonymous referees for the press, not to be missed, who provided sage counsel on achieving the volume. Additional readers of early drafts of the chapters also proved decisive in considerations of shape, tone, and extent. Alexis Burgess offered a fateful liaison.

Thoughts on the conceptual and programmatic viability of metacinema began to take the shape of consecutive remarks a little more than a decade ago in preparing *The Philosophy of Charlie Kaufman*. As with subsequent editorial projects, such as *The Philosophy of War Films*, *The Philosophy of Documentary Film*, *The Thought of Stanley Cavell and Cinema*, and *Movies with Stanley Cavell in Mind* (each of them with distinctive meta elements and meta aspects), conversations with contributors to these collections have informed what might be possible for a more explicit and extended engagement with metacinema. I remain grateful to these perceptive and innovative interlocutors.

An education that made the form and content of metacinema of abiding interest to me was inspired by and enriched at a number of inflection points: at Buffalo, with Newton Garver, Peter H. Hare, and Carolyn Korsmeyer; at Berkeley, with Anthony Cascardi, Frederick Dolan, and Michael Mascuch; at Vanderbilt, with Jay Bernstein, Gregg Horowitz, and John Lachs; at Harvard, with Giuliana Bruno, Stanley Cavell, Elizabeth Grosz, Despina Kakoudaki, Peggy Phelan, and the wider community of the Visual and Environmental Studies Department, the Harvard Film Archive, and the Sensory Ethnography Lab; in brief but impactful encounters with Maureen Gosling, Larry Gottheim, Hal Hartley, and Edward Zwick; sharing table at the Signet Society; during a term as Harvard's Sinclair Kennedy Fellow in the United Kingdom; touring venerable institutions of art and intellect with M. Jane Evans in London; working happily with and for Alessandro Subrizi in San Francisco and during the California days of Philm, Ink; taking a workshop with Edward Tufte in New York, teaming with tips and techniques; shooting documentary films in New York and Umbria with the cooperation of Brunello Cucinelli and Giorgiana Magnolfi; editing footage with Bill Jersey and Robert Elfstrom at Fantasy Studios; participating in Werner Herzog's Rogue Film School, "not for the faint-hearted"; holding fast to a stirring intellectual companionship and pedagogical partnership with Paul Cronin; reveling in a cinema workshop with Abbas Kiarostami; programming film at the Brooklyn Historical Society; appreciating the gracious encouragement of Robert Pippin; savoring summers in the company of the School of Criticism and Theory at Cornell (capably led by Hent de Vries) and calling to mind an especially generative summer with Emily Apter; taking notes with Oscar Jansson in Ithaca and Lund; reflecting on modernism with Ricardo Miguel-Alfonso; assessing undramatic achievement with Andrew Klevan; appraising ordinary language philosophy with Richard Deming; collaborating with Rita Mullaney on Jill Freedman's last film and testament by way of Chelsea Beat Productions and Fine Print Film; workshopping some forms and effects of experimental film and avant-garde cinema with participants at the New Directions conference at the University of Arizona, at the Docusophia: Documentary Film and Philosophy conference at Tel Aviv University, and during a guest visit to the Department of Comparative Literature at Lund University; curating experiences of film, literature, and philosophy with Haaris Naqvi; deliberating on ecstatic truth with Richard Eldridge; pondering temporality and memory with William Day; sorting tuitions and intuitions with William Rothman; trading in good measure the "monsters of fame" and the poetics of the everyday with Lawrence F. Rhu; liaising connections between philosophy and cinema with Mark T. Conard; contending with film traditions with Scott MacDonald; spending precious time with Thomas Elsaesser, who had patience for these kinds of questions; exploring meta modalities with Garrett Stewart; contemplating the relationship between cinema and television with Sandra Laugier; probing film pedagogy and analysis with Steven G. Affeldt, Diana Allan, Shai Biderman, Jeremy Braddock, Dan Geva, Matthew Holtmeier, Ohad Landesman, J. P. Sniadecki, Andrew Utterson, Amy Villarejo, Chelsea Wessels, Linda Williams, and Patricia R. Zimmermann; learning principles of photography from Victor Shanchuk and Diane Bush, and of painting from Philip Burke; sustaining a decades-long meditation on art with John Opera; and benefiting from the communities of moviemaking and film-philosophy

I have joined periodically in Paris, Tel Aviv, Stockholm, Montréal, New York, San Francisco, Berkeley, Cambridge, and Ithaca.

Teaching philosophy and cinema has provided occasion to think out loud with capable colleagues and students. In recent years, I am remembering the impact of courses and conversations at the State University of New York College at Cortland, Ithaca College, Cornell University, the School of Visual Arts, and in the Cinema Department at Binghamton University. A memorable discussion with Vincent Grenier helped me clarify the attributes of metacinema I most wished to critically investigate in the company of these adept interpreters of cinema and media.

Thinking of supportive family, I think immediately and gratefully of Sheldon and Lorna K. Hershinow, Ian M. Evans and Luanna H. Meyer, Frances LaRocca and Roselle Sweeney, David N. and Hi-jin Hodge. Discerning comments from informed, scholarly friends and family provided ongoing reminders of the natural, consequential coursings of everyday life and cinephilosophy.

I am perpetually mindful of the full range of gifts that come from days and seasons in the company of the ever-scintillating K. L. Evans, discovering together "the dailiness of life, its diurnal repetitiveness, as its own possibility of festivity." And I never lose a chance to marvel at the mysterious and wonderful presences of our dear girls, Ruby and Star. If moved to write a screenplay in your honor, I might name it *The Three*.

Index

For the benefit of digital users, indexed terms that span two pages (e.g., 52–53) may, on occasion, appear on only one of those pages.